Gringos in Mexico

IN

Texas Christian University Press
Fort Worth

MEXICO

An Anthology
Edited by
Edward Simmen

Library of Congress Cataloging-in-Publication Data

Gringos in Mexico: one hundred years of Mexico in the American short
story / edited by Edward Simmen; foreword by John Graves.
   p. cm.
  A collection of reprints of short stories previously published
from 1872 to 1983.
  ISBN 0-87565-029-5 (pbk.)
   1. Short stories, American. 2. Mexico—Fiction. 3. Americans—
Mexico—Fiction. 4. American fiction—20th century. 5. American
fiction—19th century. I. Simmen, Edward.
PS648.M42G75 1988   813'.01'083272—dc19   87-31186   CIP

Designed by WHITEHEAD & WHITEHEAD
Woodcut by BARBARA WHITEHEAD

Contents

Acknowledgements

Bryant, William Cullen. *Prose Writings of William Cullen Bryant.* Edited by Parke Godwin. 2 vols. New York: D. Appleton, 1884.

Crane, Stephen. *The Complete Short Stories and Sketches of Stephen Crane.* Edited by Thomas A. Cullason. Garden City: Doubleday, 1963.

Ferber, Edna. "They Brought Their Women." Copyright 1932 by Edna Ferber. Copyright renewed 1959 by Edna Ferber. Reprinted by permission of Harriet F. Pilpel, trustee & attorney for the Ferber Proprietors.

Flandrau, Charles M. *Prejudices.* New York: D. Appleton, 1911.

Gabrial, Jan. "Not With a Bang." *Story* 39, No. 121 (September–October 1946): 55–61.

Gabrial, Jan. "Voyage to the Shores of Cuautla." *New Mexico Quarterly Review* 15 (1945): 472–480.

Garber, Eugene. "An Old Dance." *The Kenyon Review,* New Series, 2, No. 1 (Winter 1980): 117–142. Reprinted with permission of the author and *The Kenyon Review.*

Graves, John. "The Aztec Dog." *The Colorado Quarterly* 9, No. 1 (Summer 1960): 31–46.

Graves, John. "The Green Fly." *Town and Country* 108, No. 4379 (April 1954).

Kerouac, Jack. "A Billowy Trip in the World." *New Directions* 16. New York: James Laughlin, 1957.

London, Jack. "Whose Business is to Live." *Dutch Courage and Other Stories.* New York: Macmillan, 1922.

Osborn, Carolyn. "Letter to a Friend Far Away." *Ascent* 8, No. 2 (1983), 13–21.

Porter, Katherine Anne. *Hacienda.* From *Flowering Judas and Other Stories,* copyright 1935, 1963 by Katherine Anne Porter. Reprinted by permission of Harcourt Brace Jovanovich, Inc.

Reed, John. "Mac-American." *Daughter of the Revolution and Other Stories*. Edited by Floyd Dell. New York: Vanguard, 1927.

Robins, Edmund J. "A Primitive." *The Mexico Quarterly Review* 3, No. 2 (1968): 61–69.

Robins, Edmund J. "A Snapped String." *The Mexico Quarterly Review* 1, No. 1 (1962): 44–55.

Shedd, Margaret. "The Dwarfs of Xlapac." *The Texas Quarterly* 3, No. 2 (Summer 1960): 64–76.

Shedd, Margaret. "I Hate You, Cruz Rivera." *Perspectivas* (Otono 1982): 24–29.

Spratling, William. *A Small Mexican World*. Copyright 1932 by William Spratling. Copyright 1964 by Little, Brown and Company, Inc.

Tefft, Dorothy. "The Dig."

Tefft, Dorothy. "Serenade."

For my mother

Preface

THIS anthology of twenty-four short stories by fifteen American writers is the first of its kind; never before has a collection been devoted entirely to Mexico as it appears in American short fiction.

When the collection was in its early stages, the Honorable John Gavin, who served from 1982–1986 as Ambassador of the United States to Mexico, was invited to comment on the project. He considered it a "timely and important anthology." He noted:

> Historically, most Americans have tended to ignore Mexico—that is until some sort of crisis has awakened us from our indifferences. Mexico is a rapidly growing country and has become the United States' third largest trading partner. Its trade with us now surpasses our commerce with Great Britain and West Germany.
>
> The two-thousand-mile border we share with Mexico is a constant reminder of both our long-standing good relations and our vulnerability to each other's problems. Debt, the crisis in Central America, and illegal immigration—among other issues—also bring home to Americans the fact that what happens in Mexico directly affects the United States.
>
> It is imperative, therefore, that we learn to respect our differences if we are to live together and continue to strengthen this relationship. Our two countries represent distinct cultures, languages, traditions, and historical ex-

periences. This first step toward mutual respect requires that we perceive these differences clearly and realistically; in other words, that we *learn* about each other.

Mr. Gavin concluded: "What better way for Americans to look at Mexico than through the eyes of our writers? These stories reveal the remarkable complexity of a country which has always fascinated and yet confounded American visitors of all backgrounds."

Included here are works by writers who are very well-known and others who are, for the most part, unknown to the general reading public. Two have been awarded the Pulitzer Prize for literature; one has been honored with the coveted National Book Award, and another has twice been a finalist in that competition. Many of the stories included in this collection first appeared in some of the most highly respected American journals and magazines, including the *New Mexico Quarterly, Story, Town and Country, Colorado Quarterly, Texas Quarterly, Kenyon Review* and *Ascent*. One was reprinted in *Best American Short Stories* and another in *Prize Stories: The O. Henry Awards.*

Together, the stories reveal how Mexico has been seen through the eyes of some of the most highly respected American writers over the last hundred years.

However, the authors whose works are presented in this collection are obviously not the only American writers to make use of a Mexican experience in their short fiction. Prominent among the others is Ray Bradbury. Over the years he has published several fine short stories and sketches that were inspired by trips south of the border. Tennessee Williams was also a frequent visitor to Mexico during his lifetime, making his first trip in 1940. The country appears prominently in several of his best plays, including *Night of the Iguana* (1962), which he wrote in 1946 as a short story with the same title and then published in his first collection of stories, *One Arm and Other Stories* (1948). And after a young Saul Bellow spent three months in Mexico, "passing from marvel to marvel from amazement to amazement," he combined his impressions of the country beyond Mexico City with Leon Trotsky's assassination and produced "The Mexican General" (*Partisan Review,* May–June 1940).

It is, in addition, curious that two great American writers—Faulkner and Hemingway—were never inspired by that country. For example, Hemingway's collection of stories entitled *Winner Take Nothing* (1922) contains a story set in Mexico, "Mother of a Queen," but he wrote it without having been there. His first visit was not until 1940, and obviously the country never attracted him as did Italy, Spain or Cuba.

As for William Faulkner, it is said that he also visited Mexico under most amusing circumstances when he was in Hollywood during the 1930s writing film scripts. One day he took off from the studio and drove to Tijuana. Once across the border, he went to a cantina, drank a beer and muttered, "Well, now I've been to Mexico." With that, he returned to Los Angeles and soon back to Mississippi. Obviously, he felt more at home in "Yoknapatawpha County."

Just the opposite of Faulkner and Hemingway is another American winner of the Nobel Prize for literature: John Steinbeck. He was apparently completely taken by the country and the plight of its poorest people, the *campesinos*. His popular novela, *The Pearl,* attests to his sympathetic understanding. A great compliment was given to Steinbeck by Mexico's internationally acclaimed motion picture director, Emilio Fernández, who after reading the work in manuscript form asked the American to adapt it for the screen. This Steinbeck did in collaboration with Fernández, and filming began two months before the novella even appeared in print. The film, starring Pedro Armendariz and María Elena Marqués, was photographed by the award-winning cinematographer Gabriel Figueroa on location in a village on the shores of the Gulf of California. Two versions were made—one in English and the other in Spanish—and released in September 1947. Then, in December of that year, the work was published in *Woman's Home Companion*. Simultaneously it appeared in book form in the United States. Since that time, *The Pearl* has seen nearly one hundred printings.

Mexico was the subject for another Steinbeck film script, *Viva Zapata,* which was released in 1952 starring Marlon Brando as the revolutionary hero. Then, too, Mexican characters figure prominently in other Steinbeck works such as *Tortilla Flat* (1935) and *The Wayward Bus* (1947). The setting for those novels, of course, is California, but the feeling of Mexico is always present.

To get a more complete picture of American writers—not just short story writers but poets, essayists, novelists and dramatists—one should consult a book mentioned in the introduction to this anthology: *British and American Writers in Mexico, 1556–1973* by Drewey Wayne Gunn. No other work on the subject can compare with it, and that book, as well as its author, has been consulted many times in the compilation of this collection. Also of great help have been Dennis Mc-Nally's detailed biography of Jack Kerouac, *Desolate Angel* (1979); Enrique Hank Lopez's *Conversations with Katherine Anne Porter* (1981); R. W. Stallman's biography, *Stephen Crane* (1968); Robert E. Quirk's *An Affair of Honor: Woodrow Wilson and the Occupation of Veracruz* (1962); and Douglas Day's National Book Award winner, *Malcolm Lowry: A Biography* (1973).

It must be noted that certain writers in this anthology have contributed more than just their stories; through interviews, conversations or letters, they—Shedd, Garber, Tefft and Osborn—have commented profoundly on their works, their lives as writers and their thoughts about Mexico. These invaluable comments appear in the introduction and bring new light to understanding how a writer feels when writing about a country as totally fascinating and engrossing and complex as Mexico.

My special gratitude goes to John Graves, who is represented by two stories in this collection, for so kindly writing a most revealing and appropriate foreword. He still has the clearest of views from his limestone ledge.

I would also like to take this opportunity to mention more than just a few of the many friends, colleagues, and students who are so directly a vital part of this collection. Some of them came into my life, stayed a while, and then disappeared. Others—fortunately for me—have remained. Among them are Rosa and Luis Ernesto Derbéz, Alicia and Ricardo Arocha, Rene and Glynn Morgan, Adriana Bianchi, Stanley Zuckerman, Andrés Sternberg, Manuel Albarrán, Miguel Hakim, Liliana and Rene Greenwald (seniors and juniors), Roberto Benitez, Jeff Teague and Paul Yandré, María Elena and Gary Mounce, Gabriela and Sergio Díaz Montaño, Diane Stanley, Sidney Hamolsky, Georgette Mondragón, Necla and Dan Tschirgi, Guadalupe Espinoza, Frieda Koeniger de Padilla, Enrique Rivera—lost with his sketch pad in Central Park—los hermanos Cruz y Celis Ellinger, Javier Arozarena, Marko Foitzig, Sigfried Pizano, Claudia Uriarte, Luís Lopez, Carlos Navarro, Roberto Ortiz Clark (1956–1988), Martín Fernandez, Guillermo Rodriguez, Victor (no sabe fallar) Faucheret, Luis Salinas, the one and ever only Jesse Reinberg, and—of course—Karen Kalteissen. And what would my life have been like during these years without Felice, Xochilquetzali, Burbujita, and Pipilzinzintili?

And special to me will always be the parents of my three favorite girls: María and Enrique Cárdenas.

Finally, my thoughts must go to Carmen López Blumenkron. Agony and frustration know no enemies like a Saturday night movie or a Sunday lunch on the patio with family and friends.

Abrazos a todos.

Edward Simmen
Universidad de las Américas-Puebla
Ex-Hacienda Santa Catarina Mártir
Puebla, México

Foreword

BOTH as a man and as a writer I've always had an incomplete feeling about Mexico, and at my present age I
suppose I'm stuck with it for good. I've got an incomplete
feeling about much of the rest of the world too, but when
young I was certain I'd get to know Mexico from the inside
when the time came for such knowledge, and in fact the time
seems never really to have come.

What I knew about it while growing up in Texas, or thought
I knew, was that it was a very romantic place. This view had
sources in my region's literature, in old family tales of bandit
raids and such south of the Nueces, in wailed norteño music
heard on the border stations at night, in stints of country
work with tough, often friendly wetback laborers, in the
mere existence of all that colorful foreignness so close to
home. . . . I managed to maintain such a feeling up until
World War II, nursing it even through the standard grub-
biness of tequila-flavored forays with college friends to the
sin towns just across the Rio Grande. It more or less peaked
out one summer when I went with a classmate to the time-
worn, populous hacienda of his mother's family not far from
Linares, riding the last few miles on horseback through rough
country. The place had an old stone fortress of a house sprad-
dled around a dusty, busy courtyard, pretty girls who were
my classmate's cousins home from school, vaqueros deft
with rawhide ropes, and soft lamplight in the evenings. The
family's men were called Don This and Don That and some

wore pistols against dangers having to do with agrarians. It was a tawny nineteenth-century setting straight out of legend, and I'm glad I saw it while I still felt as I did then, for that particular sentimentality of viewpoint, along with some others, seems not to have come intact through the war years that followed.

Late in 1945 I got out of the Marine Corps and after spending a time at home in Texas, went to Mexico not to seek romance or to immerse myself in learning about the country, but mainly because it was unconnected with things and people I knew and seemed a likely environment wherein to start getting my head straightened out. It is worth noting too that I didn't yet think of myself as a writer and indeed wasn't sure I wanted to try to be one, though that idea was lurking about. What I chiefly was at that point, I suppose, was an inward-looker and a journal-keeper, a young man trying to understand who and what he might be through contemplation of the things that had happened to him thus far, though in truth not very much had besides an average dose of war.

Hence I traveled little in any real sense but would plunk myself down in some agreeable spot for a few weeks before moving along elsewhere, pecking all the while at a portable Corona. What came out of this at the time was a rather long introspective and retrospective mass of words with in it hardly a mention of Mexico but much about war and women, both of which I found perplexing. What came out of it almost incidentally years later, after I'd turned into a writer of sorts, was a very few short stories, including the two in this collection. While engaged in mauling my own sparsely eventful past in that journal I was also, of course, existing from day to day and learning about things around me and meeting all kinds of people. But I kept no notes on these matters and the stories I built from them long afterward were based on rather hazy recollection.

I remember, for instance, going rather early in that Mexico sojourn to a quiet lodge in the mountains near Pachuca that someone had told me about. It was owned by a group of

American doctors as a vacation retreat but accepted paying guests. For a time another of the guests was an old Spanish exile, a doctor, with whom I did some friendly fishing in the pretty trout waters there. But such is the haze I referred to that I can't say now exactly what parts of "The Green Fly," when I wrote it in the fifties in New York, were connected with actual events and what part I made up.

In Mexico City I ran into an old acquaintance, an entrepreneur of international background who was the adoptive father of a Texas friend of mine and weighed about four hundred pounds. By finagling scarce American raw materials for Mexican industrialists during the war he had made a good bit of money, which he was now spending as fast as he could on high living, on bad investments, and on people he cared about, including a couple of bright waifs rescued from the capital's streets and installed in private schools. But I don't want to get off here onto this warm-hearted and unlikely man, who was impossible in any event, as I've found, to write about convincingly. . . . He had a chauffeured Cadillac and a half-floor at the old American Club, where I stayed for a time before he sent me to a down-at-the-heels hacienda in the uplands of Veracruz state in which he had acquired some sort of interest, a venture about on a par with the rest of his investments.

While there I had some experiences that led eventually to "The Aztec Dog," maybe my favorite among the few half-decent stories I've written. Again remembrance is vague, but I believe this story's setting and textural details are pretty close to the way things were, though the tale itself is a matter of what might have happened if I'd been a teen-ager in trouble and the old *hacendado* had been as much of a piece as the story represents him to be. In reality, as I recall, he was about half-crazy at times and could be quite difficult.

And afterward during that long stay in Mexico, which lasted till autumn when I went back to the States for graduate school, there were other good places or interesting places, always with people worth knowing: a primitive ranch in the Gulf Coast hot country run by hard gallego Spaniards, a tucked-away rural posada in the highlands above Tuxpan, the beaches of Acapulco before glitter took them over. . . . At some point I even wound up the damned journal, whether or not this got my head any straighter than when I'd crossed the border heading south. But even though I was enjoying life and learning a few things and speaking much better Spanish, I still was watching what was around me not with a writer's interpretive eyes, but with those of a passer-through. I hadn't *gone* there as a writer, nor did I afterward ever go there as such, except for a brief spell of wandering while doing an article for the old *Holiday* magazine on the border country, and three or four months in the late fifties spent mainly at Mazatlán, where I fought with an ill-fated novel whose material had nothing to do with Mexico.

Maybe if my footloose time of life, such as it was, had lasted longer I'd have gone back to Mexico at some point with eyes that saw more deeply. That seems doubtful to me nowadays, however, because of an uncomfortable bit of awareness that has seeped in on me over the years while visiting Mexico from time to time and thinking about it often. It has seeped in on many other people too, being in fact the very theme of quite a bit of writing in English about that nation and its people. What it amounts to is that Mexico for deep and ancient reasons is an especially, emphatically foreign country, one that has always rebuffed easy familiarity from outsiders except of a surface sort. The awareness, the suspicion I now have is that it rebuffed me too, and that's where my incomplete feeling comes from.

Thus one gringo writer's rather skimpy relationship with the land of the eagle and the serpent. . . . The diverse relationships of some other writers with that same land are imbedded in this book's assortment of stories, sometimes obviously and sometimes not. It is curious to note—astounding, really—that within this handful of authors, varying as they do in viewpoint and talent and depth of perception, is to be found perhaps a majority of the Americans who during the past century have undertaken to write honest short fiction with a Mexican setting. I have no doubt at all that a main reason for this has been that same potent and enigmatic foreignness I've mentioned, though certainly there are other reasons as well, among them a cultural heritage that has drawn literate American roamers more often eastward across an ocean than toward the Indian–Latin south.

These writers *were* drawn southward, though, whether for short stays or for long ones, whether to penetrate and understand the Mexican way of being or to keep on living their gringo lives, as I did, along its surface. The relative quality of the work they've done is separate from these matters, but all have had their say, and it's good to see examples of their work assembled in one volume. Nothing is going to make it magically simple to see Mexico's past and present complexity whole, or to understand with clarity the tangle of attitudes and reactions that have existed between its natives and us aliens from the north. But here and there among these stories, an individual reader with individual quirks and sympathies may find an image or a scene or an insight to furnish a start toward comprehension. That is one of the things that fiction can do, and it's not the least thing either.

John Graves
Glen Rose, Texas

Introduction

SINCE the early days of the Republic, American fiction writers have been a restless group, traveling the world for one reason or another, observing foreign cultures and customs and often making their experiences part of their later creative works.

Washington Irving is generally regarded as the first; in total, the writer of "Rip Van Winkle" and "The Legend of Sleepy Hollow" lived thirty-two years abroad, most of the time in England and Spain. Throughout the nineteenth century, other writers of American classics were drawn to live for lengthy periods in Europe: James Fenimore Cooper, Nathaniel Hawthorne, William Dean Howells, Stephen Crane and perhaps the most American of all, Mark Twain, who made no fewer than eight trips, the longest one lasting nine years. Henry James was the most *European* American writer; he took his first trip to Europe with his family before he was one year old, and during his lifetime he spent some forty-seven years abroad before finally becoming a naturalized British subject in 1915, the year before he died.

The beginning of the twentieth century found more young Americans sailing to Europe, primarily to serve in the "war to end all wars." Among those who became influential writers were John Dos Passos, e.e. cummings and two future Nobel Prize winners, Ernest Hemingway and William Faulkner. After the Armistice in 1918 and continuing throughout the Roaring Twenties and the Great Depression, others traveled the road to Paris to join Gertrude Stein, Alice B. Toklas,

Hemingway and their group of artists, writers, poets and as-sorted intellectuals and hangers-on; among the more success-ful of these were F. Scott Fitzgerald, Dorothy Parker, Kath-erine Anne Porter, Conrad Aiken and Thomas Wolfe.

Not all American travel experiences have been limited to Europe, however. Herman Melville took to the sea for his in-spiration, as did Jack London later in the nineteenth century. Pearl Buck made use of her many years in China to write her way to a Nobel Prize in 1938. And when another great "war to end all wars" provided substance for another generation of American writers, including Saul Bellow and J. D. Salinger, the battleground was no longer limited to Europe: the Orient and the islands of the Pacific provided settings and conflicts for a number of works by Herman Wouk, James Michener, James Jones and William Brinkley. Indeed, American writers have traveled over the globe and incorporated their experi-ences in American literature.

It does, however, seem curious that so few have been at-tracted to Mexico, considering that the two countries share a two-thousand-mile border. In fact, of all the writers previ-ously mentioned, only four visited and made use of their Mexican experiences in their short fiction: Crane, London, Porter and Bellow.

Perhaps it is easy to explain why the writers of the nine-teenth century elected to travel to Europe rather than to their southern neighbor. After all, their ancestral roots were, for the most part, in England, and what interested them was to be readily found in the sophisticated cities and picturesque countrysides of France and Italy and Spain. Consequently, instead of looking to the west and southwest, to what was still an unsettled frontier, they simply looked back across the Atlantic.

And it must be accepted that nineteenth-century Mexico was not a very attractive place for a Yankee visitor. Rebel-lions and insurrections and foreign invasions left the country in almost constant turmoil and change until very late in the nineteenth century. Violence began with Mexico's struggle to gain independence from Spain, a conflict which raged from

1810 until independence in 1821. In 1829, Spain made another—this time unsuccessful—invasion of Mexico, but in 1836 an insurrection in Texas cost Mexico that territory, which became the Republic of Texas and nine years later part of the United States. More devastating to Mexico was its two-year war with the United States, fought largely on Mexican soil; when it ended in 1848 with the Treaty of Guadalupe Hidalgo, Mexico received fifteen million dollars and deeded to the victorious Americans the territory that makes up most of the western United States. In one decade, Mexico lost more than half of its territory to the United States.

Fifteen years later, in 1861, the French armies of Napoleon III invaded and occupied the country, removed its duly elected president, Benito Juarez, and in 1864 installed Austria's Prince Maximilian as Emperor of Mexico. That occupation met steady armed resistance from Mexican nationalists led by Juarez, and in 1867 the French, realizing that the Mexicans would not submit to foreign rule, retreated.

Once Mexican forces captured Maximilian and executed him, there began a period when the country was beset by internal rebellions, struggles for political power and widespread bandit activity. Relative peace and order were finally restored after General Porfirio Díaz became president, ruling the country with an iron hand for thirty-four years.

Such was Mexico during the nineteenth century—obviously not a place for the cultivated Yankee intellectual. Before the 1890s a few American writers took their chances and ventured south, but none wrote any memorable fiction—or nonfiction, for that matter—as a result of his adventures. For example, Lewis Wallace, best remembered as the author of *Ben Hur* (1880), went as a soldier when American armies invaded Mexico in 1846. He returned in 1867 to help Juarez in his efforts to overthrow Emperor Maximilian and the French occupation forces. The results of those visits were two articles—one published in 1867 in *Harper's* magazine and another in 1879 in *Scribner's*—and a long-since-forgotten novel, *The Fair God, or the Last of the 'Tzins: A Tale of the Conquest of Mexico,* published in 1873.

Other American writers began visiting in the 1880s, after the government of General Porfirio Díaz had restored calm and brought prosperity to the country. Charles Dudley Warner, best remembered as an editor of *Harper's* and co-author with Mark Twain of *The Gilded Age* (1873), took a trip across Mexico in 1887 and published five sketches in *Harper's*. He returned again in 1897 and 1898 and wrote two more articles that also appeared in *Harper's*. Another visitor was Frederick Remington, the well-known Western painter, who in 1893 visited northern Mexico and wrote and illustrated four articles for *Harper's;* the illustrations, as might be expected, are superb. Helen Hunt Jackson, author of the classic California romance, *Ramona* (1884), crossed over the Rio Grande at El Paso during the summer of 1882 and spent several hours on the Mexican side of the border. The result was an article published in the *Atlantic* in March 1883, entitled "By Horse-Cars into Mexico."

Without question, the most interesting American writer to visit the country during the nineteenth century was William Cullen Bryant (1794–1878). Internationally respected as a poet, essayist and editor, in 1872 Bryant accepted President Benito Juarez's invitation to visit the country and become a member of the Mexican Society of Geography and Statistics, a society for Mexican intellectuals that Juarez had recently formed. Juarez had hoped, and with reason, that a visit by someone so distinguished as Bryant would help bring the prestige and recognition that Mexico not only needed but justly deserved.

The result of Bryant's visit was a lively, descriptive essay that is included in this volume as a prologue. It should do much to explain why other Americans did *not* visit Mexico, for while Bryant's visit was exciting, fascinating and enlightening, it was also an adventure, at times fraught with discomfort and danger. Likewise, Bryant's essay demonstrates what other Americans *missed* by forsaking Mexico in order to visit London, Rome and Paris. But Bryant's visit anticipated an American awareness of Mexico, and midway through the last decade of the nineteenth century, American writers began to visit Mexico and use their Mexican experiences in their fiction.

STEPHEN CRANE (1871–1900)

Stephen Crane arrived in Mexico City in March 1895. He was only twenty-four years old, but already an abridged version of his novel *The Red Badge of Courage* had appeared in numerous newspapers, and later that year it would be published as a book. As a result of his success as a reporter, the newspaper syndicate for which he worked had sent him to travel through the Midwest, down into the South and finally into the interior of Mexico, dispatching articles as he went. His trip took him to Lincoln, Nebraska; Hot Springs, Arkansas; New Orleans and the Mardi Gras festivities; Galveston, Texas; and San Antonio, where he boarded a train to Mexico, entering at Laredo and arriving two days later in Mexico City, where he spent about two months.

As a good reporter and a keen observer of humanity, Crane evidently tried to see and do everything that might provide him with an interesting article or story. He is known to have seen a bullfight—sitting on the *sombra* or shady side of the stands—and to have taken a boat trip down the Viga Canal to spend an afternoon at the floating gardens of Xochimilco. He wrote that he even had intentions of climbing the awesome volcano, Popocatepetl. Occasionally, he ventured out of the city on horseback, in the company of a guide, to try to capture the life of the *other* Mexico: the Mexico of the Indian pueblos that surrounded Mexico City. Most of the time, however, he stayed close to the city, associating with—and always observing critically—members of the American / British colony who congregated daily in the bars and restaurants near the Hotel Iturbide, where he stayed.

The time he spent in Mexico had immediate results: nine articles reflecting various aspects of Mexican life and three fables which he either invented or overheard and recorded. More significant results were three short stories that he wrote after his return home. "Horses—One Dash" first appeared in newspapers early in 1896, "The Wise Men" and "Five White Mice" in magazines in April 1898. Later that year, the three were collected and published in Crane's first collection of short fiction, *The Open Boat and Other Stories*.

Two of the stories—"The Wise Men" and "The Five White Mice"—relate the adventures of two young men from the American community in Mexico. On the surface, they appear to be simple, almost insignificant tales; when read carefully, however, they become critical commentaries on the empty and fruitless lives led by those foreigners. In addition, "The Five White Mice" makes a thoughtful statement of how explosive the clash of cultures can be.

In the third story, "Horses—One Dash"—Crane leaves the confines of Mexico City and takes his American hero, on horseback, into the surrounding countryside. But the story transcends its regional setting and traditional "conflict of cultures" theme and becomes, like "The Blue Hotel" and "The Open Boat," a universal study of arrogance and pride, of hate and fear, and of man's supreme desire to overcome all obstacles in order to survive.

CHARLES FLANDRAU (1871–1938)

The next American to write short fiction about Mexico was Charles Flandrau, best known for his still popular and highly regarded travel classic, *Viva Mexico!*, which first appeared in print in 1908.

Flandrau was born in St. Paul, Minnesota, and educated at Harvard, where he wrote sketches and stories for college magazines and graduated in 1895. Upon the death of his father, he received an inheritance that permitted him to travel leisurely. Between 1903 and 1908, he made a series of lengthy visits to his brother, who had a coffee plantation in the state of Veracruz. His travels in Mexico became the substance of not only the travel book but of a short story, "Wanderlust," that first appeared in a literary magazine in Minneapolis and in 1911 was collected and published with other stories under the title *Prejudices*.

The story concerns two young Americans who leave home in New York to have an advanture in the tropics. Landing in Veracruz, they soon find themselves forced by circumstances into an existence that threatens to destroy them. Like Crane, Flandrau provides a strong setting; the scenes of the port of

Veracruz at the turn of the century are vivid in detail. Also like Crane, Flandrau makes the most of the agony that can result when an individual unsuspectingly enters a culture that is both alien and hostile to his own.

JOHN REED (1887–1920)

A reporter's assignment took Crane to a peaceful Mexico; Flandrau's visits were prompted by a desire to spend some time on his brother's plantation and travel at his leisure. John Reed went for another reason: he was sent in December 1913 by the *Metropolitan* magazine and the *New York World* as a war correspondent, to cover the Mexican Revolution which had been raging in the northern states for two years.

Born in Portland, Oregon, to a wealthy and prominent family, Reed, like Flandrau, was educated at Harvard, where he served on the editorial board and wrote, as did Flandrau, for various college publications. After his graduation in 1910, he began his career in journalism. Almost immediately, his interest in social problems was aroused, and within only a few years, the socially prominent conservative became a vocal radical, "a champion of the oppressed and exploited." He was ripe for the Mexican Revolution.

Not long after crossing into Mexico from Texas, he met and had the first of several interviews with the revolutionary leader, Pancho Villa. For nearly four months, Reed lived among Villa's followers, who were poor uneducated *campesinos* or peasants turned revolutionaries. Reed wrote of his experiences in sixteen articles which were collected and published, during the summer of 1914, as *Insurgent Mexico,* a work that critics still regard as one of the best ever written about Mexico by a foreigner.

In addition, he wrote two short stories. The most important and revealing, "Mac-American," first appeared in 1914 in *Masses,* a magazine Reed edited; it was reprinted seven years after his death in a collection entitled *Daughter of the Revolution* (1927). His story focuses on what he considered a major contribution to the agony of the poor Mexican: the arrogant American who for decades had lived in Mexico and

exploited both the country and the people. Like Crane and
Flandrau, he kept his eye on what he knew best: the American.

JACK LONDON (1876–1916)

Not long after Reed had returned home, a bizarre incident occurred in the port city of Tampico, the consequences of which
drew Jack London, among others, to Mexico. The reason for
his visit says much about the United States' relations with its
southern neighbor.

Tampico is located on the Panuco River, ten miles from the
Gulf of Mexico, in the heart of what was to become at the
time one of the richest oil fields in the world. The oil com-
panies drilling there, however, were not Mexican-owned but
foreign—mainly American, British and Dutch. As a result,
the port city of Tampico, which from 1909 to 1914 had grown
in population from five thousand to over sixty thousand,
boasted the largest foreign population—the majority American—outside of Mexico City. Likewise, Tampico considered
itself fortunate not to have been touched by the revolution in
northern Mexico—that is, not until the spring of 1914.

On April 5, revolutionaries attacked the federal forces then
in control of the city. Immediately, ships from the United
States Navy, which for several months had been patrolling
off the coast in an effort to keep the port open, moved in and
began evacuating American oil company employees and their
families.

Four days later, on April 9, 1914, a U.S. naval officer and
nine sailors ventured in a whaleboat into dangerous waters in
order to refuel. Mexican authorities stopped the Americans
and detained them for thirty minutes while they questioned
and warned them of the dangers of being in the area. Then,
after customary apologies for any inconvenience they might
have suffered, the Mexican officials released the Americans.
The affair was so minor that the matter should have ended
there. Unfortunately, it did not, and soon the thirty-minute
detention was blown up into an international incident. The
American admiral became incensed and charged that the Mex-

icans' action was no less than a gross insult to the American flag. He insisted not only that the Mexican official who stopped the sailors be punished but that the Mexican government pay honor to the American flag with a twenty-one gun salute. The news soon reached Washington, where tempers flared. One senator was so offended that he proclaimed to his colleagues in the Senate: "I'd make them salute the flag if we have to blow up the whole place."

Eleven days later, on April 20, with the remainder of the Atlantic fleet proceeding to the neighboring port of Veracruz, a joint session of Congress was called. Some of the legislators felt that the affront was so grave that the only deserving answer would be a declaration of war on Mexico. That proposal was defeated, but a majority of the session did approve a proposal to invade the city of Veracruz. The attack, ordered by President Woodrow Wilson, began the following day, April 21, and in less than twenty-four hours, three thousand American troops had occupied the port city. By midmorning, the shooting was virtually over. The dead included nineteen American servicemen and literally hundreds of Mexican soldiers, naval cadets and civilians.

Less than two weeks had passed since the incident involving the American sailors and Mexican authorities. It had, however, been noticed by the American press, and rumors of war with Mexico began to spread. Several days prior to the invasion, Jack London, at home in California, was contracted by *Collier's* magazine to go to Mexico and cover the "war" as its own correspondent. He left California by train, arriving on April 20 in Galveston, Texas, from which the American forces were being deployed on U.S. transports.

London's request to join the other war correspondents was at first rejected. U.S. military authorities accused him of having written a letter, first published in the *International Socialist Review* in October 1913, which denounced members of the armed forces. "No man," the letter noted, "can fall lower than a soldier—it is a depth beneath which we cannot go. Keep the boys out of the army. It is hell." The pamphlet ended: "Down with the army and navy. We don't need killing institutions. We need life-giving institutions." Repeatedly London denied authorship. Finally, he was granted permission to leave, and on April 24—two days after the "war" was over—London, accompanied by his wife and a Chinese manservant, left aboard a troopship bound for Veracruz.

While London had never been to Mexico, he was certainly familiar with it and had a special interest in its revolution. In February 1911, he addressed an open letter to his "dear, brave comrades of the Mexican Revolution," telling them, "We socialists, anarchists, hobos, chicken thieves, outlaws and undesirable citizens of the United States are with you heart and soul in your effort to overthrow slavery in Mexico." At the time he wrote the letter, he was also writing a short story, "The Mexican," which appeared in the April 19, 1911, issue of the *Saturday Evening Post*. The story relates the struggles of a young Mexican patriot who had fled Mexico at the outset of the revolution and entered the United States where he was determined—albeit ill-prepared—to earn enough money to send back so that his compatriots could purchase guns and continue the revolution.

Of course, when London had written the "open letter" and the story, he had not yet been to Mexico; he obviously had been stimulated by his strong conviction that the Mexican Revolution was a revolution of "the working class" fighting the oppression and injustice of decades of dictatorial rule. However, the London who stayed six weeks in Veracruz was anything but the "chicken thief" and "outlaw" who wrote in 1911 to his "dear, brave comrades of the Mexican Revolution." In May 1914 he spent much of his time horseback riding, attending bullfights or drinking heavily, as was his habit, in the sidewalk cafes on the main plaza. Indeed, it was a rare day when the distinguished author and his wife were not lavishly entertained at lunch or dinner aboard one of the American warships anchored in the harbor or at a restaurant in the city.

The seven articles he wrote for *Collier's* make clear that he no longer saw the revolution as one waged for and by the working class; revolutionaries were plundering bandits instead. But London's flag-waving pro-Americanism is perhaps best seen in the only short story—one of his last—that was to come out of this Mexican adventure: "Whose Business Is to Live." The story, published posthumously in 1922, came out of a brief trip to Tampico and is set in that city at midnight on April 21, 1914, the day the American naval forces bombarded and invaded Veracruz. Until the Veracruz invasion, Americans working in the oil fields had been permitted to live their lives peacefully, ignored by the battling revolutionaries; now, however, the Americans had become a common enemy of the Mexicans. The action involves the adventures of two men who decide to risk the dangers and venture fifty miles up the Pánuco River from Tampico to rescue a beautiful young American woman who is totally unaware of the explosive situation. We find a familiar London theme—only the fittest survive—but this time we have determined Americans out-witting the superior Mexican forces. As is usual in many London stories, the "good"—this time, Americans—are pitted against the "bad," the Mexicans.

On May 24, 1914, London returned from Tampico to Vera-cruz and immediately came down with acute dysentery. He was bedridden for more than a week until finally, on June 9, the Londons boarded a military transport and left Mexico. Some feel that his death in 1916 was hastened by the dysen-tery; he never fully recovered.

After his return to California, London began making nu-merous notes and outlines for what he called his "Mexican stories." *Cosmopolitan* magazine even expressed a desire to publish them. However, probably because of his illness, he lost interest and discarded his plans to write about Mexico; he was only able to complete the one.

Among the four turn-of-the-century writers who used their Mexican experiences in their short fiction—Crane, Flan-drau, Reed and London—not one tried to enter the complex mind of the Mexican. Each kept his distance and concen-trated on what he knew he could do best: create an American character and describe how he acts and reacts when he is

thrown into a culture alien to his own. Perhaps that was because not one of these writers had lived in Mexico long enough
to begin to understand how or why a Mexican could think
and feel and act as he did. That cannot, however, be said of
Katherine Anne Porter; on the contrary, no other American
has had such successes in writing about Mexico, a country
which she visited often and learned to understand.

KATHERINE ANNE PORTER (1890–1980)

During one of her frequent visits to Mexico in 1964, Katherine Anne Porter was approached by an editor of a Mexican
literary magazine who asked for an interview. "I'll do anything for Mexico," she answered enthusiastically. "I've always considered it my second home."

Born in Indian Creek, Texas, near San Antonio, Porter
grew up in central Texas associating with Mexican Americans and listening to her father relate tales of the times he had
spent as a youth south of the border; thus, her personal con-
nection with Mexico was established early in her life. It evidently was not difficult for her to adapt; she later wrote that
Mexico "never seemed strange to me even at my first sight of
it," which happened when she, as a girl of ten, visited the
country with her father in 1900—only five years after Crane
and several years before Flandrau, Reed and London. She then
returned many times during and after the Mexican Revolution. For her, Mexico was always a "moving experience."

Over the years, beginning in 1921, she wrote a number of
penetrating essays on the country, its culture and its problems. In 1942, her translation of José Joaquín Fernández de
Lizardi's novel, *The Itching Parrot,* for which she also wrote a
lengthy introduction, was published. Mexico, likewise, is
important to her only novel, *Ship of Fools* (1962). Not only
are several important characters Mexican, but the story begins in Veracruz, and her descriptions indicate how accurately she could capture the vital spirit of the country and its
people.

However, it is the short stories inspired by her "second

country" that have established Porter's prominent position in American literature, beginning with her first published story "María Concepción," which she wrote—and rewrote fifteen or sixteen times—following a visit in 1921. Then came others, including "Flowering Judas" (1929), considered by many critics as one of the great American short stories.

"Hacienda" was finally published in 1934. A shorter version had appeared in 1932 in the *Virginia Quarterly Review,* but for the perfectionist Porter, it was yet to be finished. The final version is not only much longer but much larger in scope and more profound in intention than any of her others.

Set in 1929, it is a brilliantly complex portrayal of the generally negative results of the 1910 Revolution seen at every level of Mexican society. The story grew directly out of a visit Porter had made to the hacienda where Sergei Eisenstein was filming his aborted epic, *Viva Mexico!* The major upheaval of the Revolution had ended ten years before, and the critical changes to Mexico were becoming more and more clear. To someone as perceptive as Porter—who had known Mexico before, during and immediately after the Revolution—those social and cultural changes were even more obvious. Then, too, she had the advantage of a foreigner's perspective: she could stand apart, as does the narrator of "Hacienda," to observe and reflect and occasionally insert a piercing comment.

Although published in 1934, "Hacienda" is for many an accurate portrait of the country a half-century later. Much of what existed then still exists today: the staggering poverty on the one hand and the enormous wealth on the other; the corruption that grows out of the bureaucratic snarls which end only with inevitable bribes to the appropriate official; the strictly drawn social boundaries; the intensity of life at every level of society; as well as the sense, sensibility and humor of the Mexican people. At the end of it all is an optimism that keeps the country alive. As the Indian driver says to the narrator at the conclusion of the story: "If you should come back in about ten days . . . you will see a different place. It is sad now. But then the green corn will be ready, and ah, there will be enough to eat again."

"Hacienda" was the last of Porter's short stories set in Mexico. However, in its structure, large cast of characters and generally pessimistic, perhaps realistic, view of the world, the story seems to have been the genesis for *Ship of Fools,* which was published nearly three decades later and brought Porter once again to her "second country," the one she presented so accurately in her writing.

WILLIAM SPRATLING (1900–1967)

Another American, William Spratling, arrived in Mexico in 1929 with a contract and a modest advance from a New York publisher to write a book on Mexico. His plan was to settle in the then-isolated village of Taxco, spend a few months and then write the book. However, the plan soon changed; Taxco became Spratling's home for the rest of his life. Not only did Taxco change him, but Spratling completely transformed Taxco, which centuries before had been the silver capital of Mexico.

His first attempts to write the book as promised failed, so in order to make a living, he opened up a workshop, brought in a few Indian goldsmiths from a nearby pueblo and put them to work making silver. Within several years, the village's long-forgotten silver industry began to flourish, and soon Taxco became a thriving tourist center. At one time, Spratling's workshop employed 422 silversmiths, 38 cabinet-makers and 27 people in the office—all of them from the village or surrounding area. Spratling was also responsible for training many other Indian silversmiths who, after perfecting the craft, left with his blessing and set up their own small factories and shops in Taxco.

From the beginning, Spratling immersed himself in the culture, as can be seen in the collection of portraits that was published in 1932 under the title *Little Mexico* and then reissued in 1974 as *A Small Mexican World.* Three of those portraits are included in this collection: "Santa Señora," "La Virgen de la Luz" and "Of the Old Regime."

Before he settled in Taxco, Spratling had been a teacher of architecture at Tulane University in New Orleans. He lived in the French Quarter, sharing a room with William Faulkner, and in 1926 they published a collection of caricatures of their famous and not-yet-famous friends: *Sherwood Anderson and Other Famous Creoles*. During that time, Spratling also supplemented his income by writing for art and architecture magazines.

However, he soon found that writing about Mexico was something quite different. He later remarked: "There are only two ways you can do a book about a foreign country. The first is you have to do it from the outside in, in all innocence, in the first four or five days you are in the country, and be a bit silly about it, and try to be amusing. Or you can sit down and learn your material and do the same thing from the inside out. Yes, the second method was the only possible one for me." He then admitted, "It took me three and a half years to write the book."

The slim volume of literary portraits was and continues to be a critical success. Even before it was published, Spratling sent the manuscript to several of his Mexican friends and awaited their comments. Among them was the internationally known muralist, Diego Rivera, who on August 29, 1931, wrote to Spratling from his home in Mexico City:

My Dear Bill,

I have received the manuscript of your book which you were good enough to let me see. Many thanks.

The publication of this book makes me very happy; you have lived here a very long time and for this and other reasons—above all because you love Mexico and because Mexico loves you—it is your right to make a portrait of that which you know so well. You have made a portrait of Mexico composed of many small portraits of people and things.

Your portraits have the acuteness and grace of those painted by certain masters in my country who died before I was born. Those portraits were made with precision and tenderness and contain irony and love.

Your book is in itself a portrait and in that sense needs no preface; it explains itself.

Your friend who congratulates you,
Diego Rivera

Even Spratling was somewhat startled by the reception of *Little Mexico*. He once recalled, "It received wonderful reviews. I remember John Chamberlain writing two columns in the *New York Times* a couple of years later, declaring that here was one of the three classics on Mexico, lining it up with [Fanny] Calderón de la Barca [*Life in Mexico,* 1843] and Bernal Díaz del Castillo [*The True History of the Spanish Conquest of New Spain, 1519–1540*]. Stuart Chase wrote a page about it in the *Herald Tribune* and Carleton Beals wrote half a page somewhere else."

Fernando Horcasitas, the late Mexican linguist, historian and educator, rendered an excellent translation which was sold not only in Mexico but exported throughout Latin America; the translation, like the English original, also received high praise from the critics and public.

One Mexican reader, Agustín Salvát, who later became Director of Tourism in Mexico, wrote to Spratling praising the American's achievements "not only because of the eloquence and elegance of your prose or the concise Spartan-like portraits you present. What impressed me was your human approach to humans." Speaking as a Mexican, he added:

> The Indian world has been a world apart from us, something we get used to co-existing with yet without understanding it. It is a different world which we cannot comprehend if we do not plunge into it, in the nude, without impediment. This you have done and you give us glimpses of a richness that we have overlooked for centuries. . . . Your book shows that the confidence of the people can be gained if one's approach is as clean as yours; the only way to destroy a barrier of suspicion built over the years is to begin without a superiority complex and to be receptive to richness—spiritual richness—more vast than our own traditional concepts. This you did in your book, and I congratulate you.

Such praise from a Mexican critic of an American writing about Mexico is indeed rare, but in this case warranted. Spratling had obviously sat down and learned, as he said, his "material"—Mexico—and had done "the thing from the inside out." He was ready to admit that it had not been easy; he had rewritten the work "hundreds of times. I find writing," he complained, "a highly abnormal process. In fact, I hate it. When I finally had a draft of *A Small Mexican World,* I took it to bed with me and cut 122 pages before morning." He pruned until he had exactly what he wanted.

Twenty-five years after its first publication, an interviewer asked him if his collection was "completely non-fiction, or did you use a little writer's prerogative here and there." Without pausing, he blurted: "Hell, yes, it's real. It's Mexico." I know of no one who would disagree with him. His collection is a classic.

EDNA FERBER (1887–1968)

Other American writers visited Mexico in the 1930s and 1940s, but none stayed long enough to write about it as well as Porter or Spratling. For example, Edna Ferber—best known for her novels *So Big* (1924), *Cimarron* (1930), *Showboat* (1936) and *Giant* (1950)—left New York in 1931 and went to Mexico City for the same reason that she went to Hawaii, California or Europe: to rest between projects. After publishing *Cimarron* and finishing the manuscript of *American Beauty,* she was exhausted. For a change she took a train to Mexico, leaving Chicago and traveling to Texas where, as Crane had done in 1895, she crossed the border at Laredo and continued on the Aztec Eagle to Mexico City. There she stopped, staying, in general, within the limits prescribed by the English-speaking community.

However, she must have had something more on her mind than merely a vacation, for she was certainly informed about the current literature on Mexico. One of the characters in the story she wrote as a result of the trip—"They Brought Their Women"—had read everything recently published on the country including Ernest Gruening's *Mexico and Its Heritage* (1928), Stuart Chase's *Mexico* (1931) and Carleton Beals's *Mexican Maze* (1931). But then, Ferber herself often learned about places she intended to use in her fiction by reading about them as well as by experiencing them firsthand.

In her Mexican story, we see the country from the train or from a table at Sanborn's, the "American" restaurant near the Palace of Fine Arts. Her characters do all the things that most visiting Gringos would have done and still do: lunch "in the sun drenched patio of the Inn of San Angel," drift "down the Xochimilco canals" and return to the hotel "with armloads of violets and roses." They even whirl "down the dusty roads across the plains to the Pyramids of San Juan Teotihuacan."

Of the three main characters, one, a snob, is totally repulsed by Mexico. Her husband is fascinated by it but can't leave his wife to "try it out." The third character, Jeff Boyd, has the adventuresome spirit to try to know the real Mexico; absolutely enchanted by what he sees, he leaves the city for the Indian villages to discover how the Mexican peasant actually lives.

"They Brought Their Women," which became the title story of the collection she published in 1933, is typically Ferber: a group of interesting characters are placed in a setting which is alive and different and act out the human comedy as Ferber knew it. In her other works, we get Ferber on the Mississippi River or Ferber in Oklahoma or Texas or Alaska; in "They Brought Their Women" we get Ferber in Mexico— and Ferber in Mexico moves right along at an engrossing pace.

Unlike Porter and Spratling, who spoke and wrote about and literally lived in Mexico, Edna Ferber left very little about that country. Once, however, she did mention the trip that turned into the story included here when, in 1947, "They Brought Their Women" was reprinted in her collection, *One Basket:*

> On my way to Mexico . . . I was reading a book by Ernest Gruening. It was on the subject of the early settling of America by the pioneers. In it was a paragraph about the exalted position held by women in this country. Women in the early days were scarce and rare, hence they became something precious. When the American

settler went pioneering, his womenfolk came along. "The North American settlers brought their women," wrote Gruening.

This gave me the idea for the story of a modern hag-ridden husband journeying, perhaps, to a dazzling and romantic country such as Mexico. Into the mouth of this nagging wife I put certain speeches definitely uncomplimentary to Mexico itself, but these were strictly in character and certainly no reflection of my own opinion of that country. Unfortunately, the Mexican government misunderstood. After the short story appeared I was stunned to read in a New York newspaper that I was forever barred from Mexico.

I hope they have relented.

Ferber died twenty years later. No one knows if the Mexican government ever did relent. But, then, no one knows if she ever tried to return to that "dazzling and romantic country." At least we know this much: no one in the current Mexican government remembers Edna Ferber as ever being a persona non grata.

JAN GABRIAL (1906–?)

Another American woman, quite different from Porter or Ferber, went to Mexico several years later: Jan Gabrial, the first wife of Malcolm Lowry, the English author of *Under the Volcano* (1947), a novel many critics judge as the best ever written by a foreigner about Mexico.

Gabrial, who married Lowry in Paris in 1934, went with him in November 1936 to settle in Cuernavaca, where he planned to write. Their short time together obviously brought out the writer in his wife; certainly, living with Lowry gave her a lot to write about.

Lowry was a legendary drunk who sobered up long enough to let his genius influence his writing. And Gabrial was always there to watch and learn. She was present when Conrad Aiken, the American novelist who was also Lowry's friend and onetime tutor, visited the Lowrys in Cuernavaca during the spring and summer of 1937. Later, Gabrial became a character in Aiken's roman à clef, *A Heart for the Gods of Mexico* (1939); she also appears in his fictionalized autobiography *Ushant: An Essay* (1952).

Gabrial stayed with Lowry until December of 1937, when she returned to California and later obtained a divorce. Gabrial's marriage, however, amounted to more than two rather disquieting years out of her life; it produced two short stories which she wrote and published nearly ten years after she left Lowry.

In "Voyage to the Shores of Cuautla" (1945), she relates the tragic story of an Indian couple who are caught in the machinations of their own doing. Simply told, it is the story of a marriage, once so right, that goes wrong and everyone suffers. The other story, "Not With a Bang" (1946), is Gabrial's fictionalized account of the breakup of her marriage with Lowry. Set in Mexico City, it is a well-controlled study of a man who, like Lowry, is bent on self-destruction and in the course of his actions destroys everything he wants and needs; in Gabrial's story those desires become a small puppy and his marriage. The author has clearly drawn on two vital influences: her genius husband and Mexico.

Unfortunately, no one seems to know what happened to Jan Gabrial. Even Lowry's biographer, Douglas Day, was unable to find her. She simply has disappeared; to the public she lives on only as the first wife of Malcolm Lowry and the author of two stories set in Mexico.

JOHN GRAVES (1920–   )

John Graves has twice been a finalist for the National Book Award, first in 1959 for *Goodbye to a River* and again in 1981 for *From a Limestone Ridge*. He is represented in this collection by two of his finest short stories—"The Green Fly," first published in *Town and Country* in 1954 and again in *Prize Stories 1955: The O. Henry Awards,* and his favorite, "The

Aztec Dog," which appeared in the *Colorado Quarterly* in 1961 and then in *The Best American Short Stories: 1962*.

His own recollections and observations regarding himself and gringos in Mexico are vividly related in his Foreword to this anthology. Added to those comments are certain remarks that he wrote in 1978 about his life and times in Mexico:

> In truth, I have an incomplete feeling about Mexico, and I suppose at this stage, I am stuck with it. Having always been drawn toward it in terms of the toughness and starkness and leathery romance of the northern parts and in terms of the "Meskins" of rural Texas, often wet, with whom I had worked since youth and whom I liked, I suppose that in the *normal* course of events I would have followed up on my 1946 stay with numerous others, and might in the end have come to know the country well, as well, anyhow, as a foreigner can, for I have always found something about it, the Indian side especially, resistant to real understanding. But events, as is their habit, weren't normal.
>
> I did go back down for three or four months in 1959 or '60, but was chiefly working on an ill-fated novel at Mazatlán and a couple of other places, and again was focused more inward than outward.
>
> And since then there have been only occasional visits to border towns and one very good wild canoe trip down the Conchos River in Chihuahua in the middle sixties.
>
> And I know there are many things in Mexico that I would like to have known and taken part in, mainly the leathery difficult things. But you need to do that young and there is only so much time in life.

JACK KEROUAC (1922–1969)

How totally different from John Graves is Jack Kerouac, considered by many as the most prominent figure in the Beat Generation, a literary movement that flourished in the United

States in the fifties and early sixties and included such writers as poet Allen Ginsberg and novelist William Burroughs.

In fact, it was Burroughs who invited Kerouac to make his first visit to Mexico in June 1950. Burroughs was living in Mexico City with his wife, Joan, her child by a former marriage, and their own young son. Since January 1950, he had been studying anthropology in the graduate program of Mexico City College, later the Universidad de las Américas. But he and his wife had another reason for being in Mexico: both had a long history of alcohol and drug addiction and they found it easier, less expensive and much safer to obtain marijuana, morphine and other narcotics in Mexico than in the United States.

Indeed, Burroughs had written several glowing letters to Kerouac proclaiming one of the "virtues" of Mexico—the ready availability of sex, drugs and alcohol. Evidently that was enough to convince Kerouac, and in June 1950, he left Denver with two friends, Neal Cassady and Frank Shepherd, and drove to Texas, crossing into Mexico at Laredo and then continuing on to Mexico City. By the time they arrived at the Burroughs apartment, Kerouac was violently ill with dysentery. Almost immediately Cassady returned to the United States, Shepherd went off on his own, and in a short time, Kerouac recovered.

With Kerouac present and well, Burroughs lost interest in his graduate studies and withdrew during the summer semester. While he did register at the college for the fall and winter sessions, his grades—including six Fs and a D—indicate that he never again took his studies seriously. As Allen Ginsberg later commented, "Kerouac was obviously far more interesting to Burroughs than the courses he was taking at Mexico City College." Indeed, the two old friends—along with Burroughs's wife—spent the summer of 1950 either drunk on gin or tequila or stoned on marijuana or whatever other narcotic they could find.

Kerouac returned to the United States in September to work on *On the Road,* the novel that was to bring him praise from both the critics and the public.

A year later, on a "hot and drunken day" in September of 1951, a tragic accident occurred in the Burroughs apartment. Dennis McNally gives an account of the incident in his excellent biography of Kerouac, *Desolate Angel:*

> Supposedly Joan teased Bill into shooting a glass of gin off her head William Tell style. Certainly Bill was obsessed with handguns, and Joan's death wish was legendary. . . . In any case, there was a gun, a .38 revolver. Bill fired it, and it killed Joan. The newspapers were pleased with a juicy story: the [New York] *Daily News* blared *Heir's Pistol Kills His Wife: He Denies Playing William Tell* and presented Burroughs as a "wealthy Texas cotton grower" held on murder charges. Given the Mexican system of justice, it was no surprise that Bill managed to avoid prison, but he was temporarily confined to the country.

At any rate, Burroughs was still in Mexico in May 1952 when Kerouac returned to Mexico City by bus, crossing at Nogales. On that occasion—a rerun of his first visit as far as drugs and alcohol are concerned—he stayed only two months, leaving in early July. But he returned once more with Cassady in early December 1952. As he had done on their first trip in 1950, Cassady got stoned on marijuana and immediately left. Several days later, evidently the Mexican government released Burroughs and he fled Mexico for Florida. Being alone was too much for Kerouac; several days before Christmas, he too packed up and returned to the United States. This time, he stayed away until October 1956; during that two-month visit, he had experiences with a prostitute who was addicted to morphine, and that later became the novela *Tristessa* (1960). Also in that year, another of Kerouac's books, *Lonesome Traveler,* was published; one chapter, "Mexico Fellaheen," is an account of the bus trip from Nogales to Mexico City that he made in May 1952, the second time he visited Burroughs.

The story included here, "A Billowy Trip in the World," first appeared in *New Directions 16,* published early in 1956. It is, with only minor changes, the final chapter of Kerouac's most famous work *On the Road* (published in September 1957), an autobiographical rendering of the meanderings of Kerouac and some of his Beat Generation friends. The final chapter relates the experiences that Kerouac and Cassady had after they had crossed into Mexico at Laredo in June 1950.

In his biography of Kerouac, McNally records the incident as it actually happened:

> When they [Kerouac, Cassady and Shepherd] bought grass (marijuana) in [the village of] Gregória from a kid named Victor, and his aged mother came out from behind the house with a fat cigar full of guaranteed superior brain-cell destroyer, they thought they'd found paradise: "There's no *suspicion* here," whispered a delightedly shocked Neal, barely able to comprehend the possibility. Stoned to the eyeballs, they indulged in an expensive but super mini-orgy set to a mambo in a whorehouse before packing on down the road through the bugs and jungle to a second shock: a friendly cop. Too exhausted to continue, they parked by the side of the road, and with Frank in the car, Jack on top, and Neal in the road, they slept. A cop came by, and asked Jack if Neal was sleeping. Jack nodded, "*Sí, sí durmiendo,*" and assured that the dirty vagrant was not injured, the peaceful guardian sauntered off without bothering them.

This is the account by Kerouac's biographer; in "A Billowy Trip in the World," Kerouac presents his quasi-fictionalized version. Only the names are changed; what appears in the short story must have actually happened.

MARGARET SHEDD (1900–1986)

To say the least, Kerouac's experiences in Mexico and his use of them in his fiction were obviously different from those of other writers in the collection—especially Margaret Shedd, a novelist and prize-winning short story writer who *took* a great deal from but *gave* more to Mexico. She stands out from all other American writers who have traveled in and written about Mexico in one very important way: for over thirty years she had a tremendous indirect influence on contemporary Mexican literature.

That influence actually began in February 1950, when she joined the faculty of Mexico City College—at the time Burroughs was sometimes studying there—and founded the school's Creative Writing Center. However, less than two years later she left the school, and with funds from the Rockefeller Foundation, she and Alfonso Reyes, Mexico's respected poet and intellectual, inaugurated what was later to become the internationally famous *Centro Mexicano de Escritores*. Since its opening, this Mexican Writers Center has helped—through financial assistance and professional guidance—to launch the careers of more than two hundred Mexican writers, chief among them Juan Rulfo, Juan José Arreola, Marco Antonio Montes de Oca, Jorge Ibargüengoitia, Rosario Castellanos, Sergio Magaña, Carlos Fuentes, Clementina Díaz de Ovando and Gustavo Sainz. It would be impossible to speak of contemporary Mexican literature without mentioning the writers who have been associated with the Centro, which Shedd directed for fourteen years, until she was appointed the honorary director and a lifetime member of the board in 1965.

She recalled those first years at the Centro:

> At the beginning we had sessions once a week, on Wednesdays. They were wonderful sessions! We used to meet at two o'clock and would go on for hours and hours. I remember Rulfo. This was about 1954 when he was writing his first book *Pedro Paramo,* which came two years after the publication of his collection of short stories, *The Burning Plain.* I can see him standing up at the fireplace in that horrible little house we had on Río Volga near the American Embassy. Arreola was there too reading probably from *Confabulario* or one of his poems or a short story—he wrote so many. He was always prancing around. And those *wild* arguments we

had! It is much more orderly now. Anyway, we had lots of things going on. Lots of things. We sometimes went visiting. Once we went over to Guanajuato and had a great time having round-tables. We used to have a lot of round-tables on contentious subjects. Oh, it was a lovely life. And I feel the Center has contributed a great deal.

The whole time she was director, Shedd continued writing her novels and short stories which on three different occasions have appeared in the annual *Prize Stories: The O. Henry Awards,* as well as *Fifty Years of American Short Stories.* Six of those stories are set in Mexico, and two of them—"The Dwarfs of Xlapac" and her favorite, "I Hate You, Cruz Rivera"—appear in this collection.

On a trip to Mexico in 1979, she was asked to comment on a remark that Octavio Paz, the eminent poet and essayist, made in the September 17, 1979, issue of *The New Yorker:*

> The perceptions of the American novelists and poets who have written on Mexican themes have been brilliant but they have been fragmentary. Moreover, a critic who has devoted a book to this theme [Drewey Wayne Gunn, *British and American Writers in Mexico*] has said, they reveal less of Mexican reality than that of the author's personality. In general, American writers have not looked for Mexico in Mexico; they have looked for their obsessions, enthusiasms, phobias, hopes, and interests—and these are what they have found.

Without hesitation, Shedd responded:

> For one thing, it is a very pompous remark. For another thing, I'd like to know what Mexican writers writing about the U.S. have not also written about themselves. Every writer writes about himself. And that's exactly what his subject is. And he writes. And as I have just said, you can't possibly try to write about a country that you come into as a foreigner except in a very humble way. As a foreigner, you can't possibly try to point out the specialties or peculiarities of Mexico. I think it would

be presumptuous for an American writer to come here and write the "last word" about Mexico. I mean we have very fine Mexican writers who can do that. What's the matter with their doing it? I don't feel that we as foreigners are called upon to do it. And it would be very rude of us to do it.

In the stories by Margaret Shedd included here, it is obvious that she was enchanted not only by the country but also by the people and their creative capacities. "Here," she once noted,

> life and death have everything to do with creativity. And creativity has to do with despair. Despair for whatever reason! Perhaps they are dissatisfied with themselves. That is one of the main reasons for despair. Or perhaps they are hungry. For God's sake, you must know what I mean! Look, Mexico is a very creative country. Mexicans are an intense people. Dissatisfied and in despair. An essentially creative people. But I think that when you have a whole nation full of intense creativity and the people are held down for centuries, you automatically get a sense of death, you see. And there is, besides this sense of death, an equally intense and tremendous sense of life. Of living.

What Shedd said about Mexico definitely applies to the characters in the two stories included here. In both there is a strong need to struggle and fight to overcome. It is, perhaps, not by chance that what she saw in Mexico managed to surface in her own writing. For too many years, she lived and worked too closely with the most talented of Mexican writers for that *not* to have influenced her.

EDMUND J. ROBINS (1904–1978)

Shedd's stories are followed by two written by Edmund Robins, who studied creative writing with Shedd in the late 1940s when she taught in the graduate program at the University of California-Berkeley. It was, in fact, his former teacher who brought him to Mexico when she arrived in February 1950 to open the Creative Writing Center at Mexico City College; Robins became one of her faculty. Then, when Shedd left shortly thereafter, Robins took over as director, a position he held until the university discontinued the creative writing program in 1975, the year that Robins retired and was named professor emeritus.

In addition to teaching and publishing short fiction, poems and essays in journals and magazines in the United States, he also edited, with Coley Taylor, the *Mexico Quarterly Review,* a "little magazine" that presented the works of some of Mexico's most outstanding writers and artists, include Juan José Arreola, Ignacio Bernal, Ramón Beteta, Rubén Dario, Fernando Horcacitas, Miguel León Portilla, Marco Antonio Montes de Oca, José Clemente Orozco, José Emilio Pacheco, Octavio Paz, Alfonso Reyes, Juan Rulfo, Gustavo Sainz, Ramón Xirau and an entire edition dedicated to the works of Jaime Torres Bodet. In addition, Robins's journal published the works of many prominent North Americans who are closely identified with Mexico, including Arnold Belkin, Elizabeth Beteta, Richard Greenleaf, Charles Mann, Clare Mooser, John Paddock, Selden Rodman, William Spratling, Coley Taylor and Charles Wicke.

Under Robins's direction, the *Mexico Quarterly Review* flourished. Obviously, meeting and knowing the contributors to the journal as well as reading their works aided greatly in his pursuit to understand the Mexican character. Likewise, because he lived in Mexico for so many years, he had the opportunity to experience those difficulties any American expatriate has in trying to adjust and adapt to a culture so foreign to his own. Those difficulties emerge in both of his stories presented here: "A Snapped String" (1962) and "A Primitive" (1968).

Robins, like Spratling, never left Mexico; he died in Cholula, Puebla, on December 6, 1978, and at his request his ashes were interred in the walls of an eighteenth-century posada in Mitla, Oaxaca, which he had visited on numerous occasions.

EUGENE K. GARBER (1932–   )

Eugene Garber, represented here by "An Old Dance," is one of the new generation of American writers who have spent a short time in Mexico and felt the creative force of the culture and the people. When asked to comment on his own experiences in the country that led to the writing of his story, he wrote,

> I was there for about three and a half months, mostly in Guadalajara, with trips to Mexico City, Uruapan, and Pátzcuaro. I was temporarily demolished by amoebae and more or less hypnotized and frightened by the splendid barbarousness of the country. Being a myth freak, I got at least superficially into mesoamerican mythology, which obviously shows up in the story. What also obviously impressed me was the unemulsified mixture of pagan, Christian, Indian, European—a sort of toiling, grinding place. A powder keg. Violence always in the air.
>
> I wrote the story in Guadalajara hot upon my return from the trip to Mexico City and other places. This is very rare for me, maybe unique. Usually I let the material settle in my mind over a long period of time before I write about it. As a result this story has perhaps some fairly accurate local color—all obviously manipulated for symbolic purposes. Actually, I don't care much about sociological accuracy. My stories are essentially mythological.

DOROTHY TEFFT (1925–   )

Dorothy Tefft arrived in Mexico City in 1945 to study Spanish at the old UNAM Summer School and has been in Mexico ever since.

When she married the second son of Rodolfo Gaona, Mexico's fabled bullfighter (1888–1975), she began a study of Mexican personality, thought, history and culture that would interest her for the rest of her life. The elusive "Mexican character," she believes, has as many facets as there are strata in Mexican society.

Her three children were born in Mexico and, far from feeling torn between two cultural heritages, feel sorry for children who do not have at least two backgrounds to draw from.

Tefft taught English at the Universidad de las Américas for
ten years. Now retired, she is working very slowly on two
books: one, in English, a collection of stories about her handsome, talented, ill-fated family-in-law; the other, in Spanish,
a biography of her former father-in-law.

The two stories offered here—"The Dig" and "Serenade"—clearly indicate what American writers, from Crane
onward, soon discover when they encounter Mexico: the
American view of a situation is rarely the same as the Mexican one.

When asked if she could put herself into the Mexican
mind for portrayal of character in her stories, as Katherine
Anne Porter did in "María Concepción," for instance, Tefft
answered:

It would depend greatly upon *what* Mexican mind, of
course, but generally speaking, yes, I could. As an author, however, I don't feel comfortable in anyone's mind
except my own. I prefer to observe and record.

When you have lived in Mexico with a Mexican family, right there in the middle of it—sharing, grieving,
celebrating, loving, fighting, holding your own—for
more than twenty years, Mexican thought not only becomes clear to you, it becomes *your* thought to a great
extent.

And I dare say that all the members of that Mexican
family had a clear view of what small-town U.S.A. opinions were, after living with me. I told them frequently,
for a while at the beginning anyway, how things ought
to be. What they must have thought, that assured, sophisticated Mexican family, of my sophomoric observations! I blush now, remembering; but the basic values,
we all found—the biblical, human values of decency and
love and behavior—are no different in Mexico City
from those in Wellsville, New York.

The father—chief, founder, and absolute authority of this family I found myself bound into—was Rodolfo Gaona, one of the most extraordinary and, yes, glamorous personalities produced by this maddening, rewarding, wonderful country. And what he thought when his favorite son brought home for a bride a young, gauche, Protestant *gringa,* I can only imagine. There were many skirmishes there at the beginning, I can tell you, but eventually we all adapted to each other and began to trust.

Although we lived in Rodolfo Gaona's house with him for five years, we seldom saw him—usually at mealtimes. The house was large, and he spent a great deal of his time in his rooms, reading. He never mixed, in an everyday way, with his family: even at home, he made appearances. Gaona was a S-T-A-R, all the time, in private and in public.

But his influence was strong upon us. We were all tremendously proud of him, of course, but awed, and always in the house there was fear of his notoriously violent temper, easily unleashed. Fear and awe can be damaging influences on young sons: their father's act was a difficult one to follow.

As a boy, Gaona supported his widowed mother and his brother by making shoes in a factory in Leon, Guanajuato. Given one small chance to become a bullfighter, he immediately put so much bravery, grace, and personality into the role that he rose to the top of that unlikely profession, and he stayed at the top, unlike the unlucky hero of Ibañez's *Blood and Sand.*

By the age of twenty-one, he had his own private railroad car; at twenty-five he was wearing five-carat diamonds as shirt buttons, down the streets of Madrid, and sending home sums that bought large sections of downtown Mexico City real estate. Fans followed, whenever they could, to cheer each of his performances in Spain, Portugal, and Mexico.

At thirty-seven he announced suddenly that he was

leaving the bullring, refused really extraordinary offers to continue, and retired, saying that it was forever; and it was. He rarely attended a bullfight after that.

A true Gaona legend: Rich, idolized, still young at retirement, he was offered the concession of all public transport in Mexico City by an influential fan. He refused angrily, saying, "What do you think I know about buses, or street-cars? Do I look like a bus driver?" When friends remonstrated, he answered, "If they give me this today, tomorrow they'll be back asking for something. I won't be obligated to anyone in the world."

The interests of my father-in-law became, of course, those of his family, and mine, too: literature, Spanish and Mexican; horses and riding; history, Spanish and Mexican; *frontón;* the guitar, and music—*flamenco* and *cante jondo,* and *zarzuela* tunes from Spain, old songs from all parts of Mexico, waltzes from the times of Don Porfirio Díaz, *corridos* from the Revolution. The Gaonas knew them all, and I made haste to learn.

My mother-in-law, from Spain, saw to it that I took up knitting, sewing, and cooking—Spanish and Mexican; she taught me to co-exist with and manage (it isn't easy!) vast numbers of Mexican servants, too. You have to be quick indeed to keep one step ahead of a Mexican maid!

These were some of the things I learned in that great house on the Paseo de la Reforma. These, and how to bring up children in the Mexican manner. When I think back on those years now, so many stories and remembrances beat around my head that it's either weep or write. Yes, I know something of the Mexican mind.

CAROLYN OSBORN (1934–   )

The last story in this anthology—"Letter to a Friend Far Away"—is by Carolyn Osborn. Other stories by Osborn have appeared in such journals as *Paris Review, Antioch Review, Texas Quarterly, Descant* and *New Orleans Review.* In

1977, her collection of short stories, *A Horse of Another Color,* was selected as co-winner, with a work by Paul Horgan, as the Best Book Length Fiction by a Southwestern Writer.

Osborn, who lives in Austin, Texas, has been a frequent visitor to Mexico since she—along with Vance Bourjaily, William Brinkley, Tómas Rivera and José Antonio Villarreal—taught at a writers workshop at the Universidad de las Américas during the summer of 1977.

She was recently asked to comment on writing about Mexico:

> The images I have of Mexico are dramatic and appear as I write. I can't begin to use them all—the yellow baroque church blossoming between two volcanoes, a distant figure in a whole field of orange marigolds and an almost violet sky, the exhaust blackened trees lining the main streets of Mexico City. The interior slide show dims. The people crowd forward.
>
> My main characters are generally American expatriates or American visitors; obviously these are the people I know best. At the most basic level, their reactions to each other, to Mexicans, to another culture all provide the conflicts necessary to story telling. Not until I began to know Mexican people could I write about fictional Mexican characters. And the ones I've written about are always seen from an American viewpoint. I haven't lived in Mexico long enough to attempt to do otherwise.
>
> On another level, the incongruities of daily life in a third world country where a farmer drives his two-wheeled cart down the road next to the car factory are situations my characters flourish in.
>
> My people are a troubled lot. They have unhappy marriages, are divorced, drink too much, have too much or too little money, can't speak the language—usually because they refuse to learn it. Most of this could happen in any country; I have written stories about Americans set in France, in Germany, in England. Now, because I've been there more frequently lately, some of them are taking place in Mexico.

Mexico is so near yet so foreign, known yet forever novel, an archetype of flagrant contrasts, and for me a perfect mirror of my characters' flaws, desires, dreams.

Here, in this collection, is Mexico as seen and heard and experienced during the last one hundred years by fifteen different American short story writers from Stephen Crane to Carolyn Obsorn. Each one had very special reasons for coming to Mexico, for staying for a while, and then for leaving impressions on the printed page. Combined, these talents spread before the reader a mural of Mexico as colorful and startling and complex as any painted by Diego Rivera or Clemente Orozco. Here will be found a very real depiction. Real? It is best to respond to that question as did William Spratling: "Real? Hell, yes, it's real. It's Mexico."

Edward Simmen
Universidad de las Américas
Cholula, Puebla, México

Gringos in Mexico

William Cullen Bryant

A VISIT TO MEXICO

MEXICO, March 6, 1872: Our voyage from Havana to Vera Cruz was in all respects a holiday. The temperature was most agreeable, the airs the softest that ever blew, the sea like a looking-glass, and the steamer—the British steamer Corsica—comfortable and roomy. In a little more than three days we were anchored in the harbor of Vera Cruz, in the middle of the night. The morning showed us the city, somewhat picturesque in its aspect, with its spires and stuccoed houses, and with its ancient fort on a little isle in front of it. A range of blue mountains lay to the west, and high above these the peak of Orizaba, white with perpetual snow, was seen among the clouds. I was told that the captain of the port desired to speak with me; and, meeting him, was informed that, by direction of the Minister of Finance, he had come with the government boat to take me and my party to town. We landed at a wharf against which the sea was beating with its gentlest ripples, but this is not always its mood. When a strong north wind blows, it rolls up vast waves, beginning at the coast of Louisiana and Florida, and sweeps them into the roadstead before Vera Cruz. The surf is hurled against the sea-wall that protects the city, and the outer streets are drenched with the spray. No vessel can then discharge or receive its cargo, and it often happens that several days elapse before there can be a communication between ship and shore. The harbor at Tampico is no better; indeed, it is said to be worse, and equally exposed to the fury of the northers. In fact, there is no good harbor on the eastern coast of Mexico, and the proper communication between that country and all others that lie to the east of it must be by means of railways and through the United States, unless, indeed, the Mexican government should build artificial harbors for its towns on the coast, an undertaking for which it has no money. Yet, I am told, there is a pretty good harbor at Anton Lizardo, less than twenty miles south of Vera Cruz, but at Anton Lizardo there is no town. Moreover, there is the yellow fever, which broods almost perpetually over the towns on the low coasts. At Vera Cruz they told me that the place was never without it; but they made light of the distemper, as a sort of seasoning process which every stranger residing there for three months must assuredly go through.

But the far greater part of the republic of Mexico consists of high table-lands. "Nine tenths of our country," said a Mexican gentleman to me, "belongs to what we call the *tierra templada*—the region which produces the harvests of the temperate zones." Perhaps this is an excessive estimate, but no one who has the map of that country before him can fail to see that a railway, beginning at our own frontier, might convey the traveller from one cool upland valley to another, till it landed him, almost without a consciousness that he was under a tropical sun, in the capital of the republic. This will yet be the principal means of communication between the two countries.

"You will find Vera Cruz a dirty, miserable place," said the bluff English commander of our steamer, the Corsica; but he did it injustice. The city lies low, and is under the suspicion of being badly drained, but the streets are a great deal cleaner than those of New York, and the black vultures, which are seen hopping about them or sitting by scores on the cupolas of its churches, devour everything above ground that can corrupt in the heat and poison the air. The dwellings and warehouses are necessarily built each of two stories around a square court; they have lofty ceilings, spacious rooms and airy galleries, the sitting-rooms so arranged as to admit the fresh sea-breeze that comes in from the harbor.

Early the next morning we were on the railway which is partly constructed from Vera Cruz to the city of Mexico. It was a somewhat dreary road for the first fifty miles, yet not without its interest. The iron track swept by a circuitous course through vast grazing-grounds of a russet hue, thinly set with low trees, yet leafless for the most part, but now and then blossoming with great strange flowers, bright yellow, or pink, or crimson. Here and there we passed a village of the aborigines, in which the dwellings were mere wigwams, built with four stout posts sustaining a roof thatched with coarse grass or leaves of the aloe. The walls of these cabins were rows of sticks or reeds, set in the ground so thinly as scarce to afford a shelter from the wind. There were a few houses of more pretension, built of sun-dried bricks white-washed, and roofed with coarse tiles. The brown inhabitants, a race of rather low stature, but square built, loitered in the simplest possible attire about their dwellings, the women, for the most part, sitting on the ground at their doors. It could be seen at once that they were a people of few wants, and that these wants were easily supplied.

About fifty miles from Vera Cruz the country began to wear a different aspect. There were tokens of irrigation, or at least of more frequent rains, in this the dry section; the trees and shrubs were all in leaf, and there were fields green with harvests, and plantations of the banana. As we went on we found ourselves on the border of a stream flowing in a deep ravine, between almost perpendicular banks, hundreds of yards below us. A tall forest rose on each side, the trees sprouting with half a dozen parasitic plants, some of which were in bloom. The castor-bean grew by the track to the size of a tree, and the morning-glory, which here never feels the frost, climbed the trees and tied her blue or crimsoned blossoms to the branches a hundred feet from the ground.

We stopped at the present termination of the railway, seventy miles from Vera Cruz, at a place called Fortin, from which we were taken by a diligence to the city of Orizaba, situated among sugar estates, orange gardens, and coffee plantations. We had heard stories of robberies committed on the road between Vera Cruz and Mexico, and we did not feel quite sure that they were not the mere echo of what had happened some time since; but here at Orizaba the landlord of our hotel told us of a recent incident of the kind. "If you go on," he said, "you will stop for the night at San Agustin de Palmar. Not far from that place, two or three days since, the diligence was stopped, and two passengers, a Mr. Foote and companion, were robbed of fifteen thousand dollars, their trunks, and all the valuables they had with them." It therefore became a question whether it was prudent for us to proceed. We consulted together, and, concluding that the robbers would not be likely to repeat their crime immediately, we determined to go on. We threaded the long valley in which Orizaba lies, passing between banana patches and hedges in which the finest roses were in bloom, and beside little rivulets running by the wayside to water the fields. There are points in Orizaba commanding some of the most beautiful views of mountain scenery that ever met my eyes—summits, crests, ridges, spurs of mountains, interlocking each other, with valleys penetrating far between, the haunt of eternal spring, with the peak of Orizaba overlooking out from the region of eternal winter.

Coming to where the mountains bounded the valley at its western end, our vehicle ascended what are called the Heights of Aculcingo by a zigzag path cut in the rocks, and in one place crossed by a pretty waterfall. These heights are famed for the fine views they afford of the gulfy valleys below and the great mountain buttresses one behind another. But of these we had little more than a glimpse, for the mist gathered round us, and the darkness fell. A man who sat at the left hand of the driver of the diligence lighted a rope of combustibles, which served for a torch to light our way. And this was soon shown to be necessary, for the road, which since we left Fortin had been for the most part a good macadamized highway, became one of the worst on which I ever travelled.

The track was full of inequalities; it lay deep in fine dust, which concealed them from sight; and we plunged from one to another with fearful jolts, which almost seemed as if they would shake the old diligence to fragments. We drove on in a cloud of white dust, surrounding us at every step. I have never seen our good old mother, the Earth, under a more ghastly aspect than that which she wore in the light of our torch. Everything looked white—the road, the banks, the fields, as far as we could see on each side—and the vegetation which bordered our way was of the ugliest and grimmest that the earth produces: cactuses, with their angular and unshapely growth, twelve or fifteen feet in height; the stiff and pointed leaves of the *maguey,* or aloe; and, grimmer than they, a kind of palm with branches, and at the end of every branch a tuft of bayonet-shaped leaves, pointing in every direction from a common centre, like the hair of a human head standing on end with horror. It seemed the very region where one might expect a robber to spring from the bank of the road, put his pistol to your breast, and demand your money.

At eleven o'clock in the evening we were at the little town of San Agustin de Palmar, and, finding that our vehicle was to set out again at half-past one, we exchanged places with some passengers who desired to go on immediately, but whose conveyance would not be ready till five o'clock in the morning. The morning found us journeying over a broad, arid, herbless, treeless plain, encircled by mountains equally bare of vegetation, and of a pale-brown hue. We were still shrouded and almost choked with the dust. Little whirlwinds of dust crossed the highway before us and passed off toward the mountains. This is the season when the earth is at rest— the barren season of the year; in the summer, when the rains fall, these now bare fields are green and fresh with the growing harvests. The mountains gradually came nearer the highway, and we passed from this highland valley into another, which I was told is of still higher elevation, and so we journeyed on from one region enclosed by high mountains to another, the cool, spring-like airs indicating that we were in the temperate regions of the republic. Vast fields of the *maguey*, the *Agave Americana*, sometimes called the aloe, from which the intoxicating liquor called *pulque* is drawn, now made their appearance—the dark-green plants set in rows at such a distance from each other as allowed the cultivation of maize and other grains between them. Here and there was a field green with irrigation, and soon the spires of Puebla were seen against the evening sky. The roads were full of people of the aboriginal race, returning to their cabins from the town, which we entered a little after sunset.

The next morning, while waiting for the train, I walked, with my friends, the streets of Puebla, which have a cheerful look. Above all the dwellings rises the cathedral with its domes and spires. We entered it, and found the floor covered with worshippers, three fourths of whom were women, murmuring aloud their prayers in a supplicating, half-tremulous tone. The exterior of the edifice is imposing; the ribbed columns of Roman architecture are both tall and massive, and not without a certain simplicity in the detail, which, joined to the somewhat dark color of the marble, gives to the whole a grave aspect well suited to the house of prayer.

At half-past eleven the next morning we took the railway train to convey us over the hundred and fifteen miles lying between Puebla and the capital. The region was much like that over which we had travelled, save that in approaching Mexico we passed by abandoned habitations, the tokens of a dwindled population, and for a space skirted the shallow waters of Lake Texcoco, which in places covered the ground on its edge with a sediment as white as snow. The train stopped at a rather shabby station in the suburbs of the capital. Our luggage had to undergo an inspection at the custom-house, and shortly after we were installed in pleasant quarters at the Hotel Iturbide, named after the young adventurer who resided for a short time in the building, and who, aspiring to be the Emperor of Mexico, paid for his ambition with his life.[1]

MEXICO, MARCH 8th: One of the first things which we had to do on arriving at the city of Mexico was to conform our dress to the climate. We were now in a cool region nearly eight thousand feet above the level of the sea, and the temperature admonished us to resume our winter under-clothing. The sunshine at this season is perpetual and the weather spring-like. It is only from May to October that the clouds thicken into rain. In the early part of winter spangles of frost are sometimes seen on the ground. On an estate in the neighborhood of the city, and on the pleasant slopes of Tacubaya, amid stately palms and orange-trees loaded with their golden fruit, and roses in bloom, I saw a tree, more than fifteen feet high, wrapped in matting to the very top. "What does that mean?" I asked. "It is some tender tree," was the answer, "from the hot country south of us, which they have covered in that way to protect it from the frost." The summers in this region, I am told, are but little warmer than the winters, the chief difference being that the summer is the rainy season, when the afternoons and evenings are showery, and the fields are in their fullest luxuriance.

The city stands so far above the sea-level that the inhabitants breathe a thin air, which, as the stranger immediately perceived, puts him out of breath in ascending a staircase or declivity. Those who suffer from symptoms of heart-disease find them considerably aggravated here, and the remark is often made that deaths from that disease are more frequent here than in most places. The air is as dry as it is thin. It requires very brisk exercise, even in warm weather, to bring out anything like sensible perspiration. "I suppose," said a medical gentleman with whom I was talking on this subject, "that there are persons here, born in Mexico, who never in their lives experienced anything like sensible perspiration." "It is an insidious climate," said another resident. "You take cold easily; you expose yourself to a draught which is neither considerable nor unpleasant, and the next day you have a severe cold." The disease of the lungs which they call *pulmonia* in Madrid, and which is there so violent and fatal, is almost equally so here, and carries off its victims after a short illness. Yet Mexico is a healthy city, notwithstanding that it is badly drained; indeed, it can scarcely be said that it is drained at all, so slight is all the descent that can be given to the drains.

There can be no cellars to the houses, for, on digging two or three feet in the ground, you come to water. Great shallow, plashy lakes cover vast tracts in the neighborhood of the city, and sometimes, in seasons of copious rain, overflow their banks and invade the streets, and ripple against the thresholds of the dwellings. Yet is the air, so they say, never charged with moisture, and Mexico will yet be the frequent resort of those who suffer from any disease of the lungs or throat requiring a dry atmosphere. I doubt, however, whether the climate is particularly favorable to longevity, for I saw few old men, either among the aboriginal inhabitants or those of Spanish descent.

One who takes his idea of this city from photographs and engravings is apt to suppose it a city of small houses; but this is a mistake. It is true that the houses are not often of more than one story, but they are spacious and massively built, with lofty ceilings. They generally enclose a court of ample size, round which, on the second story, runs a gallery supported by sturdy columns or square pillars of heavy masonry. From these galleries the doors open into the rooms where the family live, including the sleeping-rooms, and standing in the galleries or in the roomy antechambers are vases of flowering plants of brilliant bloom, which in this spring-like climate need no other attention than the water which moistens the soil about their roots. I can scarcely imagine a pleasanter abode in a large town than some of these houses belonging to opulent families—houses airy, cheerful, and luxuriously commodious. Yet beside this opulence you see the most squalid poverty; ragged and dirty human beings, who saunter about during the day and lie down at night wherever the night surprises them. In a climate so soft as this, with a soil so genial and productive, people are tempted to be poor. It costs but little labor to obtain the means of living; slight clothing is all that is needed; slight shelter suffices; a few beans, *frijoles,* and two or three *tortillas,* or flap-jacks, wind up the living machine for the day. Where poverty is so easy a condition of life, and its few wants are so cheaply supplied, there must be many poor. "How many are there in the city of Mexico, rich

and poor taken together?" I asked a resident. "Probably somewhat over two hundred thousand," was the answer, "but no
man can speak with any certainty. The moment that any person employed by the government appears and begins to take
the enumeration, the suspicion is awakened that there is to be
a conscription, or that a new tax is to be levied. The people
disappear like a brood of young partridges, and keep out of
the way till the supposed danger is over."

Side by side with the utter poverty which I have just described there is great luxury. The day after my arrival I was a
guest at a private banquet, and, without professing an admiration for luxurious dinners, I may say that I never sat at any
in which sumptuousness exceeded it. The blaze of gaslights,
the glitter of plate, the variety and delicacy of the viands, the
exquisite wines, the rich attire of the ladies, the number and
dexterity of the attendants—were all there in as great perfection as at the tables of the most luxurious of our own mer-
chant-princes, with a dessert of fruits of such various flavors
as our climate does not afford. Nor should I leave out of the
account the profusion of flowers, both of tropical and temperate climates, which sweetened the atmosphere—all gathered
from their beds in the open air.

The day following was Sunday, and as I went to the cathedral I was struck with the number of persons whom I met
selling lottery-tickets. Gambling is one of the besetting vices
of the Mexicans, and the numerous lotteries give them the
opportunity to gamble as they are going to church. I found
the floor of the cathedral occupied by a crowd on their knees,
mostly women, while priests in their rich vestments were of-
ficiating at the principal altar. The building without is not
imposing; its front is covered with a jumble of pilasters and
capitals and scrolls, and other architectural ornaments; but
within it is grave and grand, though in some parts wanting in
simplicity.

I have spoken of the vestments of the priests. By the "laws
of reform," as they are called, no ecclesiastical costume can
be worn in the streets. You might traverse Mexico from
Sonora to Yucatan and never meet with any person whom

you would recognize as a priest, save when you entered the churches. They are obliged to dress as others do; they can get up no religious processions: all such are forbidden; the convents are suppressed; there is neither monk nor nun in all Mexico; the convent buildings and grounds have been taken by the government; many of the churches have shared the same fate, and the schools, of which at one time the priests had the sole direction, are all secularized and given to the control of laymen. So dissatisfied are the Catholic clergy with these restrictions that, as I am told, they are the most zealous friends of annexation to the United States that are found in all Mexico, in the hope of recovering by it some of their lost privileges.[2]

From the cathedral I followed the street till I came to a chapel belonging to what was called the Church of Jesus. This church and another, both of them large, have been sold by the government, at a low price, to the Protestant worshippers. In the chapel I found about four hundred persons, which were as many as could be seated, in devout attitudes, while in the pulpit a minister in a white surplice was engaged in prayer. The form of the service was partly liturgical, and there were occasional responses. After the prayer a hymn was given out, and sung by the congregation with great apparent fervor. I looked round upon the assembly, which was composed of men in the proportion of three to one of the other sex, and perceived that they were mostly of the aboriginal race. Most of them, however, were neatly dressed, and all were attentive. The minister then preached a sermon; he spoke with animation, and was apparently heard with very great interest. I inquired afterward the meaning of what I had seen. "The person whom you saw in the pulpit," was the answer, "is Father Agnas, a Catholic priest of no little eloquence, who has been converted to the Protestant faith; but the principal head of the Protestant Church here, and the composer of its liturgy, is Father Reilly, who is a citizen of the United States, although reared in Chili. He has engaged with great zeal in the cause of Protestantism, and is aided by several ministers who once belonged to the Church of Rome, and are now as zealous as he in making converts from it. The government favors them, and would doubtless be glad of their success, for the government and the Catholic priesthood bear no good-will to each other. There are now more than a score of these Protestant congregations in the city of Mexico, and more than thirty in the neighboring country. The priesthood are naturally vexed at seeing the Protestants in churches which once were theirs, but the effect upon them is salutary, for it has made them more attentive to their own personal morals."

Those who have read the accounts of Mexico given by travellers will remember that the clergy of this country are generally spoken of as exceedingly loose in their morals. The truth of this was afterward confirmed to me by a gentleman who had resided for some years in Mexico. "I am a Catholic," said he, "brought up as a Catholic in the United States. When I came here I expected to find the clergy of my Church such as they are in the country I left—men of pure lives, and watchful guardians of the morals of their flocks. I was disappointed; I found them immoral in their own lives, and indifferent to the morals of those who were under their spiritual care. I must say that they have not done their duty; and if the Mexican people are not what they ought to be, the clergy are in a good degree responsible." Afterward I saw Father Reilly, as he is often called here.[3] He assured me that all which I had heard of his success and the displeasure of the clergy was true, and expressed strong hopes of further success. I mentioned to him that by far the greater part of the worshippers whom I saw in the cathedral were women, and that, on the other hand, in his church I found that the men greatly outnumbered the women. He replied that in some of the Protestant congregations the women were most numerous. There is no question that the Catholic clergy in Mexico have been fearfully corrupted by what may be called the monopoly of religious worship which they possessed, by the immense riches of their Church, and the power of persecution which was placed in their hands. They will become better men by the effect of adversity and the formidable rivalry to which they are now subjected.

MEXICO, MARCH 10th: One of the first visits I made to the country surrounding the city of Mexico was to Chapultepec, a rocky mount rising from the midst of a plain west of the town. A grove of cypresses and other trees shaded its eastern slope, and hither the kings of Mexico, before the conquest, are said to have resorted for recreation. One of these cypresses yet bears the name of Montezuma's Tree, and even before his time must have seen several generations of the Aztec monarchs. We measured it, and found it thirty-seven feet and four inches in circumference—the largest tree that I ever saw in any part of the world. It is still in full vigor, and will outlast many generations of men yet to come. I looked into its broad extent of branches, hung with gray, thread-like mosses clinging to them like mist, and thought of the dim antiquity which dwelt there, and of the unwritten histories, both sorrowful and pleasant, bound up in the long life of that silent tree.

It was a holiday, and there were several parties of pleasure in these ancient shades. In one part was a family group at a picnic; in another a guitar was tinkling, and two or three couples dancing; in another were a young man and woman withdrawn from the rest—most likely lovers—engaged in such talk as lovers use. I climbed with my companions to the top of the hill, where is a palace which had been fitted up by Maximilian for his own residence, but in which the poor fellow, during his short and most unhappy reign, could be scarcely said to have ever resided. It stands in the midst of a garden, where the air is sweetened all the year with shrubs in bloom. Near it, on the esplanade, the Mexican gentleman who accompanied us pointed out what at first seemed to us a deep well—a circular opening in the ground—walled up with stones apparently hewn. "This," he said, "belongs to the time of the Aztecs. It communicates with a cavern below, having its issue on the west side of the hill, so that it forms an underground passage."

The view from the top of Chapultepec is very fine. The Mexicans are fond of repeating a saying ascribed to Humboldt[4]—that it is the finest view in the world; to which I should not agree, for there are finer in the neighborhood of Orizaba. But it was very striking as I saw it—the great valley of Mexico stretching away on every side, the city with its spires, the green fields artificially watered, the brown pasture-lands, the great glimmering lakes, the rows and groups of trees in full leaf that mark the place of the floating gardens, and finally the circle of mountains enclosing all. Beyond these, in clear weather, the snowy peaks of the two great and now silent volcanoes of Popocatepetl and Iztaccihuatl are seen rising to an immense height. Near at hand, and in full sight, is the building called the Molino del Rey, or King's Mill, around which was fought the bloody battle of that name, just before the entrance of the United States troops into the city in the late war with Mexico. With the narrative of that war before him, one may stand on Chapultepec and trace the progress of the American armies step by step as they drew near to the capital which was to fall into their hands.

On the slope of Chapultepec we passed the large basin of a copious spring, forty feet in depth, and so clear that the bottom seems almost close to the eye. A rapid stream rushes from it and is received in a stately aqueduct, which carried it off to the city of Mexico on its tall arches, resembling those which cross the Roman Campagna. Looking to the south, you see another and longer aqueduct, which strides across the plain, bringing water from a more distant point. Lower down gushes from the ground another spring, no less copious, which supplies commodious baths, public and private, and then flows on to irrigate the fields, marking its course by tracts of verdure. Leaving these behind us, we followed the road a little distance to the village of Tacubaya, situated on ground somewhat elevated above the plain, and noted for its beautiful country seats, the property of opulent families in the city. We entered and wandered over one of these—the Escandon estate, as it is called, from the name of the family owning it. It was a perfect labyrinth of walks among fruit-trees and flowering shrubs. The walks, twining through the grove, are somewhat neglected, to be sure. Here and there were towering over the palms the fruit-trees. A spacious mansion stood in the midst of an ample flower-garden. "Is not the family there?" I asked. "No," was the answer, "the family is safer in town. The members sometimes come out to visit this place in the daytime and return by daylight, but they never venture to remain here over night. They might be robbed, or perhaps kidnapped, and made to pay a heavy ransom." I looked round on the orange-trees dropping their fruit, and on the neglected walks, where the weeds were beginning to make their appearance, and, beautiful as the place was, I did not much wonder that it was not more carefully tended by those who were able to enjoy its beauty only by snatches, or in constant fear of a visit from banditti. That Tacubaya was not a safe place for those who had anything to lose I had a proof before I got home, for, arriving at the railway-station just before sunset, I entered the cars amid a crowd of people returning to town, and soon after, having occasion to consult my watch, I found that it was missing.

The most unsafe place, however, at present, seems to be the railway between this city and Puebla. The newspapers here give accounts of attacks made by robbers on the trains conveying *pulque,* which is the beverage drawn from the plant called here the *maguey.* These attacks, however, have been generally repulsed. Not so fortunate has been the superintendent and paymaster of the railway which is yet constructing between Puebla and Orizaba, Mr. Quin, whom I saw the day after my arrival, just returned from an adventure with the robbers. They seized him when he happened to be without money, took away his watch, and, after a detention of two hours, bargained with him for his release on the payment of fifty dollars, which he brought them, and they returned him his watch. But the watch he was not to keep, for two days afterward I heard that they found him with sixteen hundred dollars on his person, and took that and the watch also. Soon afterward news came that Mr. Quin was kidnapped a third time. He had no money with him, and after detaining him a day or two, the robbers allowed him to depart, with the message to his employers that if forty thousand dollars were not immediately sent them they would tear up the iron rails. The money, however, has not been paid, and the railway is yet untouched. The leader of these bandits is one Negrete who calls himself a general and claims to be a revolutionist, instead of a robber.

MEXICO, MARCH 11th: One of the most interesting things to be seen in Mexico is the school of Tecpan de Santiago, a charitable institution, founded and supported by a Mexican lady, the Señora Baz, wife of an opulent gentleman who has formerly filled the post of Governor of the province of Mexico. We called first at the house of Governor Baz, as he is called, one of the finest mansions in Mexico, fitted up with great taste and attention to comfort. His lady, a native Mexican of somewhat slight but elegant figure and quiet manners, came out and accompanied us in our visit to the school. Just on the skirts of the city, or perhaps a little outside of them, stands a spacious building, once the convent of Tecpan de Santiago, and this has been taken by Señora Baz for the charitable purpose to which she devotes a large income and gives her daily care. In this school five hundred boys—picked up in the city, parentless, or neglected by their parents, utterly friendless, and, if not taken from the streets, certain to belong to that miserable class called the *leperos,* and to grow up in ignorance and habits of indolence and vice—are clothed, fed, educated, taught a variety of trades and employments, and fitted to become useful members of society. We passed from room to room, in some of which the lads were studying their lessons, and in others attending to the occupations in which they were to be trained. Here were the future shoemakers of Mexico, busy over their lasts and lapstones; there the tailors learning to sew and cut out and fit garments, and in another place the printers busy at their types. "The proceedings and ordinances of the Common Council are printed here," said Señora Baz, and we were shown several samples neatly executed. In one room were the young cabinet-makers, smoothing and polishing slabs of rosewood; in another, carpenters learning to handle the saw and plane; in a third, several turning-lathes were humming. The boys were all neatly and comfortably clad in the garments made by their own tailors. We

passed through the prodigiously long halls which serve as
dormitories, with their neat beds, numerous enough to lodge
a regiment of soldiers, and came last to the kitchen, where
ample preparations were making for their meals.[5]

In this school the course of education included grammar,
drawing, and music. The benevolent founder of the school
visits it every day, observes the progress of the pupils, sees
that their comfort is not neglected, and that her plan is faithfully carried out. Such an inroad as her institution is making
into the worthless class of *leperos* must at length reduce their
number and increase the proportion of those who live in comfortable houses and follow habits of regular industry. I can
hardly imagine a fairer omen of the future peace and prosperity of Mexico than this noble example of one of her daughters, who applies her large fortune, and gives the leisure which
her large fortune allows her, to the work of rescuing such
numbers of her fellow-creatures from the degradation and
misery to which they seemed to be doomed by the circumstances of their birth.

There is yet another department of this school which answers to our House of Refuge, just as the department which I
have already described answers to our Children's Aid Society.
There are seventy-five boys sent to it from the criminal tri-
bunals for reformation. These young delinquents are all kept
by themselves, and never see the other inmates. I fancied that
I saw in the faces of some of them a peculiar expression—a
premature sharpness and slyness. One of them, and one of
the youngest, was asked for what cause he had been sent
there. His answer was a little too discreet. He was *charged,* he
said, with taking something that belonged to another.

The same day we visited the market which lies beside the
canal connecting the lake of Texcoco with that of Chalco.
There the flat-bottomed boats come in loaded with the products of the *chinampas,* or floating gardens, as they are sometimes called, though they are only narrow parallelograms of
fertile soil surrounded by canals, from which they are watered
and kept constantly green. Over a large space of this market
we saw women squatted on the ground in the dust beside

their vegetables, their fruits, and their wares, for at this season the sunshine is constant, and the showers are not to fall till May. If any shelter from the sun is wanted, a rude one is formed by a piece of matting supported on poles. No season in Mexico seems to be without its fruits; the banana may be had in perfection all the year round; the orange is now as fine as it can be; the *granadilla,* or fruit of the edible passion-flower, is at this time common in the markets, as well as the *sapote prieto,* or dark-colored sapote, a green fruit, filled with a rich, jetty pulp, like a sort of marmalade. Meantime, the *aguacate,* or what in the English West Indies is called the alligator-pear, is reserved for a later season, and the Manila mango, the finest variety of mango, is just putting forth its clusters of red blossoms; its fruits are not to be ripe before next summer. Other fruits follow in that order till the year completes its circle.

On our return to our hotel we saw a crowd of people about an open door, and, by looking in, we saw the drawing of a lottery, in which the bystanders seemed to be much interested. A hollow cylinder, full of bits of paper indicating the blanks and prizes, was made to revolve a few times; a little boy then thrust in an awl through an opening among these bits of paper, and on its point drew out either a blank or a prize, and this determined the fate of the ticket of which the number was read just before the cylinder was made to revolve. A large proportion of the earnings of the humbler class in Mexico are thrown away in the purchase of lottery tickets, and it is not to be wondered at that, where the passion for this sort of gambling is so very common, there should be such extreme poverty.

I have since visited an institution in which, until the era of Mexican independence, orphan children of the emigrants from Biscay to Mexico were educated. It was a magnificent endowment, founded by the opulent Biscayans while the country was under the rule of Spain. A million of dollars was expended in erecting a building of vast dimensions—a perfect palace, enclosing several quadrangles—and half a million dollars set aside for the support of the inmates. It was origi-

nally called the Colegio de las Biscayinas; but the Basques in
Mexico might, I suppose, now be counted on the fingers of
one's hand, and the Mexican government has taken possession of the institution and named it the National School for
Girls. Here seventy-eight orphan girls of all the different
races in Mexico are sheltered, reared, educated, and provided
with a home till they marry. Drawing and music are among
the accomplishments which they are taught—embroidery, of
course. The inmates were of all ages; some had already reached
middle life, and as spinsters were sure of a shelter till they
died of old age. We were shown over the whole, and could
not but admire the clean and comfortable appearance of everything in their airy apartments. The long sleeping-rooms, in
which were rows of neat little beds, stretched away like the
galleries of the Louvre in Paris. The matron who showed us
these rooms, and who accompanied us to the great kitchen,
where the dinner of the inmates was simmering, smoked, as
she went, a *cigarillo,* a pinch or two of fine tobacco rolled up
in paper so as to form a little cylinder. It is customary among
the elderly Mexican women and those of middle age to smoke
tobacco in this form, but when I spoke of this to a Mexican
lady she answered: "The practice is going out of vogue; the
young women now do not smoke."

But I have not yet done with the school. All these ample
accommodations are not alone for the orphans who are gra-
tuitously provided for. A hundred and forty girls of Mexican
families are received here as boarders and pupils on payment
of ten dollars monthly. Besides these, there is kept in the
building a day-school for little girls of the poorer class, who
amount to an indefinite number, and for whom nothing is
paid.

From the National School for Girls I went to the Foundling
Hospital, which is here called the *Cuna,* or Cradle. Here I
found myself in a swarm of three hundred of these parentless
creatures, from grown-up boys and girls down to the babe of
yesterday. Some of them were plump-looking infants, asleep
in their little beds, and there were one or two lying uneasily
and panting with fever. I was surprised at the small number

of boys in the hospital. "How is this?" I asked; "what is the proportion of boys to girls in this institution?" "Three fourths are girls," was the answer. "But why should they send girls to this place rather than boys?" "Simply because there are more of them. The births settle that matter. Here in Mexico are born three girls to one boy."[6] I expressed my astonishment at this, but I was assured that the statistics of the country showed the fact to be as here stated; and, indeed, the register of the Foundling Hospital is pretty good evidence of the vast preponderance of female over male births in Mexico. A smiling ecclesiastic, with an asthmatic laugh, conducted us over the building, or rather the two large private houses so connected as to form one, and caused one of the inmates, already a woman grown, to play for us on the piano, which she did very creditably. Fourteen of the girls then sang in chorus two or three songs with a precision which showed that they had been carefully trained.

We closed the day, as it is often closed here, with a drive on the *Paseo* west of the city. On our way we passed through the Alameda, a fine grove of tall trees intersected with walks and carriage-roads. Hither on holidays come crowds of the Mexican people in their best dresses. Here some sit on benches and listen to music, while others, in couples, move to the *jarabe,* a peculiar and not ungraceful dance of this country and of Cuba.[7] Hither resort on these occasions the sellers of sweetmeats and fruits, and find a ready market for their wares. The sober shadow cast by those great old trees is then lighted up through all its extent by the brilliant hues, not only of the women's dresses, but of the *sarapes,* or light shawls, with bright-colored stripes, worn by the broad-brimmed Mexicans. The Spanish minister, a most amiable man and a favorite among the Mexicans, sent from Spain, doubtless, to win their hearts and keep them in good humor, had given me a seat in his carriage, and we drove to the broad space beyond the city bounds, about an eighth of a mile in length, where the carriages were passing backward and forward and by each other, from one end of the *Paseo* to the other, a favorite amusement of the Mexicans, and adopted from the Spaniards. The earth in this dry season requires profuse watering, and on that day the place had been but slightly sprinkled, so that we were involved in clouds of dust. After several rounds we drew up on one side of the *Paseo,* where a row of carriages had already ranged themselves, and observed the handsome equipages and gayly dressed women as they passed. Two or three turns more on the *Paseo* completed the entertainment, which seemed to me excessively dull, considering the dust, and with the setting sun I returned to the Hotel Iturbide.

MEXICO, MARCH 11th: In company with my travelling companions, I have been presented to Señor Juarez, the President of the Mexican republic. We went to the palace, a spacious building of massive construction, where in the time of the Spanish dominion the viceroys dwelt in semi-regal state. Mr. Romero, the Minister of Finance,[8] had promised to accompany us, and we called on him at his cabinet in a corner of the building, where we found him, as usual, closely engaged in the business of his department. It is no holiday task to have charge of the exchequer of Mexico, the expenditures of which are greater than the income, and we wondered not that our friend should have the look of one who is greatly overworked and beset by many perplexities. We followed him through spacious antechambers and long halls to the cabinet of the President. The palace, in its present state, is large, including several quadrangles; but it was considerably larger before the time of Maximilian, who pulled down a considerable part of it, with a view of rebuilding it in a style more conformable to his taste. He had just time to demolish, but defeat and death overtook him before he had time to rebuild.

We reached the cabinet of the President, and found him expecting us. I was struck with his appearance. There stood before me a man of low stature and dark complexion, evidently of the Aztec race,[9] square-built and sturdy in figure, with a mild expression of countenance, yet with something in his aspect which indicated inflexible resolution. He is sixty-six years of age, but time seems to have dealt gently with him; his hair is not sprinkled with gray, nor his face marked with wrinkles. The image of him which remains in my memory is that of a man not much older than fifty years. I had already seen three of his daughters at an evening party, children of a lady of Italian extraction. They seemed to me to be favorable samples of the blending of the European with the Aztec race.

He received us courteously. We spoke of the signal defeat of the insurgents a few days before by the government forces under General Rocha,[10] the news of which had been received with great rejoicings at the capital. "It is," he said, "the end of the revolt. We shall hear but little more of it. After the first of May, when the rainy season begins, and the insurgents find themselves without shelter, they will come out of their hiding-places in the woods and submit." We talked of the state of the country. "We have," he said, "great advantages of soil and climate, but we want capital for enterprises important to the country, and we want the strong arms of skilled laborers to execute them." He might have added that, more than all, the country wants internal quiet. The revolt by which the republic is now disturbed will certainly be suppressed; the rebels will submit; the roads will be again safe from robberies perpetrated in the name of revolution; but those who have lived for some years in the country do not feel certain that the quiet will last. "We shall have a peaceful condition of things," said one of them to me, "for about two years; then these fellows who are now running away from Rocha will become uneasy again; we shall have another *pronunciamiento* and another revolt, and fresh robberies on the highways." I hope this anticipation will not become a reality. It is founded on the restlessness of the mixed race in Mexico, who are about one-fifth part of the inhabitants. The Aztec race, who form the greater part of the population, I was told, are generally mild, docile, and submissive to the government. Hardworking they are not, but nearly all the labor of the fields in Mexico is performed by their hands. It is they who are the handicraftsmen for the most part, and the regular industry of the country, such as it is, is theirs. In the mixed race, I was told, are found the men who will not work, and are ready to engage in a revolt against the government, which gives them an opportunity of living by extorting contributions from the peaceable part of the population. These fellows will fight on any side indiscriminately, and, when beaten, enlist in the victorious army.

President Juarez dismissed me with words which I may cite as a characteristic example of Spanish courtesy. Taking both my hands in his, he said: "Remember, Señor, that in me you have a servant and a friend. If at any time you have occasion for my aid, apply to me confidently, and the service you desire shall be performed."

To understand the nature of the revolt which now seems to have received its death-blow, it should be remembered that at the last election of President in Mexico there were three candidates—Juarez, who now fills that post; Lerdo, now the principal judge of the highest tribunal in Mexico,[11] and Porfirio Diaz, who had distinguished himself as an able general in the war which ended in the overthrow of Maximilian. Juarez obtained the office; his rivals complained of unfairness in the election; Lerdo and his friends submitted, but Porfirio Diaz took up arms, issued a *pronunciamiento,* and attempted to seize upon the government by force. He drew to his standard the desperate men who are too numerous in Mexico, and who saw in the revolt an opportunity of living by contributions wrung from the people. They have met the fate which they deserved. A few of their chiefs yet seem to hold out, but their principal leader, whose military fame and prowess were their boast and their great reliance, has disappeared; and whether he be dead or concealed in some hiding-place in Mexico, or has run away, nobody knows.[13]

Of course, Mexico cannot prosper until these disturbances cease, without a probability of their being renewed. Capital will not flow into Mexico without some assurance that it shall be secure, and that its earnings shall not be wrested from the hands of the owner. Skilled laborers will not seek employment in Mexico unless they can be sure of keeping the accumulations of their wages. Ten years of perfect quiet would make an immense difference in the condition of the country.

Capital would enter from other regions, and bring with it the skilled and energetic labor that is wanted. Railways would be constructed and safely guarded; highways would be opened; the waters that fall on the mountains would be gathered in great reservoirs on the declivities, and in winter led in rivulets over the fertile valleys which for half the year are now beds of dust, and would keep them, through all the dry season, green and overspread with perpetual harvests. The only difficulty which I see in the way of these enterprises is a certain jealousy of foreigners, which influences, to some extent, not the government, but the mass of the people. At one time since the independence of Mexico was declared, the expulsion of all foreigners from the republic was decreed, and, in obedience to the fierce demand of the populace, they were all driven out. That feeling has since been greatly moderated, but it is not yet wholly extinct. I asked an intelligent member of the Mexican Congress how it was that, instead of submitting quietly to the result of an election, as we here submit, even when it is pretty manifest that the successful party has used unfair means, his countrymen so often resort to the sword, as if the question of fairness could be settled by cutting each others' throats. "It is in our blood," he answered; "it is owing to the impatience of our temperament. The cure must be to invite emigration from countries like yours, where the popular vote decides the matter, and the beaten party takes its revenge by obtaining the majority at the next election." The remedy is a sure one, but there is this difficulty in applying it, that the emgirants will not arrive until the evil shall be already cured and the country in a state of perfect quiet.

Yet there are changes going on in Mexico as great as would be this of quietly submitting to an election without an immediate revolt. I once heard Mr. Peter Cooper, the New York philanthropist, relate an incident which happened some years since, while his brother was residing for a few months in the city of Mexico. A procession passed through the streets bearing the Host, or consecrated wafer, probably to some rich person. All the people in the street kneeled save an American who kept a little shoe-shop and happened to be standing at its door. One of the crowd struck at him to make him kneel, on which he retreated into his shop. This so enraged the people in the street that several rushed after him into the shop, and one of them, with a dagger, gave him a mortal wound. The American consul was informed of the murder without delay, and he applied to the proper authorities, requiring them to bring the offender to justice. He was told that nothing could be done, for such was the temper of the populace that, if any steps were taken to punish the guilty man, the house of his victim would undoubtedly be pulled down and its inmates torn in pieces. Such was Mexico not long since. This savage fanaticism has had its day. Now the Host is not permitted to be openly carried through the streets. Protestant worship is held in churches with doors opening upon the public way, and the worshippers are not molested.

I have heard of a method taken to put an end to these demonstrations of reverence for the Host in the streets which is more remarkable for its ingenuity than its decorum. After the laws of reform had required the Host to be carried only in a close carriage, the priests made the driver lay aside his hat while he passed slowly on his way. The populace were given to understand that when they saw a carriage slowly driven by a man without a hat, it contained the consecrated wafer, and, of course, the real presence. Accordingly, all kneeled as they had been wont to do when the Host was borne openly by the priests. One day a carriage was seen to pass, driven with great deliberation by a solemn-looking coachman without a hat, through one of the principal streets. The foot-passengers on the right and left all kneeled in worship. At a place where the crowd was most numerous the carriage stopped, and two women, notoriously of the most degraded and shameless class, got out of it, to the great confusion of the worshippers. This, I was told, put an end to the adoration of the Host in the public streets, and nobody is likely hereafter to be murdered for declining to show it the accustomed reverence.

Other changes have been made in the customs of the country. There is scarce any public entertainment so well adapted to encourage and cherish a spirit of cruelty in a people as the bull-fights of Spain. When I came to Vera Cruz I heard something said about the *Plaza de Toros.* "Where are your bull-fights held?" I innocently asked. "They are held no longer," I was answered. "They are forbidden by law." Here are two important steps taken in civilization—the extinction of a fierce religious fanaticism, and the suppression of one of the most cruel of public spectacles known to modern times. Who shall say that the country which has made these advances may not yet accustom itself to submit quietly to the arbitrament of the ballot, as a lesson learned from a long series of bloody experiences?[13]

There is one peculiarity in the political constitution of Mexico which must be done away, or it will prove a serious obstacle to her prosperity. Spain left, as an unhappy legacy to the republic, the practice of requiring duties to be paid at the frontiers of the different provinces on merchandise conveyed from one of them to another. The several states which comprise the republic are now accustomed in this way to raise the revenue which each state requires, and there seems to be little disposition to renounce the system. According to the doctrine of the protectionists, this should result in making each state the richer by taxing heavily the products of its sister states. It is felt, however, as a cruel burden upon the industry and internal trade of the country, and it must be thrown off before the republic can fully avail itself of its own rich and numerous resources.

MEXICO, MARCH 11th: One of the curiosities of Mexico is the *Peñon Nuevo,* or New Crag, a rocky eminence close to the Lake of Texcoco, which I visited the other morning. It is a great volcanic rock of no very remote origin, from the summit of which you have a noble view of the plain of Mexico, of its mountain barriers, and the city, and the broad lakes. The crest of the rock leans to the south, and there overhangs its base, looking as if, when the huge billow of molten lava was spouted into the air, the wind had swayed it from the perpendicular, and it had cooled and stiffened as it was about to fall, forming several caverns on the side opposite to the wind. In these chambers of the rock live two or three Indian families and their dogs. The wild-looking inmates, with their children, came about us, as we peeped into these strange abodes, and wanted money. The women were cooking fish, caught in the lake close at hand. I went to the lake, and on my way passed a warm spring smoking from the ground; the internal fires which caused the eruption of the lava are smouldering yet. The water of the lake is salt, though not intensely so, and the neighboring soil is so impregnated with salt that the Indians extract from it a dark-colored salt by passing water through it. Not far from the *Peñon* are some half-ruinous buildings enclosing a hot spring, to which invalids resort, and an old church, in the shadow of which some of them have found a grave.

We returned to town over the extensive low grounds, now dry, but elevated only two or three feet above the level of the lake, and therefore sure to be laid under water when the copious summer rains, falling on the sides of the mountains, are gathered in the great basin of the Mexican valley. We breakfasted at the Tivoli Gardens, to which we were taken by the American consul, Dr. Skelton. This is a favorite resort of the Mexicans, and often the place of their public banquets. For this purpose there are broad galleries open to the air, but under a roof, while for small parties there are little summerhouses beneath the shade of great trees. Rivulets of water keep up a perpetual verdure; there is a turf always green, and flowers always in bloom. For the recreation of visitors, there are three or four bowling-alleys.

It was a holiday, and we went to the Véga, a public drive just without the city, beside the canal which connects the salt lake of Texcoco with the fresh-water lake of Chalco. This time we found the ground sufficiently watered to keep the dust in its place, and all the finest equipages in Mexico were out, with many of humbler pretensions, passing and repassing each other as they drove backward and forward. Sometimes the equipage was a neat carriage drawn by a pair of mules, the handsomest creatures of their kind that I ever saw, with a spirited look which they certainly do not inherit from the parent donkey. Mingled among these were horsemen with their handsome barbs, their massive glittering stirrups and spurs and showy saddles, their slashed pantaloons, their gay *sarapes* of many colors, and their broad-brimmed white hats, with ornaments of silver. The Mexicans ride well and gracefully, and sit their horses in such a manner that the rider seems a part of the animal. On the canal, which bordered this public drive, flat-boats, some of them quite large, were passing, filled with people from the Indian villages south of the city: women with chaplets of flowers on their heads, and young people dancing, with a slow, swaying motion—for there was no capering—to the light sound of some musical instrument as their boat slid along the water. By the canal, and under the trees which bordered it, sat people who seemed to enjoy the spectacle of the showy equipages, and still more showy cavaliers on horseback, quite as much as those who sat in the carriages. On the opposite side of the Véga were people grouped about the houses of entertainment under the trees, some of whom were amusing themselves with swings. As the sun touched the horizon the carriages turned homeward, the foot-passengers trooped toward the town, and the flat-boats disappeared from the canals.

The next day, in company with Mr. Porter Bliss, the American Secretary of Legation, we explored the canal. Going to the Paseo de la Véga, we took one of the boats, with two men carrying poles to push it forward and guide its course, and soon came to the narrow fields enclosed by canals which are called the *chinampas,* and are all that remains of the floating gardens spoken of in Mexican history. They are as fast at the present time as any of the meadows in the valley of Mexico. Here are cultivated all the garden vegetables of temperate climates—every root that comes upon the dinnertable, and a great variety of fruits. The peach and almond were now in full bloom, and the fruit of the apricot was, as the gardeners say, already set. The brown cultivators of these gardens were busy in place with a sort of long-handled ladle, scooping up the water from the canals and flinging it upon the thirsty little islands. We passed the Indian town of Santa Anita to another named Ixtacaleo, where we landed. There an artesian well

had been sunk, where the cool water of the brightest trans-
parency gushes up with force from the ground, filling a spacious tank, and then running off into the canal. An old church
was near, with graves by its side, only one or two of which
had any monumental stone. The rest were dusty hillocks, the
newest of which had little crosses made of reed planted at the
head. We returned to the town of Santa Anita, where the Indian cooks gave us a breakfast of chocolate, which here in
Mexico is excellently well prepared, eggs, and *frijoles,* or
beans, together with a roast chicken. But the most palatable
dish—so I thought—was that which they call *tamales,* made
of the meal of Indian-corn baked in the husks of the ear. The
Indians often eat them seasoned with red pepper, *enchilados,*
as their phrase is, but a single trial of the *tamales* prepared in
this manner set my mouth on fire and satisfied me.

While the Indian women were preparing our breakfast we
looked about us. The place which we were in was evidently a
great resort on holidays, for here were counters for dispens-
ing *pulque* and other beverages, on the walls of which were
drawings rudely executed by Aztec artists, accompanied by
ill-spelled inscriptions, mostly in rhyme, by the village poets.
I could not help comparing this simple breakfast, furnished
by the coarse cookery of these Indian villagers, with one at
which I was present a few days before, at Tacubaya, on the
gentle declivities which overlook the city from the west. A
Scottish merchant invited a large party, including several
ladies, to breakfast on the Barron estate, a fine country seat,
kept in the most scrupulous order, although no one ventures
to live there, or even to pass the night, on account of the frequent robberies which are committed in the neighborhood.
The founder of the Barron family was from Ireland, and is
said to have made his immense wealth by trade, not without
the suspicion of having benefited the community in the way
approved by Jeremy Bentham—that is to say, by redressing
the rigors of a tyrannical system of revenue laws. However,
this may be, the mansion of the place is a palace, and the
grounds—with their shady walks, and fragrant, blossoming
thickets, and smooth lawns, and groups of trees laden with

tropical fruits, and little streams traversing the ever-verdant groves, and sheets of water reflecting beds of roses in bloom— are as beautiful as any one can imagine. We were on the spot at eleven o'clock, and the breakfast was to begin not far from that time; but one or two of the guests, the most distinguished, were late in arriving, and we did not sit down till nearly one. But the breakfast—if I were to describe it, I could hardly do better than to borrow the words of Milton in "Paradise Regained," in which he gives the bill of fare provided by the Tempter in the wilderness. It was too sumptuous and exquisite to be soon over; and when we rose from the table the rain, a most unusual circumstance at this season of the year, was beating on the roof. Ere long, however, the clouds dispersed, the air was the clearer for the shower, and the volcano of Popocatepetl, which in the winter is generally concealed from sight by the haze, showed its white summit in the bright sunshine of mid-heaven. Then there were the grounds to look at again, and the bowling-alley to visit, where the ladies distinguished themselves by their address in knocking down the pins, and thus the short space between the breakfast and the hour of sunset was passed. Suddenly toward sunset we saw the attendants busy in packing up the plate and china in order to take them back to the city, and we all got into our carriages again, to return from a breakfast which might be almost said to have taken up the whole day.

In the afternoon we visited the Museum of Antiquities, to which the Minister of Justice, Señor Alcarras, was kind enough to accompany us. The samples of ancient Aztec pottery, the hideous idols, the implements and ornaments of stone, and the sharp blades of obsidian, or volcanic glass, which before the Spanish conquest were used as knives, are curious, but the description of them would be tiresome; only engravings can give anything like an accurate idea of them. Under the same roof is a cabinet of natural history, which seemed to me well arranged. I should here mention an earlier visit to the Mexican Academy of Arts. Here is an ample collection of casts from the antique, much larger than I expected to see; here are also a great number of Mexican pictures, centuries old, of quaint designs, yet not without talent; but of the works of eminent European painters, by the example of which the pupil might be guided in his art, there are very few. I saw, however, recent pictures by native artists, which bespeak the possession of a decided talent for the art. Among them was a picture of Dante and Virgil looking over a precipice into the fiery gulf prepared for the wicked, by Raphael Flores. Other pictures of merit were "Cimabue, in Company with Giotto," by Obregon; "The Sacrifice of Isaac," by Santiago Rabull; "Ishmael," by Pablo Valdez; "San Carlos Borromeo Distributing Alms," by Salome Piña, and a "Christ," by Ramon Sagrado.[14] There were also some creditable samples of Mexican statuary, among which I saw a statue, yet in plaster, of San Carlos Borromeo and a child. Of Mexican engravings I saw no example. The artist here finds two obstacles in the way of his success. In the first place, there are few good pictures from which he can obtain an idea of his art in its highest forms of excellence. In the second place—and perhaps I ought to have put this first—there are few persons here who buy pictures. I was told of native artists, who had given proofs of no little talent, that they had been obliged to take to making shoes.

The art of music is cultivated with some zeal. There is a philharmonic society here, and I attended one of its concerts, as an honorary member newly installed. The piano was played with a skilful execution, and a choral melody was sung by several young girls in white. They sang with a precision which showed, I thought, careful training and accurate musical perception; but there was something sharp and stridulous in their voices. A few evenings since I heard, at an evening party, Señorita Peratta,[15] famed for the sweetness of her voice. "The Mexicans," said a gentleman who was present, "are proud of Peratta, and with reason. She sings well; but she did not succeed in Paris. Her very plain face and ungraceful action carried the day against the voice, and she returned to Mexico."

But what of the literature of Mexico? Of that, as I know but little yet, I can say but little. But Mexico has her men of science, her eloquent orators, her eminent antiquaries, her historians, her successful novelists, and her poets, who, I am told, are numerous, so easily does the melodious language spoken here run into verse. All who have obtained distinction in this way are gathered into an association called the Geographical and Statistical Society—a very narrow appellation for one which embraces so wide a circle of notabilities.[16]

I was present the other day at one of the meetings of this society, at which several persons were admitted as members, of whom I had the honor to be one. It was held in the *Minería,* or School of Mines, one of the finest buildings in Mexico, stately and spacious, with airy galleries surrounding an inner square, and with ample rooms for its cabinets of minerals and its fossil animal remains, which had a somewhat meagre appearance in so extensive a receptacle. The members assembled in a large hall capable of holding several thousand people; the *Ministro de Fomento,* an officer of the government who answers to our Secretary of the Interior, presided, and honored the occasion with an animated speech. By his side sat a gentleman, evidently of the pure Aztec race, who, I was told, generally presided at the meetings of the society; it was Señor Ramirez, the vice-president. At a desk in front of the president sat Señor Allamirano,[17] the first secretary, who bore equally manifest tokens of Aztec descent. Many of these descendants of the people subdued by Cortes are men of cultivated minds and engaging manners. The greater part of the works of art in the galleries of which I have spoken are from their hands.

I was curious to see the *Monte Pio,* a national institution for lending money on pledges of personal property, and, accordingly, Mr. Bliss conducted us thither. It occupies what was once the palace of Cortes, looking upon the cathedral square, and built, it is said, on the very spot where stood the royal dwelling of Montezuma. Cortes must have brought over from Spain his artisans to hew and lay the stones of this massive structure, which has furnished a pattern for all the mansions of the wealthy residents of Mexico which have been built since.

I found the great building filled, from the ground-floor to the roof, with articles pawned by persons in need. The lower part, under the galleries, was crowded with every kind of carriage, from the heavy family coach to the light gig, and with every movable that could be sold for money. In another part of the building, in a well-secured apartment, and kept in drawers safely locked, are jewels of every kind—diamonds, rubies, pearls, sapphires, and the like, in the shape of wreaths for the brow, necklaces, bracelets, ear-drops, and every kind of ornament worn by women. Elsewhere I saw garments of various kinds, from the most costly silks and shawls to the plainest chintzes and coarsest handkerchiefs. All these things are appraised at their just value, from which the interest for six months is deducted and the remainder paid to the owner. At the end of six months the objects pawned are sold by auction, and if they bring more than the original valuation, the owner receives the difference. It is worth remarking that the institution is managed with perfect integrity—at least in such a manner that there is no complaint of unfairness or wrong. I could not help thinking, with shame, of the extent to which some of our own savings banks, established under pretence of aiding the poorer class, have swindled those who gave them their confidence, and was obliged to own to myself that Mexico, in this respect, was more honest than New York.

VERA CRUZ, MARCH 20th: I left Mexico by rail on the morning of the 13th of March, regretting that my plans did not allow me to give more time to a place so interesting in many respects—the history of which is so full of remarkable incidents, the people of which have so many quaint peculiarities, and the physical geography of which is so different from that of any country which I had ever seen. Several of the acquaintances whom we had made at Mexico kindly came to see us off at the station.

Soon after issuing from the city, we passed, at a considerable distance from us on the right, a small village of mud cabins, to which a fellow-passenger directed our attention. "There lives," he said, "a peculiar tribe of people, of the most degraded and beastly habits. There are no marriages among them, and their practices are free love in its grossest form. Incest of the most revolting kind is common, and there is the utmost confusion of kindred."

One of the cars attached to the train on which we travelled was full of armed men, so that we regarded ourselves as secure against any attack from those who rob travellers in the name of what they call the revolution. At one of the stations where we stopped we found an intrenchment and breastworks thrown up to defend the trains, while they stopped, against robbers coming upon them from the hills that lay to the north of the track.

Soon after leaving the capital we were among the fields of *maguey,* the plant with stiff, thick, dark-green leaves, from which the common drink of the country, called *pulque,* is drawn. On each side we saw them stretching away over the champaign country to the bare hills that enclose it. Near at hand the broad spaces, left for other crops, between the rows were visible to the eye, but at a distance the rows seemed to run together, and the earth was completely hidden, for leagues around, under what seemed to the sight a close mass of dark-green leaves. This plant, after several years' cultivation and growth, suddenly sends up a thick, vigorous stem. Into this the sap of the plant, a milky juice, flows rapidly, pushing it upward to the height of some fifteen feet, when its summit puts forth horizontal branches hung with flowers. If left to itself, it there perfects its seeds, and then the plant perishes. But the Mexican, while the sap is rushing upward, cuts off the stem at its base, and there scoops out a sort of basin among the leaves near the root. Into this the sap intended for the stem—the Mexicans call it the milk, from its color—flows in great abundance, and, with the help of a tube at the mouth of an Aztec laborer, is drawn out by suction. This, when fermented, is the *pulque,* the ordinary drink of the country, and by distillation yields a spirit like whiskey. To one who at this season casts his eyes over the country it would almost seem as if there was nothing but the *maguey* cultivated, so few are the other crops at this time of the year, and such is the great breadth of the region occupied by this plant.

The railways also attest the extent of this traffic. The freight-trains drag huge cars loaded with it in barrels, and also in skins, the primitive method of keeping wine in Spain. At the railway stations were piles of barrels and huge heaps of skins filled with *pulque* waiting their turn to be transported to market. "This *pulque*," said a Mexican gentleman to me, "this *pulque* and the spirit drawn from it are the bane of our country. It is drunk immoderately, and our people, when full of *pulque,* are good for nothing. We must contrive to wean them from its use if we mean that our country shall advance in civilization." Of course, here is an ample field for the apostles of temperance. I was amused by hearing a young Englishman, lately arrived, whom we saw at Fortin, say very innocently that he had fallen in with some Indians who had been drinking a kind of sour wine—meaning their *pulque.* It disagreed with them, he said, and made them sick.

The train arrived at Puebla a little before two o'clock in the afternoon, and we hired a carriage to take us to the pyramid of Cholula, in the neighborhood. We had been told in Mexico that this excursion would not be quite safe without an escort, but at Puebla they laughed at this apprehension, and we determined to go. So we went by one of these rough, neglected Mexican roads, through brown pasture-grounds, and russet fallows, and fields of *maguey,* and, crossing a little river overhung with trees in full leaf, came at length to the decayed little town of Cholula. Here is a conical hill, apparently of dark-colored earth, two hundred feet high. Examine it, and you see that it is composed of tiers of sun-dried brick, with many fragments of pottery and small, rough stones, and here and there a horizontal line of a whitish mortar—all evidently built up from the level plain. On its broad sides grew shrubs and trees, and in one or two places the ground had been terraced and cultivated. At the top is a broad, level space where the Aztecs once worshipped, but now a church is standing— an old building, but undergoing repairs, which, I was told, were done by subscription, the government neither building nor repairing any more churches. The interior of the building was in good taste and really beautiful. From the summit we had an extensive view—the little town of Cholula, immediately below, once swarming with inhabitants, but now scarcely more than a hamlet, yet with half a dozen churches; green fields artificially watered, roads crossing each other, bordered with rows of the dark-green *maguey,* the spires of Puebla in the distance, and that circle of mountains which everywhere embraces these upland plains. Near this pyramid is a smaller one, on the top of which we found small Aztec knife-blades of obsidian or volcanic glass; and yet another, the sloping parts of which had been cut down and carried away, leaving the sides completely perpendicular, and, as I judged, almost forty feet high.

Returning to Puebla, I waited on General Alatorre, to whom I had a letter from the Minister of War, Señor Balcárcel, procured for me by the kindness of Señor Romero, requiring him to furnish me with an escort to Orizaba. I found a handsome man of a fine military presence, who asked me if it was necessary that I should set out next day. "It is necessary," I answered, "in order to arrive seasonably at Vera Cruz." "Then, said he, "I must send a messenger to some distance for the cavalry you will want."

The escort was ready to proceed with us the next morning—thirteen men, good riders, all well mounted, and armed with carbines. There were four of our party; we had taken a diligence as far as Orizaba for ourselves only, and we were about to set out, when two gentlemen from Guadalajara, who were about to proceed first to the United States and then to England, asked leave to take seats with us. We gave our consent, and had no reason to regret it. They were courteous, intelligent men, and no smokers, one of them about thirty-two years of age, and the other a little more than ten years younger. They were lawyers going abroad to make themselves acquainted with the jurisprudence of our own country and that of England. Both had some knowledge of English; the memory of the elder one was well stored with passages from Milton's "Paradise Lost," and he repeated them with an accent which the residence of a few months among those who speak our language can hardly fail to improve.

We were joined by another diligence, containing a Mexican family, and traversed again those arid plains encircled by mountains, our armed escort trotting faithfully by our side. We met with no enemy save the dust rising from roads where the earth, by the constant passing of heavy vehicles, had been ground into powder, from which we protected our eyes and nostrils by gauze veils. Before the day ended, our escort had stopped and had been relieved by another of the same number. But instead of caps, our new protectors wore broad-brimmed white hats, and leathern pantaloons instead of woolen ones. Another night at San Agustin de Palmar and another day on the dusty, uneven road to the heights of Aculcingo, upon reaching which our escort was again changed. Let me say here that there will be no occasion for any further complaints of this road after the present year has closed. On the 31st of December the railway from Mexico to Vera Cruz is to be finished, and the journey between the cities will be made in a single day.

NOTES for Bryant's "A Visit to Mexico" (1872)

1. Mexico's independence from Spain came in 1821. A leader of that victorious movement was Agustín de Iturbide, a conservative Creole who was a former officer in the Spanish army. On 19 May 1822, he was proclaimed the Emperor of Mexico: Agustín I. His son, the Prince Imperial, was declared heir to the throne and his other sons and daughters were designated princes and princesses. However, less than a year later, during the middle of February 1823, a rebellion led by the military forced him to abdicate. He and his family were banished to exile in Italy; later, they moved to England. He returned to Mexico in May of the following year hoping to regain his throne; instead, he was quickly captured and on 19 July 1824, ex-Emperor Agustín I was executed. In 1852, his "palace" became a hotel and stagecoach terminal under the name Hotel Diligencias. Then, in 1867, a new owner renovated and reopened it as the luxurious Hotel de Iturbide; soon it became a favorite with English-speaking foreigners in Mexico. In 1895, Stephen Crane stayed at the palace and made the restaurant-bar his headquarters during his March-through-May visit to Mexico.

2. The first "laws of reform" that Bryant refers to were passed during the period that General Ignacio Comonfort ruled Mexico: 1855–1858. Written by his Secretary of the Treasury, Miguel Lerdo de Tejada, the reforms, which became law on 25 June 1856, were part of an effort to break the powerful economic force of the Roman Catholic Church. Among the actions taken were the expropriation of all lands belonging to the church with the exception of church buildings, the suppression of all religious orders of priests and nuns, and the creation of a civil marriage ceremony that was obligatory. Three years later, on 12 July 1859, President Benito Juarez promulgated another law—Nacionalización de los bienes del Clero—confiscating all church property and publishing an attack on the Church. Then, in January 1861, Juarez ordered the liquidation of the property of the clergy

and anything else of value found in a church. Some of the properties were sold to Protestant denominations which were now very welcome in Mexico as part of the government's attempts to de-Catholicize the nation.

3. Matías Romero—who served Juarez and Diaz as Mexico's ambassador to the United States—wrote of his participation in the "laws of church reform" in his book, *Mexico and the United States,* published in 1898 by the New York firm of G. P. Putnam's Sons. In it he notes, "after having lived for ten years in the United States, from 1859 to 1868, I returned to Mexico and took charge of the Treasury Department there, just at the time when the religious question was being solved. . . ." He states that he "favored the establishment of a Protestant community as planned by Mr. Henry C. Riley . . . (who) . . . eagerly desired to establish a Mexican National Church in competition with the Roman Catholic. . . . He proposed to buy one of the finest churches, the main church of the Franciscan convent, which had been built by the Spaniards, located in the best section of the City of Mexico, and which could not now be duplicated but for a very large amount of money; and with the hearty support of President Juarez, who shared my views and who was perhaps a great deal more radical than I was myself on such subjects, I sold the building which had become national property after the confiscation of the Church property, for a mere trifle, if I remember rightly about $4000, most of that amount being paid in Government bonds which were then at a nominal price" (p. 96).

4. Alexander von Humboldt (1769–1859), the highly regarded German naturalist and world-wanderer, is best known for the geographical and botanical work he conducted during the first years of the nineteenth century off the western coast of South America, after which he visited Mexico. He arrived at the port of Acapulco on 22 March 1803 and spent until the following March conducting research in various cities including Guanajuato, Toluca, Cholula, Perote, Jalapa, and Veracruz. He later published several definitive works on the country, including his classic economic study, *A Political Essay on* *the Kingdom of New Spain* (1803), as well as various pictorial maps of the regions he visited. Of course, Bryant would have known of von Humboldt and his works. It is said that the Baron's international fame was second only to Napoleon's during the nineteenth century.

5. Señora Baz's husband, Juan José Baz (1820–1887), was a lawyer who became wealthy and influential by being active from an early age in politics. In 1847, when he was twenty-seven years old, acting-President Dr. Valentín Gómez Farias appointed him to his first of several terms as Governor of the Federal District. Baz was again governor when in 1856 the first laws of church reform were passed. Then, in 1861, when Juarez ordered the liquidation of all church properties, Baz was placed in charge of selling those properties in the Federal District, of which he was governor once again. It must have been at this time that he acquired the ex-convent of Tepcan de Santiago, used later by his wife for the school that so impressed Bryant. See also notes 2 and 3 on the confiscation of church property.

6. The information regarding male and female births during this period is incorrect. In general, there were always more male births than female although the male infant death rate was considerably higher than that of the female child. However, Bryant is speaking of the foundling hospital—an orphanage especially for the abandoned newborn children of the poor. During the nineteenth century in Mexico, it was generally accepted that male children of the lower socioeconomic classes were more "highly prized"—that is to say, useful—than female children since the boys would grow up and take their places as laborers. It stands to reason, therefore, that more female infants than male would have been abandoned at the orphanage.

7. According to the Mexican dance critic, Alberto Dallal, there were at this time numerous versions of the *jarabe* dance, with each region having its own version. The dances came to Mexico with the Spaniards from Andalucia during the seventeenth and eighteenth centuries, but they were, according to Maestro Dallal, "Mexicanized."

8. See note 3. In the preface to his book *Mexico and the United States,* Matías Romero notes that he served his country at the Mexican embassy in Washington from 24 December 1859, becoming Envoy Extraordinary and Minister Plenipotentiary of Mexico and presenting his credentials to President Lincoln on 29 October 1863. He remained in that capacity until 16 July 1868, when he returned to Mexico to serve as Juarez's Secretary of the Treasury. He writes, "It was my fortune to meet the most prominent men of this country, both in political and social life, and to hold very friendly personal relations with many of them such as Secretary [of State William] Seward and General Grant" (p. iii). When Bryant met him at the national palace, Romero had been back in Mexico for less than four years. The American must have been quite happy to have made such an acquaintance; after all, Bryant spoke no Spanish and the Treasury Secretary was completely bilingual. Romero returned as Mexican Ambassador to the United States in 1882 and served in that post until his death in 1898.

9. Bryant—like many uninformed gringos of the period who might have read Prescott's *Conquest of Mexico* (1843)— had obviously believed the misconception that all Mexican Indians were Aztec. Indeed, there were many other important groups of Indians in Mexico, such as the Mayan, Tarascan, Mixtec, Otomi, and Chichimecas. Juarez was proud to identify himself as the son of full-blooded Zapotec Indian peasants from Oaxaca.

10. General Sostenes Rocha (1831–1897) was graduated from the Colegio Militar in 1853; throughout his early career, he was firmly on the side of Juarez. He fought against and defeated a variety of rebellious officers—including Porfirio Diaz—who tried on occasion to overthrow Juarez. Rocha was, indeed, one of Juarez's most trusted advisors. When, in 1876, Diaz overthrew the government of Lerdo de Tejada, General Rocha left Mexico for four years which he passed writing several works on military tactics. In 1880, he returned and was appointed director of the Colegio Militar, a post he held until 1886.

11. Sebastian Lerdo de Tejada (1823–1889), then the Chief

Justice of the Supreme Court, became president of Mexico with the death of Juarez on 19 July 1872, less than five months after Bryant and his party returned to the United States. See also note 2.

12. Porfirio Diaz (1830–1915) was quite alive and well and in hiding, awaiting the propitious moment for his return. A part-Mixtec Indian from Oaxaca and one of the heroes of the Cinco de Mayo, 1862, Battle of Puebla when the Mexicans defeated the French forces of Napoleon, Diaz returned in 1876 to fight against the reelection of Lerdo de Tejada, but the attempt was thwarted. After a six-month exile in the United States, he tried again; this time he was successful in overthrowing Lerdo. In May 1877, Porfirio Diaz was formally elected president and served with a dictatorial hand in that capacity—with the exception of the four-year period from 1880 to 1884—until May 1911, when he left Mexico to live in exile in Paris until his death on 2 July 1915.

13. Bryant, without a doubt, would be most disillusioned to learn the real reason why Juarez abolished bull-fighting after his return to the presidency in 1867. It was in no way part of a plan to "civilize" the country. Rather, his reasons were purely nationalistic: the bull-fights—imported from Spain by Cortes—brought back too many bad memories of the centuries of Spanish rule. Bull-fights did not return to the Plazas de Toros of Mexico until Porfirio Diaz reinstated them in the latter part of the century.

14. Many of the works of art that Bryant refers to are in the permanent collection of the Museum del Palacio de Bellas Artes in Mexico City. Others found their way into private collections. For additional information on the artists and their works, consult Justino Fernandez's definitive work, *El arte del siglo XIX en México* (México: Imprenta Universitaria, 1967).

15. Angela Peralta (1845–1883)—el ruiseñor mexicano/ the Mexican nightingale—made a highly successful debut at the age of 15 singing in Verdi's "Leonora" at the Teatro Nacional. She immediately left for Spain with her father where she sang in various cities, including Cádiz and Madrid, before settling in Milan where she made her La Scala debut at the age of 17.

16. On 18 April 1833, acting-President Dr. Valentin Go-
mez Farias established the Instituto de Geografía y Estadís-
tica; the first members, however, were not appointed until
January 1835. Chosen for this honor were highly regarded intellectuals from throughout Mexico. In December 1849, the
name of the organization was changed to the Sociedad Mexi-
cana de Geografía y Estadísticas. Maximilian, when he arrived in 1864, weakened the Society by forming a rival group
which he called Imperial Academy of Science and Literature.
But in 1866, Juarez, once he realized the value and importance of the institution, immediately regenerated interest in it
by inviting a number of foreigners to become members. The
Society, after all, was the first such institution in the western
hemisphere as well as the third oldest society of that type in
the world. For over 150 years, prominent Mexicans—and a
select few foreigners like William Cullen Bryant—have been
honored with membership in the society.

17. Ignacio Manuel Altamirano (1843–1893), the son of
poor Indians, did not learn Spanish until he was fourteen
years old, when he received an appointment to study at the
Instituto Literario of Toluca and became the disciple of the
institute's founder, Ignacio Ramirez. Later, Ramirez and Altamirano became collaborators, founding first, in 1867, the
influential newspaper, *El Correo de Mexico,* and then, in 1869,
El Renacimiento (The Renaissance), the period's most highly
respected literary journal. Altamirano is best remembered for
his poetry and several novels including *El Zarco* (1888) and
Clemencia (1869), considered by critics as the first modern
Mexican novel. Ramirez (1818–1879) spent his life being active in both the political and literary worlds of the time. He
served several presidents in various capacities as well as writing numerous political, scientific and literary works. It is not
surprising that Juarez appointed them to the Society of which
they were both officers. And considering their talents and contributions, it is even less surprising that Bryant was impressed.

Stephen Crane

THE FIVE WHITE MICE

F REDDIE was mixing a cocktail. His hand with the long spoon was whirling swiftly, and the ice in the glass hummed and rattled like a cheap watch. Over by the window, a gambler, a millionaire, a railway conductor, and the agent of a vast American syndicate were playing seven-up. Freddie surveyed them with the ironical glance of a man who is mixing a cocktail.

From time to time a swarthy Mexican waiter came with his tray from the rooms at the rear, and called his orders across the bar. The sounds of the indolent stir of the city awakening from its siesta floated over the screens which barred the sun and the inquisitive eye. From the far-away kitchen could be heard the roar of the old French chef, driving, herding, and abusing his Mexican helpers.

A string of men came suddenly in from the street. They stormed up to the bar. There were impatient shouts. "Come, now, Freddie, don't stand there like a portrait of yourself. Wiggle!" Drinks of many kinds and colours—amber, green, mahogany, strong and mild—began to swarm upon the bar, with all the attendants of lemon, sugar, mint, and ice. Freddie, with Mexican support, worked like a sailor in the provision of them, sometimes talking with that scorn for drink and admiration for those who drink which is the attribute of a good barkeeper.

At last a man was afflicted with a stroke of dice-shaking. A herculean discussion was waging, and he was deeply engaged in it, but at the same time he lazily flirted the dice. Occasionally he made great combinations. "Look at that, would you?" he cried proudly. The others paid little heed. Then violently the craving took them. It went along the line like an epidemic, and involved them all. In a moment they had arranged a carnival of dice-shaking, with money penalties and liquid prizes. They clamorously made it a point of honour with Freddie that he too should play, and take his chance of sometimes providing this large group with free refreshment. With bent heads, like football players, they surged over the tinkling dice, jostling, cheering, and bitterly arguing. One of the quiet company playing seven-up at the corner table said profanely that the row reminded him of a bowling contest at a picnic.

After the regular shower, many carriages rolled over the smooth *calle,* and sent a musical thunder through the Casa Verde. The shop windows became aglow with light, and the walks were crowded with youths, callow and ogling, dressed vainly according to supposititious fashions. The policemen had muffled themselves in their gnome-like cloaks and placed their lanterns as obstacles for the carriages in the middle of the street. The City of Mexico gave forth the deep, mellow organ-tones of its evening resurrection.

But still the group at the bar of the Casa Verde were shaking dice. They had passed beyond shaking for drinks for the crowd, for Mexican dollars, for dinner, for the wine at dinner. They had even gone to the trouble of separating the cigars and cigarettes from the dinner's bill, and causing a distinct man to be responsible for them. Finally they were aghast. Nothing remained within sight of their minds which even remotely suggested further gambling. There was a pause for deep consideration.

"Well!"

"Well!"

A man called out in the exuberance of creation: "I know!

Let's stake for a box to-night at the circus! A box at the circus!" The group was profoundly edified. "That's it! That's it! Come on, now! Box at the circus!" A dominating voice cried: "Three dashes—high man out!" An American, tall, and with a face of copper red from the rays that flash among the Sierra Madres and burn on the cactus deserts, took the little leathern cup, and spun the dice out upon the polished wood. A fascinated assemblage hung upon the bar rail. Three kings turned their pink faces upward. The tall man flourished the cup, burlesquing, and flung the two other dice. From them he ultimately extracted one more pink king. "There," he said. "Now, let's see! Four kings!" He began to swagger in a sort of provisional way.

The next man took the cup, and blew softly on the top of it. Poising it in his hand, he then surveyed the company with a stony eye, and paused. They knew perfectly well that he was applying the magic of deliberation and ostentatious indifference, but they could not wait in tranquillity during the performance of all these rites. They began to call out impatiently: "Come, now! Hurry up!" At last the man, with a gesture that was singularly impressive, threw the dice. The others set up a howl of joy. "Not a pair!" There was another solemn pause. The men moved restlessly. "Come, now! Go ahead!" In the end, the man, induced and abused, achieved something that was nothing in the presence of four kings. The tall man climbed on the foot-rail, and leaned hazardously forward. "Four kings! My four kings are good to go out," he bellowed into the middle of the mob; and, although in a moment he did pass into the radiant region of exemption, he continued to bawl advice and scorn.

The mirrors and oiled woods of the Casa Verde were now dancing with blue flashes from a great buzzing electric lamp. A host of quiet members of the Anglo-Saxon colony had come in for their pre-dinner cocktails. An amiable person was exhibiting to some tourists this popular American saloon. It was a very sober and respectable time of day. Freddie reproved courageously the dice-shaking brawlers, and, in return, he received the choicest advice in a tumult of seven combined vocabularies. He laughed. He had been compelled to retire from the game, but he was keeping an interested, if furtive, eye upon it.

Down at the end of the line there was a youth at whom everybody railed for his flaming ill luck. At such disaster, Freddie swore from behind the bar, in a sort of affectionate contempt. "Why, this Kid has had no luck for two days. Did you ever see such throwin'?"

The contest narrowed eventually to the New York Kid and an individual who swung about placidly on legs that moved in nefarious circles. He had a grin that resembled a bit of carving. He was obliged to lean down and blink rapidly to ascertain the facts of his venture, but fate presented him with five queens. His smile did not change, but he puffed gently, like a man who has been running.

The others, having emerged scatheless from this part of the conflict, waxed hilarious with the Kid. They smote him on either shoulder. "We've got you stuck for it, Kid! You can't beat that game! Five queens!"

Up to this time the Kid had displayed only the temper of the gambler; but the cheerful hoots of the players, supplemented now by a ring of guying non-combatants, caused him to feel profoundly that it would be fine to beat the five queens. He addressed a gambler's slogan to the interior of the cup:

> Oh, five white mice of chance,
> Shirts of wool and corduroy pants,
> Gold and wine, women and sin,
> All for you if you let me come in—
> Into the house of chance.

Flashing the dice sardonically out upon the bar, he displayed three aces. From two dice in the next throw he achieved one more ace. For his last throw he rattled the single die for a long time. He already had four aces; if he accomplished another one, the five queens were vanquished, and the box at the circus came from the drunken man's pocket. All of the

Kid's movements were slow and elaborate. For his last throw he planted the cup bottom up on the bar, with the one die hidden under it. Then he turned and faced the crowd with the air of a conjuror or a cheat. "Oh, maybe it's an ace," he said in boastful calm—"maybe it's an ace." Instantly he was presiding over a little drama in which every man was absorbed. The Kid leaned with his back against the bar rail and with his elbows upon it. "Maybe it's an ace," he repeated.

A jeering voice in the background said: "Yes, maybe it is, Kid."

The Kid's eyes searched for a moment among the men. "I'll bet fifty dollars it is an ace," he said.

Another voice asked: "American money?"

"Yes," answered the Kid.

"Oh!" There was a general laugh at this discomfiture. However, no one came forward at the Kid's challenge, and presently he turned to the cup. "Now I'll show you." With the manner of a mayor unveiling a statue, he lifted the cup. There was revealed naught but a ten-spot. In the roar which arose could be heard each man ridiculing the cowardice of his neighbour, and above all the din rang the voice of Freddie berating every one.

"Why, there isn't one liver to every five men in the outfit. That was the greatest cold bluff I ever saw worked. He wouldn't know how to cheat with dice if he wanted to. Don't know the first thing about it. I could hardly keep from laughin' when I seen him drillin' you around. Why, I tell you I had that fifty dollars right in my pocket, if I wanted to be a chump. You're an easy lot!"

Nevertheless, the group who had won in the circus-box game did not relinquish their triumph. They burst like a storm about the head of the Kid, swinging at him with their fists. "'Five white mice'!" they quoted, choking—"'five white mice'!"

"Oh, they are not so bad," said the Kid.

Afterward it often occurred that a man would suddenly jeer a finger at the Kid, and derisively say: "'Five white mice'!"

On the route from the dinner to the circus, others of the

party often asked the Kid if he had really intended to make his appeal to mice. They suggested other animals—rabbits, dogs, hedgehogs, snakes, opossums. To this banter the Kid replied with a serious expression of his belief in the fidelity and wisdom of the five white mice. He presented a most eloquent case, decorated with fine language and insults, in which he proved that, if one was going to believe in anything at all, one might as well choose the five white mice. His companions, however, at once and unanimously pointed out to him that his recent exploit did not place him in the light of a convincing advocate.

The Kid discerned two figures in the street. They were making imperious signs at him. He waited for them to approach, for he recognized one as the other Kid—the 'Frisco Kid: there were two Kids. With the 'Frisco Kid was Benson. They arrived almost breathless. "Where you been?" cried the 'Frisco Kid. It was an arrangement that, upon meeting, the one that could first ask this question was entitled to use a tone of limitless injury. "What you been doing? Where you going? Come on with us! Benson and I have got a little scheme."

The New York Kid pulled his arm from the grapple of the other. "I can't. I've got to take these sutlers to the circus. They stuck me for it, shaking dice at Freddie's. I can't, I tell you."

The two did not at first attend to his remarks. "Come on; we've got a little scheme."

"I can't. They've stuck me. I've got to take 'm to the circus."

At this time it did not suit the men with the scheme to recognize these objections as important. "Oh, take 'm some other time." "Well, can't you take 'm some other time?" "Let 'm go." "Damn the circus." "Get cold feet!" "What did you get stuck for?" "Get cold feet!"

But despite their fighting, the New York Kid broke away from them. "I can't, I tell you. They stuck me."

As he left them, they yelled with rage. "Well, meet us, now, do you hear?—in the Casa Verde, as soon as the circus quits! Hear?" They threw maledictions after him.

In the City of Mexico a man goes to the circus without descending in any way to infant amusements, because the Circo Teatro Orrin is one of the best in the world, and too easily surpasses anything of the kind in the United States, where it is merely a matter of a number of rings, if possible, and a great professional agreement to lie to the public. Moreover, the American clown who in the Mexican arena prances and gabbles is the clown to whom writers refer as the delight of their childhood and lament that he is dead. At this circus the Kid was not debased by the sight of mournful prisoner elephants and caged animals, forlorn and sickly. He sat in his box until late, and laughed, and swore, when past laughing, at the comic, foolish, wise clown.

When he returned to the Casa Verde, there was no display of the 'Frisco Kid and Benson. Freddie was leaning upon the bar, listening to four men terribly discuss a question that was not plain. There was a card-game in the corner, of course. Sounds of revelry pealed from the rear rooms.

When the Kid asked Freddie if he had seen his friend and Benson, Freddie looked bored. "Oh, yes; they were in here just a minute ago; but I don't know where they went. They've got their skates on. Where've they been? Came in here rolling across the floor like two little gilt gods. They wobbled around for a time, and then 'Frisco wanted me to send six bottles of wine around to Benson's rooms; but I didn't have anybody to send this time of night, and so they got mad and went out. Where did they get their loads?"

In the first deep gloom of the street the Kid paused a moment, debating. But presently he heard quavering voices: "Oh, Kid! Kid! Come'ere!" Peering, he recognized two vague figures against the opposite wall. He crossed the street, and they said: "Hellokid."

"Say, where did you get it?" he demanded sternly. "You Indians better go home. What did you want to get scragged for?" His face was luminous with virtue.

As they swung to and fro they made angry denials: "We ain' load'. We ain' load. Big chump! Comonangetadrink."

The sober youth turned then to his friend. "Hadn't you better go home, Kid? Come on; it's late. You'd better break away."

The 'Frisco Kid wagged his head decisively. "Got take Benson home first. He'll be wallowing round in a minute. Don't mind me; I'm all right."

"Ce'r'ly he's all right," said Benson, arousing from deep thought. "He's all right. But better take 'm home, though. That's ri-right. He's load'. But he's all right. No need go home any more'n you. But better take'm home. He's load'." He looked at his companion with compassion. "Kid, you're load'."

The sober Kid spoke abruptly to his friend from San Francisco. "Kid, pull yourself together, now. Don't fool. We've got to brace this ass of a Benson all the way home. Get hold of his other arm."

The 'Frisco Kid immediately obeyed his comrade, without a word or a glower. He seized Benson, and came to attention like a soldier. Later, indeed, he meekly ventured: "Can't we take cab?" But when the New York Kid snapped out that there were no convenient cabs, he subsided to an impassive silence. He seemed to be reflecting upon his state without astonishment, dismay, or any particular emotion. He submitted himself woodenly to the direction of his friend.

Benson had protested when they had grasped his arms. "W'asha doing?" he said in a new and guttural voice. "W'asha doing? I ain' load. Comonangetadrink. I——"

"Oh, come along, you idiot," said the New York Kid. The 'Frisco Kid merely presented the mien of a stoic to the appeal of Benson, and in silence dragged away at one of his arms. Benson's feet came from that particular spot on the pavement with the reluctance of roots, and also with the ultimate suddenness of roots. The three of them lurched out into the street in the abandon of tumbling chimneys. Benson was meanwhile noisily challenging the others to produce any reasons for his being taken home. His toes clashed into the kerb when they reached the other side of the *calle,* and for a moment the Kids hauled him along, with the points of his shoes scraping musically on the pavement. He balked formidably as they were about to pass the Casa Verde. "No, no! Leshavanothdrink! Anothdrink! Onemore!"

But the 'Frisco Kid obeyed the voice of his partner in a manner that was blind, but absolute, and they scummed Benson on past the door. Locked together, the three swung into a dark street. The sober Kid's flank was continually careering ahead of the other wing. He harshly admonished the 'Frisco child, and the latter promptly improved in the same manner of unthinking, complete obedience. Benson began to recite the tale of a love-affair—a tale that didn't even have a middle. Occasionally the New York Kid swore. They toppled on their way like three comedians playing at it on the stage.

At midnight a little Mexican street burrowing among the walls of the city is as dark as a whale's throat at deep sea. Upon this occasion heavy clouds hung over the capital, and the sky was a pall. The projecting balconies could make no shadows.

"Shay," said Benson, breaking away from his escort suddenly, "what want g'ome for? I ain' load'. You got reg'lar spool-fact'ry in your head—you N' York Kid, there. Thish oth' Kid, he's mos' proper—mos' proper shober. He's drunk, but—but he's shober."

"Ah, shut up, Benson," said the New York Kid. "Come along, now. We can't stay here all night." Benson refused to be corralled, but spread his legs and twirled like a dervish, meanwhile under the evident impression that he was conducting himself most handsomely. It was not long before he gained the opinion that he was laughing at the others. "Eight purple dogsh—dogs! Eight purple dogs! Tha's what Kid'll see in the morn'. Look ou' for 'em. They——"

As Benson, describing the canine phenomena, swung wildly across the sidewalk, it chanced that three other pedestrians were passing in the shadowy rank. Benson's shoulder jostled one of them.

A Mexican wheeled upon the instant. His hand flashed to

his hip. There was a moment of silence, during which Benson's voice was not heard raised in apology. Then an indescribable comment, one burning word, came from between the Mexican's teeth.

Benson, rolling about in a semi-detached manner, stared vacantly at the Mexican, who thrust his lean yellow face forward, while his fingers played nervously at his hip. The New York Kid could not follow Spanish well, but he understood when the Mexican breathed softly: "Does the señor want fight?"

Benson simply gazed in gentle surprise. The woman next to him at dinner had said something inventive—his tailor had presented his bill—something had occurred which was mildly out of the ordinary, and his surcharged brain refused to cope with it. He displayed only the agitation of a smoker temporarily without a light.

The New York Kid had almost instantly grasped Benson's arm, and was about to jerk him away when the other Kid, who up to this time had been an automaton, suddenly projected himself forward, thrust the rubber Benson aside, and said: "Yes."

There was no sound nor light in the world. The wall at the left happened to be of the common prison-like construction—no door, no window, no opening at all. Humanity was enclosed and asleep. Into the mouth of the sober Kid came a wretched, bitter taste, as if it had filled with blood. He was transfixed, as if he was already seeing the lightning ripples on the knife-blade.

But the Mexican's hand did not move at that time. His face went still further forward, and he whispered: "So?" The sober Kid saw this face as if he and it were alone in space—a yellow mask, smiling in eager cruelty, in satisfaction, and, above all, it was lit with sinister decision. As for the features, they were reminiscent of an unplaced, a forgotten type, which really resembled with precision those of a man who had shaved him three times in Boston in 1888. But the expression burned his mind as sealing-wax burns the palm, and, fascinated, stupefied, he actually watched the progress of the man's thought toward the point where a knife would be wrenched from its sheath. The emotion, a sort of mechanical fury, a breeze made by electric fans, a rage made by vanity, smote the dark countenance in wave after wave.

Then the New York Kid took a sudden step forward. His hand was also at his hip. He was gripping there a revolver of robust size. He recalled that upon its black handle was stamped a hunting scene in which a sportsman in fine leggings and a peaked cap was taking aim at a stag less than one eighth of an inch away.

His pace forward caused instant movement of the Mexicans. One immediately took two steps to face him squarely. There was a general adjustment, pair and pair. The opponent of the New York Kid was a tall man and quite stout. His sombrero was drawn low over his eyes; his serape was flung on his left shoulder; his back was bent in the supposed manner of a Spanish grandee. This concave gentleman cut a fine and terrible figure. The lad, moved by the spirits of his modest and perpendicular ancestors, had time to feel his blood roar at sight of the pose.

He was aware that the third Mexican was over on the left, fronting Benson; and he was aware that Benson was leaning against the wall, sleepily and peacefully eyeing the convention. So it happened that these six men stood, side fronting side, five of them with their right hands at their hips, and with their bodies lifted nervously, while the central pair exchanged a crescendo of provocations. The meaning of their words rose and rose. They were travelling in a straight line toward collision.

The New York Kid contemplated his Spanish grandee. He drew his revolver upward until the hammer was surely free of the holster. He waited, immovable and watchful, while the garrulous 'Frisco Kid expended two and a half lexicons on the middle Mexican.

The Eastern lad suddenly decided that he was going to be killed. His mind leaped forward and studied the aftermath. The story would be a marvel of brevity when first it reached the far New York home, written in a careful hand on a bit of cheap paper, topped and footed and backed by the printed fortifications of the cable company. But they are often as stones flung into mirrors, these bits of paper upon which are laconically written all the most terrible chronicles of the times. He witnessed the uprising of his mother and sister, and the invincible calm of his hard-mouthed old father, who would probably shut himself in his library and smoke alone. Then his father would come, and they would bring him here, and say: "This is the place." Then, very likely, each would remove his hat. They would stand quietly with their hats in their hands for a decent minute. He pitied his old financing father, unyielding and millioned, a man who commonly spoke twenty-two words a year to his beloved son. The Kid understood it at this time. If his fate was not impregnable, he might have turned out to be a man and have been liked by his father.

The other Kid would mourn his death. He would be preternaturally correct for some weeks, and recite the tale without swearing. But it would not bore him. For the sake of his dead comrade he would be glad to be preternaturally correct and to recite the tale without swearing.

These views were perfectly stereopticon, flashing in and away from his thought with an inconceivable rapidity, until, after all, they were simply one quick, dismal impression. And now, here is the unreal real: Into this Kid's nostrils, at the expectant moment of slaughter, had come the scent of new-mown hay, a fragrance from a field of prostrate grass, a fragrance which contained the sunshine, the bees, the peace of meadows, and the wonder of a distant crooning stream. It had no right to be supreme, but it was supreme, and he breathed it as he waited for pain and a sight of the unknown.

But in the same instant, it may be, his thought flew to the 'Frisco Kid, and it came upon him like a flicker of lightning that the 'Frisco Kid was not going to be there to perform, for instance, the extraordinary office of respectable mourner. The other Kid's head was muddled, his hand was unsteady, his agility was gone. This other Kid was facing the determined and most ferocious gentleman of the enemy. The New

York Kid became convinced that his friend was lost. There was going to be a screaming murder. He was so certain of it that he wanted to shield his eyes from sight of the leaping arm and the knife. It was sickening—utterly sickening. The New York Kid might have been taking his first sea-voyage. A combination of honourable manhood and inability prevented him from running away.

He suddenly knew that it was possible to draw his own revolver, and by a swift manœuvre face down all three Mexicans. If he was quick enough he would probably be victor. If any hitch occurred in the draw he would undoubtedly be dead with his friends. It was a new game. He had never been obliged to face a situation of this kind in the Beacon Club in New York. In this test the lungs of the Kid still continued to perform their duty:

> Oh, five white mice of chance,
> Shirts of wool and corduroy pants,
> Gold and wine, women and sin,
> All for you if you let me come in—
> Into the house of chance.

He thought of the weight and size of his revolver, and dismay pierced him. He feared that in his hands it would be as unwieldly as a sewing-machine for his quick work. He imagined, too, that some singular providence might cause him to lose his grip as he raised his weapon; or it might get fatally entangled in the tails of his coat. Some of the eels of despair lay wet and cold against his back.

But at the supreme moment the revolver came forth as if it were greased, and it arose like a feather. This somnolent machine, after months of repose, was finally looking at the breasts of men.

Perhaps in this one series of movements the Kid had unconsciously used nervous force sufficient to raise a bale of hay. Before he comprehended it, he was standing behind his revolver, glaring over the barrel at the Mexicans, menacing first one and then another. His finger was tremoring on the trigger. The revolver gleamed in the darkness with a fine silver light.

The fulsome grandee sprang backward with a low cry. The man who had been facing the 'Frisco Kid took a quick step away. The beautiful array of Mexicans was suddenly disorganized.

The cry and the backward steps revealed something of great importance to the New York Kid. He had never dreamed that he did not have a complete monopoly of all possible trepidations. The cry of the grandee was that of a man who suddenly sees a poisonous snake. Thus the Kid was able to understand swiftly that they were all human beings. They were unanimous in not wishing for too bloody a combat. There was a sudden expression of the equality. He had vaguely believed that they were not going to evince much consideration for his dramatic development as an active factor. They even might be exasperated into an onslaught by it. Instead, they had respected his movement with a respect as great even as an ejaculation of fear and backward steps. Upon the instant he pounced forward, and began to swear, unreeling great English oaths as thick as ropes, and lashing the faces of the Mexicans with them. He was bursting with rage because these men had not previously confided to him that they were vulnerable. The whole thing had been an absurd imposition. He had been seduced into respectful alarm by the concave attitude of the grandee. And, after all, there had been an equality of emotion—an equality! He was furious. He wanted to take the serape of the grandee and swaddle him in it.

The Mexicans slunk back, their eyes burning wistfully. The Kid took aim first at one and then at another. After they had achieved a certain distance, they paused and drew up in a rank. They then resumed some of their old splendour of manner. A voice hailed him in a tone of cynical bravado, as if it had come from between high lips of smiling mockery: "Well, señor, it is finished?"

The Kid scowled into the darkness, his revolver drooping at his side. After a moment he answered: "I am willing." He found it strange that he should be able to speak after this silence of years.

"Good night, señor."

"Good night."

When he turned to look at the 'Frisco Kid, he found him in his original position, his hand upon his hip. He was blinking in perplexity at the point where the Mexicans had vanished.

"Well," said the sober Kid, crossly, "are you ready to go home now?"

The 'Frisco Kid said: "Where they gone?" His voice was undisturbed, but inquisitive.

Benson suddenly propelled himself from his dreamful position against the wall. "'Frisco Kid's all right. He's drunk's fool, and he's all right. But you New York Kid, you're shober." He passed into a state of profound investigation. "Kid shober 'cause didn't go with us. Didn't go with us 'cause went to damn circus. Went to damn circus 'cause lose shakin' dice. Lose shakin' dice 'cause—what make lose shakin' dice, Kid?"

The New York Kid eyed the senile youth. "I don't know. The five white mice, maybe."

Benson puzzled so over this reply that he had to be held erect by his friends. Finally the 'Frisco Kid said: "Let's go home."

Nothing had happened.

Stephen Crane

THE WISE MEN

THEY were youths of subtle mind. They were very wicked, according to report, and yet they managed to have it reflect credit upon them. They often had the well-informed and the great talkers of the American colony engaged in reciting their misdeeds, and facts relating to their sins were usually told with a flourish of awe and fine admiration.

One was from San Francisco, and one was from New York; but they resembled each other in appearance. This is an idiosyncrasy of geography.

They were never apart in the City of Mexico, at any rate, excepting perhaps, when one had retired to his hotel for a respite; and then the other was usually camped down at the office, sending up servants with clamorous messages: "Oh, get up, and come on down."

They were two lads—they were called the Kids—and far from their mothers. Occasionally some wise man pitied them, but he usually was alone in his wisdom; the other folk frankly were transfixed at the splendour of the audacity and endurance of these Kids.

"When do these two boys ever sleep?" murmured a man, as he viewed them entering a café about eight o'clock one morning. Their smooth, infantile faces looked bright and fresh enough, at any rate. "Jim told me he saw them still at it about four-thirty this morning."

"Sleep?" ejaculated a companion, in a glowing voice. "They never sleep! They go to bed once in every two weeks." His boast of it seemed almost a personal pride.

"They'll end with a crash, though, if they keep it up at this pace," said a gloomy voice from behind a newspaper.

The Café Colorado has a front of white and gold, in which are set larger plate-glass windows than are commonly to be found in Mexico. Two little wings of willow, flip-flapping incessantly, serve as doors. Under them small stray dogs go furtively into the café, and are shied into the street again by the waiters. On the sidewalk there is always a decorative effect in loungers, ranging from the newly arrived and superior tourist to the old veteran of the silver-mines bronzed by violent suns. They contemplate, with various shades of interest, the show of the street—the red, purple, dusty white, glaring forth against the walls in the furious sunshine.

One afternoon the Kids strolled into the Café Colorado. A half-dozen of the men who sat smoking and reading with a sort of Parisian effect at the little tables which lined two sides of the room looked up, and bowed, smiling; and although this coming of the Kids was anything but an unusual event, at least a dozen men wheeled in their seats to stare after them. Three waiters polished tables, and moved chairs noisily, and appeared to be eager. Distinctly these Kids were of importance.

Behind the distant bar the tall form of old Pop himself awaited them, smiling with broad geniality. "Well, my boys, how are you?" he cried in a voice of profound solicitude. He allowed five or six of his customers to languish in the care of Mexican bartenders, while he himself gave his eloquent attention to the Kids, lending all the dignity of a great event to their arrival. "How are the boys to-day, eh?"

"You're a smooth old guy," said one, eyeing him. "Are you giving us this welcome so we won't notice it when you push your worst whisky at us?"

Pop turned in appeal from one Kid to the other Kid. "There, now! Hear that, will you?" He assumed an oratorical pose.

"Why, my boys, you always get the best—the very best—that this house has got."

"Yes, we do!" The Kids laughed. "Well, bring it out, anyhow; and if it's the same you sold us last night, we'll grab your cash-register and run."

Pop whirled a bottle along the bar, and then gazed at it with a rapt expression. "Fine as silk," he murmured. "Now just taste that, and if it isn't the finest whisky you ever put in your face, why, I'm a liar, that's all."

The Kids surveyed him with scorn, and poured out their allowances. Then they stood for a time, insulting Pop about his whisky. "Usually it tastes exactly like new parlour furniture," said the San Francisco Kid. "Well, here goes; and you want to look out for your cash-register."

"Your health, gentlemen," said Pop, with a grand air; and as he wiped his bristling grey moustache he wagged his head with reference to the cash-register question. "I could catch you before you got very far."

"Why, are you a runner?" said one, derisively.

"You just bank on me, my boy," said Pop, with deep emphasis. "I'm a flier."

The Kids set down their glasses suddenly, and looked at him. "You must be," they said. Pop was tall and graceful, and magnificent in manner, but he did not display those qualities of form which mean speed in the animal. His hair was grey; his face was round and fat from much living. The buttons of his glittering white vest formed a fine curve, so that if the concave surface of a piece of barrel-hoop had been laid against Pop it would have touched each button. "You must be," observed the Kids again.

"Well, you can laugh all you like, but—no jolly, now, boys—I tell you I'm a winner. Why, I bet you I can skin anything in this town on a square go. When I kept by place in Eagle Pass, there wasn't anybody who could touch me. One of these sure things came down from San Anton'. Oh, he was a runner, he was—one of these people with wings. Well, I skinned 'im. What? Certainly I did. Never touched me."

The Kids had been regarding him in grave silence, but at

this moment they grinned, and said, quite in chorus: "Oh, you old liar!"

Pop's voice took on a whining tone of earnestness: "Boys, I'm telling it to you straight. I'm a flier."

One of the Kids had had a dreamy cloud in his eye, and he cried out suddenly: "Say, what a joke to play this on Freddie!"

The other jumped ecstatically. "Oh, wouldn't it be, though? Say, he wouldn't do a thing but howl! He'd go crazy!"

They looked at Pop as if they longed to be certain that he was, after all, a runner. "Say, now, Pop—on the level," said one of them, wistfully, "can you run?"

"Boys," swore Pop, "I'm a peach! On the dead level, I'm a peach."

"By golly, I believe the old Indian can run," said one to the other, as if they were alone in conference.

"That's what I can," cried Pop.

The Kids said: "Well, so long, old man." They went to a table, and sat down. They ordered a salad. They were always ordering salads. This was because one Kid had a wild passion for salads, and the other did not care much. So at any hour of the day or night they might be seen ordering a salad. When this one came, they went into a sort of executive session. It was a very long consultation. Some of the men noted it; they said there was deviltry afoot. Occasionally the Kids laughed in supreme enjoyment of something unknown. The low rumble of wheels came from the street. Often could be heard the parrot-like cries of distant vendors. The sunlight streamed through the green curtains and made some little amber-coloured flitterings on the marble floor. High up among the severe decorations of the ceiling—reminiscent of the days when the great building was a palace—a small white butterfly was wending through the cool air-spaces. The long billiard-hall stretched back to a vague gloom. The balls were always clicking, and one could see endless elbows crooking. Beggars slunk through the wicker doors, and were ejected by the nearest waiter.

At last the Kids called Pop to them. "Sit down, Pop! Have

a drink!" They scanned him carefully. "Say, now, Pop, on your solemn oath, can you run?"

"Boys," said Pop, piously, and raising his hand, "I can run like a rabbit."

"On your oath?"

"On my oath."

"Can you beat Freddie?"

Pop appeared to look at the matter from all sides. "Well, boys, I'll tell you: no man is cock-sure of anything in this world, and I don't want to say that I can best any man; but I've seen Freddie run, and I'm ready to swear I can beat 'im. In a hundred yards I'd just about skin 'im neat—you understand—just about neat. Freddie is a good average runner, but I—you understand—I'm just—a little—bit—better."

The Kids had been listening with the utmost attention. Pop spoke the latter part slowly and meaningly. They thought that he intended them to see his great confidence.

One said: "Pop, if you throw us in this thing, we'll come here and drink for two weeks without paying. We'll back you, and work a josh on Freddie! But oh—if you throw us!"

To this menace Pop cried: "Boys, I'll make the run of my life! On my oath!"

The salad having vanished, the Kids arose. "All right, now," they warned him. "If you play us for duffers, we'll get square. Don't you forget it!"

"Boys, I'll give you a race for your money. Bank on that. I may lose—understand, I may lose—no man can help meeting a better man, but I think I can skin 'im, and I'll give you a run for your money, you bet."

"All right, then. But look here," they told him. "You keep your face closed. Nobody but us gets in on this. Understand?"

"Not a soul," Pop declared.

They left him, gesturing a last warning from the wicker doors.

In the street they saw Benson, his cane gripped in the middle, strolling among the white-clothed, jabbering natives on the shady side. They semaphored to him eagerly, their faces a-shine with a plot. He came across cautiously, like a man who ventures into dangerous company.

"We're going to get up a race—Pop and Fred. Pop swears he can skin 'im. This is a tip; keep it dark, now. Say, won't Freddie be hot?"

Benson looked as if he had been compelled to endure these exhibitions of insanity for a century. "Oh, you fellows are off. Pop can't beat Freddie. He's an old bat. Why, it's impossible. Pop can't beat Freddie."

"Can't he? Want to bet he can't?" said the Kids. "There, now; let's see—you're talking so large."

"Well, you——"

"Oh, bet! Bet, or else close your trap. That's the way!"

"How do you know you can pull off the race? Seen Freddie?"

"No; but——"

"Well, see him, then. Can't bet now, with no race arranged. I'll bet with you all right, all right. I'll give you fellows a tip, though—you're a pair of asses. Pop can't run any faster than a brick schoolhouse."

The Kids scowled at him, and defiantly said: "Can't he?"

They left him, and went to the Casa Verde. Freddie, beautiful in his white jacket, was holding one of his innumerable conversations across the bar. He smiled when he saw them. "Where you boys been?" he demanded in a paternal tone. Almost all the proprietors of American cafés in the city used to adopt a paternal tone when they spoke to the Kids.

"Oh, been round," they replied.

"Have a drink," said the proprietor of the Casa Verde, forgetting his other social obligations.

During the course of this ceremony one of the Kids remarked: "Freddie, Pop says he can beat you running."

"Does he?" observed Freddie, without excitement. He was used to various snares of the Kids.

"That's what. He says he can leave you at the wire, and not see you again."

"Well, he lies," replied Freddie, placidly.

"And I'll bet you a bottle of wine that he can do it, too."

"Rats!" said Freddie.

"Oh, that's all right," pursued a Kid. "You can throw bluffs all you like; but he can lose you in a hundred-yard dash, you bet."

Freddie drank his whisky, and then settled his elbows on the bar. "Say, now, what do you boys keep coming in here with some pipe-story all the time for? You can't josh me. Do you think you can scare me about Pop? Why, I know I can beat 'im. He's an old man. He can't run with me; certainly not. Why, you fellows are just jollying me."

"Are we, though?" said the Kids. "You daresn't bet the bottle of wine."

"Oh, of course I can bet you a bottle of wine," said Freddie, disdainfully. "Nobody cares about a bottle of wine, but——"

"Well, make it five, then," advised one of the Kids.

Freddie hunched his shoulders. "Why, certainly I will. Make it ten if you like, but——"

"We do," they said.

"Ten, is it? All right; that goes." A look of weariness came over Freddie's face. "But you boys are foolish. I tell you, Pop is an old man. How can you expect him to run? Of course I'm no great runner, but, then, I'm young and healthy, and—and a pretty smooth runner, too. Pop is old and fat, and, then, he doesn't do a thing but tank all day. It's a cinch."

The Kids looked at him, and laughed rapturously. They waved their fingers at him. "Ah, there!" they cried. They meant that they had made a victim of him.

But Freddie continued to expostulate: "I tell you, he couldn't win—an old man like him. You're crazy! Of course I know that you don't care about ten bottles of wine, but then—to make such bets as that! You're twisted."

"Are we, though?" cried the Kids, in mockery. They had precipitated Freddie into a long and thoughtful treatise on every possible chance of the thing as he saw it. They disputed with him from time to time, and jeered at him. He laboured on through his argument. Their childish faces were bright with glee.

In the midst of it Wilburson entered. Wilburson worked—
not too much, though. He had hold of the Mexican end of a
great importing house of New York, and, as he was a junior
partner, he worked—but not too much, though.

"What's the howl?" he said.

The Kids giggled. "We've got Freddie rattled."

"Why," said Freddie, turning to him, "these two Indians
are trying to tell me that Pop can beat me running."

"Like the devil!" said Wilburson, incredulously.

"Well, can't he?" demanded a Kid.

"Why, certainly not," said Wilburson, dismissing every
possibility of it with a gesture. "That old bat? Certainly not!
I'll bet fifty dollars that Freddie——"

"Take you," said a Kid.

"What?" said Wilburson. "That Freddie won't beat Pop?"

The Kid that had spoken now nodded his head.

"That Freddie won't beat Pop?" repeated Wilburson.

"Yes; is it a go?"

"Why, certainly," retorted Wilburson. "Fifty? All right."

"Bet you five bottles on the side," ventured the other Kid.

"Why, certainly," exploded Wilburson, wrathfully. "You
fellows must take me for something easy. I'll take all those
kind of bets that I can get. Cer-tain-ly."

They settled the details. The course was to be paced off on
the asphalt of one of the adjacent side streets; and then, at
about eleven o'clock in the evening, the match would be run.
Usually in Mexico the streets of a city grow lonely and dark
but a little time after nine o'clock. There are occasional lurking figures, perhaps, but no crowds, lights, noise. The course
would doubtless be undisturbed. As for the policemen in the
vicinity, they—well, they were conditionally amiable.

The Kids went to see Pop. They told him of the arrangements; and then in deep tones they said: "Oh, Pop, if you
throw us!"

Pop appeared to be a trifle shaken by the weight of responsibility thrust upon him, but he spoke out bravely: "Boys, I'll
pinch that race. Now you watch me. I'll pinch it!"

The Kids went then on some business of their own, for they were not seen again until evening. When they returned to the neighbourhood of the Café Colorado, the usual evening stream of carriages was whirling along the *calle*. The wheels hummed on the asphalt, and the coachmen towered in their great sombreros. On the sidewalk a gazing crowd sauntered, the better classes self-satisfied and proud in their derby hats and cutaway coats, the lower classes muffling their dark faces in their blankets, slipping along in leather sandals. An electric light sputtered and fumed over the throng. The afternoon shower had left the pave wet and glittering; the air was still laden with the odour of rain on flowers, grass, leaves.

In the Café Colorado a cosmopolitan crowd ate, drank, played billiards, gossiped, or read in the glaring yellow light. When the Kids entered, a large circle of men that had been gesticulating near the bar greeted them with a roar:

"Here they are now!"

"Oh, you pair of peaches!"

"Say, got any more money to bet with?"

The Kids smiled complacently. Old Colonel Hammigan, grinning, pushed his way to them. "Say, boys, we'll all have a drink on you now, because you won't have any money after eleven o'clock. You'll be going down the back stairs in your stocking-feet."

Although the Kids remained unnaturally serene and quiet, argument in the Café Colorado became tumultuous. Here and there a man who did not intend to bet ventured meekly that perchance Pop might win; and the others swarmed upon him in a whirlwind of angry denial and ridicule.

Pop, enthroned behind the bar, looked over at this storm with a shadow of anxiety upon his face; this wide-spread flouting affected him; but the Kids looked blissfully satisfied with the tumult they had stirred.

Blanco, honest man, ever worrying for his friends, came to them. "Say, you fellows, you aren't betting too much? This think looks kind of shaky, don't it?"

The faces of the Kids grew sober, and after consideration

one said: "No; I guess we've got a good thing, Blanco. Pop is going to surprise them, I think."

"Well, don't——"

"All right, old boy. We'll watch out."

From time to time the Kids had much business with certain orange, red, blue, purple, and green bills. They were making little memoranda on the backs of visiting-cards. Pop watched them closely, the shadow still upon his face. Once he called to them; and when they came, he leaned over the bar, and said intensely: "Say, boys, remember, now—I might lose this race. Nobody can ever say for sure, and if I do—why——"

"Oh, that's all right, Pop," said the Kids, reassuringly. "Don't mind it. Do your durnedest, and let it go at that."

When they had left him, however, they went to a corner to consult. "Say, this is getting interesting. Are you in deep?" asked one, anxiously, of his friend.

"Yes; pretty deep," said the other, stolidly. "Are you?"

"Deep as the devil," replied the other, in the same tone.

They looked at each other stonily, and went back to the crowd. Benson had just entered the café. He approached them with a gloating smile of victory. "Well, where's all that money you were going to bet?"

"Right here," said the Kids, thrusting into their vest pockets.

At eleven o'clock a curious thing was learned. When Pop and Freddie, the Kids, and all, came to the little side street, it was thick with people. It seems that the news of this great race had spread like the wind among the Americans, and they had come to witness the event. In the darkness the crowd moved, gesticulating and mumbling in argument.

The principals, the Kids, and those with them surveyed this scene with some dismay. "Say, here's a go." Even then a policeman might be seen approaching, the light from his little lantern flickering on his white cap, gloves, brass buttons, and on the butt of the old-fashioned Colt's revolver which hung at his belt. He addressed Freddie in swift Mexican. Freddie listened, nodding from time to time. Finally Freddie turned to the others to translate: "He says he'll get into trouble if he allows this race when all this crowd is here."

There was a murmur of discontent. The policeman looked at them with an expression of anxiety on his broad brown face.

"Oh, come on. We'll go hold it on some other fellow's beat," said one of the Kids.

The group moved slowly away, debating.

Suddenly the other Kid cried: "I know! The Paseo!"

"By jiminy!" said Freddie, "just the thing. We'll get a cab, and go out to the Paseo. S-s-sh! Keep it quiet. We don't want all this mob."

Later they tumbled into a cab—Pop, Freddie, the Kids, old Colonel Hammigan, and Benson. They whispered to the men who had wagered: "The Paseo." The cab whirled away up the back street. There were occasional grunts and groans—cries of "Oh, get off me feet!" and "Quit! You're killing me!" Six people do not have fun in one cab. The principals spoke to each other with the respect and friendliness which comes to good men at such times.

Once a kid put his head out of the window and looked backward. He pulled it in again, and cried: "Great Scott! Look at that, would you!"

The others struggled to do as they were bid, and afterward shouted: "Holy smoke!" "Well, I'll be blowed!" "Thunder and Turf!"

Galloping after them came innumerable other cabs, their lights twinkling, streaming in a great procession through the night. "The street is full of them," ejaculated the old colonel.

The Paseo de la Reforma is the famous drive of the City of Mexico, leading to the castle of Chapultepec, which last ought to be well known in the United States.

It is a broad, fine avenue of macadam, with a much greater quality of dignity than anything of the kind we possess in our own land. It seems of the Old World, where to the beauty of the thing itself is added the solemnity of tradition and history, the knowledge that feet in buskins trod the same stones, that cavalcades of steel thundered there before the coming of carriages.

When the Americans tumbled out of their cabs, the giant

bronzes of Aztec and Spaniard loomed dimly above them like towers. The four rows of poplar-trees rustled weirdly off there in the darkness. Pop took out his watch, and struck a match. "Well, hurry up this thing. It's almost midnight."

The other cabs came swarming, the drivers lashing their horses; for these Americans, who did all manner of strange things, nevertheless always paid well for it. There was a mighty hubbub then in the darkness. Five or six men began to pace off the distance and quarrel. Others knotted their handkerchiefs together to make a tape. Men were swearing over bets, fussing and fuming about the odds. Benson came to the Kids, swaggering. "You're a pair of asses." The cabs waited in a solid block down the avenue. Above the crowd, the tall statues hid their visages in the night.

At last a voice floated through the darkness: "Are you ready, there?" Everybody yelled excitedly. The men at the tape pulled it out straight. "Hold it higher, Jim, you fool!" A silence fell then upon the throng. Men bended down, trying to pierce the darkness with their eyes. From out at the starting-point came muffled voices. The crowd swayed and jostled.

The racers did not come. The crowd began to fret, its nerves burning. "Oh, hurry up!" shrilled some one.

The voice called again: "Ready, there?"

Everybody replied: "Yes; all ready! Hurry up!"

There was more muffled discussion at the starting-point. In the crowd a man began to make a proposition: "I'll bet twenty——" But the throng interrupted with a howl: "Here they come!" The thickly packed body of men swung as if the ground had moved. The men at the tape shouldered madly at their fellows, bawling: "Keep back! Keep back!"

From the profound gloom came the noise of feet pattering furiously. Vague forms flashed into view for an instant. A hoarse roar broke from the crowd. Men bended and swayed and fought. The Kids, back near the tape, exchanged another stolid look. A white form shone forth. It grew like a spectre. Always could be heard the wild patter. A barbaric scream broke from the crowd: "By Gawd, it's Pop! Pop! Pop's ahead!"

The old man spun toward the tape like a madman, his chin thrown back, his grey hair flying. His legs moved like maniac machinery. And as he shot forward a howl as from forty cages of wild animals went toward the imperturbable chieftains in bronze. The crowd flung themselves forward. "Oh, you old Indian! You savage! You cuss, you! Durn my buttons, did you ever see such running?"

"Ain't he a peach? Well!"

"Say, this beats anything!"

"Where's the Kids? H-e-y Kids!"

"Look at 'im, would you? Did you ever think?"

These cries flew in the air, blended in a vast shout of astonishment and laughter.

For an instant the whole great tragedy was in view. Freddie, desperate, his teeth shining, his face contorted, whirling along in deadly effort, was twenty feet behind the tall form of old Pop, who, dressed only in his—only in his underclothes—gained with each stride. One grand, insane moment, and then Pop had hurled himself against the tape—victor!

Freddie, falling into the arms of some men, struggled with his breath, and at last managed to stammer: "Say—can't—can't that old—old man run!"

Pop, puffing and heaving, could only gasp: "Where's my shoes? Who's got my shoes?"

Later Freddie scrambled, panting, through the crowd, and held out his hand. "Good man, Pop!" And then he looked up and down the tall, stout form. "Smoke! Who would think you could run like that?"

The Kids were surrounded by a crowd, laughing tempestuously.

"How did you know he could run?"

"Why didn't you give me a line on him?"

"Say—great snakes!—you fellows had a nerve to bet on Pop."

"Why, I was cock-sure he couldn't win."

"Oh, you fellows must have seen him run before!"

"Who would ever think it!"

Benson came by, filling the midnight air with curses. They turned to jeer him. "What's the matter, Benson?"

"Somebody pinched my handkerchief. I tied it up in that string. Damn it!"

The Kids laughed blithely. "Why, hullo, Benson!" they said.

There was a great rush for cabs. Shouting, laughing, wondering, the crowd hustled into their conveyances, and the drivers flogged their horses toward the city again.

"Won't Freddie be crazy! Say, he'll be guyed about this for years."

"But who would ever think that old tank could run so?"

One cab had to wait while Pop and Freddie resumed various parts of their clothing.

As they drove home, Freddie said: "Well, Pop, you beat me!"

Pop said: "That's all right, old man."

The Kids, grinning, said: "How much did you lose, Benson?"

Benson said defiantly: "Oh, not so much. How much did you win?"

"Oh, not so much!"

Old Colonel Hammigan, squeezed down in a corner, had apparently been reviewing the event in his mind, for he suddenly remarked: "Well, I'll be damned!"

They were late in reaching the Café Colorado; but when they did, the bottles were on the bar as thick as pickets on a fence.

Stephen Crane

HORSES—ONE DASH

RICHARDSON pulled up his horse and looked back over the trail, where the crimson serape of his servant flamed amid the dusk of the mesquit. The hills in the west were carved into peaks, and were painted the most profound blue. Above them, the sky was of that marvellous tone of green—like still sun-shot water—which people denounce in pictures.

José was muffled deep in his blanket, and his great toppling sombrero was drawn low over his brow. He shadowed his master along the dimming trail in the fashion of an assassin. A cold wind of the impending night swept over the wilderness of mesquit.

"Man," said Richardson, in lame Mexican, as the servant drew near, "I want eat! I want sleep! Understand no? Quickly! Understand?"

"Si, señor," said José, nodding. He stretched one arm out of his blanket, and pointed a yellow finger into the gloom. "Over there, small village! Si, señor."

They rode forward again. Once the American's horse shied and breathed quiveringly at something which he saw or imagined in the darkness, and the rider drew a steady, patient rein and leaned over to speak tenderly, as if he were addressing a frightened woman. The sky had faded to white over the mountains, and the plain was a vast, pointless ocean of black.

Suddenly some low houses appeared squatting amid the bushes. The horsemen rode into a hollow until the houses rose against the sombre sundown sky, and then up a small hillock, causing these habitations to sink like boats in the sea of shadow.

A beam of red firelight fell across the trail. Richardson sat sleepily on his horse while the servant quarrelled with somebody—a mere voice in the gloom—over the price of bed and board. The houses about him were for the most part like tombs in their whiteness and silence, but there were scudding black figures that seemed interested in his arrival.

José came at last to the horses' heads, and the American slid stiffly from his seat. He muttered a greeting as with his spurred feet he clicked into the adobe house that confronted him. The brown, stolid face of a woman shone in the light of the fire. He seated himself on the earthen floor, and blinked drowsily at the blaze. He was aware that the woman was clinking earthenware, and hieing here and everywhere in the manœuvres of the housewife. From a dark corner of the room there came the sound of two or three snores twining together.

The woman handed him a bowl of tortillas. She was a submissive creature, timid and large-eyed. She gazed at his enormous silver spurs, his large and impressive revolver, with the interest and admiration of the highly privileged cat of the adage. When he ate, she seemed transfixed off there in the gloom, her white teeth shining.

José entered, staggering under two Mexican saddles large enough for building-sites. Richardson decided to smoke a cigarette, and then changed his mind. It would be much finer to go to sleep. His blanket hung over his left shoulder, furled into a long pipe of cloth, according to a Mexican fashion. By doffing his sombrero, unfastening his spurs and his revolver-belt, he made himself ready for the slow, blissful twist into the blanket. Like a cautious man, he lay close to the wall, and all his property was very near his hand.

The mesquit brush burned long. José threw two gigantic wings of shadow as he flapped his blanket about him—first across his chest under his arms, and then around his neck and across his chest again, this time over his arms, with the end tossed on his right shoulder. A Mexican thus snugly enveloped can nevertheless free his fighting arm in a beautifully brisk way, merely shrugging his shoulder as he grabs for the weapon at his belt. They always wear their serapes in this manner.

The firelight smothered the rays which, streaming from a moon as large as a drum-head, were struggling at the open door. Richardson heard from the plain the fine, rhythmical trample of the hoofs of hurried horses. He went to sleep wondering who rode so fast and so late. And in the deep silence the pale rays of the moon must have prevailed against the red spears of the fire until the room was slowly flooded to its middle with a rectangle of silver light.

Richardson was awakened by the sound of a guitar. It was badly played—in this land of Mexico, from which the romance of the instrument ascends to us like a perfume. The guitar was groaning and whining like a badgered soul. A noise of scuffling feet accompanied the music. Sometimes laughter arose, and often the voices of men saying bitter things to each other; but always the guitar cried on, the treble sounding as if some one were beating iron, and the bass humming like bees.

"Damn it! they're having a dance," muttered Richardson, fretfully. He heard two men quarrelling in short, sharp words like pistol-shots; they were calling each other worse names than common people know in other countries.

He wondered why the noise was so loud. Raising his head from his saddle-pillow, he saw, with the help of the valiant moonbeams, a blanket hanging flat against the wall at the farther end of the room. Being of the opinion that it concealed a door, and remembering that Mexican drink made men very drunk, he pulled his revolver closer to him and prepared for sudden disaster.

Richardson was dreaming of his far and beloved North.

"Well, I would kill him, then!"

"No, you must not!"

"Yes, I will kill him! Listen! I will ask this American beast for his beautiful pistol and spurs and money and saddle, and if he will not give them—you will see!"

"But these Americans—they are a strange people. Look out, señor."

Then twenty voices took part in the discussion. They rose in quivering shrillness, as from men badly drunk.

Richardson felt the skin draw tight around his mouth, and his knee-joints turned to bread. He slowly came to a sitting posture, glaring at the motionless blanket at the far end of the room. This stiff and mechanical movement, accomplished entirely by the muscles of the wrist, must have looked like the rising of a corpse in the wan moonlight, which gave everything a hue of the grave.

My friend, take my advice, and never be executed by a hangman who doesn't talk the English language. It, or anything that resembles it, is the most difficult of deaths. The tumultuous emotions of Richardson's terror destroyed that slow and careful process of thought by means of which he understood Mexican. Then he used his instinctive comprehension of the first and universal language, which is tone. Still, it is disheartening not to be able to understand the detail of threats against the blood of your body.

Suddenly the clamour of voices ceased. There was a silence—a silence of decision. The blanket was flung aside, and the red light of a torch flared into the room. It was held high by a fat, round-faced Mexican, whose little snake-like moustache was as black as his eyes, and whose eyes were black as jet. He was insane with the wild rage of a man whose liquor is dully burning at his brain. Five or six of his fellows crowded after him. The guitar, which had been thrummed doggedly during the time of the high words, now suddenly stopped.

They contemplated each other. Richardson sat very straight and still, his right hand lost in the folds of his blanket. The

Mexicans jostled in the light of the torch, their eyes blinking and glittering.

The fat one posed in the manner of a grandee. Presently his hand dropped to his belt, and from his lips there spun an epithet—a hideous word which often foreshadows knife-blows, a word peculiarly of Mexico, where people have to dig deep to find an insult that has not lost its savour.

The American did not move. He was staring at the fat Mexican with a strange fixedness of gaze, not fearful, not dauntless, not anything that could be interpreted; he simply stared.

The fat Mexican must have been disconcerted, for he continued to pose as a grandee with more and more sublimity, until it would have been easy for him to fall over backward. His companions were swaying in a very drunken manner. They still blinked their beady eyes at Richardson. Ah, well, sirs, here was a mystery. At the approach of their menacing company, why did not this American cry out and turn pale, or run, or pray them mercy? The animal merely sat still, and stared, and waited for them to begin. Well, evidently he was a great fighter; or perhaps he was an idiot. Indeed, this was an embarrassing situation, for who was going forward to discover whether he was a great fighter or an idiot?

To Richardson, whose nerves were tingling and twitching like live wires, and whose heart jolted inside him, this pause was a long horror; and for these men who could so frighten him there began to swell in him a fierce hatred—a hatred that made him long to be capable of fighting all of them, a hatred that made him capable of fighting all of them. A .44-caliber revolver can make a hole large enough for little boys to shoot marbles through, and there was a certain fat Mexican, with a moustache like a snake, who came extremely near to have eaten his last tamale merely because he frightened a man too much.

José had slept the first part of the night in his fashion, his body hunched into a heap, his legs crooked, his head touching his knees. Shadows had obscured him from the sight of the invaders. At this point he arose, and began to prowl quakingly over toward Richardson, as if he meant to hide behind him.

Of a sudden the fat Mexican gave a howl of glee. José had come within the torch's circle of light. With roars of singular ferocity the whole group of Mexicans pounced on the American's servant.

He shrank shuddering away from them, beseeching by every device of word and gesture. They pushed him this way and that. They beat him with their fists. They stung him with their curses. As he grovelled on his knees, the fat Mexican took him by the throat and said: "I'm going to kill you!" And continually they turned their eyes to see if they were to succeed in causing the initial demonstration by the American.

Richardson looked on impassively. Under the blanket, however, his fingers were clenched as rigidly as iron upon the handle of his revolver.

Here suddenly two brilliant clashing chords from the guitar were heard, and a woman's voice, full of laughter and confidence, cried from without: "Hello! hello! Where are you?"

The lurching company of Mexicans instantly paused and looked at the ground. One said, as he stood with his legs wide apart in order to balance himself: "It is the girls! They have come!" He screamed in answer to the question of the woman: "Here!" And without waiting he started on a pilgrimage toward the blanket-covered door. One could now hear a number of female voices giggling and chattering.

Two other Mexicans said: "Yes; it is the girls! Yes!" They also started quietly away. Even the fat Mexican's ferocity seemed to be affected. He looked uncertainly at the still immovable American. Two of his friends grasped him gaily. "Come, the girls are here! Come!" He cast another glower at Richardson. "But this——" he began. Laughing, his comrades hustled him toward the door. On its threshold, and holding back the blanket with one hand, he turned his yellow face with a last challenging glare toward the American. José, bewailing his state in little sobs of utter despair and woe, crept to Richardson and huddled near his knee. Then the cries of the Mexicans meeting the girls were heard, and the guitar burst out in joyous humming.

The moon clouded, and but a faint square of light fell through the open main door of the house. The coals of the fire were silent save for occasional sputters. Richardson did not change his position. He remained staring at the blanket which hid the strategic door in the far end. At his knees José was arguing, in a low, aggrieved tone, with the saints. Without, the Mexicans laughed and danced, and—it would appear from the sound—drank more.

In the stillness and night Richardson sat wondering if some serpent-like Mexican was sliding toward him in the darkness, and if the first thing he knew of it would be the deadly sting of the knife. "Sssh," he whispered to José. He drew his revolver from under the blanket and held it on his leg.

The blanket over the door fascinated him. It was a vague form, black and unmoving. Through the opening it shielded was to come, probably, menace, death. Sometimes he thought he saw it move.

As grim white sheets, the black and silver of coffins, all the panoply of death, affect us because of that which they hide, so this blanket, dangling before a hole in an adobe wall, was to Richardson a horrible emblem, and a horrible thing in itself. In his present mood Richardson could not have been brought to touch it with his finger.

The celebrating Mexicans occasionally howled in song. The guitarist played with speed and enthusiasm.

Richardson longed to run. But in this threatening gloom, his terror convinced him that a move on his part would be a signal for the pounce of death. José, crouching abjectly, occasionally mumbled. Slowly and ponderous as stars the minutes went.

Suddenly, Richardson thrilled and started. His breath, for a moment, left him. In sleep his nerveless fingers had allowed his revolver to fall and clang upon the hard floor. He grabbed it up hastily, and his glance swept apprehensively over the room.

A chill blue light of dawn was in the place. Every outline

was slowly growing; detail was following detail. The dread blanket did not move. The riotous company had gone or become silent.

Richardson felt in his blood the effect of this cold dawn. The candour of breaking day brought his nerve. He touched José. "Come," he said. His servant lifted his lined, yellow face and comprehended. Richardson buckled on his spurs and strode up; José obediently lifted the two great saddles. Richardson held two bridles and a blanket on his left arm; in his right hand he held his revolver. They sneaked toward the door.

The man who said that spurs jingled was insane. Spurs have a mellow clash—clash—clash. Walking in spurs—notably Mexican spurs—you remind yourself vaguely of a telegraphic lineman. Richardson was inexpressibly shocked when he came to walk. He sounded to himself like a pair of cymbals. He would have known of this if he had reflected; but then he was escaping, not reflecting. He made a gesture of despair, and from under the two saddles José tried to make one of hopeless horror. Richardson stooped, and with shaking fingers unfastened the spurs. Taking them in his left hand, he picked up his revolver, and they slunk on toward the door.

On the threshold Richardson looked back. In a corner he saw, watching him with large eyes, the Indian man and woman who had been his hosts. Throughout the night they had made no sign, and now they neither spoke nor moved. Yet Richardson thought he detected meek satisfaction at his departure.

The street was still and deserted. In the eastern sky there was a lemon-coloured patch.

José had picketed the horses at the side of the house. As the two men came around the corner, Richardson's animal set up a whinny of welcome. The little horse had evidently heard them coming. He stood facing them, his ears cocked forward, his eyes bright with welcome.

Richardson made a frantic gesture, but the horse, in his happiness at the appearance of his friends, whinnied with enthusiasm.

The American felt at this time that he could have strangled his well-beloved steed. Upon the threshold of safety he was being betrayed by his horse, his friend. He felt the same hate for the horse that he would have felt for a dragon. And yet, as he glanced wildly about him, he could see nothing stirring in the street, nor at the doors of the tomb-like houses.

José had his own saddle-girth and both bridles buckled in a moment. He curled the picket-ropes with a few sweeps of his arm. The fingers of Richardson, however, were shaking so that he could hardly buckle the girth. His hands were in invisible mittens. He was wondering, calculating, hoping about his horse. He knew the little animal's willingness and courage under all circumstances up to this time, but then— here it was different. Who could tell if some wretched instance of equine perversity was not about to develop? Maybe the little fellow would not feel like smoking over the plain at express speed this morning, and so he would rebel and kick and be wicked. Maybe he would be without feeling of interest, and run listlessly. All men who have had to hurry in the saddle know what it is to be on a horse who does not understand the dramatic situation. Riding a lame sheep is bliss to it. Richardson, fumbling furiously at the girth, thought of these things.

Presently he had it fastened. He swung into the saddle, and as he did so his horse made a mad jump forward. The spurs of José scratched and tore the flanks of his great black animal, and side by side the two horses raced down the village street. The American heard his horse breathe a quivering sigh of excitement.

Those four feet skimmed. They were as light as fairy puff-balls. The houses of the village glided past in a moment, and the great, clear, silent plain appeared like a pale blue sea of mist and wet bushes. Above the mountains the colours of the sunlight were like the first tones, the opening chords, of the mighty hymn of the morning.

The American looked down at his horse. He felt in his heart the first thrill of confidence. The little animal, unurged and quite tranquil, moving his ears this way and that way with an air of interest in the scenery, was nevertheless bounding into the eye of the breaking day with the speed of a frightened antelope. Richardson, looking down, saw the long, fine reach of forelimb as steady as steel machinery. As the ground reeled past, the long dried grasses hissed, and cactus-plants were dull blurs. A wind whirled the horse's mane over his rider's bridle hand.

José's profile was lined against the pale sky. It was as that of a man who swims along in an ocean. His eyes glinted like metal fastened on some unknown point ahead of him, some mystic place of safety. Occasionally his mouth puckered in a little unheard cry; and his legs, bent back, worked spasmodically as his spurred heels sliced the flanks of his charger.

Richardson consulted the gloom in the west for signs of a hard-riding, yelling cavalcade. He knew that, whereas his friends the enemy had not attacked him when he had sat still and with apparent calmness confronted them, they would certainly take furiously after him now that he had run from them—now that he had confessed to them that he was the weaker. Their valour would grow like weeds in the spring, and upon discovering his escape they would ride forth dauntless warriors.

Sometimes he was sure he saw them. Sometimes he was sure he heard them. Continually looking backward over his shoulder, he studied the purple expanses where the night was marching away. José rolled and shuddered in his saddle, persistently disturbing the stride of the black horse, fretting and worrying him until the white foam flew and the great shoulders shone like satin from the sweat.

At last Richardson drew his horse carefully down to a walk. José wished to rush insanely on, but the American spoke to him sternly. As the two paced forward side by side, Richardson's little horse thrust over his soft nose and inquired into the black's condition.

Riding with José was like riding with a corpse. His face resembled a cast in lead. Sometimes he swung forward and almost pitched from his seat. Richardson was too frightened himself to do anything but hate this man for his fear. Finally he issued a mandate which nearly caused José's eyes to slide out of his head and fall to the ground like two silver coins.

"Ride behind me—about fifty paces."

"Señor—" stuttered the servant.

"Go!" cried the American, furiously. He glared at the other and laid his hand on his revolver. José looked at his master wildly. He made a piteous gesture. Then slowly he fell back, watching the hard face of the American for a sign of mercy.

Richardson had resolved in his rage that at any rate he was going to use the eyes and ears of extreme fear to detect the approach of danger; and so he established his servant as a sort of outpost.

As they proceeded he was obliged to watch sharply to see that the servant did not slink forward and join him. When José made beseeching circles in the air with his arm he replied menacingly gripping his revolver.

José had a revolver, too; nevertheless it was very clear in his mind that the revolver was distinctly an American weapon. He had been educated in the Rio Grande country.

Richardson lost the trail once. He was recalled to it by the loud sobs of his servant.

Then at last José came clattering forward, gesticulating and wailing. The little horse sprang to the shoulder of the black. They were off.

Richardson, again looking backward, could see a slanting flare of dust on the whitening plain. He thought that he could detect small moving figures in it.

José's moans and cries amounted to a university course in theology. They broke continually from his quivering lips. His spurs were as motors. They forced the black horse over the plain in great headlong leaps.

But under Richardson there was a little insignificant rat-coloured beast who was running apparently with almost as much effort as it requires for a bronze statue to stand still. As a matter of truth, the ground seemed merely something to be touched from time to time with hoofs that were as light as blown leaves. Occasionally Richardson lay back and pulled stoutly at his bridle to keep from abandoning his servant.

José harried at his horse's mouth, flopped around in the saddle, and made his two heels beat like flails. The black ran like a horse in despair.

Crimson serapes in the distance resemble drops of blood on the great cloth of plain.

Richardson began to dream of all possible chances. Although quite a humane man, he did not once think of his servant. José being a Mexican, it was natural that he should be killed in Mexico; but for himself, a New Yorker—

He remembered all the tales of such races for life, and he thought them badly written.

The great black horse was growing indifferent. The jabs of José's spurs no longer caused him to bound forward in wild leaps of pain. José had at last succeeded in teaching him that spurring was to be expected, speed or no speed, and now he took the pain of it dully and stolidly, as an animal who finds that doing his best gains him no respite.

José was turned into a raving maniac. He bellowed and screamed, working his arms and his heels like one in a fit. He resembled a man on a sinking ship, who appeals to the ship. Richardson, too, cried madly to the black horse.

The spirit of the horse responded to these calls, and, quivering and breathing heavily, he made a great effort, a sort of final rush, not for himself apparently, but because he understood that his life's sacrifice, perhaps, had been invoked by these two men who cried to him in the universal tongue. Richardson had no sense of appreciation at this time—he was too frightened— but often now he remembers a certain black horse.

From the rear could be heard a yelling, and once a shot was fired—in the air, evidently. Richardson moaned as he looked back. He kept his hand on his revolver. He tried to imagine the brief tumult of his capture—the flurry of dust from the hoofs of horses pulled suddenly to their haunches, the shrill biting curses of the men, the ring of the shots, his own last contortion. He wondered, too, if he could not somehow manage to pelt that fat Mexican, just to cure his abominable egotism.

It was José, the terror-stricken, who at last discovered

safety. Suddenly he gave a howl of delight, and astonished his horse into a new burst of speed. They were on a little ridge at the time, and the American at the top of it saw his servant gallop down the slope and into the arms, so to speak, of a small column of horsemen in grey and silver clothes. In the dim light of the early morning they were as vague as shadows, but Richardson knew them at once for a detachment of rurales, that crack cavalry corps of the Mexican army which polices the plain so zealously, being of themselves the law and the arm of it—a fierce and swift-moving body that knows little of prevention, but much of vengeance. They drew up suddenly, and the rows of great silver-trimmed sombreros bobbed in surprise.

Richardson saw José throw himself from his horse and begin to jabber at the leader of the party. When he arrived he found that his servant had already outlined the entire situation, and was then engaged in describing him, Richardson, as an American señor of vast wealth, who was the friend of almost every governmental potentate within two hundred miles. This seemed to profoundly impress the officer. He bowed gravely to Richardson and smiled significantly at his men, who unslung their carbines.

The little ridge hid the pursuers from view, but the rapid thud of their horses' feet could be heard. Occasionally they yelled and called to each other.

Then at last they swept over the brow of the hill, a wild mob of almost fifty drunken horsemen. When they discerned the pale-uniformed rurales they were sailing down the slope at top speed.

If toboggans half-way down a hill should suddenly make up their minds to turn around and go back, there would be an effect somewhat like that now produced by the drunken horsemen. Richardson saw the rurales serenely swing their carbines forward, and, peculiar-minded person that he was, felt his heart leap into his throat at the prospective volley. But the officer rode forward alone.

It appeared that the man who owned the best horse in this astonished company was the fat Mexican with the snaky moustache, and, in consequence, this gentleman was quite a distance in the van. He tried to pull up, wheel his horse, and scuttle back over the hill as some of his companions had done, but the officer called to him in a voice harsh with rage.

"—!" howled the officer. "This señor is my friend, the friend of my friends. Do you dare pursue him, —? —! —! —! —!" These lines represent terrible names, all different, used by the officer.

The fat Mexican simply grovelled on his horse's neck. His face was green; it could be seen that he expected death.

The officer stormed with magnificent intensity: "—! —! —!"

Finally, he sprang from his saddle and, running to the fat Mexican's side, yelled: "Go!" and kicked the horse in the belly with all his might. The animal gave a mighty leap into the air, and the fat Mexican, with one wretched glance at the contemplative rurales, aimed his steed for the top of the ridge. Richardson again gulped in expectation of a volley, for, it is said, this is one of the favourite methods of the rurales for disposing of objectionable people. The fat, green Mexican also evidently thought that he was to be killed while on the run, from the miserable look he cast at the troops. Nevertheless, he was allowed to vanish in a cloud of yellow dust at the ridge-top.

José was exultant, defiant, and, oh! bristling with courage. The black horse was drooping sadly, his nose to the ground. Richardson's little animal, with his ears bent forward, was staring at the horses of the rurales as if in an intense study. Richardson longed for speech, but he could only bend forward and pat the shining, silken shoulders. The little horse turned his head and looked back gravely.

Charles Flandrau

WANDERLUST

THE crew, much to its surprise, was paid off at Havana and furnished with a variety of explanations that did not particularly explain. Most of the men were bitter about it, but Lansing and Hayward were too unsophisticated, too new to the ways of the sea, to realize at first that they had been imposed upon. They had shipped on the wretched little steamer in New York in a sudden and curiously belated access of romanticism. For Hayward, who was twenty-three, had worked as an electrician since he was seventeen, and Lansing, who could scarcely remember a time he had not driven a grocer's wagon, was twenty-four. The sea had never been a boyish passion with them; they, indeed, had rarely seen it. As far as their previous relations with it had been concerned, New York might almost have been situated in the middle of a Dakota prairie. Their lives had always been city lives, but not of the kind that finds its way into popular fiction. For, in expressing themselves, they were not accustomed to employ a semi-unintelligible jargon of new slang, and from personal experience they knew almost as little about the Bowery as they knew about the sea. Their vocabularies, instead of being large and florid, were small and simple; their lapses from grammar were too usual to be interesting. They knew a few streets of the immense place exceedingly well, but they were, for the most part, lower-middle-class, commonplace, entirely respectable streets. They both had lived at home and worked hard—conscientiously, one would say, except that in the routine of their existences conscience played but little part. They had worked hard from habit, from the realization that they could easily be replaced and from an innate desire to keep their "jobs."

It was strange, or perhaps it wasn't strange (How do I know?), that the sea had all at once irrelevantly called to them. If they had been fond of reading, their embarkation might plausibly have been the practical attempt to make a dream come true. But they rarely read anything except the larger headlines of one-cent newspapers. The voluminous literature of adventure in foreign countries, of a wild, free life on the high seas, was almost as unknown to them as the thing itself. And yet, one day, they went to sea.

Early in April, an electric car smashed into Lansing's delivery wagon and hurt the horse, to say nothing of the wagon itself and its valuable contents. The fault was neither Lansing's nor the motorman's, but the grocer both discharged Lansing and collected two hundred and fifty dollars from the street railway company. Out of employment, Lansing saw something of New York. He had been faithful and careful, and in a dumb, uncomplaining sort of way he felt aggrieved and rebellious. His long, aimless walks, during the first few days of idleness, sometimes took him to the water's edge, and one morning he found himself on a Wall Street wharf, just as a steamer was about to leave for the tropics. Although he didn't precisely know what it all meant, the experience was, somehow, a moving one. There was an army of half-savage negroes—unlike any negroes he had ever seen—wheeling baggage on trucks and, with incoherent yelps, filling with freight a coarse net of rope that lifted, swung, sank, disappeared, and then reappeared limp and hungrily empty. There were fat, inexplicable women with improbable complexions, accompanied by lean, sallow, gesticulating men, who darted from their trunks to the ship and back again in a frenzy of excitement; and there were smells. Lansing did not know it (he knew very little) but it was the smells that, vulgarly speaking, "did the business." There was a kind of background—a fundamental smell—of pitch, of tar, of resin; but here and there, protruding from this, as he strolled up and down the long, inclosed wharf, was the rank, searching smell of unroasted coffee, the fruity fragrance of pineapples, the pungent acidity of tomatoes, the heavy sweetness of vanilla. As each odor came to him he inhaled it deeply, curiously, and for him, somewhat excitedly.

After the vessel had slipped away and disappeared around the corner of the wharf, Lansing had emerged with the intention of traversing Wall Street and taking an uptown car, but a young and slightly drunken sailor from a warship in the harbor had, àpropos of nothing at all, thrown an arm about his waist and led him to a saloon across the way. They had together only a glass of beer apiece, but they had sat down to it at a little table and the sailor had talked.

In the sphere of life to which they both belonged there is a directness and a frankness in the matter of intercourse that would be impossible for persons higher in the social order. Lansing had made many acquaintances and even a few friends by speaking or being spoken to by detached young men of his own age standing on street corners. Most of his acquaintances among girls had been begun in the same way. They had spoken to him or he had spoken to them—it was immaterial—and if they found each other congenial they sometimes met again; sometimes they didn't. But in any event meeting, talking, parting, involved nothing. It was merely an incident, often a pleasant one, of the kind the so-called upper classes know but little. It seemed perfectly natural to Lansing that the sailor, whom he never had seen before and probably would never see again, should offer him a glass of beer and tell him of his voyage around the world, and that he himself should respond with his accident, his discharge from the grocery—in a word, his "troubles," as he finally called them.

"A sailor *has* no troubles," the other declared as they got up to go; and he altogether looked it. After that, Lansing spent most of his time on the wharves and on Sunday afternoon he took Hayward with him.

Hayward's experience and education was as limited as his friend's, but he was of finer clay. What Lansing only felt, Hayward both felt and translated into words.

"Gee, look at them turtles!" he would exclaim at a row of the huge, grasping tortured creatures, lying on their backs and bound to a board by ropes punched through their bleeding flippers. "They come out of the water to lay eggs in the sand, and then you run out of the bushes and turn them over on their backs with a pole. I bet there's money in turtles." Or, "Gosh, what a lot of pineapples! How would you like to go down there, Lansing, where it's always summer, and just sit around while the niggers work, and send millions of pineapples back here to be sold at fifty cents apiece?"

"Forty-five," corrected Lansing, who had "delivered" them all his life, but who, until recently, had impartially given them the same consideration he had been accustomed to bestow upon a potato. Once they stood for an hour in front of ten cages full of white and yellow cockatoos. They were even more disturbing, more convincing than the incoherent negroes, the excitement of departure, the odor of exotic fruits.

"Down there you can see them flying around wild," Hayward meditated aloud. "Down there!" The words began to mean wonderful, incommunicable things to both of them. "Down there" was the shimmering, beautiful, hot, mysterious and seductive end of the earth that a Frenchman is always able to evoke for an instant, when, in a certain languid, reminiscent tone, he pronounces the words "là bas."

So they shipped on a tramp steamer and after a week they had been paid off at Havana. In Havana they spent an entrancing day and evening (Hayward bought an imitation diamond brooch at a place on Obispo Street where the revolving electric lights in the window elicited the last glitter), but the next day was a good deal of a bore. They had seen the town, there was no point in seeing it over again, and they were unused to idleness. Both of them would have jumped at the opportunity of returning to New York, but as no opportunity of doing so presented itself neither of them had been obliged to admit it. On the third day, however, they did move on to Vera Cruz. To Hayward, Vera Cruz was a name he had heard (Lansing had never even heard it), but had he been asked what country it was in he could not have told. He had an idea that it was near New Orleans and Galveston. In another week they were there—paid off again and turned loose in the Plaza.

Again they spent a notable day. They wandered about the streets, they went to a wedding in a church, they marveled at the unmolested buzzards filching garbage from the open drains along the curbstones, they walked at sunset to the end of the long breakwater and watched the fishermen come in with their gorgeous catch of red snapper. In the evening they went to a moving-picture show where they saw a realistic bull fight and a manufactured American train robbery. (This last gave them their first twinge of homesickness; the Pullman cars and the passengers looked so natural.) When it was over, they again sought the Plaza, where, in the sultry air, a compact mass of people was slowly forcing its way around and around to the music of an enormous band high above them among the trees in the center. They slept at an inexpensive lodging house to which they had been taken by one of the stokers.

But the next day was very like the second day at Havana, except that the possibilities of Vera Cruz seemed to be fewer. They could not walk in any direction without soon coming to the water or to a hot and dreary stretch of sand, and in their unconsciously blasé New York fashion they had become, by the second day, hardened to ragged Indians, enormous straw hats and scarlet *sarapes*. They sat on a shady bench in the Plaza and discussed an immediate return to New York. Lansing was for going overland; he had a hazy idea that they were near the border, and he was amazed and troubled for a moment when the stoker, whom they several times met again, laughed and told them that the border was a half a week away in a train. This, of course, they knew they could

not afford, and they decided to work their way back, as they
had come, on a steamer.

After that they spent most of their time on the docks, or in
front of the hotels and cafés near them, waylaying skippers
and mates. But places on ships bound for New York were apparently not to be had for the asking. The men to whom they
applied were invariably curt and definite when they weren't,
as sometimes happened, brutally abusive. This was annoying
although it was also, now and then, amusing. They, as yet,
had not begun to regard matters in the light of a "situation,"
for they still had a little money. At this period of their ebbing
fortunes it seemed to them that they were making a sort of
humiliating concession when they ceased to specify New
York as their destination, and resolved to sail on any ship
bound for any American port. But here, again, they were met
with the same irritated outbursts, or brief, cold denials.

They did not know it, because outside of the little ruts in
which they had always moved back and forth, they knew
nothing, but Mexico, in winter, is one of the great goals of
the American tramp. Thousands of them, in perpetually following at the heels of summer, drift across the border and
gradually wander from Laredo to San Luis Potosi, to the City
of Mexico, to Tampico and to Vera Cruz. They approach one
in the Plaza, in the Alameda, at the doors of hotels and theaters and restaurants, and, with an always interesting fiction,
extract twenty-five cents from one in the name of patriotism.
When the spring comes and it is once more warm at home,
they haunt the seaports, endeavoring to return by water. For
short-handed ships at Vera Cruz in April and May there is an
embarrassment of choice—a glut. Without in the least suspecting it, Hayward and Lansing had, in the eyes of the
world, become tramps, seeking a return passage.

The heat had begun to be intense and the invariable refusal
of their services was discouraging, but far more so were the
interminable mornings and afternoons and evenings when,
for the time being, they gave up their quest and sat on a bench
in the Plaza, or, at sunset, strolled down to the breakwater
for the red snappers and the evening breeze. They had left

home together and they stayed together as a matter of course, for they did not know anyone else, but they no longer had anything in particular to say to each other. For the most part they were silent and listless. They spoke only when something occurred to them relevant to what, at last, had begun to strike them as their "situation."

"It'll save money if we have one room instead of two, and sleep in the same bed," Hayward declared one night, after a day in which they had scarcely spoken at all.

"If we don't get up so early—What's the use anyhow?—We won't have to pay for breakfast. Two meals is enough if you're asleep," suggested Lansing a day or so later. And as long as they had money they spent it only for their bed and their two daily meals. Then came the inevitable day when they no longer had money, when they realized that the few cents they were spending for their supper were the last. It was disagreeable and they had begun to hate Vera Cruz—the monotony of it, the enforced idleness, the blistering heat, the rumor (they heard it from some English sailors on the dock) of yellow fever, and their inability to leave it all behind them. But although they were alarmed they were not yet panic-stricken. They each had a dress-suit case, an extra suit of clothes, an extra pair of shoes, some shirts and underclothes, a hat as well as a cap, three razors and a cheap watch.

The watch went first. They didn't need a watch. When they wished to know the time they could glance up from their bench at the clock on the tower of the "municipal palace." After this they parted on two successive days with the dress-suit cases, then the hats, the clothes and shoes and shirts and underclothes, one by one. The disposal of two of the razors gave them for forty-eight hours almost a sense of opulence. Lansing did not know there was a third razor and Hayward did not tell him of it. Hayward was an innately neat person, and at the Y.M.C.A., to which he belonged in New York, he had grown to look upon free soap and unending hot and cold shower-baths in a light that was spiritual as well as physical. He was good-looking and he knew it. The thought of becoming an unshaven thing was abhorrent to him. Starvation, just then, he felt he could face, but the prospect of a week's beard revolted him. So he twisted the razor into a piece of newspaper and secreted it in his pocket. As long as he and Lansing were together he knew he would not be able to shave; he could not confess to the possession of anything so convertible into money without immediately converting it. But the sensation of guilt was at first dispelled by an anticipatory thrill at the thought of the day when he could once more look clean and fresh and pink under his sunburn. He did not work it out in words, but the razor was to him a tangible symbol of self-respect, and he clung to it, although it would have bought them both the food they had begun to need.

"We've got to beat it. We've got to beat it right away," he said one morning, when they awoke to the prospect of a foodless day.

"They don't want us on the ships, but they'll have to take us anyhow. We'll sneak on board and hide. After they get started they'll have to keep us. They can't throw us overboard, and we'll work. Gee, how I want to work!"

That day they ate nothing, but in the evening they marvelously succeeded in smuggling themselves on a steamer bound for New Orleans, and in the prospect of getting away they forgot that they were hungry. One of the crew, with whom they struck up an acquaintance on the dock, seemed impressed by the sincerity with which they swore they would pay him if he would make it possible for them to return to where they could once more work. He agreed to help them conditionally; that is, he would get them on board and stow them away, if he could do it without too much risk to himself. The attendant conditions had to be just right; sometimes it was easy enough and sometimes it couldn't be done at all.

In their case the right conditions were unexpectedly furnished in the fraction of a second that it takes a cable to snap and drop a large piece of locomotive from the main deck on a dozen barrels of apples in the hold below. In the uproar that followed and continued for five or six minutes, the only cool and competent person was the new friend of Hayward and Lansing. He had been waiting for something of the kind to happen, and he took instant advantage of it. While everyone else was screaming Spanish oaths and peering into the hatchway at the ruins, he hustled the two on board and hid them. An hour and a half later, Hayward, dazed and suffocated, was dragged out by the feet and kicked down the gang plank. Lansing did not reappear. From the dock, Hayward watched the vessel become first a black speck and then a suggestion of low-lying smoke in the dusk.

He was all at once horribly alone and lonely, but it did not occur to him to feel resentful. Lansing's luck had been good; his own had been bad. That was all there was to it. He was glad someone had been lucky. That night he went back to the lodging house and slept in the bed—it was the last bed he ever slept in—and as he had no money, he in the morning gave the *patron* his razor.

Then began for him an existence, the absolute hopelessness of which appalled and crushed him. At first a ship to New York had seemed to him the only solution of his predicament; then the idea of a ship to anywhere had become a vision of paradise; now he saw that ships were an impossibility. As the season advanced the officers became more and more vigilant. A shabby, unshaven young man could not go within speaking distance of a ship. He made the rounds of the hotels and asked for work—any kind of work—but there was none. He tried to get employment as a laborer on the dock, but the foreman, who spoke English, laughed and asked him why he wished to commit suicide.

"An American keeping one of us out of a job would be stabbed in an hour," he declared, and refused to hire him. He managed for a time to keep alive, because one day he remembered that on the little finger of his left hand he had a gold ring. For years it had been so much a part of him that it had not occurred to him to sell it. The discovery of it came as a kind of revelation and made it possible for him to eat, sparingly, for two days. Then a brisk little American woman, in a white duck suit, approached him in the Plaza and gave him twenty-five centavos for delivering hand bills. She was a fortune teller—a "seeress," and had recently opened a "Studio for the Occult" in the Hotel Segurança, across the way. She seemed like a kind, capable little creature and once, when he had not eaten for two days, he went to the hotel and asked for her; but as he was unshaven and dazed and rather vague, they assumed him to be a drunken tramp and drove him away. Then he made the acquaintance, in the Plaza, of an utterly unreal person of no particular age, who dragged out of the hotel and in again every afternoon for half an hour or so, with the aid of a cane. His face was bloated and discolored, but his body was no more than a semi-upright arrangement of bones. Hayward at first thought he was an invalid in the last stages, then felt sure he was a drunkard, and, finally, it came to him that the man was a slave to some drug. He would occasionally give Hayward the twenty-five centavos on which he could exist for several days, and then, after a long silence on a bench, petulantly demand: "What do you do with all the money I give you? The day before yesterday I gave you three hundred dollars. I'm afraid you're extravagant." In one of his more lucid intervals, he suggested the American consul, and Hayward went to the consulate.

"I don't want to beg, I want to work," he said when the consul wheeled from a desk and impatiently eyed him.

"Oh, I hear that twenty times a day. Get out and don't come back," exclaimed the consul wearily. He "got out" and he did not go back. Something in the man's dumpy, coarse, dirty-fingernailed personality told him it would be useless. Then he tried to steal a ride on a freight train bound for the City of Mexico, and was discovered and thrown out at the second station, twelve miles away. It merely meant his walking back to Vera Cruz in the blistering heat over the endless sand dunes and past the fever-stricken marshes where the mosquitoes devoured him. He spent as much as he dared of that night on a bench in the Plaza, but for fear the policemen might begin to think he was sitting too long in one place, he, from time to time, aroused himself and walked down to the docks, or to the railway stations at opposite ends of the town. The humiliation of it was worse, somehow, than his hunger and his fatigue. The next night, however, the need of sleep was overpowering, and he lay down on the beach at the edge of the town. In spite of the ants that swarmed up under his clothes and stung him from his neck to his ankles, he slept the sleep of exhaustion. But to sleep on the beach at Vera Cruz is against the law, and at three o'clock in the morning he was arrested and thrown into a vile and crowded room under the tower, whose clock of late had struck for him so many aimless, hopeless hours. In the morning the judge dismissed him with the reminder (a negro from Havana translated the ultimatum) that the second offense would mean thirty days.

Then followed a horrible week—a last nightmare. He heard from a trainman that there was work at the machine shops of Casa Blanca, forty miles away, and, in the incredible heat, he walked there, and when he found the rumor was untrue, he walked back again. On the way, he lived on poisonous water and a yellow nut that looked like dates and grew on scrubby palm trees by the roadside. He did not know how long it had taken him to make the journey. When he once more reached the inevitable Plaza, he was dizzy with hunger, and as he thought he was going to die, he reeled over to where the world was dining under the arcade on the sidewalk. There were fifteen or twenty tables, and after passing them all he picked out one where five Americans, three men and two women, had finished eating and were lolling back in their chairs, waiting for their plates of half-consumed meat to be removed.

"I'm not a beggar," he began hurriedly, taking off his hat. "I'm not asking you for money, but I haven't had anything to eat today. Please let me have some of what you've left before the waiter takes it away." They might have given it to him, and then again they might not have. He never knew. The waiter came back just then and authoritatively slapped him away with a soiled napkin.

"What pretty hair he had," one of the women reflected. "It grows back from his forehead in a kind of proud way. Of course he's a fake."

"I didn't notice his hair, but he had perfect teeth," said the other. "This country's just full of tramps."

Late that night, when a young man skeptically gave him a Mexican dollar he wished to get rid of, as he was sailing for New York in the morning, Hayward suddenly burst into tears and, with his head on the back of the bench, sobbed for half an hour. He lived on the dollar for five days. In the meantime, the drug fiend died, and the seeress departed for the City of Mexico.

Hayward had never read "Les Misérables," but on the sixth day after the young man had given him the dollar, he remembered that on one of his teeth was a gold crown, and without success, he asked a dentist to pull and buy it. He had nothing to eat that day, and at night the desire to lie down and sleep instead of hypocritically walking about as if he were going somewhere became irresistable. So he went again to the beach and lay down among the ants, and in the morning a policeman scared away the buzzards that had already begun to hop about him and crane their hideously naked necks. The American consul, greatly bored (the heat was frightful), officially glanced at him and then they dumped him into a hole with an Indian who had been stabbed in a drunken row the night before.

John Reed

MAC—AMERICAN

I met Mac down in Mexico—Chihuahua City—on New Year's Eve. He was a breath from home, an American in the raw. I remember that as we sallied out of the hotel for a Tom-and-Jerry at Chee Lee's, the cracked bells in the ancient cathedral were ringing wildly for midnight mass. Above us were the hot desert stars. All over the city, from the *cuartels* where Villa's army was quartered, from the distant outposts on the naked hills, from the sentries in the streets, came the sound of exultant shots. A drunken officer passed us, and mistaking the *fiesta,* yelled "Christ is born!" At the next corner down a group of soldiers, wrapped to their eyes in *serapes,* sat around a fire chanting the interminable ballad called "Morning Song to Francisco Villa." Each singer had to make up a new verse about the exploits of the Great Captain. . . .

At the great doors of the church, through the shady paths of the Plaza, visible and vanishing again at the mouths of dark streets, the silent, sinister figures of black-robed women gathered to wash away their sins. And from the cathedral itself, a pale red light streamed out—and strange Indian voices singing a chant that I had heard only in Spain.

"Let's go in and see the service," I said. "It must be interesting."

"Hell, no!" said Mac, in a slightly strained voice. "I don't want to butt in on a man's religion."

"Are you a Catholic?"

"No," he replied. "I don't guess I'm anything. I haven't been in a church for years."

"Bully for you!" I cried. "So you're not superstitious, either!"

Mac looked at me with some distaste. "I'm not a religious man." He spat. "But I don't go around knocking God. There's too much risk in it."

"Risk of what?"

"Why, when you die—you know. . . ." Now he was disgusted and angry.

In Chee Lee's we met up with two more Americans. They were the kind that preface all remarks by "I've been in this country seven years, and I know the people down to the ground!"

"Mexican women," said one, "are the rottenest on earth. Why, they never wash more than twice a year. And as for Virtue—it simply doesn't exist! They don't get married even. They just take anybody they happen to like. Mexican women are all whores, that's all there is to it!"

"I got a nice little Indian girl down in Torreon," began the other man. "Say, it's a crime. Why, she don't even care if I marry her or not! I—"

"That's the way with 'em," broke in the other. "Loose! That's what they are. I've been in the country seven years."

"And do you know," the other man shook his finger severely at me. "You can tell all that to a Mexican Greaser and he'll just laugh at you! That's the kind of dirty skunks they are!"

"They've got no pride," said Mac, gloomily.

"Imagine," began the first compatriot. "Imagine what would happen if you said that to an *American!*"

Mac banged his fist on the table. "The American Woman, God bless her!" he said. "If any man dared to dirty the fair name of the American Woman to me, I think I'd kill him."

He glared around the table, and as none of us besmirched the reputation of the Femininity of the Great Republic, he proceeded. "She is a Pure Ideal, and we've got to keep her so. I'd like to hear anybody talk rotten about a woman in my hearing!"

We drank our Tom-and-Jerries with the solemn righteousness of a Convention of Galahads.

"Say, Mac," the second man said abruptly. "Do you remember them two little girls you and I had in Kansas City that winter?"

"*Do* I?" glowed Mac. "And remember the awful fix you thought you were in?"

"Will I ever forget it!"

The first man spoke. "Well," he said, "you can crack up your pretty señoritas all you want to. But for *me,* give me a clean little American girl." . . .

Mac was over six feet tall—a brute of a man, in the magnificent insolence of youth. He was only twenty-five, but he had seen many places and been many things: railroad foreman, plantation overseer in Georgia, box mechanic in a Mexican mine, cow-puncher, and Texas deputy-sheriff. He came originally from Vermont. Along about the fourth Tom-and-Jerry, he lifted the veil of his past.

"When I came down to Burlington to work in the lumber mill, I was only a kid about sixteen. My brother had been working there already a year, and he took me up to board at the same house as him. He was four years older than me—a big guy, too; but a little soft. . . . Always kept bulling around about how wrong it was to fight, and that kind of stuff. Never would hit me—even when he got hot at me because he said I was smaller.

"Well, there was a girl in the house, that my brother had been carrying on with for a long time. Now I've got the cussedest damn disposition," laughed Mac. "Always did have. Nothing would do me but I should get that girl away from my brother. Pretty soon I did it. Well, gentlemen, do you know what that devil of a girl did? One time when my brother was kissing her, she suddenly says, 'Why, you kiss just like Mac does!' . . .

"He came to find me. All his ideas about not fighting were gone, of course—not worth a damn with a real man. He was so white around the gills that I hardly knew him—eyes shooting fire like a volcano. He says, 'Damn you, what have you been doing with my girl?' He was a great big fellow, and for a minute I was a little scared. But then I remembered how soft he was, and I was game. 'If you can't hold her,' I says, 'leave her go!'

"It was a bad fight. He was out to kill me. I tried to kill him, too. A big, red cloud came over me, and I went raging, tearing mad. See this ear?" Mac indicated the stump of the member alluded to. "He did that. I got him in one eye, though, so he never saw again. We soon quit using fists; we scratched, and choked, and bit, and kicked. They say my brother let out a roar like a bull every few minutes, but I just opened my mouth and screamed all the time. . . . Pretty soon I landed a kick in—a place where it hurt, and he fell like he was dead." . . . Mac finished his Tom-and-Jerry.

Somebody ordered another. Mac went on.

"A little while after that I came away South, and my brother joined the Northwest Mounted Police. You remember that Indian who murdered the fellow out in Victoria in '06? Well, my brother was sent out after him, and got shot in the lung. I happened to be up visiting the folks—only time I ever went back—when my brother came home to die. . . . But he got well. I remember the day I went away he was just out of bed. He walked to the station with me, begging me to speak just one word to him. He held out his hand for me to shake, but I just turned on him and says, 'You son of a bitch!' A little later he started back to the job but died on the way. . . ."

"Gar!" said the first man. "Northwestern Mounted Police! That must be a job. A good rifle and a good horse and no closed season on Indians! That's what I call Sport!"

"Speaking of Sport," said Mac, "the greatest sport in the

world is hunting niggers. After I left Burlington, you remember, I drifted down South. I was out to see the world
from top to bottom, and I had just found out I could scrap.
God! The fights I used to get into. . . . Well, anyway, I
landed up on a cotton plantation down in Georgia, near a
place called Dixville; and they happened to be shy of an overseer, so I stuck.

"I remember the night perfectly, because I was sitting in
my cabin writing home to my sister. She and I always hit it
off, but we couldn't seem to get along with the rest of the
family. Last year she got into a scrape with a drummer—and
if I ever catch that—Well, as I say; I was sitting there writing
by the light of a little oil lamp. It was a sticky, hot night, and
the window screen was just a squirming mass of bugs. It
made me itch all over to see 'em crawling around. All of a
sudden, I pricked up my ears, and the hair began to stand
right up on my head. It was dogs—blood hounds—coming
lickety-split in the dark. I don't know whether you fellows
ever heard a hound bay when he's after a human. . . . Any
hound baying at night is about the lonesomest, *doomingest*
sound in the world. But this was worse than that. It made
you feel like you were standing in the dark, waiting for somebody to strangle you to death—*and you couldn't get away!*

"For a minute all I heard was the dogs, and then somebody, or some Thing, fell over my fence, and heavy feet running went right past my window, and a sound of breathing.
You know how a stubborn horse breathes when they're choking him around the neck with a rope? That way.

"I was out on my porch in one jump, just in time to see the
dogs scramble over my fence. Then somebody I couldn't see
yelled out, so hoarse he couldn't hardly speak, 'Where'd
he go?'

"'Past the house and out back!'" says I, and started to run.
There was about twelve of us. I never did find out what that
nigger did, and I guess most of the men didn't either. We
didn't care. We ran like crazy men, through the cotton field,
and the woods swampy from floods, swam the river, dove

over fences, in a way that would tire out a man ordinarily in a hundred yards. And we never felt it. The spit kept dripping out of my mouth,—that was the only thing that bothered me. It was full moon, and every once in a while when we came to an open place somebody would yell, 'There he goes!' and we'd think the dogs had made a mistake, and take after a shadow. Always the dogs ahead, baying like bells. Say, did you ever hear a bloodhound when he's after a human? It's like a bugle! I broke my shins on twenty fences, and I banged my head on all the trees in Georgia, but I never felt it. . . ."

Mac smacked his lips and drank.

"Of course," he said, "when we got up to him, the dogs had just about torn that coon to pieces."

He shook his head in shining reminiscence.

"Did you finish your letter to your sister?" I asked.

"Sure," said Mac, shortly. . . .

"I wouldn't like to live down here in Mexico," Mac volunteered. "The people haven't got any Heart. I like people to be friendly, like Americans."

Jack London

WHOSE BUSINESS IS TO LIVE

STANTON Davies and Jim Wemple ceased from their talk to listen to an increase of uproar in the street. A volley of stones thrummed and boomed the wire mosquito nettings that protected the windows. It was a hot night, and the sweat of the heat stood on their faces as they listened. Arose the incoherent clamor of the mob, punctuated by individual cries in Mexican-Spanish. Least terrible among the obscene threats were: "Death to the Gringos!" "Kill the American pigs!" "Drown the American dogs in the sea!"

Stanton Davies and Jim Wemple shrugged their shoulders patiently to each other, and resumed their conversation, talking louder in order to make themselves heard above the uproar.

"The question is *how*," Wemple said. "It's forty-seven miles to Panuco, by river—"

"And the land's impossible, with Zaragoza's and Villa's men on the loot and maybe fraternizing," Davies agreed.

Wemple nodded and continued: "And she's at the East Coast Magnolia, two miles beyond, if she isn't back at the hunting camp. We've got to get her—"

"We've played pretty square in this matter, Wemple," Davies said. "And we might as well speak up and acknowledge what each of us knows the other knows. You want her. I want her."

Wemple lighted a cigarette and nodded.

"And now's the time when it's up to us to make a show as if we didn't want her and that all we want is just to save her and get her down here."

"And a truce until we do save her—I get you," Wemple affirmed.

"A truce until we get her safe and sound back here in Tampico, or aboard a battleship. After that . . . ?"

Both men shrugged shoulders and beamed on each other as their hands met in ratification.

Fresh volleys of stones thrummed against the wire-screened windows; a boy's voice rose shrilly above the clamor, proclaiming death to the Gringos; and the house reverberated to the heavy crash of some battering ram against the street-door downstairs. Both men, snatching up automatic rifles, ran down to where their fire could command the threatened door.

"If they break in we've got to let them have it," Wemple said.

Davies nodded quiet agreement, then inconsistently burst out with a lurid string of oaths.

"To think of it!" he explained his wrath. "One out of three of those curs outside has worked for you or me—lean-bellied, bare-footed, poverty-stricken, glad for ten centavos a day if they could only get work. And we've given them steady jobs and a hundred and fifty centavos a day, and here they are yelling for our blood."

"Only the half breeds," Davies corrected.

"You know what I mean," Wemple replied. "The only peons we've lost are those that have been run off or shot."

The attack on the door ceasing, they returned upstairs. Half a dozen scattered shots from farther along the street seemed to draw away the mob, for the neighborhood became comparatively quiet.

A whistle came to them through the open windows, and a man's voice calling:

"Wemple! Open the door! It's Habert! Want to talk to you!"

Wemple went down, returning in several minutes with a tidily-paunched, well-built, gray-haired American of fifty. He shook hands with Davies and flung himself into a chair, breathing heavily. He did not relinquish his clutch on the Colt's .44 automatic pistol, although he immediately addressed himself to the task of fishing a filled clip of cartridges from the pocket of his linen coat. He had arrived hatless and breathless, and the blood from a stone-cut on the cheek oozed down his face. He, too, in a fit of anger, springing to his feet when he had changed clips in his pistol, burst out with mouth-filling profanity.

"They had an American flag in the dirt, stamping and spitting on it. And they told me to spit on it."

Wemple and Davies regarded him with silent interrogation.

"Oh, I know what you're wondering!" he flared out. "Would I a-spit on it in the pinch? That's what's eating you. I'll answer. Straight out, brass tacks, I WOULD. Put that in your pipe and smoke it."

He paused to help himself to a cigar from the box on the table and to light it with a steady and defiant hand.

"Hell!—I guess this neck of the woods knows Anthony Habert, and you can bank on it that it's never located his yellow streak. Sure, in the pinch, I'd spit on Old Glory. What the hell d'ye think I'm going on the streets for a night like this? Didn't I skin out of the Southern Hotel half an hour ago, where there are forty buck Americans, not counting their women, and all armed? That was safety. What d'ye think I came here for?—to rescue you?"

His indignation lumped his throat into silence, and he seemed shaken as with an apoplexy.

"Spit it out," Davies commanded dryly.

"I'll tell you," Habert exploded. "It's Billy Boy. Fifty miles up country and twenty-thousand throat-cutting federals and rebels between him and me. D'ye know what that boy'd do, if he was here in Tampico and I was fifty miles up the Panuco? Well, I know. And I'm going to do the same—go and get him."

"We're figuring on going up," Wemple assured him.

"And that's why I headed here—Miss Drexel, of course?"

Both men acquiesced and smiled. It was a time when men dared speak of matters which at other times tabooed speech.

"Then the thing's to get started," Habert exclaimed, looking at his watch. "It's midnight now. We've got to get to the river and get a boat—"

But the clamor of returning mob came through the windows in answer.

Davies was about to speak, when the telephone rang, and Wemple sprang to the instrument.

"It's Carson," he interjected, as he listened. "They haven't cut the wires across the river yet.—Hello, Carson. Was it a break or a cut? . . . Bully for you. . . . Yes, move the mules across to the portero beyond Tamcochin. . . . Who's at the water station? . . . Can you still 'phone him? . . . Tell him to keep the tanks full, and to shut off the main to Arico. Also, to hang on till the last minute, and keep a horse saddled to cut and run for it. Last thing before he runs, he must jerk out the 'phone. . . . Yes, yes, yes. Sure. No breeds. Leave full-blooded Indians in charge. Gabriel is a good *hombre*. Heaven knows, once we're chased out, when we'll get back. . . . You can't pinch down Jaramillo under twenty-five hundred barrels. We've got storage for ten days. Gabriel'll have to handle it. Keep it moving, if we have to run it into the river—"

"Ask him if he has a launch," Habert broke in.

"He hasn't," was Wemple's answer. "The federals commandeered the last one at noon."

"Say, Carson, how are you going to make your get-away?" Wemple queried.

The man to whom he talked was across the Panuco, on the south side, at the tank farm.

"Says there isn't any get-away," Wemple vouchsafed to the other two. "The federals are all over the shop, and he can't understand why they haven't raided him hours ago."

" . . . Who? Campos? That skunk! . . . all right . . . Don't be worried if you don't hear from me. I'm going up river with Davies and Habert. . . . Use your judgment, and if you get a safe chance at Campos, pot him. . . . Oh, a hot time over here. They're battering our doors now. Yes, by all means . . . Good-by, old man."

Wemple lighted a cigarette and wiped his forehead.

"You know Campos, José H. Campos," he volunteered. "The dirty cur's stuck Carson up for twenty thousand pesos. We had to pay, or he'd have compelled half our peons to enlist or set the wells on fire. And you know, Davies, what we've done for him in past years. Gratitude? Simple decency? Great Scott!"

It was the night of April twenty-first. On the morning of the twenty-first the American marines and bluejackets had landed at Vera Cruz and seized the custom house and the city. Immediately the news was telegraphed, the vengeful Mexican mob had taken possession of the streets of Tampico and expressed its disapproval of the action of the United States by tearing down American flags and crying death to the Americans.

There was nothing save its own spinelessness to deter the mob from carrying out its threat. Had it battered down the doors of the Southern Hotel, or of other hotels, or of residences such as Wemple's, a fight would have started in which the thousands of federal soldiers in Tampico would have joined their civilian compatriots in the laudable task of decreasing the Gringo population of that particular portion of Mexico. There should have been American warships to act as deterrents; but through some inexplicable excess of delicacy, or strategy, or heaven knows what, the United States, when it gave its orders to take Vera Cruz, had very carefully withdrawn its warships from Tampico to the open Gulf a dozen miles away. This order had come to Admiral Mayo by wireless from Washington, and thrice he had demanded the order to be repeated, ere, with tears in his eyes, he had turned his back on his countrymen and countrywomen and steamed to sea.

"Of all asinine things, to leave us in the lurch this way!" Habert was denouncing the powers that be of his country.

"Mayo'd never have done it. Mark my words, he had to take program from Washington. And here we are, and our dear ones scattered for fifty miles back up country. . . . Say, if I lose Billy Boy I'll never dare go home to face the wife.— Come on. Let the three of us make a start. We can throw the fear of God into any gang on the streets."

"Come on over and take a squint," Davies invited from where he stood, somewhat back from the window, looking down into the street.

It was gorged with rioters, all haranguing, cursing, crying out death, and urging one another to smash the doors, but each hanging back from the death he knew waited behind those doors for the first of the rush.

"We can't break through a bunch like that, Habert," was Davies' comment.

"And if we die under their feet we'll be of little use to Billy Boy or anybody else up the Panuco," Wemple added. "And if—"

A new movement of the mob caused him to break off. It was splitting before a slow and silent advance of a file of white-clad men.

"Bluejackets—Mayo's come back for us after all," Habert muttered.

"Then we can get a navy launch," Davies said.

The bedlam of the mob died away, and, in silence, the sailors reached the street door and knocked for admittance. All three went down to open it, and to discover that the callers were not Americans but two German lieutenants and half a dozen German marines. At sight of the Americans, the rage of the mob rose again, and was quelled by the grounding of the rifle butts of the marines.

"No, thank you," the senior lieutenant, in passable English, declined the invitation to enter. He unconcernedly kept his cigar alive at such times that the mob drowned his voice. "We are on the way back to our ship. Our commander conferred with the English and Dutch commanders; but they declined to cooperate, so our commander has undertaken the entire responsibility. We have been the round of the hotels.

They are to hold their own until daybreak, when we'll take them off. We have given them rockets such as these.—Take them. If your house is entered, hold your own and send up a rocket from the roof. We can be here in force, in forty-five minutes. Steam is up in all our launches, launch crews and marines for shore duty are in the launches, and at the first rocket we shall start."

"Since you are going aboard now, we should like to go with you," Davies said, after having rendered due thanks.

The surprise and distaste on both lieutenants' faces was patent.

"Oh, no," Davies laughed. "We don't want refuge. We have friends fifty miles up river, and we want to get to the river in order to go up after them."

The pleasure on the officers' faces was immediate as they looked a silent conference at each other.

"Since our commander has undertaken grave responsibility on a night like this, may we do less than take minor responsibility?" queried the elder.

To this the younger heartily agreed. In a trice, upstairs and down again, equipped with extra ammunition, extra pistols, and a pocket-bulging supply of cigars, cigarettes and matches, the three Americans were ready. Wemple called last instructions up the stairway to imaginary occupants being left behind, ascertained that the spring lock was on, and slammed the door.

The officers led, followed by the Americans, the rear brought up by the six marines; and the spitting, howling mob, not daring to cast a stone, gave way before them.

As they came alongside the gangway of the cruiser, they saw launches and barges lying in strings to the boat-booms, filled with men, waiting for the rocket signal from the beleaguered hotels. A gun thundered from close at hand, up river, followed by the thunder of numerous guns and the reports of many rifles fired very rapidly.

"Now what's the *Topila* whanging away at?" Habert complained, then joined the others in gazing at the picture.

A searchlight, evidently emanating from the Mexican gunboat, was stabbing the darkness to the middle of the river, where it played upon the water. And across the water, the center of the moving circle of light, flashed a long, lean speedboat. A shell burst in the air a hundred feet astern of it. Somewhere, outside the light, other shells were bursting in the water; for they saw the boat rocked by the waves from the explosions. They could guess the whizzing of the rifle bullets.

But for only several minutes the spectacle lasted. Such was the speed of the boat that it gained shelter behind the Germans, when the Mexican gunboat was compelled to cease fire. The speedboat slowed down, turned in a wide and heeling circle, and ranged up alongside the launch at the gangway.

The lights from the gangway showed but one occupant, a tow-headed, greasy-faced blond youth of twenty, very lean, very calm, very much satisfied with himself.

"If it ain't Peter Tonsburg!" Habert ejaculated, reaching out a hand to shake. "Howdy, Peter, howdy. And where in hell are you hell-bent for, surging by the *Topila* in such scandalous fashion?"

Peter, a Texas-born Swede of immigrant parents, filled with the old Texas traditions, greasily shook hands with Wemple and Davies as well, saying "Howdy," as only the Texan born can say it.

"Me," he answered Habert. "I ain't hell-bent nowhere exceptin' to get away from the shell-fire. She's a caution, that *Topila*. Huh! but I limbered 'em up some. I was goin' every inch of twenty-five. They was like amateurs blazin' away at canvasback."

"Which *Chill* is it?" Wemple asked.

"*Chill II*," Peter answered. "It's all that's left. *Chill I* a Greaser—you know'm—Campos—commandeered this noon. I was runnin' *Chill III* when they caught me at sundown. Made me come in under their guns at the East Coast outfit, and fired me out on my neck.

"Now the boss'd gone over in this one to Tampico in the early evening, and just about ten minutes ago I spots it landin' with a sousy bunch of Federals at the East Coast, and swipes it back according. Where's the boss? He ain't hurt, is he? Because I'm going after him."

"No, you're not, Peter," Davies said. "Mr. Frisbie is safe at the Southern Hotel, all except a five-inch scalp wound from a brick that's got him down with a splitting headache. He's safe, so you're going with us, going to take us, I mean, up beyond Panuco town."

"Huh?—I can see myself," Peter retorted, wiping his greasy nose on a wad of greasy cotton waste. "I got some cold. Besides, this night-drivin' ain't good for my complexion."

"My boy's up there," Habert said.

"Well, he's bigger'n I am, and I reckon he can take of himself."

"And there's a woman there—Miss Drexel," Davies said quietly.

"Who? Miss Drexel? Why didn't you say so at first?" Peter demanded grievedly. He sighed and added, "Well, climb in an' make a start. Better get your Dutch friends to donate me about twenty gallons of gasoline if you want to get anywhere."

"Won't do you no good to lay low," Peter Tonsburg remarked as, at full speed, headed up river, the *Topila's* searchlight stabbed them. "High or low, if one of them shells hits in the vicinity—*good night!*"

Immediately thereafter the *Topila* erupted. The roar of the *Chill's* exhaust nearly drowned the roar of the guns, but the fragile hull of the craft was shaken and rocked by the bursting shells. An occasional bullet thudded into or pinged off the *Chill,* and, despite Peter's warning that, high or low, they were bound to get it if it came to them, every man on board, including Peter, crouched, with chest contracted by drawn-in shoulders, in an instinctive and purely unconscious effort to lessen the area of body he presented as a target or receptacle for flying fragments of steel.

The *Topila* was a federal gunboat. To complicate the affair,

the constitutionalists, gathered on the north shore in the siege
of Tampico, opened up on the speedboat with many rifles
and a machine gun.

"Lord, I'm glad they're Mexicans, and not Americans,"
Habert observed, after five mad minutes in which no damage
had been received. "Mexicans are born with guns in their
hands, and they never learn to use them."

Nor was the *Chill* or any man aboard damaged when at last
she rounded the bend of river that shielded her from the
searchlight.

"I'll have you in Panuco town in less'n three hours, . . . if
we don't hit a log," Peter leaned back and shouted in Wemple's ear. "And if we do hit driftwood, I'll have you in the
swim quicker than that."

Chill II tore her way through the darkness, steered by the
tow-headed youth who knew every foot of the river and who
guided his course by the loom of the banks in the dim star-
light. A smart breeze, kicking up spiteful wavelets on the
wider reaches, splashed them with sheeted water as well as
fine-flung spray. And, in the face of the warmth of the tropic
night, the wind, added to the speed of the boat, chilled them
through their wet clothes.

"Now I know why she was named the *Chill*," Habert observed betwixt chattering teeth.

But conversation languished during the nearly three hours
of drive through the darkness. Once, by the exhaust, they
knew that they passed an unlighted launch bound down
stream. And once, a glare of light, near the south bank, as
they passed through the Toreno field, aroused brief debate as
to whether it was the Toreno wells, or the bungalow of Mer-
rick's banana plantation that flared so fiercely.

At the end of an hour, Peter slowed down and ran in to the
bank.

"I got a cache of gasoline here—ten gallons," he explained,
"and it's just as well to know it's here for the back trip."
Without leaving the boat, fishing arm-deep into the brush, he
announced, "All hunky-dory." He proceeded to oil the engine. "Huh!" he soliloquized for their benefit. "I was just

readin' a magazine yarn last night. 'Whose Business Is to Die,' was its title. An' all I got to say is, 'The hell it is.' A man's business is to live. Maybe you thought it was our business to die when the *Topila* was pepperin' us. But you was wrong. We're alive, ain't we? We beat her to it. That's the game. Nobody's got any business to die. I ain't never goin' to die, if I've got any say about it."

He turned over the crank, and the roar and rush of the *Chill* put an end to speech.

There was no need for Wemple or Davies to speak further in the affair closest to their hearts. Their truce to love-making had been made as binding as it was brief, and each rival honored the other with a firm belief that he would commit no infraction of the truce. Afterward was another matter. In the meantime they were one in the effort to get Beth Drexel back to the safety of riotous Tampico or of a war vessel.

It was four o'clock when they passed by Panuco town. Shouts and songs told them that the federal detachment holding the place was celebrating its indignation at the landing of American bluejackets in Vera Cruz. Sentinels challenged the *Chill* from the shore and shot at random at the noise of her in the darkness.

A mile beyond, where a lighted river steamer with steam up lay at the north bank, they ran in at the Asphodel wells. The steamer was small, and the nearly two hundred Americans—men, women, and children—crowded her capacity. Blasphemous greetings of pure joy and geniality were exchanged between the men, and Habert learned that the steamboat was waiting for his Billy Boy, who, astride a horse, was rounding up isolated drilling gangs who had not yet learned that the United States had seized Vera Cruz and that all Mexico was boiling.

Habert climbed out to wait and to go down on the steamer, while the three that remained on the *Chill,* having learned that Miss Drexel was not with the refugees, headed for the Dutch Company on the south shore. This was the big gusher, pinched down from one hundred and eighty-five thousand daily barrels to the quantity the company was able to handle.

Mexico had no quarrel with Holland, so that the superintendent, while up, with night guards out to prevent drunken
soldiers from firing his vast lakes of oil, was quite unemo-
tional. Yes, the last he had heard was that Miss Drexel and
her brother were back at the hunting lodge. No; he had not
sent any warning, and he doubted that anybody else had. Not
till ten o'clock the previous evening had he learned of the
landing at Vera Cruz. The Mexicans had turned nasty as soon
as they heard of it, and they had killed Miles Forman at the
Empire Wells, run off his labor, and looted the camp. Horses?
No; he didn't have horse or mule on the place. The federals
had commandeered the last animal weeks back. It was his belief, however, that there were a couple of plugs at the lodge,
too worthless even for the Mexicans to take.

"It's a hike," Davies said cheerfully.

"Six miles of it," Wemple agreed, equally cheerfully. "Let's
beat it."

A shot from the river, where they had left Peter in the
boat, started them on the run for the bank. The scattering of
shots, as from two rifles, followed. And while the Dutch superintendent, in execrable Spanish, shouted affirmations of
Dutch neutrality into the menacing dark, across the gunwale
of *Chill II* they found the body of the tow-headed youth
whose business it had been not to die.

For the first hour, talking little, Davies and Wemple stumbled along the apology for a road that led through the jungle
to the lodge. They did discuss the glares of several fires to the
east along the south bank of Panuco River, and hoped fer-
vently that they were dwellings and not wells.

"Two billion dollars worth of oil right here in the Ebaño
field alone," Davies grumbled.

"And a drunken Mexican, whose whole carcass and immortal soul aren't worth ten pesos including hair, hide, and
tallow, can start the bonfire with a lighted wad of cotton
waste," was Wemple's contribution. "And if ever she starts,
she'll gut the field of its last barrel."

Dawn, at five, enabled them to accelerate their pace; and

six o'clock found them routing out the occupants of the lodge.

"Dress for rough travel, and don't stop for any frills," Wemple called around the corner of Miss Drexel's screened sleeping porch.

"Not a wash, nothing," Davies supplemented grimly, as he shook hands with Charley Drexel, who yawned and slippered up to them in pajamas. "Where are those horses, Charley? Still alive?"

Wemple finished giving orders to the sleepy peons to remain and care for the place, occupying their spare time with hiding the more valuable things, and was calling around the corner to Miss Drexel the news of the capture of Vera Cruz, when Davies returned with the information that the horses consisted of a pair of moth-eaten skates that could be depended upon to lie down and die in the first half mile.

Beth Drexel emerged, first protesting that under no circumstances would she be guilty of riding the creatures, and, next, her brunette skin and dark eyes still flushed warm with sleep, greeting the two rescuers.

"It would be just as well if you washed your face, Stanton," she told Davies; and, to Wemple: "You're just as bad, Jim. You are a pair of dirty boys."

"And so will you be," Wemple assured her, "before you get back to Tampico. Are you ready?"

"As soon as Juanita packs my hand bag."

"Heavens, Beth, don't waste time!" exclaimed Wemple. "Jump in and grab up what you want."

"Make a start—make a start," chanted Davies. "Hustle! Hustle!—Charley, get the rifle you like best and take it along. Get a couple for us."

"Is it as serious as that?" Miss Drexel queried.

Both men nodded.

"The Mexicans are tearing loose," Davies explained. "How they missed this place I don't know." A movement in the adjoining room startled him. "Who's that?" he cried.

"Why, Mrs. Morgan," Miss Drexel answered.

"Good heavens, Wemple, I'd forgotten *her*," groaned Davies. "How will we ever get her anywhere?"

"Let Beth walk and relay the lady on the nags."

"She weighs a hundred and eighty," Miss Drexel laughed. "Oh, hurry, Martha! We're waiting on you to start!"

Muffled speech came through the partition, and then emerged a very short, stout, much-flustered woman of middle age.

"I simply can't walk, and you boys needn't demand it of me," was her plaint. "It's no use. I couldn't walk half a mile to save my life, and it's six of the worst miles to the river."

They regarded her in despair.

"Then you'll ride," said Davies. "Come on, Charley. We'll get a saddle on each of the nags."

Along the road through the tropic jungle, Miss Drexel and Juanita, her Indian maid, led the way. Her brother, carrying the three rifles, brought up the rear, while in the middle Davies and Wemple struggled with Mrs. Morgan and the two decrepit steeds. One, a flea-bitten roan, groaned continually from the moment Mrs. Morgan's burden was put upon him till she was shifted to the other horse. And this other, a mangy sorrel, invariably lay down at the end of a quarter of a mile of Mrs. Morgan.

Miss Drexel laughed and joked and encouraged; and Wemple, in brutal fashion, compelled Mrs. Morgan to walk every third quarter of a mile. At the end of an hour the sorrel refused positively to get up, and, so, was abandoned. Thereafter, Mrs. Morgan rode the roan alternate quarters of miles, and between times walked—if *walk* may describe her stumbling progress on two preposterously tiny feet with a man supporting her on either side.

A mile from the river, the road became more civilized, running along the side of a thousand acres of banana plantation.

"Parslow's," young Drexel said. "He'll lose a year's crop now on account of this mixup."

"Oh, look what I've found!" Miss Drexel called from the lead.

"First machine that ever tackled this road," was young Drexel's judgment, as they halted to stare at the tire-tracks.

"But look at the tracks," his sister urged. "The machine must have come right out of the bananas and climbed the bank."

"Some machine to climb a bank like that," was Davies' comment. "What it did do was to go down the bank—take a scout after it, Charley, while Wemple and I get Mrs. Morgan off her fractious mount. No machine ever built could travel far through those bananas."

The flea-bitten roan, on its four legs upstanding, continued bravely to stand until the lady was removed, whereupon, with a long sigh, it sank down on the ground. Mrs. Morgan likewise sighed, sat down, and regarded her tiny feet mournfully.

"Go on, boys," she said. "Maybe you can find something at the river and send back for me."

But their indignant rejection of the plan never attained speech, for, at that instant, from the green sea of banana trees beneath them, came the sudden purr of an engine. A minute later the splutter of an exhaust told them the silencer had been taken off. The huge-fronded banana trees were violently agitated as by the threshing of a hidden Titan. They could identify the changing of gears and the reversing and going ahead, until, at the end of five minutes, a long low, black car burst from the wall of greenery and charged the soft earth bank, but the earth was too soft, and when, two-thirds of the way up, beaten, Charley Drexel braked the car to a standstill, the earth crumbled from under the tires, and he ran it down and back, the way he had come, until half-buried in the bananas.

"'A Merry Oldsmobile!'" Miss Drexel quoted from the popular song, clapping her hands. "Now, Martha, your troubles are over."

"Six-cylinder, and sounds as if it hadn't been out of the shop a week, or may I never ride in a machine again," Wemple remarked, looking to Davies for confirmation.

Davies nodded.

"It's Allison's," he said. "Campos tried to shake him down for a private loan, and—well, you know Allison. He told

Campos to go to. And Campos, in revenge, commandeered his new car. That was two days ago, before we lifted a hand at Vera Cruz. Allison told me yesterday the last he'd heard of the car it was on a steamboat bound up river. And here's where they ditched it—but let's get a hustle on and get her into the running."

Three attempts they made, with young Drexel at the wheel; but the soft earth and the pitch of the grade baffled.

"She's got the power all right," young Drexel protested. "But she can't bite into that mush."

So far, they had spread on the ground the robes found in the car. The men now added their coats, and Wemple, for additional traction, unsaddled the roan, and spread the cinches, stirrup leathers, saddle blanket, and bridle in the way of the wheels. The car took the treacherous slope in a rush, with churning wheels biting into the woven fabrics; and, with no more than a hint of hesitation, it cleared the crest and swung into the road.

"Isn't she the spunky devil!" Drexel exulted. "Say, she could climb the side of a house if she could get traction."

"Better put on that silencer again, if you don't want to play tag with every soldier in the district," Wemple ordered, as they helped Mrs. Morgan in.

The road to the Dutch gusher compelled them to go through the outskirts of Panuco town. Indian and half breed women gazed stolidly at the strange vehicle, while the children and barking dogs clamorously advertised its progress. Once, passing long lines of tethered federal horses, they were challenged by a sentry; but at Wemple's "Throw on the juice!" the car took the rutted road at fifty miles an hour. A shot whistled after them. But it was not the shot that made Mrs. Morgan scream. The cause was a series of hog-wallows masked with mud, which nearly tore the steering wheel from Drexel's hands before he could reduce speed.

"Wonder it didn't break an axle," Davies growled. "Go on and take it easy, Charley. We're past any interference."

They swung into the Dutch camp and into the beginning of their real troubles. The refugee steamboat had departed down river from the Asphodel camp; *Chill II* had disappeared, the superintendent knew not how, along with the body of Peter Tonsburg; and the superintendent was dubious of their remaining.

"I've got to consider the owners," he told them. "This is the biggest well in Mexico, and you know it—a hundred and eighty-five thousand barrels daily flow. I've no right to risk it. We have no trouble with the Mexicans. It's you Americans. If you stay here, I'll have to protect you. And I can't protect you, anyway. We'll all lose our lives and they'll destroy the well in the bargain. And if they fire it, it means the entire Ebaño oil field. The strata's too broken. We're flowing twenty thousand barrels now, and we can't pinch down any further. As it is, the oil's coming up outside the pipe. And we can't have a fight. We've got to keep the oil moving."

The men nodded. It was cold-blooded logic; but there was no fault to it.

The harassed expression eased on the superintendent's face, and he almost beamed on them for agreeing with him.

"You've got a good machine there," he continued. "The ferry's at the bank at Panuco, and once you're across, the rebels aren't so thick on the north shore. Why, you can beat the steamboat back to Tampico by hours. And it hasn't rained for days. The road won't be at all bad."

"Which is all very good," Davies observed to Wemple as they approached Panuco, "except for the fact that the road on the other side was never built for automobiles, much less for a long-bodied one like this. I wish it were the Four instead of the Six."

"And it would bother you with a Four to negotiate that hill at Aliso where the road switchbacks above the river."

"And we're going to do it with a Six or lose a perfectly good Six in trying," Beth Drexel laughed to them.

Avoiding the cavalry camp, they entered Panuco with all the speed the ruts permitted, swinging dizzy corners to the squawking of chickens and barking of dogs. To gain the ferry, they had to pass down one side of the great plaza which was the heart of the city. Peon soldiers, drowsing in the sun or clustering around the *cantinas,* stared stupidly at them as they flashed past. Then a drunken major shouted a challenge from the doorway of a *cantina* and began vociferating orders, and as they left the plaza behind they could hear rising the familiar mob-cry, "*Kill the Gringos!*"

"If any shooting begins, you women get down in the bottom of the car," Davies commanded. "And there's the ferry all right. Be careful, Charley."

The machine plunged directly down the bank through a cut so deep that it was more like a chute, struck the gangplank with a terrific bump, and seemed fairly to leap on board. The ferry was scarcely longer than the machine, and Drexel, visibly shaken by the closeness of the shave, managed to stop only when six inches remained between the front wheels and overboard.

It was a cable ferry, operated by gasoline, and, while Wemple cast off the mooring lines, Davies was making swift acquaintance with the engine. The third turn-over started it, and he threw it into gear with the windlass that began winding up the cable from the river's bottom.

By the time they were in midstream a score of horsemen rode out on the bank they had just left and opened a scattering fire. The party crowded in the shelter of the car and listened to the occasional ricochet of a bullet. Once, only, the car was struck.

"Here!—what are you up to?" Wemple demanded suddenly of Drexel, who had exposed himself to fish a rifle out of the car.

"Going to show the skunks what shooting is," was his answer.

"No, you don't," Wemple said. "We're not here to fight, but to get this party to Tampico." He remembered Peter Tonsburg's remark. "Whose business is to live, Charley—that's our business. Anybody can get killed. It's too easy these days."

Still under fire, they moored at the north shore, and when Davies had tossed overboard the igniter from the ferry engine and commandeered ten gallons of its surplus gasoline, they took the steep, soft road up the bank in a rush.

"Look at her climb," Drexel uttered gleefully. "That Aliso hill won't bother us at all. She'll put a crimp in it, that's what she'll do."

"It isn't the hill, it's the sharp turn of the zig-zag that's liable to put a crimp in her," Davies answered. "That road was never laid out for autos, and no auto has ever been over it. They steamboated this one up."

But trouble came before Aliso was reached. Where the road dipped abruptly into a small jag of hollow that was almost V-shaped, it arose out and became a hundred yards of deep sand. In order to have speed left for the sand after he cleared the stiff up-grade of the V, Drexel was compelled to hit the trough of the V with speed. Wemple clutched Miss Drexel as she was on the verge of being bounced out. Mrs. Morgan, too solid for such airiness, screamed from the pain of the bump; and even the imperturbable Juanita fell to crossing herself and uttering prayers with exceeding rapidity.

The car cleared the crest and encountered the sand, going slower from moment to moment, slewing and writhing and squirming from side to side. The men leaped out and began shoving. Miss Drexel urged Juanita out and followed. But the car came to a standstill, and Drexel, looking back and pointing, showed the first sign of being beaten. Two things he pointed to: a constitutional soldier on horseback a quarter of a mile in the rear; and a portion of the narrow road that had fallen out bodily on the far slope of the V.

"Can't get at this sand unless we go back and try over, and we ditch the car if we try to back up that."

The ditch was a huge natural sump-hole, the stagnant surface of which was a-crawl with slime twenty feet beneath.

Davies and Wemple sprang to take the boy's place.

"You can't do it," he urged. "You can get the back wheels past, but right there you hit that little curve, and if you make it your front wheel will be off the bank. If you don't make it, your back wheel'll be off."

Both men studied it carefully, then looked at each other.

"We've got to," said Davies.

"And we're going to," Wemple said, shoving his rival aside

in comradely fashion and taking the post of danger at the wheel. "You're just as good as I at the wheel, Davies," he explained. "But you're a better shot. Your job's cut out to go back and hold off any Greasers that show up."

Davies took a rifle and strolled back with so ominous an air that the lone cavalryman put spurs to his horse and fled. Mrs. Morgan was helped out and sent plodding and tottering unaided on her way to the end of the sand stretch. Miss Drexel and Juanita joined Charley in spreading the coats and robes on the sand and in gathering and spreading small branches, brush, and armfuls of a dry, brittle shrub. But all three ceased from their exertions to watch Wemple as he shot the car backward down the V and up. The car seemed first to stand on one end, then on the other, and to reel drunkenly and to threaten to turn over into the sump-hole when its right front wheel fell into the air where the road had ceased to be. But the hind wheels bit and climbed the grade and out.

Without pause, gathering speed down the perilous slope, Wemple came ahead and up, gaining fifty feet of sand over the previous failure. More of the alluvial soil of the road had dropped out at the bad place; but he took the V in reverse, overhung the front wheel as before, and from the top came ahead again. Four times he did this, gaining each time, but each time knocking a bigger hole where the road fell out, until Miss Drexel begged him not to try again.

He pointed to a squad of horsemen coming at a gallop along the road a mile in the rear, and took the V once again in reverse.

"If only we had more stuff," Drexel groaned to his sister, as he threw down a meager, hard-gathered armful of the dry and brittle shrub, and as Wemple once more, with rush and roar, shot down the V.

For an instant it seemed that the great car would turn over into the sump, but the next instant it was past. It struck the bottom of the hollow a mighty wallop, and bounced and upended to the steep pitch of the climb. Miss Drexel, seized by inspiration or desperation, with a quick movement stripped off her short, corduroy tramping-skirt, and, looking very lithe and boyish in slender-cut pongee bloomers, ran along the sand and dropped the skirt for a foothold for the slowly revolving wheels. Almost, but not quite, did the car stop, then, gathering way, with the others running alongside and shoving, it emerged on the hard road.

While they tossed the robes and coats and Miss Drexel's skirt into the bottom of the car and got Mrs. Morgan on board, Davies overtook them.

"Down on the bottom!—all of you!" he shouted, as he gained the running board and the machine sprang away. A scattering of shots came from the rear.

"Whose business is to live!—hunch down!" Davies yelled in Wemple's ear, accompanying the instruction with an open-handed blow on the shoulder.

"Live yourself," Wemple grumbled as he obediently hunched. "Get your head down. You're exposing yourself."

The pursuit lasted but a little while, and died away in an occasional distant shot.

"They've quit," Davies announced. "It never entered their . stupid heads that they could have caught us on Aliso Hill."

"It can't be done," was Charley Drexel's quick judgment of youth, as the machine stopped and they surveyed the acute-angled turn on the stiff up-grade of Aliso. Beneath was the swift-running river.

"Get out everybody!" Wemple commanded. "Up-side, all of you, if you don't want the car to turn over on you. Spread traction wherever she needs it."

"Shoot her ahead, or back—she can't stop," Davies said quietly, from the outer edge of the road, where he had taken position. "The earth's crumbling away from under the tires every second she stands still."

"Get out from under, or she'll be on top of you," Wemple ordered, as he went ahead several yards.

But again, after the car rested a minute, the light, dry earth began to crack and crumble away from under the tires, rolling in a miniature avalanche down the steep declivity into the water. And not until Wemple had backed fifty yards down the narrow road did he find solid resting for the car. He came ahead on foot and examined the acute angle formed by the two zig-zags. Together with Davies he planned what was to be done.

"When you come you've got to come a-humping," Davies advised. "If you stop anywhere for more than seconds, it's good night, and the walking won't be fine."

"She's full of fight, and she can do it. See that hard formation right there on the inside wall. It couldn't have come at a better spot. If I don't make her hind wheels climb half way up it, we'll start walking about a second thereafter."

"She's a two-fisted piece of machinery," Davies encouraged. "I know her kind. If she can't do it, no machine can that was ever made. Am I right, Beth?"

"She's a regular, spunky she-devil," Miss Drexel laughed agreement. "And so are the pair of you—er—of the male persuasion, I mean."

Miss Drexel had never seemed so fascinating to either of them as she was then, in the excitement quite unconscious of her abbreviated costume, her brown hair flying, her eyes sparkling, her lips smiling. Each man caught the other in that moment's pause to look, and each man sighed to the other and looked frankly into each other's eyes ere he turned to the work at hand.

Wemple came up with his usual rush, but it was a gauged rush; and Davies took the post of danger, the outside running board, where his weight would help the broad tires to bite a little deeper into the treacherous surface. If the road-edge crumbled away it was inevitable that he would be caught under the car as it rolled over and down to the river.

It was ahead and reverse, ahead and reverse, with only the briefest of pauses in which to shift the gears. Wemple backed up the hard formation on the inside bank till the car seemed standing on end, rushed ahead till the earth of the outer edge broke under the front tires and splashed in the water. Davies, now off, and again on the running board when needed, accompanied the car in its jerky and erratic progress, tossing robes and coats under the tires, calling instructions to Drexel similarly occupied on the other side, and warning Miss Drexel out of the way.

"Oh, you Merry Olds, you Merry Olds, you Merry Olds," Wemple muttered aloud, as if in prayer, as he wrestled the car about the narrow area, gaining sometimes inches in pivoting it, sometimes fetching back up the inner wall precisely at the spot previously attained, and, once, having the car, with the surface of the roadbed under it, slide bodily and sidewise, two feet down the road.

The clapping of Miss Drexel's hands was the first warning Davies received that the feat was accomplished, and, swinging on to the running board, he found the car backing in the straight-away up the next zig-zag and Wemple still chanting ecstatically, "Oh, you Merry Olds, you Merry Olds!"

There were no more grades nor zigzags between them and Tampico, but, so narrow was the primitive road, two miles farther were backed before the space was found in which to turn around. One thing of importance did lie between them and Tampico—namely the investing lines of the constitutionalists. But here, at noon, fortune favored in the form of three American soldiers of fortune, operators of machine guns, who had fought the entire campaign with Villa from the beginning of the advance from the Texan border. Under a white flag, Wemple drove the car across the zone of debate into the federal lines, where good fortune, in the guise of an ubiquitous German naval officer, again received them.

"I think you are nearly the only Americans left in Tampico," he told them. "About all the rest are lying out in the Gulf on the different warships. But at the Southern Hotel there are several, and the situation seems quieter."

As they got out at the Southern, Davies laid his hand on the car and murmured, "Good old girl!" Wemple followed suit. And Miss Drexel, engaging both men's eyes and about to say something, was guilty of a sudden moisture in her own eyes that made her turn to the car with a caressing hand and repeat, "Good old girl!"

Katherine Anne Porter

HACIENDA

IT was worth the price of a ticket to see Kennerly take possession of the railway train among a dark inferior people. Andreyev and I trailed without plan in the wake of his gigantic progress (he was a man of ordinary height merely, physically taller by a head, perhaps, than the nearest Indian; but his moral stature in this moment was beyond calculation) through the second-class coach into which we had climbed, in our haste, by mistake. . . . Now that the true revolution of blessed memory has come and gone in Mexico, the names of many things are changed, nearly always with the view to an appearance of heightened well-being for all creatures. So you cannot ride third-class no matter how poor or humble-spirited or miserly you may be. You may go second in cheerful disorder and sociability, or first in sober ease; or, if you like, you may at great price install yourself in the stately plush of the Pullman, isolated and envied as any successful General from the north. "Ah, it is beautiful as a *pulman!*" says the middle-class Mexican when he wishes to truly praise anything. . . . There was no Pullman with this train or we should most unavoidably have been in it. Kennerly traveled like that. He strode mightily through, waving his free arm, lunging his portfolio and leather bag, stiffening his nostrils as conspicuously as he could against the smell that "poured," he said, "simply poured like mildewed pea soup!" from the teeming clutter of wet infants and draggled turkeys and indignant baby pigs and food baskets and bundles of vegetables and bales and hampers of domestic goods, each little mountain of confusion yet drawn into a unit, from the midst of which its owners glanced up casually from dark pleased faces at the passing strangers. Their pleasure had nothing to do with us. They were pleased because, sitting still, without even the effort of beating a burro, they were on the point of being carried where they wished to go, accomplishing in an hour what would otherwise have been a day's hard journey, with all their households on their backs. . . . Almost nothing can disturb their quiet ecstasy when they are finally settled among their plunder, and the engine, mysteriously and powerfully animated, draws them lightly over the miles they have so often counted step by step. And they are not troubled by the noisy white man because, by now, they are accustomed to him. White men look all much alike to the Indians, and they had seen this maddened fellow with light eyes and leather-colored hair battling his way desperately through their coach many times before. There is always one of him on every train. They watch his performance with as much attention as they can spare from their own always absorbing business; he is a part of the scene of travel.

He turned in the door and motioned wildly at us when we showed signs of stopping where we were. "No, no!" he bellowed. "NO! Not here. This will never do for you," he said, giving me a great look, protecting me, a lady. I followed on, trying to reassure him by noddings and hand-wavings. Andreyev came after, stepping tenderly over large objects and small beings, exchanging quick glances with many pair of calm, lively dark eyes.

The first-class coach was nicely swept, there were no natives about to speak of, and most of the windows were open. Kennerly hurled bags at the racks, jerked seatbacks about rudely, and spread down topcoats and scarves until, with great clamor, he had built us a nest in which we might curl up facing each other, temporarily secure from the appalling situation of being three quite superior persons of the intellectual caste of the ruling race at large and practically defenseless in what a country! Kennerly almost choked when he tried to talk about it. It was for himself he built the nest, really: he was certain of what he was. Andreyev and I were included by courtesy: Andreyev was a Communist, and I was a writer, or so Kennerly had been told. He had never heard of me until a week before, he had never known anyone who had, and it was really up to Andreyev, who had invited me on this trip, to look out for me. But Andreyev took everything calmly, was not suspicious, never asked questions, and had no sense of social responsibility whatever—not, at least, what Kennerly would ever call by such a name; so it was hopeless to expect anything from him.

I had already proved that I lacked something by arriving at the station first and buying my own ticket, having been warned by Kennerly to meet them at the first-class window, as they were arriving straight from another town. When he discovered this, he managed to fill me with shame and confusion. "You were to have been our guest," he told me bitterly, taking my ticket and handing it to the conductor as if I had appropriated it to my own use from his pocket, stripping me publicly of guesthood once for all, it seemed. Andreyev also rebuked me: "We none of us should throw away our money when Kennerly is so rich and charitable." Kennerly, tucking away his leather billfold, paused, glared blindly at Andreyev for a moment, jumped as if he had discovered that he was stabbed clean through, said, "Rich? Me, rich? What do you mean, rich?" and blustered for a moment, hoping that somehow the proper retort would emerge; but it would not. So he sulked for a moment, got up and shifted his bags, sat down, felt in all his pockets again to make certain of something, sat back and wanted to know if I had noticed that he carried his own bags. It was because he was tired of being gypped by these people. Every time he let a fellow carry his bags, he had to fight to the death in simple self-defense. Literally, in his whole life he had never run into such a set of bandits as these train porters. Besides, think of the risk of infection from their filthy paws on your luggage handles. It was just damned dangerous, if you asked him.

I was thinking that foreigners anywhere traveling were three or four kinds of phonograph records, and of them all I liked Kennerly's kind the least. Andreyev hardly ever looked at him out of his clear, square gray eyes, in which so many different kinds of feeling against Kennerly were mingled, the total expression had become a sort of exasperated patience. Settling back, he drew out a folder of photographs, scenes from the film they had been making all over the country, balanced them on his knees and began where he left off to talk about Russia. . . . Kennerly moved into his corner away from us and turned to the window as if he wished to avoid overhearing a private conversation. The sun was shining when we left Mexico City, but mile by mile through the solemn valley of the pyramids we climbed through the maguey fields towards the thunderous blue cloud banked solidly in the east, until it dissolved and received us gently in a pallid, silent rain. We hung our heads out of the window every time the train paused, raising false hopes in the hearts of the Indian women who ran along beside us, faces thrown back and arms stretching upward even after the train was moving away.

"Fresh pulque!" they urged mournfully, holding up their clay jars filled with thick gray-white liquor. "Fresh maguey worms!" they cried in despair above the clamor of the turning wheels, waving like nosegays the leaf bags, slimy and lumpy with the worms they had gathered one at a time from the cactus whose heart bleeds the honey water for the pulque. They ran along still hoping, their brown fingers holding the bags lightly by the very tips, ready to toss them if the travelers should change their minds and buy, even then, until the engine outran them, their voices floated away and they were left clustered together a little knot of faded blue skirts and shawls, in the indifferent rain.

Kennerly opened three bottles of luke-warm bitter beer. "The water is filthy!" he said earnestly, taking a ponderous, gargling swig from his bottle. "Isn't it horrible, the things they eat and drink?" he asked, as if, no matter what we might in our madness (for he did not trust either of us) say, he already knew the one possible answer. He shuddered and for a moment could not swallow his lump of sweet American chocolate: "I have just come back," he told me, trying to account for his extreme sensitiveness in these matters, "from God's country," meaning to say California. He ripped open an orange trademarked in purple ink. "I'll simply have to get used to all this all over again. What a relief to eat fruit that isn't full of germs. I brought them all the way back with me." (I could fairly see him legging across the Sonora desert with a knapsack full of oranges.) "Have one. Anyhow it's clean."

Kennerly was very clean, too, a walking reproach to untidiness: washed, shaven, clipped, pressed, polished, smelling of soap, brisk and firm-looking in his hay-colored tweeds. So far as that goes, a fine figure of a man, with the proper thriftiness of a healthy animal. There was no fault to find with him in this. Some day I shall make a poem to kittens washing themselves in the mornings; to Indians scrubbing their clothes to rags and their bodies to sleekness, with great slabs of sweet-smelling strong soap and wisps of henequen fiber, in the shade of trees, along river banks at midday; to horses rolling sprawling snorting rubbing themselves against the grass to cleanse their healthy hides; to naked children shouting in pools; to hens singing in their dust baths; to sober fathers of families forgetting themselves in song under the discreet flood of tap-water; to birds on the boughs ruffling and oiling their feathers in delight; to girls and boys arranging themselves like baskets of fruit for each other: to all thriving creatures making themselves cleanly and comely to the greater glory of life. But Kennerly had gone astray somewhere: he had overdone it; he wore the harried air of a man on the edge of bankruptcy, keeping up an expensive establishment because he dared not retrench. His nerves were bundles of dried twigs, they jabbed his insides every time a thought stirred in his head, they kept his blank blue eyes fixed in a white stare. The muscles of his jaw jerked in continual helpless rage. Eight months spent as business manager for three Russian moving-picture men in Mexico had about finished him off, he told me, quite as though Andreyev, one of the three, were not present.

"Ah, he should have business-managed us through China and Mongolia," said Andreyev, to me, as if speaking of an absent Kennerly. "After that, Mexico could never disturb him."

"The altitude!" said Kennerly. "My heart skips every other beat. I can't sleep a wink!"

"There was no altitude at all in Tehuantepec," said Andreyev, with stubborn gayety, "and you should have been there to see him."

Kennerly spewed up his afflictions like a child being sick.

"It's these Mexicans," he said as if it were an outrage to find them in Mexico. "They would drive any man crazy in no time. In Tehuantepec it was frightful." It would take him a week to tell the whole story; and, besides, he was keeping notes and was going to write a book about it some day; but "Just for example, they don't know the meaning of time and they have absolutely no regard for their word." They had to bribe every step of the way. Graft, bribe, graft, bribe it was from morning to night, anything from fifty pesos to the Wise Boys in the municipal councils to a bag of candy for a provincial mayor before they were even allowed to set up their cameras. The mosquitoes ate him alive. And with the bugs and cockroaches and the food and the heat and the water, everybody got sick: Stepanov, the camera-man, was sick: Andreyev was sick . . .

"Not seriously," said Andreyev.

The immortal Uspensky even got sick; and as for himself, Kennerly, he thought more than once he'd never live through it. Amoebic dysentery. You couldn't tell him. Why, it was a miracle they hadn't all died or had their throats cut. Why, it was worse than Africa. . . .

"Were you in Africa, too?" asked Andreyev. "Why do you always choose the inconvenient countries?"

Well, no, he had not been there, but he had friends who made a film among the pygmies and you wouldn't believe what they had gone through. As for him, Kennerly, give him pygmies or headhunters or cannibals outright, every time. At least you knew where you stood with them. Now take for example: they had lost ten thousand dollars flat by obeying the laws of the country—something nobody else does!—by passing their film of the Oaxaca earthquake before the board of censorship in Mexico City. Meanwhile, some unscrupulous native scoundrels who knew the ropes had beaten them to it and sent a complete newsreel to New York. It doesn't pay to have a conscience, but if you've got one what can you do about it? Just throw away your time and your money, that's all. He had written and protested to the censors, charging them with letting the Mexican film company get away with murder, accusing them of favoritism and deliberate malice in holding up the Russian film—everything, in a five-page typewritten letter. They hadn't even answered it. Now what can you do with people like that? Graft, bribe, bribe, graft, that's the way it went. Well, he had been learning, too. "Whatever they ask for, I give 'em half the amount, straight across the board," he said. "I tell 'em, 'Look here, I'll give you just half that amount, and anything more than that is bribery and corruption, d'you understand?' Do they take it? Like a shot. Ha!"

His overwhelming unmodulated voice brayed on agonizingly, his staring eyes accused everything they looked upon. Crickle crackle went the dried twigs of his nerve ends at every slightest jog of memory, every present touch, every cold wind from the future. He talked on. . . . He was afraid of his brother-in-law, a violent prohibitionist who would be furious if he ever heard that Kennerly had gone back to drinking beer openly the minute he got out of California. In a way, his job was at stake, for his brother-in-law had raised most of the money among his friends for this expedition and might just fire him out, though how the fellow expected to get along without him Kennerly could not imagine. He was the best friend his brother-in-law had in the world. If the man could only realize it. Moreover, the friends would be soon, if they were not already, shouting to have some money back on their investment. Nobody but himself ever gave a thought to that side of the business! . . . He glared outright at Andreyev at this point.

Andreyev said: "I did not ask them to invest!"

Beer was the only thing Kennerly could trust—it was food and medicine and a thirst-quencher all in one, and everything else around him, fruit, meat, air, water, bread, were poisoned. . . . The picture was to have been finished in three months and now they'd been there eight months and God knew how much longer they'd have to go. He was afraid the picture would be a failure, now it hadn't been finished on time.

"What time?" asked Andreyev, as if he had made this answer many times before. "When it is finished it is finished."

"Yes, but it isn't merely enough to finish a job just when you please. The public must be prepared for it on the dot." He went on to explain that making good involves all sorts of mysterious interlocking schedules: it must be done by a certain date, it must be art, of course, that's taken for granted, and it must be a hit. Half the chance of making a hit depends upon having your stuff ready to go at the psychological moment. There are thousands of things to be thought of, and if they miss one point, bang goes everything! . . . He sighted along an imaginary rifle, pulled the trigger, and fell back exhausted. His whole life of effort and despair flickered like a film across his relaxed face, a life of putting things over in spite of hell, of keeping up a good front, of lying awake nights fuming with schemes and frothing with beer, rising of mornings gray-faced, stupefied, pushing himself under cold showers and filling himself up on hot coffee and slamming himself into a fight in which there are no rules and no referee and the antagonist is everywhere. "God," he said to me, "you don't know. But I'm going to write a book about it. . . ."

As he sat there, talking about his book, eating American chocolate bars and drinking his third bottle of beer, sleep took him suddenly, upright as he was, in the midst of a sentence. Assertion failed, sleep took him mercifully by the nape and quelled him. His body cradled itself in the tweed, the collar rose above his neck, his closed eyes and limp mouth looked ready to cry.

Andreyev went on showing me pictures from that part of the film they were making at the pulque hacienda. . . . They had chosen it carefully, he said; it was really an old-fashioned feudal estate with the right kind of architecture, no modern improvements to speak of, and with the purest type of peons. Naturally a pulque hacienda would be just such a place. Pulque-making had not changed from the beginning, since the time the first Indian set up a rawhide vat to ferment the liquor and pierced and hollowed the first gourd to draw with his mouth the juice from the heart of the maguey. Nothing had happened since, nothing could happen. Apparently there was no better way to make pulque. The whole thing, he said, was almost too good to be true. An old Spanish gentleman had revisited the hacienda after an absence of fifty years, and had gone about looking at everything with delight. "Nothing has changed," he said, "nothing at all!"

The camera had seen this unchanged world as a landscape with figures, but figures under a doom imposed by the landscape. The closed dark faces were full of instinctive suffering, without individual memory, or only the kind of memory animals may have, who when they feel the whip know they suffer but do not know why and cannot imagine a remedy. . . . Death in these pictures was a procession with lighted candles, love a matter of vague gravity, of clasped hands and two sculptured figures inclining towards each other. Even the figure of the Indian in his ragged loose white clothing, weathered and molded to his flat-hipped, narrow-waisted body, leaning between the horns of the maguey, his mouth to the gourd, his burro with the casks on either side waiting with hanging head for his load, had this formal traditional tragedy, beautiful and hollow. There were rows of girls, like dark statues walking, their mantles streaming from their smooth brows, water jars on their shoulders; women kneeling at washing stones, their blouses slipping from their shoulders—"so picturesque, all this," said Andreyev, "we shall be accused of dressing them up." The camera had caught and fixed in moments of violence and senseless excitement, of cruel living and tortured death, the almost ecstatic death-expectancy which is in the air of Mexico. The Mexican may know when the danger is real, or may not care whether the thrill is false or true, but strangers feel the acid of death in their bones whether or not any real danger is near them. It was this terror that Kennerly had translated into fear of food, water, and air around him. In the Indian the love of death had become a habit of the spirit. It had smoothed out and polished the faces to a repose so absolute it seemed studied, though studied for so long it was held now without effort; and in them all was a common memory of defeat. The pride of their bodily posture was the mere outward shade of passive, profound resistance; the lifted, arrogant features were a mockery of the servants who lived within.

We looked at many scenes from the life of the master's house, with the characters dressed in the fashion of 1898. They were quite perfect. One girl was especially clever. She was the typical Mexican mixed-blood beauty, her mask-like face powdered white, with a round hard full mouth, and hard slanting dark eyes. Her black waved hair was combed back from a low forehead, and she wore her balloon sleeves and small stiff sailor hat with marvelous elegance.

"But this must be an actress," I said.

"Oh, yes," said Andreyev, "the only one. For that rôle we needed an actress. That is Lolita. We found her at the Jewel Theater."

The story of Lolita and Doña Julia was very gay. It had begun by being a very usual story about Lolita and Don Genaro, the master of the pulque hacienda. Doña Julia, his wife, was furious with him for bringing a fancy woman into the house. She herself was modern, she said, very modern, she had no old-fashioned ideas at all, but she still considered that she was being insulted. On the contrary, Don Genaro was very old-fashioned in his taste for ladies of the theater. He had thought he was being discreet, besides, and was truly apologetic when he was found out. But little Doña Julia was fearfully jealous. She screamed and wept and made scenes at night, first. Then she began making Don Genaro jealous with other men. So that the men grew very frightened of Doña Julia and almost ran when they saw her. Imagine all the things that might happen! There was the picture to think of, after all. . . . And then Doña Julia threatened to kill Lolita— to cut her throat, to stab her, to poison her. . . . Don Genaro simply ran away at this, and left everything in the air. He went up to the capital and stayed two days.

When he came back, the first sight that greeted his eyes was his wife and his mistress strolling, arms about each other's waists, on the upper terrace, while a whole scene was being delayed because Lolita would not leave Doña Julia and get to work.

Don Genaro, who prided himself on his speed, was thunderstruck by the suddenness of this change. He had borne with his wife's scenes because he really respected her rights and privileges as a wife. A wife's first right is to be jealous and threaten to kill her husband's mistress. Lolita also had her definite prerogatives. Everything, until he left, had gone with automatic precision exactly as it should have. This was thoroughly outrageous. He could not get them separated, either. They continued to walk and talk on the terrace under the trees all morning, affectionately entwined, heads together, one a cinema Chinese—Doña Julia loved Chinese dress made by a Hollywood costumer—the other in the stiff elegance of 1898. They remained oblivious to the summons from the embattled males: Uspensky calling for Lolita to get into the scene at once, Don Genaro sending messages by an Indian boy that the master had returned and wished to see Doña Julia on a matter of the utmost importance. . . .

The women still strolled, or sat on the edge of the fountain, whispering together, arms lying at ease about each

other's waists, for all the world to see. When Lolita finally
came down the steps and took her place in the scene, Doña
Julia sat nearby, making up her face by her round mirror in
the blinding sunlight, getting in the way, smiling at Lolita
whenever their eyes met. When they asked her to sit somewhere else, a little out of camera range, she pouted, moved
three feet away, and said, "I want to be in this scene too, with
Lolita."

Lolita's deep throaty voice cooed at Doña Julia. She tossed
strange glances at her from under her heavy eyelids, and
when she mounted her horse, she forgot her rôle, and swung
her leg over the saddle in a gesture unknown to ladies of
1898. . . . Doña Julia greeted her husband with soft affection,
and Don Genaro, who had no precedent whatever for a husband's conduct in such a situation, made a terrible scene, and
pretended he was jealous of Betancourt, one of the Mexican
advisers to Uspensky.

We turned over the pictures again, looked at some of them
twice. In the fields, among the maguey, the Indian in his
hopeless rags; in the hacienda house, theatrically luxurious
persons, posed usually with a large chromo portrait of Porfirio Díaz looming from a gaudy frame on the walls. "That is
to show," said Andreyev, "that all this really happened in the
time of Díaz, and that all this," he tapped the pictures of the
Indians, "has been swept away by the revolution. It was the
first requirement of our agreement here." This without cracking a smile or meeting my eye. "We have, in spite of everything, arrived at the third part of our picture."

I wondered how they had managed it. They had arrived
from California under a cloud as politically subversive characters. Wild rumor ran before them. It was said they had been
invited by the government to make a picture. It was said they
had not been so invited, but were being sponsored by Communists and various other shady organizations. The Mexican
government was paying them heavily; Moscow was paying
Mexico for the privilege of making the film: Uspensky was
the most dangerous agent Moscow had ever sent on a mis-

sion; Moscow was on the point of repudiating him altogether, it was doubtful he would be allowed to return to Russia. He was not really a Communist at all, but a German spy.
American Communists were paying for the film; the Mexican anti-government party was at heart in sympathy with
Russia and had paid secretly an enormous sum to the Russians for a picture that would disgrace the present régime.
The government officials themselves did not seem to know
what was going on. They took all sides at once. A delega-
tion of officials met the Russians at the boat and escorted
them to jail. The jail was hot and uncomfortable. Uspensky,
Andreyev, and Stepanov worried about their equipment,
which was being turned over very thoroughly at the customs:
and Kennerly worried about his reputation. Accustomed as
he was to the clean, four-square business methods of God's
own Hollywood, he trembled to think what he might be getting into. He had, so far as he had been able to see, helped to
make all the arrangements before they left California. But he
was no longer certain of anything. It was he who started the
rumor that Uspensky was not a Party Member, and that one
of the three was not even a Russian. He hoped this made the
whole business sound more respectable. After a night of confusion another set of officials, more important than the first,
arrived, all smiles, explanations and apologies, and set them
free. Someone then started a rumor that the whole episode
was invented for the sake of publicity.

The government officials still took no chance. They wanted
to improve this opportunity to film a glorious history of
Mexico, her wrongs and sufferings and her final triumph
through the latest revolution; and the Russians found themselves surrounded and insulated from their material by the
entire staff of professional propagandists, which had been put
at their disposal for the duration of their visit. Dozens of
helpful observers, art experts, photographers, literary talents, and travel guides swarmed about them to lead them
aright, and to show them all the most beautiful, significant,
and characteristic things in the national life and soul: if by
chance anything not beautiful got in the way of the camera,

there was a very instructed and sharp-eyed committee of censors whose duty it was to see that the scandal went no further than the cutting room.

"It has been astonishing," said Andreyev, "to see how devoted all of them are to art."

Kennerly stirred and muttered; he opened his eyes, closed them again. His head rolled uneasily.

"Wait. He is going to wake up," I whispered.

We sat still watching him.

"Maybe not yet," said Andreyev. "Everything," he added, "is pretty mixed up, and it's going to be worse."

We sat a few moments in silence, Andreyev still watching Kennerly impersonally.

"He would be something nice in a zoo," he said, with no particular malice, "but it is terrible to carry him around this way, all the time, without a cage." After a pause, he went on telling about Russia.

At the last station before we reached the hacienda, the Indian boy who was playing the leading rôle in the film came in looking for us. He entered as if on the stage, followed by several of his hero-worshipers, underfed, shabby youths, living happily in reflected glory. To be an actor in the cinema was enough for him to capture them utterly; but he was already famous in his village, being a pugilist and a good one. Bull-fighting is a little out of fashion; pugilism is the newest and smartest thing, and a really ambitious young man of the sporting set will, if God sends him the strength, take to boxing rather than to bulls. Fame added to fame had given this boy a brilliant air of self-confidence and he approached us, brows drawn together, with the easy self-possession of a man of the world accustomed to boarding trains and meeting his friends.

But the pose would not hold. His face, from high cheekbones to square chin, from the full wide-lipped mouth to the low forehead, which had ordinarily the expression of professional-boxer histrionic ferocity, now broke up into a charming open look of simple, smiling excitement. He was happy to see Andreyev again, but there was something more: he had news worth hearing, and would be the first to tell us.

What a to-do there had been at the hacienda that morning! . . . Even while we were shaking hands all around, he broke out with it. "Justino—you remember Justino?–killed his sister. He shot her and ran to the mountains. Vicente—you know which one Vicente is?—chased him on horseback and brought him back." And now they had Justino in jail there in the village we were just leaving.

We were all astounded and full of curiosity as he had hoped we would be. Yes, it had happened that very morning, at about ten o'clock. . . . No, nothing had gone wrong before that anyone knew about. No, Justino had not quarrelled with anybody. No one had seen him do it. He had been in good humor all morning, working, making part of a scene on the set.

Neither Andreyev nor Kennerly spoke Spanish. The boy's words were in a jargon hard for me to understand, but I snatched key words and translated quickly as I could. Kennerly leaped up, white-eyed. . . .

"On the set? My God! We are ruined!"

"But why ruined? Why?"

"Her family will have a damage suit against us!"

The boy wanted to know what this meant.

"The law! the law!" groaned Kennerly. "They can collect money from us for the loss of their daughter. It can be blamed on us."

The boy was fairly baffled by this.

"He says he doesn't understand," I told Kennerly. "He says nobody ever heard of such a thing. He says Justino was in his own house when it happened, and nobody, not even Justino, was to blame."

"Oh," said Kennerly. "Oh, I see. Well, let's hear the rest of it. If he wasn't on the set, it doesn't matter."

He collected himself at once and sat down.

"Yes, do sit down," said Andreyev softly, with a venomous look at Kennerly. The Indian boy seized upon the look, visibly turned it over in his mind, obviously suspected it to refer to him, and stood glancing from one to another, deep frowning eyes instantly on guard.

"Do sit down," said Andreyev, "and don't be giving them all sorts of strange notions not necessary to anybody's peace of mind."

He reached out a free hand and pulled the boy down to sit on the arm of the seat. The other lads had collected near the door.

"Tell us the rest," said Andreyev.

After a small pause, the boy melted and talked. Justino had gone to his hut for the noon meal. His sister was grinding corn for the tortillas, while he stood by waiting, throwing the pistol into the air and catching it. The pistol fired; shot her through here. . . . He touched his ribs level with his heart. . . . She fell forward on her face, over the grinding stone, dead. In no time at all a crowd came running from everywhere. Seeing what he had done, Justino ran, leaping like a crazy man, throwing away the pistol as he went, and struck through the maguey fields toward the mountains. His friend Vicente went after him on horseback, waving a gun and yelling: "Stop or I'll shoot!" and Justino yelled back: "Shoot, I don't care! . . ." But of course Vicente did not: he just galloped up and bashed Justino over the head with the gun butt, threw him across the saddle, and brought him back. Now he was in jail, but Don Genaro was already in the village getting him out. Justino did not do it on purpose.

"This is going to hold up everything," said Kennerly. "Everything! It just means more time wasted."

"And that isn't all," said the boy. He smiled ambiguously, lowered his voice a little, put on an air of conspiracy and discretion, and said: "The actress is gone too. She has gone back to the capital. Three days ago."

"A quarrel with Doña Julia?" asked Andreyev.

"No," said the boy, "it was with Don Genaro she quarreled, after all."

The three of them laughed mightily together, and Andreyev said to me:

"You know that wild girl from the Jewel Theater."

The boy said: "It was because Don Genaro was away on other business at a bad moment." He was being more discreet than ever.

Kennerly sat with his chin drawn in severely, almost making faces at Andreyev and the boy in his efforts to hush them. Andreyev stared back at him in hardy innocence. The boy saw the look, again lapsed into perfect silence, and sat very haughtily on the seat arm, clenched fist posed on his thigh, his face turned partly away. As the train slowed down, he rose suddenly and dashed ahead of us.

When we swung down the high narrow steps he was already standing beside the mule car, greeting the two Indians who had come to meet us. His young hangers-on, waving their hats to us, set out to walk a shortcut across the maguey fields.

Kennerly was blustering about, handing bags to the Indians to store away in the small shabby mule car, arranging the party, settling all properly, myself between him and Andreyev, tucking my skirts around my knees with officious hands, to keep a thread of my garments from touching the no doubt infectious foreign things facing us.

The little mule dug its sharp hoof points into the stones and grass of the track, got a tolerable purchase at last on a cross tie, and set off at a finicking steady trot, the bells on its collar jingling like a tambourine.

We jogged away, crowded together facing each other three in a row, with bags under the seats, and the straw falling out of the cushions. The driver, craning around toward the mule now and then, and snapping the reins on its back, added his comments: An unlucky family. This was the second child to be killed by a brother. The mother was half dead with grief and Justino, a good boy, was in jail.

The big man sitting by him in striped riding trousers, his hat bound under his chin with red-tasseled cord, added that Justino was in for it now, God help him. But where did he get the pistol? He borrowed it from the firearms being used in the picture. It was true he was not supposed to touch the pistols, and there was his first mistake. He meant to put it back at once, but you know how a boy of sixteen loves to play with a pistol. Nobody would blame him. . . . The girl was nineteen years old. Her body had been sent already to the village to be buried. There was too much excitement over her; nothing was done so long as she was on the place. Don Genaro had gone, according to custom, to cross her hands, close her eyes, and light a candle beside her. Everything was done in order, they said piously, their eyes dancing with rich, enjoyable feelings. It is always regrettable and exciting when somebody you know gets into such dramatic trouble. Ah, we were alive under that deepening sky, jingling away through the yellow fields of blooming mustard with the pattern of spiked maguey shuttling as we passed, from straight lines to angles, to diamond shapes, and back again, miles and miles of it spreading away to the looming mountains.

"Surely they would not have had loaded pistols among those being used in the picture?" I asked, rather suddenly, of the big man with the red-tasseled cord on his hat.

He opened his mouth to say something and snapped it shut again. There was a pause. Nobody spoke. It was my turn to be uncomfortable under a quick exchange of glances between the others.

There was again the guarded watchful expression of the Indian faces. An awful silence settled over us.

Andreyev, who had been trying his Spanish boldly, said, "If I cannot talk, I can sing," and began in his big gay Russian voice: "Ay, Sandunga, Sandunga, Mamá, por Diós!" All the Indians shouted with joy and delight at the new thing his strange tongue made of the words. Andreyev laughed, too. This laughter was an invitation to their confidence. With a burst of song in Russian, the young pugilist threw himself in turn on the laughter of Andreyev. Everybody then seized the opportunity to laugh madly in fellowship, even Kennerly. Eyes met eyes through the guard of crinkled lids, and the little mule went without urging into a stiff-legged gallop.

A big rabbit leaped across the track, chased by lean hungry

dogs. It was cracking the strings of its heart in flight; its eyes started from its head like crystal bubbles. "Run, rabbit, run!" I cried. "Run, dogs!" shouted the big Indian with the red cords on his hat, his love of a contest instantly aroused. He turned to me with his eyes blazing: "What will you bet, señorita?"

The hacienda lay before us, a monastery, a walled fortress, towered in terra cotta and coral, sheltered against the mountains. An old woman in a shawl opened the heavy double gate and we slid into the main corral. The upper windows in the near end were all alight. Stepanov stood on one balcony; Betancourt, on the next; and for a moment the celebrated Uspensky appeared with waving arms at a third. They called to us, even before they recognized us, glad to see anyone of their party returning from town to relieve the long monotony of the day which had been shattered by the accident and could not be gathered together again. Thin-boned horses with round sleek haunches, long rippling manes and tails were standing under saddle in the patio. Big polite dogs of expensive breeds came out to meet us and walked with dignity beside us up the broad shallow steps.

The room was cold. The round-shaded hanging lamp hardly disturbed the shadows. The doorways, of the style called Porfirian Gothic, in honor of the Díaz period of domestic architecture, soared towards the roof in a cloud of gilded stamped wallpaper, from an undergrowth of purple and red and orange plush armchairs fringed and tassled, set on bases with springs. Such spots as this, fitted up for casual visits, interrupted the chill gloom of the rooms marching by tens along the cloisters, now and again casting themselves around patios, gardens, pens for animals. A naked player-piano in light wood occupied one corner. Standing together here, we spoke again of the death of the girl, and Justino's troubles, and all our voices were vague with the vast incurable boredom which hung in the air of the place and settled around our heads clustered together.

Kennerly worried about the possible lawsuit.

"They know nothing about such things," Betancourt assured him. "Besides, it is not our fault."

The Russians were thinking about tomorrow. It was not only a great pity about the poor girl, but both she and her brother were working in the picture; the boy's rôle was important and everything must be halted until he should come back, or if he should never come back everything must be done all over again.

Betancourt, Mexican by birth, French-Spanish by blood, French by education, was completely at the mercy of an ideal of elegance and detachment perpetually at war with a kind of Mexican nationalism which afflicted him like an inherited weakness of the nervous system. Being trustworthy and of cultured taste it was his official duty to see that nothing hurtful to the national dignity got in the way of the foreign cameras. His ambiguous situation seemed to trouble him not at all. He was plainly happy and fulfilled for the first time in years. Beggars, the poor, the deformed, the old and ugly, trusted Betancourt to wave them away. "I am sorry for everything," he said, lifting a narrow, pontifical hand, waving away vulgar human pity which always threatened, buzzing like a fly at the edges of his mind. "But when you consider"— he made an almost imperceptible inclination of his entire person in the general direction of the social point of view supposed to be represented by the Russians—"what her life would have been like in this place, it is much better that she is dead. . . ."

He had burning fanatic eyes and a small tremulous mouth. His bones were like reeds.

"It is a tragedy, but it happens too often," he said.

With his easy words the girl was dead indeed, anonymously entombed. . . .

Doña Julia came in silently, walking softly on her tiny feet in gay shoes like a Chinese woman's. She was probably twenty years old. Her black hair was sleeked to her round skull, eyes painted, apparently, in the waxed semblance of her face.

"We never really live here," she said, in a gentle smooth

voice, glancing vaguely about her strange setting, in which she appeared to be an exotic speaking doll. "It's very ugly, but you must not mind that. It is hopeless to try keeping the place up. The Indians destroy everything with neglect. We stay here now for the excitement about the film. It is thrilling." Then she added, "It is sad about the poor girl. It makes every kind of trouble. It is sad about the poor brother. . . ." As we went towards the dining-room, she murmured along beside me, "It is sad . . . very sad . . . sad. . . ."

Don Genaro's grandfather, who had been described to me as a gentleman of the very oldest school, was absent on a prolonged visit. In no way did he approve of his granddaughter-in-law, who got herself up in a fashion unknown to the ladies of his day, a fashion very upsetting to a man of the world who had always known how to judge, grade, and separate women into their proper categories at a glance. A temporary association with such a young female as this he considered a part of every gentleman's education. Marriage was an altogether different matter. In his day, she would have had at best a career in the theater. He had been silenced but in no wise changed in his conviction by the sudden, astonishing marriage of his grandson, the sole inevitable heir, who was already acting as head of the house, accountable to no one. He did not understand the boy and he did not waste time trying. He had moved his furniture and his keepsakes and his person away, to the very farthest patio in the old garden, above the terraces to the south, where he lived in bleak dignity and loneliness, without hope and without philosophy, perhaps contemptuous of both, joining his family only at mealtimes. His place at the foot of the table was empty, the week-end crowds of sightseers were gone and our party barely occupied part of the upper end.

Uspensky sat in his monkey-suit of striped overalls, his face like a superhumanly enightened monkey's now well overgrown with a simian beard.

He had a monkey attitude towards life, which amounted almost to a personal philosophy. It saved explanation, and threw off the kind of bores he could least bear with. He amused himself at the low theaters in the capital, flattering the Mexicans by declaring they really were the most obscene he had found in the whole world. He liked staging old Russian country comedies, all the players wearing Mexican dress, on the open roads in the afternoon. He would then shout his lines broadly and be in his best humor, prodding the rear of a patient burro, accustomed to grief and indignity, with a phallus-shaped gourd. "Ah, yes, I remember," he said gallantly, on meeting some southern women, "you are the ladies who are always being raped by those dreadful negroes!" But now he was fevered, restless, altogether silent, and his bawdy humor, which served as cover and disguise for all other moods, was gone.

Stepanov, a champion at tennis and polo, wore flannel tennis slacks and polo shirt. Betancourt wore well-cut riding trousers and puttees, not because he ever mounted a horse if he could avoid it, but he had learned in California, in 1921, that this was the correct costume for a moving-picture director: true, he was not yet a director, but he was assisting somewhat at the making of a film, and when in action, he always added a greenlined cork helmet, which completed some sort of precious illusion he cherished about himself. Andreyev's no-colored wool shirt was elbow to elbow with Kennerly's brash tweeds. I wore a knitted garment of the kind which always appears suitable for any other than the occasion on which it is being worn. Altogether, we provided a staggering contrast for Doña Julia at the head of the table, a figure from a Hollywood comedy, in black satin pajamas adorned with rainbow-colored bands of silk, loose sleeves falling over her babyish hands with pointed scarlet finger ends.

"We musn't wait for my husband," said Doña Julia; "he is always so busy and always late."

"Always going at top speed," said Betancourt, pleasantly, "seventy kilometers an hour at least, and never on time anywhere." He prided himself on his punctuality, and had theories about speed, its use and abuse. He loved to explain that man, if he had concentrated on his spiritual development, as he should have done, would never have needed to rely on mechanical aids to conquer time and space. In the meantime, he admitted that he himself, who could communicate telepathically with anyone he chose, and who had once levitated himself three feet from the ground by a simple act of the will, found a great deal of pleasurable stimulation in the control of machinery. I knew something about his pleasure in driving an automobile. He had for one thing a habit of stepping on the accelerator and bounding across tracks before approaching trains. Speed, he said, was "modern" and it was everyone's duty to be as modern as one's means allowed. I surmised from Betancourt's talk that Don Genaro's wealth allowed him to be at least twice as modern as Betancourt. He could afford high-powered automobiles that simply frightened other drivers off the road before him; he was thinking of an airplane to cut distance between the hacienda and the capital; speed and lightness at great expense was his ideal. Nothing could move too fast for Don Genaro, said Betancourt, whether a horse, a dog, a woman or something with metal machinery in it. Doña Julia smiled approvingly at what she considered praise of her husband and, by pleasant inference, of herself.

There came a violent commotion along the hall, at the door, in the room. The servants separated, fell back, rushed forward, scurried to draw out a chair, and Don Genaro entered, wearing Mexican country riding dress, a gray buckskin jacket and tight gray trousers strapped under the boot. He was a tall, hard-bitten, blue-eyed young Spaniard, stringy-muscled, thin-lipped, graceful, and he was in a fury. This fury he expected us to sympathize with; he dismissed it long enough to greet everybody all around, then dropped into his chair beside his wife and burst forth, beating his fist on the table.

It seemed that the imbecile village judge refused to let him have Justino. It seemed there was some crazy law about criminal negligence. The law, the judge said, does not recognize accidents in the vulgar sense. There must always be careful inquiry based on suspicion of bad faith in those nearest the victim. Don Genaro gave an imitation of the imbecile judge showing off his legal knowledge. Floods, volcanic eruptions, revolutions, runaway horses, smallpox, train wrecks, street fights, all such things, the judge said, were acts of God. Personal shootings, no. A personal shooting must always be inquired into severely. "All that has nothing to do with this case, I told him," said Don Genaro. "I told him, Justino is my peon, his family have lived for three hundred years on our hacienda, this is MY business. I know what happened and all about it, and you don't know anything and all you have to do with this is to let me have Justino back at once. I mean today, tomorrow will not do, I told him." It was no good. The judge wanted two thousand pesos to let Justino go. "Two thousand pesos!" shouted Don Genaro, thumping on the table; "try to imagine that!"

"How ridiculous!" said his wife with comradely sympathy and a glittering smile. He glared at her for a second as if he did not recognize her. She gazed back, her eyes flickering, a tiny uncertain smile in the corners of her mouth where the rouge was beginning to melt. Furiously he ignored her, shook the pause off his shoulders and hurried on, turning as he talked, hot and blinded and baffled, to one and another of his audience. It was not the two thousand pesos, it was that he was sick of paying here, paying there, for the most absurd things; every time he turned around there at his elbow was some thievish politician holding out his paw. "Well, there's one thing to do. If I pay this judge there'll be no end to it. He'll go on arresting my peons every time one of them shows his face in the village. I'll go to Mexico and see Velarde. . . ."

Everybody agreed with him that Velarde was the man to see. He was the most powerful and successful revolutionist in Mexico. He owned two pulque haciendas which had fallen to his share when the great repartition of land had taken place. He operated also the largest dairy farm in the country, furnishing milk and butter and cheese to every charitable institution, orphans' home, insane asylum, reform school and workhouse in the country, and getting just twice the prices for them that any other dairy farm would have asked. He also owned a great aguacate hacienda; he controlled the army; he controlled a powerful bank; the president of the Republic made no appointments to any office without his advice. He fought counter-revolution and political corruption, daily upon the front pages of twenty newspapers he had bought for that very purpose. He employed thousands of peons. As an employer, he would understand what Don Genaro was contending with. As an honest revolutionist, he would know how to handle that dirty, bribe-taking little judge. "I'll go to see Velarde," said Don Genaro in a voice gone suddenly flat, as if he despaired or was too bored with the topic to keep it up any longer. He sat back and looked at his guests bleakly. Everyone said something, it did not matter what. The episode of the morning now seemed very far away and not worth thinking about.

Uspensky sneezed with his hands over his face. He had spent two early morning hours standing up to his middle in the cold water of the horse fountain, with Stepanov and the camera balanced on the small stone ledge, directing a scene which he was convinced could be made from no other angle. He had taken cold; he now swallowed a mouthful of fried beans, drank half a glass of beer at one gulp, and slid off the long bench. His too-large striped overalls disappeared in two jumps through the nearest door. He went as if he were seeking another climate.

"He has a fever," said Andreyev. "If he does not feel better tonight we must send for Doctor Volk."

A large lumpish person in faded blue overalls and a flannel shirt inserted himself into a space near the foot of the table. He nodded to nobody in particular, and Betancourt punctiliously acknowledged the salute.

"You do not even recognize him?" Betancourt asked me in a low voice. "That is Carlos Montaña. You find him changed?"

He seemed anxious that I should find Carlos much changed.

I said I supposed we had all changed somewhat after ten years. Besides, Carlos had grown a fine set of whiskers. Betancourt's glance at me plainly admitted that I, like Carlos, had changed and for the worse, but he resisted the notion of change in himself. "Maybe," he said, unwillingly, "but most of us, I think, for the better. It's poor Carlos. It's not only the whiskers, and the fat. He has, you know, become a failure."

"A Puss Moth," said Don Genaro to Stepanov. "I flew it half an hour yesterday; awfully *chic*. I may buy it. I need something really fast. Something light, too, but it must be fast. It must be something I can depend upon at any minute." Stepanov was an expert pilot. He excelled in every activity that Don Genaro respected. Don Genaro listened attentively while Stepanov gave him some clear sensible advice about airplanes: what kind to buy, how to keep them in order, and what one might expect of airplanes as a usual thing.

"Airplanes!" said Kennerly, listening in. "I wouldn't go up with a Mexican pilot for all the money in—"

"Airplane! At last!" cried Doña Julia, like a gently enraptured child. She leaned over the table and called in Spanish softly as if waking someone, "Carlos! Do you hear? Genarito is going to buy me an airplane, after all!"

Don Genaro talked on with Stepanov as if he had not heard.

"And what will you do with it?" asked Carlos, eyes round and amiable from under his brushy brows. Without lifting his head from his hand, he went on eating his fried beans and green chile sauce with a spoon, good Mexican country fashion, and enjoying them.

"I shall turn somersaults in it," said Doña Julia.

"A Failure," Betancourt went on, in English, which Carlos could not understand, "though I must say he looks worse today than usual. He slipped and hurt himself in the bathtub this morning." It was as if this accident were another point against Carlos, symbolic proof of the fatal downward tendency in his character.

"I thought he had composed half the popular songs in

Mexico," I said. "I heard nothing but his songs here, ten years ago. What happened?"

"Ah, that was ten years ago, don't forget. He does almost nothing now. He hasn't been director of the Jewel for, oh ages!"

I observed the Failure. He seemed cheerful enough. He was beating time with the handle of his spoon and humming a song to Andreyev, who listened, nodding his head. "Like that, for two measures," said Carlos in French, "then like this," and he beat time, humming. "Then this for the dance. . . ." Andreyev hummed the tune and tapped on the table with his left forefinger, his right hand waving slightly. Betancourt watched them for a moment. "He feels better just now, poor fellow," he said, "now I have got him this job. It may be a new beginning for him. But he is sometimes tired, he drinks too much, he cannot always do his best."

Carlos had slumped back in his chair, his round shoulders drooped, his swollen lids covered his eyes, he poked fretfully at his plate of enchiladas with sour cream. "You'll see," he said to Andreyev in French, "how Betancourt will not like this idea either. There will be something wrong with it. . . ." He said it not angrily, not timidly, but with an unhappy certainty. "Either it will not be modern enough, or not enough in the old style, or just not Mexican enough. . . . You'll see."

Betancourt had spent his youth unlocking the stubborn secrets of Universal Harmony by means of numerology, astronomy, astrology, a formula of thought-transference and deep breathing, the practice of will-to-power combined with the latest American theories of personality development; certain complicated magical ceremonies; and a careful choice of doctrines from the several schools of Oriental philosophies which are, from time to time, so successfully introduced into California. From this material he had constructed a Way of Life which could be taught to anyone, and once learned led the initiate quietly and surely toward Success: success without pain, almost without effort except of a pleasurable kind, success accompanied by moral and esthetic beauty, as well as the most desirable material reward. Wealth, naturally, could not be an end in itself: alone, it was not Success. But it was the unobtrusive companion of all true Success. . . . From this point of view he was cheerfully explicit about Carlos. Carlos had always been contemptuous of the Eternal Laws. He had always simply written his tunes without giving a thought to the profounder inferences of music, based as it is upon the harmonic system of the spheres. . . . He, Betancourt, had many times warned Carlos. It had done no good at all. Carlos had gone on inviting his own doom.

"I have warned you, too," he said to me kindly. "I have asked myself many times why you will not or cannot accept the Mysteries which would open a whole treasure house for you. . . . All," he said, "is possible through scientific intuition. If you depend on mere intellect, you must fail."

"You must fail," he had been saying all this time to poor simple Carlos. "He has failed," he said of him to others. He now looked almost fondly upon his handiwork, who sat there, somewhat grubby and gloomy, a man who had done a good day's work in his time, and was not altogether finished yet. The neat light figure beside me posed gracefully upon its slender spine, the too-beautiful slender hands waved rhythmically upon insubstantial wrists. I remembered all that Carlos had done for Betancourt in other days; he had, in his thoughtless hopelessly human way, piled upon these thin shoulders a greater burden of gratitude than they could support. Betancourt had set in motion all the machinery of the laws of Universal Harmony he could command to help him revenge himself on Carlos. It was slow work, but he never tired.

"I don't, of course, understand just what you mean by failure, or by success either," I told him at last. "You know, I never could understand."

"It is true, you could not," he said, "that was the great trouble."

"As for Carlos," I said, "you should forgive him. . . ."

Betancourt said with perfect sincerity, "You know I never blame anyone for anything at all."

Carlos came round and shook hands with me as everybody pushed back his chair and began drifting out by the several doorways. He was full of humanity and good humor about Justino and his troubles. "These family love affairs," he said, "what can you expect?"

"Oh, no, now," said Betancourt, uneasily. He laughed his twanging tremulous little laugh.

"Oh, yes, now," said Carlos, walking beside me. "I shall make a *corrido* about Justino and his sister." He began to sing almost in a whisper, imitating the voice and gestures of a singer peddling broadsides in the market. . . .

> *Ah, poor little Rosalita*
> *Took herself a new lover,*
> *Thus betraying the heart's core*
> *Of her impassioned brother . . .*
> *Now she lies dead, poor Rosalita,*
> *With two bullets in her heart. . . .*
> *Take warning, my young sisters,*
> *Who would from your brothers part.*

"One bullet," said Betancourt, wagging a long finger at Carlos. "One bullet!"

Carlos laughed. "Very well, one bullet! Such a precisionist! Good night," he said.

Kennerly and Carlos disappeared early. Don Genaro spent the evening playing billiards with Stepanov, who won always. Don Genaro was very good at billiards, but Stepanov was a champion, with all sorts of trophies to show, so it was no humiliation to be defeated by him.

In the drafty upper-hall room fitted up as a parlor, Andreyev turned off the mechanical attachment of the piano and sang Russian songs, running his hands over the keys while he waited to remember yet other songs. Doña Julia and I sat listening. He sang for us, but for himself mostly, in the same kind of voluntary forgetfulness of his surroundings, the same self-induced absence of mind that had kept him talking about Russia in the afternoon.

We sat until very late. Doña Julia smiled steadily every time she caught the glance of Andreyev or myself, yawning now and then under her hand, her Pekinese sprawling and snoring on her lap. "You're not tired?" I asked her. "You wouldn't let us stay up too late?"

"Oh, no, let's go on with the music. I love sitting up all night. I never go to bed if I can possibly sit up. Don't go yet."

At half-past one Uspensky sent for Andreyev, for Stepanov. He was restless, in a fever, he wished to talk. Andreyev said, "I have already sent for Doctor Volk. It is better not to delay."

Doña Julia and I looked on in the billiard room downstairs, where Stepanov and Don Genaro were settling the score. Several Indians leaned in at the windows, their vast straw hats tilted forward, watching in silence. Doña Julia asked her husband, "Then you're not going to Mexico tonight?"

"Why should I?" he inquired sullenly without looking at her.

"I thought you might," said Doña Julia. "Good night, Stepanov," she said, her black eyes shining under her long lids painted silver blue.

"Good night, Julita," said Stepanov, his frank Northern smile meaning anything or nothing at all. When he was not smiling, his face was severe, expressive, and intensely alive. His smile was misleadingly simple, like a very young boy's. He was anything but simple; he smiled now like a merry open book upon the absurd little figure strayed out of a marionette theater. Turning away, Doña Julia slanted at him the glittering eye of a femme fatale in any Hollywood film. He examined the end of his cue as if he looked through a microscope. Don Genaro said violently, "Good night!" and disappeared violently through the door leading to the corral.

Doña Julia and I passed through her apartment, a long shallow room between the billiard and the vat-room. It was puffy with silk and down, glossy with bright new polished wood and wide mirrors, restless with small ornaments, boxes of sweets, French dolls in ruffled skirts and white wigs. The air was thick with perfume which fought with another heavier smell. From the vat-room came a continual muffled shouting, the rumble of barrels as they rolled down the wooden trestles to the flat mule-car standing on the tracks running past the wide doorway. The smell had not been out of my nostrils since I came, but here it rose in a thick vapor through the heavy drone of flies, sour, stale, like rotting milk and blood; this sound and this smell belonged together, and both belonged to the intermittent rumble of barrels and the long chanting cry of the Indians. On the narrow stairs I glanced back at Doña Julia. She was looking up, wrinkling her little nose, her Pekinese with his wrinkled nose of perpetual disgust held close to her face. "Pulque!" she said. "Isn't it horrid? But I hope the noise will not keep you awake."

On my balcony there was no longer any perfume to disturb the keen fine wind from the mountains, or the smell from the vat-room. "Twenty-one!" sang the Indians in a long, melodious chorus of weariness and excitement, and the twenty-first barrel of fresh pulque rolled down the slide, was seized by two men and loaded on the flat-car under my window.

From the window next to mine, the three Russian voices murmured along quietly. Pigs grunted and rooted in the soft wallow near the washing fountain, where the women were still kneeling in the darkness, thumping wet cloth on the stones, chattering, laughing. All the women seemed to be laughing that night: long after midnight, the high bright sound sparkled again and again from the long row of peon quarters along the corral. Burros sobbed and mourned to each other, there was everywhere the drowsy wakefulness of creatures, stamping hoofs, breathing and snorting. Below in the vat-room a single voice sang suddenly a dozen notes of some rowdy song; and the women at the washing fountain were silenced for a moment, then tittered among themselves. There occurred a light flurry at the arch of the gate leading into the inner patio: one of the polite, expensive dogs had lost his dignity and was chasing, with snarls of real annoyance, a little fat-bottomed soldier back to his proper place, the bar-

racks by the wall opposite the Indian huts. The soldier scrambled and stumbled silently away, without resistance, his dim
lantern agitated violently. At a certain point, as if here was the
invisible boundary line, the dog stopped, watched while the
soldier ran on, then returned to his post under the archway.
The soldiers, sent by the government as a guard against the
Agrarians, sprawled in idleness eating their beans at Don
Genaro's expense. He tolerated and resented them, and so did
the dogs.

I fell asleep to the long chanting of the Indians, counting
their barrels in the vat-room, and woke again at sunrise,
summer sunrise, to their long doleful morning song, the clatter of metal and hard leather, and the stamping of mules as
they were being harnessed to the flat-cars. . . . The drivers
swung their whips and shouted, the loaded cars creaked and
slid away in a procession, off to meet the pulque train for
Mexico City. The field workers were leaving for the maguey
fields, driving their donkeys. They shouted, too, and
whacked the donkeys with sticks, but no one was really
hurrying, nor really excited. It was just another day's work,
another day's weariness. A three-year-old man-child ran beside his father; he drove a weanling donkey carrying two
miniature casks on its furry back. The two small creatures
imitated each in his own kind perfectly the gestures of their
elders. The baby whacked and shouted, the donkey trudged
and flapped his ears at each blow.
"My God!" said Kennerly over coffee an hour later. "Do
you remember—" he beat off a cloud of flies and filled his cup
with a wobbling hand—"I thought of it all night and couldn't
sleep—*don't* you remember," he implored Stepanov, who
held one palm over his coffee cup while he finished a cigarette, "those scenes we shot only two weeks ago, when Justino played the part of a boy who killed a girl by accident,
tried to escape, and Vicente was one of the men who ran him
down on horseback? Well, the same thing has happened to
the same people in *reality!* And—" he turned to me, "the

strangest thing is, we have to make that scene again, it didn't turn out so well, and look, my God, we had it happening really, and nobody thought of it then! Then was the time. We could have got a close-up of a girl, really dead, and real blood running down Justino's face where Vicente had hit him, and my God! we never even thought of it. That kind of thing," he said, bitterly, "has been happening ever since we got here. Just happens over and over. . . . Now, what was the matter, I wonder?"

He stared at Stepanov full of accusation. Stepanov lifted his palm from his cup, and beating off flies, drank. "Light no good, probably," he said. His eyes flickered open, clicked shut in Kennerly's direction, as if they had taken a snapshot of something and that episode was finished.

"If you want to look at it that way," said Kennerly, with resentment, "but after all, there it was, it had happened, it wasn't our fault, and we might as well have had it."

"We can always do it again," said Stepanov. "When Justino comes back, and the light is better. The light," he said to me, "it is always our enemy. Here we have one good day in five, or less."

"Imagine," said Kennerly, pouncing, "just try to imagine that—when that poor boy comes back he'll have to go through the same scene he has gone through twice before, once in play and once in reality. *Reality!*" He licked his chops. "Think how he'll feel. Why, it ought to drive him crazy."

"If he comes back," said Stepanov, "we must think of that."

In the patio half a dozen Indian boys, their ragged white clothes exposing their tawny smooth skin, were flinging over the sleek-backed horses great saddles of deerskin encrusted with silver embroidery and mother-of-pearl. The women were returning to the washing fountain. The pigs were out rooting in their favorite wallows, and in the vat-room, silently, the day-workers were already filling the bullhide vats with freshly drawn pulque juice. Carlos Montaña was out early too, enjoying himself in the fresh morning air, watching three dogs chase a long-legged pig from wallow to barn. The pig, screaming steadily, galloped like a rocking horse towards the known safety of his pen, the dogs nipping at his heels just enough to keep him up to his best speed. Carlos roared with joy, holding his ribs, and the Indian boys laughed with him.

The Spanish overseer, who had been cast for the rôle of villain—one of them—in the film, came out wearing a new pair of tight riding trousers, of deerskin and silver embroidery, like the saddles, and sat slouched on the long bench near the arch, facing the great corral where the Indians and soldiers were. There he sat nearly all day, as he had sat for years and might ·it for years more. His long wry North-Spanish face was dead with boredom. He slouched, with his English cap pulled over his close-set eyes, and did not even glance to see what Carlos was laughing at. Andreyev and I waved to Carlos and he came over at once. He was still laughing. It seemed he had forgotten the pig and was laughing at the overseer, who had already forty pairs of fancy charro trousers, but had thought none of them quite good enough for the film and had caused to be made, at great expense, the pair he was now wearing, which were entirely too tight. He hoped by wearing them every day to stretch them. He was miserable, entirely, for his trousers were all he had to live for, anyhow. "All he can do with his life," said Andreyev, "is to put on a different pair of fancy trousers every day, and sit on that bench hoping that something, anything, may happen."

I said I should have thought there had been enough happening for the past few weeks . . . or at any rate the past few days.

"Oh, no," said Carlos, "nothing that lasts long enough. I mean real excitement like the last Agrarian raid. . . . There were machine guns on the towers, and every man on the place had a rifle and pistol. They had the time of their lives. They drove the raiders off, and then they fired the rest of their ammunition in the air by way of celebration; and the next day they were bored. They wanted to have the whole show over again. It was very hard to explain to them that the fiesta was ended."

"They do really hate the Agrarians, then?" I asked.

"No, they love excitement," said Carlos.

We walked through the vat-room, picking our way through the puddles of sap sinking into the mud floor, idly stopping to watch, without comment, the flies drowning in the stinking liquor which seeped over the hairy bullhides sagging between the wooden frames. María Santísima stood primly in her blue painted niche in a frame of fly-blown paper flowers, with a perpetual light at her feet. The walls were covered with a faded fresco relating the legend of pulque; how a young Indian girl discovered this divine liquor, and brought it to the emperor, who rewarded her well; and after her death she became a half-goddess. An old legend: maybe the oldest: something to do with man's confused veneration for, and terror of, the fertility of women and vegetation. . . .

Betancourt stood in the door sniffing the air bravely. He glanced around the walls with the eye of an expert. "This is a very good example," he said, smiling at the fresco, "the perfect example, really. . . . The older ones are always the best, of course. It is a fact," he said, "that the Spaniards found wall paintings in the pre-Conquest pulquerías . . . always telling this legend. So it goes on. Nothing ever ends," he waved his long beautiful hand, "it goes on being and becomes little by little something else."

"I'd call that an end, of a kind," said Carlos.

"Oh, well, *you*," said Betancourt, smiling with immense indulgence upon his old friend, who was becoming gradually something else.

At ten o'clock Don Genaro emerged on his way to visit the village judge once more. Doña Julia, Andreyev, Stepanov, Carlos, and I were walking on the roofs in the intermittent sun-and-cloud light, looking out over the immense landscape of patterned field and mountain. Stepanov carried his small camera and took snapshots of us, with the dogs. We had already had our pictures taken on the steps with a nursling burro, with Indian babies; at the fountain on the long upper terrace to the south, where the grandfather lived; before the closed chapel door (with Carlos being a fat pious priest); in the patio still farther back with the ruins of the old monastery stone bath; and in the pulquería.

So we were tired of snapshots, and leaned in a row over the roof to watch Don Genaro take his leave. . . . He leaped down the shallow steps with half a dozen Indian boys standing back for him to pass, hurled himself at the saddle of his Arab mare, his man let go the bridle instantly and leaped to his own horse, and Don Genaro rode hell-for-leather out of the corral with his mounted man pounding twenty feet behind him. Dogs, pigs, burros, women, babies, boys, chickens, scattered and fled before him, little soldiers hurled back the great outer gates at his approach, and the two went through at a dead run, disappearing into the hollow of the road. . . .

"That judge will never let Justino go without the money, I know that, and everybody knows it. Genaro knows it. Yet he will still go fight and fight," said Doña Julia in her toneless soft voice, without rebuke.

"Oh, it is barely possible he may," said Carlos. "If Velarde sends word, you'll see—Justino will pop out! like that!" He shot an imaginary pea between forefinger and thumb.

"Yes, but think how Genaro will have to pay Velarde!" said Doña Julia. "It's too tiresome, just when the film was going so well." She looked at Stepanov.

He said, "Stay just that way one little second," raised his camera and pressed the lever; then turned, gazed through the lens at a figure standing in the lower patio. Foreshortened, dirty gray-white against dirty yellow-gray wall, hat pulled down over his eyes, arms folded, Vicente stood without moving. He had been standing there for some time, staring. At last he did move; walked away suddenly with some decision, almost to the gate; then stood again staring, framed in the archway. Stepanov took another picture of him.

I said, to Andreyev, walking a little apart, "I wonder why

he did not let his friend Justino escape, or at least give him a chance to try. . . . Why did he go after him, I wonder?"

"Revenge," said Andreyev. "Imagine a man's friend betraying him so, and with a woman, and a sister! He was furious. He did not know what he was doing, maybe. . . . Now I imagine he is regretting it."

In two hours Don Genaro and his servant were back; they approached the hacienda at a reasonable pace, but once fairly in sight they whipped up their horses and charged into the corral in the same style as when they left it. The servants, suddenly awake, ran back and forth, up and down steps, round and round; the animals scurried for refuge as before. Three Indian boys flew to the mare's bridle, but Vicente was first. He leaped and danced as the mare plunged and fought for her head, his eyes fixed on Don Genaro, who flung himself to the ground, landed lightly as an acrobat, and strode away with a perfectly expressionless face.

Nothing had happened. The judge still wanted two thousand pesos to let Justino go. This may have been the answer Vicente expected. He sat against the wall all afternoon, knees drawn up to his chin, hat over his eyes, his feet in their ragged sandals fallen limp on their sides. In half an hour the evil news was known even to the farthest man in the maguey fields. At the table, Don Genaro ate and drank in silent haste, like a man who must catch the last train for a journey on which his life depends. "No, I won't have this," he broke out, hammering the table beside his plate. "Do you know what the imbecile judge said to me? He asked me why I worried so much over one peon. I told him it was my business what I chose to worry about. He said he had heard we were making a picture over here with men shooting each other in it. He said he had a jailful of men waiting to be shot, and he'd be glad to send them over for us to shoot in the picture. He couldn't see why, he said, we were pretending to kill people when we could have all we needed to kill really. He thinks Justino should be shot, too. Let him try it! But never in this world will I give him two thousand pesos!"

At sunset the men driving the burros came in from the maguey fields. The workers in the vat-room began to empty the fermented pulque into barrels, and to pour the fresh maguey water into the reeking bullhide vats. The chanting and counting and the rolling of barrels down the incline began again for the night. The white flood of pulque flowed without pause; all over Mexico the Indians would drink the corpse-white liquor, swallow forgetfulness and ease by the riverful, and the money would flow silver-white into the government treasury; Don Genaro and his fellow-hacendados would fret and curse, the Agrarians would raid, and ambitious politicians in the capital would be stealing right and left enough to buy such haciendas for themselves. It was all arranged.

We spent the evening in the billiard room. Doctor Volk had arrived, had passed an hour with Uspensky, who had a simple sore throat and a threat of tonsilitis. Doctor Volk would cure him. Meantime he played a round of billiards with Stepanov and Don Genaro. He was a splendid, conscientious, hard-working doctor, a Russian, and he could not conceal his delight at being once more with Russians, having a little holiday with a patient who was not very sick, after all, and a chance to play billiards, which he loved. When it was his turn, he climbed, smiling, on the edge of the table, leaned halfway down the green baize, closed one eye, balanced his cue and sighted and balanced again. Without taking his shot, he rolled off the table, smiling, placed himself at another angle, sighted again, leaned over almost flat, sighted, took his shot, and missed, smiling. Then it was Stepanov's turn. "I simply cannot understand it," said Doctor Volk, shaking his head, watching Stepanov with such an intensity of admiration that his eyes watered.

Andreyev sat on a low stool playing the guitar and singing Russian songs in a continuous murmur. Doña Julia curled up on the divan near him, in her black pajamas, with her Pekinese slung around her neck like a scarf. The beast snuffled and groaned and rolled his eyes in a swoon of flabby enjoyment. The big dogs sniffed around him with pained knotted foreheads. He yammered and snapped and whimpered at them. "They cannot believe he is really a dog," said Doña Julia in delight. Carlos and Betancourt sat at a small table with music and costume designs spread before them. They were talking as if they were going over again a subject which wearied them both. . . .

I was learning a new card game with a thin dark youth who was some sort of assistant to Betancourt. He was very sleek and slim-waisted and devoted, he said, to fresco painting, "only modern," he told me, "like Rivera's, the method, but not old-fashioned style like his. I am decorating a house in Cuernavaca, come and look at it. You will see what I mean. You should not have played the dagger," he added; "now I shall play the crown, and there you are, defeated." He gathered up the cards and shuffled them. "When Justino was here," he said, "the director was always having trouble with him in the serious scenes, because Justino thought everything was a joke. In the death scenes, he smiled all over his face and ruined a great deal of film. Now they are saying that when Justino comes back no one will ever have to say again to him, 'Don't laugh, Justino, this is death, this is not funny.'"

Doña Julia turned her Pekinese over and rolled him back and forth on her lap. "He will forget everything, the minute it is over . . . his sister, everything," she said, gently, looking at me with soft empty eyes. "They are animals. Nothing means anything to them. And," she added, "it is quite possible he may not come back."

A silence like a light trance fell over the whole room in which all these chance-gathered people who had nothing to say to each other were for the moment imprisoned. Action was their defense against the predicament they were in, all together, and for the moment nothing was happening. The suspense in the air seemed ready to explode when Kennerly came in almost on tiptoe, like a man entering a church. Everybody turned toward him as if he were in himself a whole rescue party. He announced his bad news loudly:

"I've got to go back to Mexico City tonight. There's all sorts of trouble there. About the film. I better get back there and have it out with the censors. I just talked over the telephone there and he says there is some talk about cutting out a whole reel . . . you know, that scene with the beggars at the fiesta."

Don Genaro laid down his cue. "I'm going back tonight," he said; "you can go with me."

"Tonight?" Doña Julia turned her face towards him, her eyes down. "What for?"

"Lolita," he said briefly and angrily. "She must come back. They have to make three or four scenes over again."

"Ah, that's lovely!" said Doña Julia. She buried her face in the fur of her little dog. "Ah, lovely! Lolita back again! Do go for her—I can't wait!"

Stepanov spoke over his shoulder to Kennerly with no attempt to conceal his impatience—"I shouldn't worry about the censors—let them have their way!"

Kennerly's jaw jerked and his voice trembled: "My God! I've *got* to worry and *somebody* has got to think of the future around here!"

Ten minutes later Don Genaro's powerful car roared past the billiard room and fled down the wild dark road towards the capital.

In the morning there began a gradual drift back to town, by train, by automobile. "Stay here," said each to me in turn, "we are coming back tomorrow, Uspensky will be feeling better, the work will begin again." Doña Julia was stopping in bed. I said good-by to her in the afternoon. She was sleepy and downy, curled up with her Pekinese on her shoulder. "Tomorrow," she said, "Lolita will be here, and there will be great excitement. They are going to do some of the best scenes over again." I could not wait for tomorrow in this deathly air. "If you should come back in about ten days," said the Indian driver, "you would see a different place. It is very sad here now. But then the green corn will be ready, and ah, there will be enough to eat again!"

William Spratling

SANTA SEÑORA

IT is on Sunday morning that Doña Petra Zaragoza transacts her business. Outside her house in the pleasant turmoil of a sunny market few of the townspeople give her a thought or have any idea as to what her business may be. They only see the poor peasants, fathers and sons, big sombreros gripped nervously in front of them, squatting outside or entering her zaguan. Her business concerns lands which lie in a score of remote villages.

The Doña Petra is a capitalist, even though not of the kind interested in stocks and bonds. More properly, she is a Mexican small-town capitalist, typical of the sort who are most fearful of appearance of wealth and spend half their lives in dissimulation of too-evident riches.

She is rarely seen in public and it is probably consciousness of her silver which prevents her walking and talking in the plaza with her neighbours, as all the world does here. When she does sally forth, a solitary figure in folds of voluminous black silk and enveloping rebozo of similar stuff, it is only to step across to the parróquia to confess to the priest or to sit with the Doña Victoria Ybañez and the other old ladies in their special little prayer stalls with their little tin candlesticks and their names all in gilt. There, of course, she is one of the

Honourable Guardians of the Sacred Image of the Virgin of Guadalupe.

Her house is the fine old shady one that occupies half one side of the plaza, between the big limestone archangel of the church corner and the pink and yellow front of Borda's palace. It is very dignified and very quiet.

The Doña Petra herself is very dignified and very quiet. Her bearing bespeaks the accumulated importance of seventy years of being rich and also maiden. She is fastidious. When she hires a new servant, for the first six months or so, they say, there is no such thing in her house as a single sweeping of her floors. Two, three, sometimes four times must the poor *pinche* bend her back to the task, and even then the Doña Petra will come along with little hen-clucking sounds and touch the palm of her soft white old hand to the surface just swept and order the creature, usually very young and dark and humble, to repeat the process yet once again. No one particularly loves the Doña Petra, yet few actually dislike her. The town in general is impressed with her. She is a long-accepted and familiar fact, to be regarded as one regards the ancient and elegant iron *reja* around the atrium of the church, or the inevitable and inscrutable hills above and below town where the silver comes from. But unlike those other local phenomena, one might live in Taxco for five years and not chance to see the old lady.

Her zaguan is the big blue and white gate, quaintly marbleized, that is between the Botica of Don Miguel Casarrubias and the pulque shop of the Señor Chavarrieta; her first-floor rooms on the street are always well rented for small shops. Within the big gate one glimpses red-tiled and vaulted passageways and the snow-white squat columns and arches beyond which is the compact green of plants in her garden, which is the patio. There are rows of bird cages of split bamboo attached to the walls of this court and in them sing *calandrias* and *tzintzontles* and *clarines,* birds called by ancient Aztec and Tarascan names, which have voices like exquisite flutes. Serving women are always in and out, busy washing, scrubbing, and interminably cleaning. When they sit in the late afternoons, the Doña Petra has them sew or embroider in order, as she says, that the devil may not perturb their thoughts with passions.

Upstairs the rooms are big and cool and darkened with Victorian plush curtains and lace next the windows. Plants are set along the balconies in the old black pottery they used to make forty years ago at the shrine of Guadalupe. In the corners of this *sala* are tall whatnots of apple and rosewood and in them, behind glass, securely locked, are contained Doña Petra's strangely assorted collection of bibelots. There are some beautiful pieces of old Spanish crystal, carved and gilded, miniature automobiles in silver filigree (1900 epoch), priceless old *talavera-de-puebla* majolica, and the spaces are filled in with modern doll sets of toy china, complete with miniature tin knives and forks. On the walls there are framed diplomas from ladies' societies in the church and several bad paintings of various virgins. And there are four rocking chairs with twisted arms, besides the usual dozen quaint little Mexican straight chairs which have woven bottoms and backs stencilled in gilt and silver indicating their owners' initials. These bear the legend,

NI ME PRESTO NI ME DOY
SOLO DE MI DUEÑA SOY
AVE AVE AVE MARIA!

which means "I" (in this case the chair) "neither lend nor give myself, belonging solely to my owner—ave, ave, etc." Which might have been written about the Doña Petra herself, so apt is it in expressing the sentiments of the mistress of the house.

It is more than twenty years since the old lady has been outside the town. Instead of visiting her properties she has the renters come in to her. No one knows just how much land she possesses, but it is all well scattered in small tracts, and for this reason the agrarians have not been able to confiscate and repartition any of it. In this she has had an enormous advantage over all the big hacendados of the region, who have lived to see their entire system of production supplanted. But then, too, the Doña Petra is a defenceless old woman and a maiden.

The Doña Petra wasted little time in changing the old manner of working which was her uncle's, when he died and left her the property. He was a sort of pioneer and believed in hard work and constructive methods. But she has eliminated all that. She does no planting herself, nor does she send to have it done; neither does she construct houses, though she always has a little lime or adobe or a few hundred tiles on hand to sell when offered a good price. The thing that most profoundly interests the Doña Petra is what the yearly rental of the lands is going to bring her in good hard pesos, and that they in turn continue to multiply. Also she enjoys hearing her servants refer to her as the *santa señora*. And she attends mass regularly.

The Doña Petra does not invest her silver, nor does she entrust it to the Banco de México. She is a sort of small banking institution in herself. She lends money and receives good security for it in land. Anyone may borrow money from her with the sole security of good land. Her interest rate is twenty to forty per cent a month, which is not uncommonly high in these parts.

Not since she was a young woman has the Doña Petra been in person to one of her villages. True, these trips are tiresome for a woman, but she has had her properties now nearly a lifetime and there are still people who can recall her regular visits to far off haciendas. Some people wonder how she can even remember which tract of land she is renting and which lies fallow. But the fact is that she does know and she does remember the boundaries of her well-watered fields in Cacalotenango and she even remembers the long tortuous path to Juliantla and Tlamacuzapa.

It was along that same road, a long time ago, that something occurred that properly belongs to the old lady's private history. Not that there was any scandal, and it may even be that the story is not true. However, knowing the Doña Petra and her countrymen, I suspect that it is true, and, anyway, I feel that if the details are a bit vague and inaccurate, something of a similar nature must surely have happened to her which would not be difficult to imagine.

She was very good-looking in those days, according to the old coloniales. She had smooth cheeks and firm legs and she rode horseback English-lady style when out inspecting her properties. She was infinitely more direct in dealing with her countrymen than she is now. She would pause on her trips to pass a word in greeting with all the small farmers and land-owners over there.

No one will ever know in how many good Mexican hearts she stirred passions. After all, how could they resist her strange blonde attractions when the only women they had known were all dark? Certain it is that no such thoughts passed through the mind of the Doña Petra. In her genera-tion, Spanish traditions still held. And even though she were Mexican, it had not yet become fashionable to admit, much less to exult in, a few drops of Indian blood. As for the Indian race itself, it existed only to work and produce for the class to which she belonged.

One day in passing on her way to Tlamacuzapa—it was at the crossing of a small stream where she invariably stopped to water her horses—she found, thrust in the fork of an ahue-huete tree, at eye level, a little flat rock scribbled on. It said merely SEÑORITA, and there was a flaming heart. The Doña Petra smiled, but took no further note of the thing.

Some fellow from the hills there was anxious to become her *novio,* to be her lover. Since not even the Doña Petra her-self ever knew him, his name remains unknown. It requires but slight effort to imagine what he was like. He probably worked a small milpa or ranch. He wore huaraches on his feet and a broad sombrero, given a certain style by the curve of its brim; on horseback he fastened it with a handwoven band of horsehair dangling under his jaw. His calzones were of white cotton and his shirt pink, maybe lavender. He belonged to that class of Mexicans whose faces are like Aztec masks, beardless, dark, like fine bronze. He had black, mysterious and childishly observant eyes. From time to time the dignity of his face would relax into a flashing smile, revealing incredibly white teeth and frank good humour. He considered himself the equal of any *catrín,* as the mountain people like to refer to people who wear town clothes.

There were no results from the first note so the boy wrote another.

The next time she passed this way recollection of the little scribbled stone flashed back to the Doña Petra. As she approached the spot she glanced toward the ahuehuete and there in the fork was another smooth flat rock. This time it was written all over, but nearly illegible, because the words had been merely scratched on the surface with another pointed rock. So the Doña Petra, with a mild access of curiosity, took the little slab of rock and put it in her saddlebag. She probably thought no more of it until she was back in her house in Taxco that night. Then she got it out and with difficulty deciphered it. It said, in gravely smooth Spanish:

SEÑORITA SINCE THE HAPPY MOMENT IN WHICH I FIRST SAW YOU I HAVE HAVE FELT AN ARDENT DESIRE FOR YOUR PERSON GOD GRANTING AND WITH THE AID OF SAINT PETER AND SAINT PAUL MAY THE DAY BE NOT LONG DELAYED WHEN YOUR BODY BE JOINED WITH MY BODY

One may only conjecture what may have been the Doña Petra's immediate reaction to his love note which did not speak of love. Certainly that night she broke the thin slab of stone in small pieces and scattered them. Perhaps it was no problem for her at all. The boy's note was serious enough, but it concerned earthy, basic matters and those things had never entered into the Doña Petra's scheme of things. She had never been—nor did she intend to be—in contact with the soil.

About that time, so they say, the Doña Petra ceased altogether to make trips to her villages. No one ever knew if there was a reason for this. However, she has often been heard to remark, even as she has remarked to me, that the Inditos—as she calls all descendants of the Aztecs—are all right seen in town, but that out there in their villages they are *muy naturales!*—indicating, as though there were a grave moral attached, that these little Mexicans are not only primitive but are given to "natural impulses."

William Spratling

VIRGEN DE LA LUZ

Greater, more colourful masses of flowers are carried to the little chapel of the Virgen de la Luz than to any other of the town's eleven shrines. Purple, white, and green orchids, *clavelin* in heavily odorous, thickly strung chains, *rosal, flor-de-los-muertos,* armfuls of lilies find their way there from far places. They enter by many and devious routes, including the twisting little passage dominated by the mass of the parroquia which is called in Aztec "Little Street of the Land of the Gods." Following that direction one finds the Virgin. To see her place and her people is to understand what has happened to religion in Mexico.

This shrine has that feeling of being at once simple, inscrutable, and vastly significant.

The image of the Virgin is a small chromo print, darkly stained and without glass. Even with the sun at mid-day outside it is obscure in the gloom, even less distinguishable for the matted accumulation of gold and silver *milagros* with which it is framed to the extent of several feet. This chapel is not a part of the Catholic church, neither does it pay taxes as belonging to its holy dueña, the venerable Doña María. It is something very special and apart.

Her shrine is particularly sacred to the Indians. They travel long distances, coming down from the mountains or up from the hot country below Taxco. Thousands come all unannounced and they bring tribute. The Virgin is worshipped unquestioningly by these dark, unemphatically moving people who decorously supplicate alleviation or who come to render thanks for favours received. She is a most powerful virgin and renowned for countless miracles. Hundreds of votive offerings, painted *retablos,* hung on the adobe walls of her humble chapel attest her willingness to oblige.

As in all the houses of the poor, there are no windows to her shrine. Only a door. It is so dark one must have a candle to make out the retablos. In one corner, the same colour as the sombre walls, sits the Doña María, piously, gravely squinting, occasionally scattering pecking chickens with a movement of her cane. There are many animals. Chickens mingle with cats and outside are roped mongrel dogs which snap at one's back. The entrance is dusty. There is nothing elegant or pretentious here.

The old woman, the Doña María, looks incredibly wise. Not merely wise but shrewd and cunning. Sitting there in her dingy gown she piously prays, interceding, with lengthy, placating words, for the benefit of a barefoot mother in rebozo who kneels with her home-made candle of brown tallow in front of the obscure chromo Virgin; or, as I myself saw and heard there one morning, she accepts a gold coin from a poor Indian and his young son, telling them as they stand there humbly with battered sombreros in their hands, that they must also bring oil, "*Eso es*"—oil is the thing!

Her role is more than that of priest, she is both intercessor and oracle. There is much more here than meets the eye. From where does the Doña María derive and how has she, a woman, achieved her holy office of priestess among a presumably Catholic people? One day she told me, in the same half-persecuted, pious voice with which the Doña Petra also speaks, that she has not been outside the house for twenty-five years—not since her holy mother died. Perhaps the chapel is an inheritance.

Socially, of course, she has no place in Taxco, no more than has the holy Niño Fidencio in Guadalajara. She is not of the people, she is of a world apart. And she is distantly removed from the conventional religious formula of the Mexican bourgeoisie. She is Taxqueña and she is mestiza; but her lot has been thrown with the Indians of pure blood, the *campesinos,* on whom depend her office and her sustenance. And she is well connected. Don Blas, the sacristan of the parroquia, claims cousinship. Her daughter is named María-de-la-Luz for her shrine. And she is an aunt of the Señorita Otilia, she of the cantina on the corner. Otilia would probably not advertise the fact, being at that ugly stage of social development where one tries to forget Indian tradition in order to become *gente decente.* It is a process akin to "crossing the line" among the habitants of Harlem. Neither extreme is bad, but the middle stage is one of presumption and a bad mixture of native with bourgeois taste. The women begin by treating their hair and using cosmetics, which are never quite right with brown skin. Men of this class, as a first evidence of the new order, leave off their gracious, comfortable huaraches for bulbous, shiny shoes, in which they can no longer walk with the quiet unpretentious movement of their race.

But the Little Indians who worship at the shrine of the Virgen de la Luz approach her with an immaculate simplicity. They are continuing, in all innocence, a religious impulse which certainly antedates the conquest, which is probably older than the Catholic church. They are the same people who have idols from the graves of their ancestors placed to guard their corn, who set up an image of Tonantzin, goddess of fertility, for the success of their crops. They call these idols of polished, finely carved green and black stone, *chanes*— spirits. The efficiency of these spirits acquires such fame that, among a community, they are frequently rented out for the season. In Huahuastla, in Titzicapán, in Tetipac these things exist. To these people it is no secret that for her service Tonantzin requires oil. . . . But more of that later.

All over Mexico these shrines exist. Presumably they are

private chapels about each of which has grown an aura of
faith in the miraculous. It is a strange compromise between
an imposed religion and embedded tradition. With the weakening of social and economic power of the orthodox church
their popularity increases. They seize the imagination of the
poor, providing a sense of intimacy, of proximity to the
Source. And their ideology unconsciously gravitates to that
which is, after all, Aztec.

That the keepers of these shrines are more or less venal
goes without saying. Their stock in trade, in the form of
milagros or precious metals and of painted retablos, which
attest marvellous cures, or rescues from bandits (or of bandits
from federals) or immunity from the bite of a serpent or ala-
crán, is incontrovertible evidence of supernatural and desirable aid. Their testimony is more effective than guide-book
recommendations. The shrines may be frequently brazen in-
ventions, becoming veritable gold mines for their owners. A
fancied apparition of a cross on the floor, an unexpected re-
covery, or a dream like a visitation, provide basis for origin
and capitalization.

The actual origin of the Doña María's shrine to the Virgen
de la Luz is a mystery. No one can remember the circumstances of the event. Her power increases day by day. But in
this unspacious adobe shack, sombre with votive offerings,
its floor of earth pressed by countless Indian knees, amidst an
atmosphere thick with the odour of the Aztec flor-de-la-
muerte and impure with the person of the revered Doña María and her horde of cats, Tonantzin, Mother of the Gods, still
lives and is well adored.

William Spratling

OF THE OLD REGIME

HE must have been nearly ninety. His mind harked back to the time of Carlota and Maximiliano and to the days when he was a child selling mangoes in the plaza. His job was more a matter of tradition than anything else. No one ever expected him to be exact. As a matter of fact, the tolling of the hours after eleven o'clock in the morning meant nothing. They were merely a pleasant sound, because Tata Luis, about eleven, had found his buddy, old Timoteo, and together they had gone for their morning cup of mezcal. From then on, they were in and out of the cantina, arguing and drooling and gesticulating. When he happened to think of it, Tata Luis went off to the tower and his bells, where, filled with a sense of high duty, he pulled heartily on the old ropes. It was not unusual for two o'clock to be rung three times and four o'clock was apt to be sounded thirteen o'clock. By three o'clock, he was on his way up the hill to his home and family and you could hear him all the way to Guadalupe if he happened to be in the mood for advising the neighbours. This was an almost daily occurrence and his querulous old voice, attempting to bellow at people, gave vent to all his most personal opinions about the world in general and his neighbours' wives in particular. Tata Luis, as he used to say himself, was as full of stories as a dog is of fleas. He would grasp my hand earnestly, telling me that he had much to talk to me about. Only what he had to tell were not stories, but endless chronicles. For him, the church was still the only institution in Mexico. Politics and government and education were just so much applied ornament.

We were in the bell tower one day and he waved his hand toward Tierra Caliente. In his day, he would say, the church was master of all the land, it needed no one's charity. Over there, he said, as far as you can see, all that was property of the church. And here below us, all the grand houses you see within a block of this church, all of them were of the church. What did the people do for land? I asked, ingenuously. Why, they paid a sort of gratification to the church, he said. And the church paid all its workers. Not like it is today. Everyone had some duty to the church. Some kept books, there were the sacristans, the choir-singers, the organist, even the official dog-runner. Yes, they had a *perrero,* whose office it was to keep the dogs off the church steps. He even had his holy uniform and a long whip. In the evenings he had to go through the cemetery, running out the dogs. Otherwise, they would dig up and eat the corpses of the recently buried. The workers were all paid.

Yes, he continued, they were all paid. But that didn't keep them from claiming property of the church in payment for salary, when Juarez came to sell the church's lands. There was Juan Mollano, the first sacristan. He kept that palace there by the plaza, which is now the jail. And Lorenzo Adán, he of the organ, he passed three houses on to his family. They all belonged to the church. It was that way with the uncle of Doña Petra Zaragoza. He had never had anything before. . . .

But my brother, he would never take anything. He was bell-ringer for thirty-five years. He died. Yes, he died, and he passed the job on to me. And the church has always paid us. It was a peso twenty-five centavos a week. Now they pay me one fifty—and don't think it wasn't hard work to get it. I had to beg for it and I even threatened to turn in my keys. For what can one do with one twenty-five a week these days.

His talk, like his life, was full of simple and profound incident, without any glory or any particular plot. He could have written an intimate history of Mexico since the days of the great liberator, but he could not even read. His face preserved the features of his land, of the rude cliffs of the Huitzteco and the hidden beauties of strange plants, like thoughts, in the interstices.

He lived through the thirty odd years of Díaz' reign without ever forgetting that he himself was a *religioso,* that this Don Porfirio was an outsider. It was as though it were just yesterday that Díaz and his army were arriving on top of the hill above town, asking permission to come in. He was in flight, coming down from Toluca, just beginning his amazing campaign, the same that finished in Oaxaca far to the south. Yes, he said, Don Porfirio had seventeen thousand men, but he sent his ambassadors to beg permission to enter this town. And then there was a council and Marcos Toledo, who was commandant then, sent him word that they were welcome to stay the night, but that they must pass on the next day. Díaz thought it was an ambush, so he waited. And it was nine o'clock and then it was ten o'clock and they had not come down. So Marcos took thirty men from his guard and went up the hill and talked to Porfirio Díaz, to tell him that they could come through. But Díaz disarmed him and his thirty men and he put them in the files under guard, and then he came down to occupy the plaza. He was here three days and there was fighting all the time. It took him that long to get forty-five men out of the towers of the parroquia. And each day they killed cattle for food, until there was none left in all the town. But Díaz lost six thousand men in those three days and he used up all his arms and ammunition. And when it was over he wanted to see the dead among the townspeople. But there were none. No, señor, there were no dead. . . . But yes, there was, there was one. He had his brains blown out by a cannon when he tried to get some mezcal from his house one night. (Tata Luis' statistics, as may be seen, always fitted the occasion.) When Porfirio Díaz left the town he conscripted every male inhabitant above twelve years of age. Yes, I was with them, and so were my three brothers. The rays of the sun poured down on us and there were many who fell and had to be carried. In one day we marched all the way to Tepecuacuilco in Tierra Caliente. Before arriving at Zumpango we brothers managed to get away. We would wrap our heads in our sarapes and simply walk off into the night. How well I remember that after walking all night, I climbed into the tall greenness of an *amate* tree and I tied myself there with rope. Yes, they say that Porfirio Díaz with that army went all the way to Tehuantepec. He passed by Tlapa and Huahuapam. And then Juarez died and Porfirio was President. But he never came back to this town. We never loved him here. Though he used to say that he would give ten soldiers of his army for one from here. . . .

But I remember much more than that. When I was just a *chamaco* there was Maximiliano and Carlota. They came down in their coach one time and, because my grandfather was the oldest man in town—he was a hundred and sixteen—they gave him a premium of silver. And I remember my father's brother. He was married to four women at the same time. He was truly a man. And he was chief of the plaza in Iguala. And just because he tried to help the other side with a little ammunition, they were going to shoot him. But his wife, his new one, came and she said to them, let me pay you not to kill him. And they laughed at her and they said, how do we know you can pay for him and besides how do we know what he is worth. So she said do not worry, you put him in the scales and weigh him equally with the silver I will bring. And it was much, much silver, because he was a man with a heavy shadow. . . . But he had had part in many revolutions. And just before that time he had been helping my general Salgado make silver pesos. That was here in the town and they coined them in the house where Don Jesús Llorado lives now. The silver they lifted from the mines at Xitinga and Atlixtac. Yes, they were badly made, but the silver in them was good, it had much gold along with it. And they were bigger than the federal pesos.

Tata Luis paused. The invitation was for a little drink—
meaning would I lend him the wherewithal. He came in and
we sat down to a bottle of Habanero. *Ay, que bueno!* he said,
this must be cognac. Any liquor other than mezcal would be
cognac. And this was certainly fine. He talked about the wine
they used to have in the church. The sacristan was always
"lending" him a pull on the bottle. But what a sacristan! It
seems there was something between Father Lupe, the priest,
and that man's wife. The sacristan always had wine, and
sometimes he sold it in Iguala, but no one thought anything
of it. The Father once tried to find out where his wine went.
He called everyone to solemn confession. But no one could
tell him anything about it. Then he remembered that the sacristan had not confessed in a long time and he said, My dear
Eulalio, for the good of your soul come and confess. All
right! They went to the confessional stall, the Father in his
little box and Eulalio outside. The Father listened to all the
sacristan had to say and then he said from his side of the grill,
but my son have you never taken wine from the church? The
sacristan said, I cannot hear, Father, what you are saying. I
asked, said the Father, if you have never taken wine from the
church. I still cannot hear you, Father, says the sacristan. So
the priest said, that is strange, let us change places, so that I
may see for myself what is the matter. So they changed places
and the Father said, now tell me again, my son, what you
said. And the sacristan said, when did you last see my wife,
Father? And then the Father said, Truly, one cannot hear. So
the sacristan received the Father's blessing and went about his
business. Tata Luis said that there was always plenty in the
family of the sacristan. God, he said, gives to those he loves.

He always spoke of serving God in the parroquia, but he
admitted that God moves about, from one church to another.
He said that the most powerful saint in the town was the
Nuestro Señor in the little church of the Holy True Cross.
That he was famous all the way to the Pacific and over into
the state of Morelos. Once, over in Acuitlapán, there was
such a drouth as never had been before. The Acuitlapeños
begged for the loan of the Nuestro Señor, and six men car-

ried him there on their backs. It was a two day trip over the mountains, but no sooner were they there than the rain came down in torrents. Truly, it was miraculous. But then, afterward, the Acuitlapeños wanted to keep the saint in their church, and there was fighting, but finally the men from our town carried him off triumphantly. There were no casualties among them, but among the Acuitlapeños there were three men killed and a señora with a black eye. After that, they always called him the Little General.

Again and again had the Little General been brought forth in procession so that the rains might come, and every time had there been a good downpour. Just last year, he said, as we brought him out from his shrine, there appeared a tiny cloud over the highest peak of the Huitzteco. We took him over to the church of San Miguel and from there to the chapel of the Ojeda and by the time we had reached the neighbourhood of the White Cross there was thunder and the clouds had joined themselves in dark array. And as we were passing the convent, it was already raining on both sides of the town. What was truly a miracle was that the waters fell copiously on every hand, except in the direction of the shrine of Nuestro Señor and there they left a narrow pass, quite dry, for his return. And though the waters fell we were not wet.

He said the Virgin of Guadalupe was strangely eccentric about bringing the waters, that once she almost washed the town away with a cloudburst when they had taken her in a procession. After that, he said, grinning, we brought out the Child Jesus when we wanted rain. That was so he could show his holy mother a thing or two!

His funeral was just at dusk. I had been off in the hills and as I approached the town I could see the flares of pitch-pine as the little single file of mourners rounded the knob of a hill this side of his house. There were three pieces of music, a violin, a bass viol and a flute, and they were playing some old-fashioned waltz. It was sad enough. As darkness crept over the scene it became a little weird. By the time I had reached the plaza they were already there. The coffin was resting on the cobbles, outside Rafael's cantina, and the women were grouped silently together. They looked as though they had been used to waiting for such things all their lives, standing there with black rebozos enveloping head and arms and shoulders in a single gesture and with one hand pressing the black folds of the garment across the lower half of their faces. The ancient Doña Clotilde, she who had borne Tata Luis so many children, who had quieted him so many times when he had returned drunk and shouting from this same little cantina, sat huddled on the stones of the pavement, her two arms covering her face and head. Not a sound came from her.

The coffin was very large and splendid, I thought, for the remains of one so poor and shrivelled as Tata Luis. It was of beautifully varnished red cedar.

As I returned to the plaza again after supper the cortège was just getting under way. Old Timoteo and his three companions came out from the cantina and very solemnly, staggering slightly, but not under the weight of Tata Luis, raised the coffin to their shoulders. The music struck up Sonny Boy and they were off to the Holy Field to bury him. The single file of women and children followed the coffin and the music and then came the rest of us. People in the street stopped to listen ceremoniously and raised sombreros from their heads, as a matter of course, as the coffin passed in front of them. There were two more stops for rest. Both times—it may have been by accident—the coffin was set down in front of a cantina. The pall-bearers and their friends sought liquid solace. Timoteo came forth from the last with a large bottle of mezcal sagging his coat pocket. . . . I recalled the story that it was this same Timoteo who, during the revolution, when Tata Luis was carried off bound to a burro by the Zapatistas to be executed, followed him and begged to be allowed to kiss his friend good-bye, and that he embraced him and kissed him on the mouth, passing him by that means a small knife. And that Tata Luis then managed to cut the cords with it and that he rolled over the cliff at Aguatitlan, escaping with his life.

At the burial ground, the coffin, shiny and resplendent in

the light of the pine torches, was set down and opened, the slender little old body which only partly filled it was taken out and wrapped in an old sarape and lowered without further ceremony to its final rest. . . . The coffin, it seems, belonged to the sacristan, who keeps it there in the church for this purpose, renting it for two pesos a burial, providing it is returned the same day and in good condition.

So we left Tata Luis, a servant of the church and of the old regime, one who had never presumed. He appeared no more formal in the wrappings of his old sarape than he had actually been in life.

Edna Ferber

THEY BROUGHT THEIR WOMEN

MURIEL is a name you cannot trifle with. She herself was like that. Even her husband called her Muriel. It was queer about her. Her skin was so fair, her eyes were so blue, her hair held such glints, that unobservant strangers, dazzled by all that pink and white and gold, failed to notice her jawline and the set of her thin red lips. They soon learned.

All the other youngish married women of her crowd were known by nicknames, or by cozy abbreviations—Bunny, Bee, Lil, Peg. Jeff Boyd's wife, Claire, actually was known to everyone as Hank Boyd, so that her own lovely name was almost forgotten. When first she had come, a bride, to Chicago's far South Side, Jeff had declaimed, "It's just a rag, a bone, and a hank of hair—a poor thing, but mine own." Hence Hank.

Then, as now, after nine years of marriage and two children, she was a skinny little thing: enormous brown eyes in a sallow, pointed face; white teeth in a rare grin; a straight bob; a beret hung precariously over one ear; her fists jammed into the shapeless pockets of a leather jacket against the stiff Lake Michigan winds. She was Hank Boyd to the whole crowd of steel-mill aristocracy living in the Chicago suburb that was a magic circle of green just within sight of the searing glare of the steel-mill chimneys—those stark chimneys bristling high above the slag-tortured Illinois prairie.

Muriel never called her Hank. She addressed her as Mrs. Boyd; or—somehow, it sounded even more formal—occasionally Claire. But Hank never called Muriel anything but Mrs. Starrett. "It—it's the long *u*," she said once, in unconvincing explanation. "Funniest thing. I can't pronounce it. I've struggled with it since childhood. I think I must have been marked, prenatally. I was sixteen before I could say funeral."

"Rilly!" said Muriel Starrett.

The two women, so nearly of an age, yet so unlike, probably never would have exchanged ten words had it not been for the friendship existing between their husbands. And that was strange, for the two men were as unlike as their wives. They had been classmates—Leonard Starrett, the son of a South Chicago steel millionaire; Jeff Boyd, a pseudo-Socialist, working his way through the engineering course with the help of a scholarship.

Jeff was not one of your gloomy, portentous haranguers. Gay, redheaded, loud-voiced, free, he was possessed of a genius for friendship. He talked too much, he made execrable puns, he ramped and roared; and was fundamentally as sound as Marx himself, and ten times as charming.

The first thing that welded the friendship between the two men was an accidental look at a portfolio of drawings Jeff had idly come across while waiting in Starrett's room at college. Leonard Starrett, entering hurriedly, late and apologetic, had found a red-faced and vociferous Boyd charging about the room, the drawings spread on every table, chair, cushion, and shelf.

"Listen. Whose are these?"

"They're mine."

"No, no, fathead! I mean, who did them! Who drew 'em!"

"I did." ·

"The hell you did!"

"Why not?"

"Say! Gosh!" He was so moved that Starrett was a little embarrassed.

They were drawings, in charcoal and in pencil, of steel-mill workers and their girls and their wives and their smoke-blackened dwellings. Hunkies. Bohemians, Poles, Hungarians, Czechs, Lithuanians, Negroes. There were men, stripped to the thighs, feeding the furnaces. You could see the muscles, like coiled pythons, writhing under the skin; smell the sweat; feel the strain of the eye sockets.

There were puddlers and rollers, in their shoddy store clothes and their silk shirts, their yellow snub-nosed shoes and round haircuts, the Saturday-night cigar between their teeth, standing on the street corner watching the high-heeled girls switch by. The watchers' Slavic eyes were narrower still, their lips more sensually curled. Their shoulders threatened the seams of their ridiculous clothing. There were big-hipped women in shanty doorways, a child at the breast. Through the open door a glimpse of a man sprawled asleep on a cot, in his mill clothes, his mouth open, his limbs distorted in dreadful repose.

"Holy gosh!" said Jeff Boyd again, inadequately.

Leonard Starrett explained, politely. "That one I call *The Boarder.* Couple of rooms, family of seven, then they take in a boarder or two. Half of them work on the night shift and sleep in the beds during the day; the other half work the day shift and they use the beds at night. Neat little arrangement, what?"

"Say, listen, Len. Len, listen——"

"I call this one *The Open Hearth,* which isn't very bright of me because that's what it is. The big furnace where the stuff flows out white-hot. It's called the open hearth. One splash and you're burned through to the bone. It's exactly like a Doré picture of hell. I love the name of it. So cozy and homelike."

"You mean to tell me you been doing those things and

never said a—Why, say, Starrett, you've got to exhibit these, see! Exhibition of original drawings by Leonard Starrett. Boy, won't Prexy sit up!

"Don't be dumb. I can't do that."

"Why can't you?"

"Can't."

"Now, listen. I don't know what I like, but I know about drawing. And you know's well as I do that these things are so good they're god-awful, so don't simper. Why, they're—they'll bust something wide open. You wait."

"I'm not simpering." He was gathering up the drawings and stacking them neatly into the portfolio. "My old man would have a stroke."

"Let him." Suddenly Jeff Boyd's high-colored, boyish face grew thoughtful and almost stern. "What're you doing here, engineering and chemistry and slop, when you can draw like that, my God!"

"Oh, these are just—amuse myself."

"Amuse, hell! This is important stuff and you know it. What's the idea—Papa'll have a stroke!"

Leonard Starrett hesitated a moment. Confidences came hard to him who had known a misunderstood childhood. He even looked a little sheepish.

"Uh—well, my father's a great guy but he's one of those from-the-ground-up boys. That's the way he began, and so that's the way he wanted me to start. Summers, since I was sixteen, I used to have one month in Europe and two months in the mills. Can you beat it! That's how I began to draw. When the time came for me to start here in the scientific end I got kind of desperate and blabbed I wanted to go abroad and study.

"I showed him and my mother some sketches—these, and some others. What a row! White hair in sorrow to the grave, and all that stuff. So I agreed to come here for four years, anyway, and learn to be a good little steel official. Mother took me aside and explained that if these things ever came to light they'd let Dad down the toboggan. I guess they might, at that. He got in early, of course, and made his pile, but he isn't one of the big shots."

Jeff Boyd lowered his head pugnaciously. "I'll tell you what. When you get through here, if your father's got enough soaked away to live on—which you damn well know he will have—and you don't go on drawing and refuse to go into the mills if they won't let you exhibit, I'll never speak to you again, so help me, for a white-livered, sniveling this-and-that."

But Leonard Starrett did not exhibit, and Jeff broke his oath, though the portfolio of drawings lay dusty and neglected through the months, through the years. For along came the war, and then along came Muriel, and then along came Junior. The big steel mills became monster mills, breathing fire and sulphur and gas over the sand dunes, over the prairie, over the lake, so that steel might be made wherewith Len and Jeff might kill the Germans and the Germans might kill Len and Jeff.

But the two came back, miraculously, whole; Leonard to his father's steel mills and to Muriel—Muriel so strong, so enveloping, so misleadingly pink and white and gold, so terrible in her possessive love. And Jeff took a job there in the South Chicago mills, for there was the postwar disillusionment, and there was Hank. And Leonard Starrett went back and forth between the roar of the steel-mill offices and the quiet of his big house facing the lake. And the boy must have this and the boy must have that and the Whatnots are coming for dinner and bridge and Oh, darling, what a lovely bracelet, you shouldn't have done it.

Jeff Boyd was known as a brilliant engineer, but too quick on the trigger, and what's this about his palling around with the Bohunks? He sounds like a Red, or something. His name came up occasionally and uneasily at board meetings.

"There's nothing red about Jeff except his hair," Leonard Starrett would say, smiling. "You pay him less than men who are worth half as much to us as he is. He doesn't ask for a raise. The Youngstown people would grab him at double the salary if he'd go."

Muriel protested, too, the sharp edge of her dislike sheathed in the velvet of loving pretense.

"Darling, I don't know what you see in that Boyd."

"That's all right, Muriel. You needn't."

"But it is important, in a way, dear, because it's kind of embarrassing for me. If you're a friend of his, and ask him here, I have to invite his wife."

"Have to invite her! Why, everybody's crazy about her. She's a wonderful girl. Jeff says she——" He broke off. "And she runs that house with one maid, sees to the kids, and keeps her job at the Welfare Station three full days a week."

"I always say, welfare begins at home. I don't think those Boyd children look any too well cared for, if you ask me."

"They're not Little Lord Fauntleroys, if that's what you mean." His tone was tinged with bitterness.

"Fauntleroy! You don't think I've made a Fauntleroy of Junior, do you?"

"You'll pin a lace collar and curls on him yet."

"You're not very kind, dear. But that's because you're not well. Goodness knows I'm not the sort of wife to come between her husband and his friends. But it does seem queer for you, whose father was one of the founders of the mills—they say the Boyds often have the Hunkies in, evenings, not for welfare work, but as friends, as social equals. They had four of the mill Negroes in to sing last week. Imagine!"

"Yeah, that's terrible. We met Robeson at Alice Longworth's in Washington last year."

"Oh, well, look at her father!"

"Yes. Low character he was."

"Darling, you hurt me very much when you talk like that, so bitterly. If you were really well you wouldn't do it. You couldn't."

It was a queer thing about Leonard's health. Muriel explained that he wasn't really ill. He was delicate. Not strong.

The least thing upset him. That was why she never left him. When he traveled, she traveled with him. I've left Junior many a time when it almost broke my heart. But a wife's place is with her husband. Leonard comes first.

Jeff and Hank Boyd sometimes talked of it. "He was strong as an ox at college. Crew man, and out of training could drink beer like a Munich Vereiner."

"It's her," said Hank, earnest and ungrammatical. "She wants him to be sick so that she can have him all to herself."

"That," he agreed thoughtfully, "and not doing what he wants. He has hated the mills for—oh, almost twenty years, I suppose. I told you about the way he can draw—or could. Well, you take twenty years of frustration, and believe me you've got enough poison in you to put you in a wheel chair."

"Can't we do something about her?"

"They hang you for murder in Illinois."

When the plan for the Mexican business trip first came up Muriel fought it like a tigress.

"Mexico! You simply can't go. I won't hear of it. Let them send somebody else. Why do you have to go?"

"Because we need what they've got, and because I think I can get it, and because we can't afford to overlook any bets these days and because the steel business, along with a lot of others, is, if I may coin a phrase, Mrs. Starrett, shot to hell-and-gone."

"That Boyd. Why are we taking that Boyd?"

He ignored the plural pronoun. "I'm taking Jeff because he speaks Spanish and because he knows more about manganese than any white man in North America and because he's a swell person to travel with."

"He won't be with us all the time, will he?"

"Now listen, Muriel. This is a trip you can't possibly take with me."

"But I'm going."

"It's impossible. You don't know Mexico. The altitude's seventy-five hundred feet. It's in the tropics. The air's cool and the sun knocks you flat. They say the food is terrible, you can't drink the water, the country's full of typhoid and malaria and dysentery." He was improvising and rather overdoing it.

When she set her jaw like that he knew it was no use. "I can stand it better than you can. I'm stronger. I come of pioneer stock. If my great-grandmother could cross the country from New England to Illinois in a covered wagon, with Indians and drought and all sorts of hardship, and if her great-grandmother could come over the ocean from England . . ."

He had heard all this many times. So had everyone else. Muriel was very proud of her ancestry. Her family had been "old North Side." Her marriage to Leonard Starrett, which had brought her, perforce, to dwell on the despised South Side, amounted in itself to a pioneer pilgrimage. Muriel, fortunately, was all ignorant of the fact that, among the more ribald of the younger mill office set, she was known as The Covered Wagon.

Her overweening pride of ancestry had once caused even Hank Boyd to show a rare claw. It was at a dinner at the Starretts' and Muriel had been more queenly than usual. In evening clothes Muriel looked her best and Hank her worst. Hank was the cardigan type. Muriel was all creamy shoulders and snowy bosom and dimpled back and copper-gold wave and exquisite scent and lace over flesh-colored satin. Hank, in careless and unbecoming black, looked as if she had slipped the dress over her shoulders, run a comb through her hair, and called it a costume. Which she had.

Muriel's blue eyes were fixed on Hank. There were eight at dinner—four North Siders of cerulean corpuscles; the Boyds; Muriel and Leonard. "You can't know what it means to one like myself, whose ancestors—well, I'm afraid that sounds like boasting—but I mean, when I read of all these dreadful, new, vulgar people crowding in, getting their names on committees, trying to push the fine old families out of their rightful place!"

"Oh, but I do know," said Hank warmly. Her voice was

clear and light. "At least, I can imagine how my ancestors must have felt."

"Your an——"

"Yes indeedy. There they were, down at the dock, to welcome the *Mayflower* girlies when they stepped off the boat onto Plymouth Rock."

Muriel allowed herself a cool smile as her contribution to the shout that went up. Then, slowly, that smile stiffened into something resembling a grimace of horror, as the possible import of Hank's words was realized. She stared, frozen, at the smiling, impish face, the eyes so deeply brown as to seem black, the straight black hair, that dusky tint of the bosom above the crepe of her gown.

"You don't—mean you've got Indian blood!"

"Only about one eighth, I'm afraid. My great-great-grandpappy, they tell me, was old Mud-in-Your-Eye, or approximately that."

It got round. Perhaps Starrett himself told it, or the jovial Jeff. For days it enlivened South Side bridge tables, dinner tables, golf games, office meetings. "And then she kind of stiffened and said, 'You don't mean you've got Indian blood!'"

Hank was a little ashamed of herself—but not much.

Leonard Starrett quietly went ahead with his preparations for the Mexican trip. So, less quietly, did Muriel. He might have uttered, simply, the truth. I don't want you. I want to be alone. Remember the man in *The Moon and Sixpence.* He did say something like this, finally, when it was too late.

"The firm won't pay your expenses, Muriel. This isn't a pleasure jaunt."

"Then I'll pay my own—if you won't pay them."

"How do I know how long I'll have to be down there! It may be a week, it may be a month. How about Junior? Planning to take him along, too, I suppose."

"Mother'll move right in for as long as we need her."

"Remember the last time, when we came home from Europe? She'd darned near ruined him. Now listen, Muriel. I

want to make this trip alone. I've taken a drawing room for
Jeff and me from here to St. Louis, and from St. Louis on the
Sunshine straight through to Mexico City. Please understand
that interior Mexico is no tourist country, no matter what the
ads say."

"I know more about it than you do," Muriel retorted. "I've
been reading Gruening and Stuart Chase and Beals and all of
them. I wouldn't let you go down there alone for a million
dollars, with your indigestion and your colds and your——"

"Stop making an invalid of me, will you!" he shouted.

"There! You're a bundle of nerves."

"Oh——"

"What kind of clothes, I wonder. They say it's cold,
evenings, and in the shade. Knitted things, I imagine, for
daytime."

Defeat.

Hank Boyd, when she heard of it, flushed in deep rage—
the slow, rare flush of the dark-skinned woman. "It's a rotten, filthy shame, that's what it is."

"Oh, I won't let her bother me much."

"I wasn't thinking so much of you—you'll have an interesting time, no matter what. But poor Len."

"I wish you were going along, Hank."

"No, you don't, dolling. Thanks just the same. Though
I've wanted all my life to see Mexico. Maybe, someday.
Maybe it isn't as dazzling as they say it is. But, Jeff, manganese or no manganese, find out all you can about the Indians;
you know—if they're really as superb as I think they are, after
the dirty deal Cortés gave them. Take a good look at the
Riveras in Mexico City—and the ones at Cuernavaca, too.
Find out if they pronounce Popocatepetl the way we were
taught in school. Betcha dollar they don't. If you bring me
home a serape, I'll make you wear it to the office. Those
things look terrible outside their native background. If there
are any bandits or shooting, you run. I don't want no dead
hero for a husband. I would relish one of those lumpy old
gold Aztec necklaces, though I understand you have to tunnel

a pyramid to get one. Don't touch water, except bottled. . . ."

Hank and some of their friends came down to the train to bid Jeff good-by. Two men and a girl. They were very cheerful. Muriel watched them from her drawing-room window as, at the last moment, they shouted to Jeff on the car platform.

"Good-by, dolling!" Hank called, above the noise of departure. "Remember, drink three Bacardis for me the minute you strike Mexican soil."

"Don't do anything I wouldn't do!" From one of the men. Then they all roared, as at something exquisitely witty. Then the four of them, arm in arm, began to execute a little tap dance there on the station platform, chanting meanwhile a doggerel which—Jeff explained, later—Hank had made up at the farewell cocktail party.

Tap-tap-tappity-tap.

> *If you would live a life of ease,*
> *Go hunt the wary manganese,*
> *The manganese so shy and yet so docile.*
> *The manganese it aims to please,*
> *The thing to do is just to seize*
> *Upon it, be it fowl or fish or fossil.*
> *The manganese . . .*

The train moved; the quartet began to recede from view. Muriel and Len, at their window, caught just a glimpse of Hank's face, the smile wiped from it. One of the men tucked his hand under Hank's arm. They turned to go. The train sped through Chicago's hideous outskirts.

"Well," said Muriel, taking off her topcoat. "She didn't seem to be very brokenhearted."

Jeff appeared in the drawing-room doorway. He had a lower in the same car. His face was wreathed in smiles.

"What a gal!" he said. "What a kid!"

"I was just saying to Leonard, you two don't seem to be much cut up at parting." Her voice was playful; her eyes were cold.

"The smile that hides a br-r-reaking heart." He glanced at

his wrist watch. "Well, I'm going in and feed the featyures before the stampede begins. You people coming in, or is it too early for you?"

"We had an early dinner before we left at six," Leonard said.

Muriel took off her hat, began to open a suitcase, rang the bell for the porter. She was the kind of woman who starts housekeeping instantly she sets foot on a train. "I don't eat any more meals on a diner than I can possibly help. Miserable, indigestible stuff."

Jeff laughed good-naturedly. "Ever since I could afford it I've liked to eat on a train. You'd think I'd be cured of it by now. I guess it comes of having watched the trains go by, when I was a kid on the farm in Ohio, with all the grand people eating at tables with flowers and lamps. I thought it must be heaven to be able to do that. I always order things you only get on trains. You know—dining-car stuff. Individual chicken pie and planked shad and those figs with cream that come in a bottle, and deep-dish blueberry tart and pork chops with candied yams. It's never as good as it sounds, but I just won't learn."

Leonard laughed. "That's the way to travel."

"Doesn't it make you sick?" Muriel asked primly.

"Sick as a dawg. That's part of traveling. You can be careful at home." He was off down the car aisle, humming.

"Where's that porter!" Muriel demanded. "If a drawing room can't get service I'd like to know what can."

By the time Jeff returned from the diner she evidently had got the porter, for the drawing room was swathed in sheets like a mortuary chamber. Shrouded coats, like angry ghosts, leaped out at you from hooks. Books were neatly stacked, bottles stood on shelves, an apple sat primly on a plate, flanked by a knife; an open suitcase over which Muriel was busy revealed almost geometric contents.

Jeff stood surveying this domestic scene. "Len, didn't you break the news to Muriel?"

She turned from her housewifely tasks. "News? What!"

Jeff grinned. "We get off this train, you know, Muriel, at

St. Louis, and take another whole entirely different train for Mexico City."

"This is nothing," Len replied for her, rather wearily. "Muriel puts up sash curtains and a rubber plant when she's in a telephone booth."

Muriel bridled. "I can't help it. I'm a home woman. And I'm not ashamed of it."

"You'd have a fit at the way Hank and I travel. But boy! Do we see things!"

Muriel sniffed. "We'll see you in the morning, Jeff."

"Say, what do you mean—morning! It's only eight-thirty. Come on back in the buffet car, Len. I met a fellow in the diner name of Shields. Lives in Mexico City. Knows the whole works. He says Mateos is square enough, but the Monterey outfit is crooked as a dog's hind leg. He's with the Universal people at San Luis Potosí. Quite a guy! He wants to meet you. Good idea, too, I think. Come on back."

"Now, Leonard, dear, you're going to do nothing of the kind. Sitting there smoking and drinking till all hours. You need a good night's sleep after the week you've had. You look perfectly haggard."

During the days and nights of steady travel that followed the change of trains at St. Louis, Jeff Boyd was up and down the length of the train and in and out of it at every stop of more than thirty seconds. He talked to passengers, conductor, waiters, porters, brakemen, and loungers at railway stations. He spoke Spanish, English, and bad German, as occasion demanded.

Muriel read and sewed. The scene in the Starrett drawing room was very domestic. Muriel kept the shades down about halfway, and a sheet across the windows because of the Texas glare and dust. She read books on Mexico. The very first day out of St. Louis, she had looked up from her book with a little exclamation. Then, leaning toward Len, she had pointed a triumphant finger at a paragraph.

"Listen to this, Leonard! Listen to what Gruening says." She began to read aloud.

"'The diversity between the two cultures south and north

of the Rio Grande is sharply discernible in the respective
status of their women. The North American settlers brought
their women. The squaw man was outcast. The exalted position of woman in the American ideology dates from the pioneer days of companionate hardship and effort. . . . The Aztec female, on the other hand, played the part of handmaiden
to the warrior male.'"

She looked up, beaming. "There!"

Len looked about him, one eyebrow cocked a little, as
when he was amused. "A drawing room on a limited train
may be your idea of companionate hardship and effort——"

He went back to his book. It was not a book on Mexico,
but a slim little volume given him by Hank as a parting gift.
Muriel had picked it up and looked at it. *Walden,* by Henry
David Thoreau.

"Well, what in the world did she give you that for!"

He had wondered, too, at her choice of the plain chronicle
of the man who had lived alone, in rigorous simplicity, at
Walden Pond. He had opened the book, idly. He read a few
pages. On page five he came to a line. Something shot straight
to his heart, so that he jumped a little, as though he had been
hit. Then he knew.

The mass of men live lives of quiet desperation.

"You seem to be enjoying that book Mrs. Boyd gave you."

"Yes."

Every two or three hours Jeff charged in, bursting with
facts valuable or fascinating or both. "That fat fellow with
the fancy vest and one arm used to be the richest man in Mexico. They got him in the Revolution and did they take him
for a ride! Burned down his hacienda, destroyed the crops,
chopped up a couple of daughters, shot his right arm off. . . .
Next time the conductor goes by get a load of him. He's
Mex, named Cordoba, wears a wing collar and a plaid tie
with an opal in it as big as your eye, and a gold cable watch
chain from here to here, with a sixteen-peso gold piece size of
a dinner plate as a charm. . . . Say, Muriel, if you'll take
down the Turkish-harem drape at the window and look at

what's going by, you'll learn more about Mexico than from any book on Mexico—*How to Tell the Flora from the Fauna.*"

At San Antonio they had had an hour and a half. The train drew in at eight. It would not leave until half-past nine.

"Come on, folks. Let's shake a leg. Get some of the train stiffness out of our bones. We can walk up into town, take a look around, and beat it back in plenty of time."

"Walk! At night! Through this district!"

Then it began in maddening futility: "But what do you want to ride for, Muriel, when we've been riding for days? . . ." "Well, you two go and I'll just wait here. . . ." "No, I wouldn't do that. . . ." "But I don't mind being here all alone at the station, really. I can just sit in the train. . . ." "A walk will do you good. . . ." "Jeff, you walk, and Muriel and I will take a taxi. . . ." "Good God, you can't see anything in a taxi. Besides, the idea is the walk. . . ." "What is there to see? . . ." "Well, good gosh, let's not stand here arguing, or none of us will be able to go. . . ." "Leonard, this porter says it's a good mile and a half to the main street. . . ." "Well, what if it is? . . ." "Now listen, fifteen minutes wasted . . ."

After the train passed the border at Laredo and they were in Mexico, Leonard put down his book to stare out of the window, denuded now of Muriel's protecting sheet. She continued to read, placidly, while all the stark, cruel beauty of Mexico went by. The mesa; a cluster of adobe walls and huts, half-naked children, dogs, chickens, mules; cactus as high as a man's head marching like an army of meager Indians across the desert; dusky women in pink petticoats and dark *rebozos;* swarthy men in dirty white pajamas, their unwashed, powerful toes thrust into rope sandals; enormous straw sombreros, brilliant serapes flung across shoulders; white fences; crumbling Spanish churches, pale pink and white and misty gray— and always, against the sky, purple at dusk, rose at sunrise, the Sierras.

"God, it's beautiful! I didn't know Mexico was so beautiful."

"Look at them!" Jeff explained. "Look, Len. Those are the

peons Rivera's been painting. Some magnificent, what! Makes you realize how darn good he is, doesn't it?"

Leonard Starrett said nothing.

"My, they're dirty!" Muriel exclaimed.

"That woman with the child slung in the *rebozo* and the jar balanced on her shoulder."

The hotel to which they went in Mexico City had been recommended because it was said to be clean and to have artesian-well water. These turned out to be its only virtues. In all other respects it was like one of those fourth-rate little Paris hotels on the Left Bank in which the chambermaids run up and down the corridors on their heels, doors and windows slam, voices bellow or screech across the echoing court, and the mysterious custom of hurling what seem to be stove lids occurs every morning at five.

They could eat nothing there, though Muriel took her morning coffee and orange juice in her room. Len and Jeff breakfasted at Sanborn's, in the Avenida Madero. After three days of visiting other recommended restaurants, Muriel insisted on Sanborn's three times a day. In its American-Spanish patio hung with red velvet and bird cages she found, in all Mexico, the cleanliness, the familiar American language, and the creamed chicken, buttered beets, and apple pie to which she was accustomed.

"But this isn't Mexico," Len objected. "Might as well be eating at Childs. The other restaurants are full of people who seem healthy."

"'When you're in Rome——'" quoted Jeff.

Muriel was adamant. "At least you're not getting malaria and typhoid. Those other places are impossible."

Jeff said she had pleasantly condensed two hackneyed sayings into the single "When you are in Rome, do as the Romans do, and die."

Jeff bounded off alone. He tried them all—native restaurants, open-front cafés, cantinas and *pulquerías*—while Len accompanied Muriel drearily to Sanborn's. Jeff took a good deal of bicarb, but he ate all the fearful native dishes, the frijoles, the enchiladas, the tortillas. "Hot dog! They burn the vitals to a cinder. Len, you got to taste *mole de guajalote*. Turkey cooked in twenty spices, any one of them guaranteed to eat a hole through asbestos." He even drank pulque. He insisted that they go with him for cocktails to a place he had discovered called Mac's Bar. He was enthusiastic about it. "Mac's an Irishman. He's lived in Mexico for forty years, without leaving it. He speaks of the United States as 'the old country.' Wait till you taste his Mac Special."

It turned out to be a dingy little vestibule of a place. Muriel said she certainly didn't think much of it. Jeff seemed a little chagrined and even bewildered. "I don't know. I guess I was wrong. I thought it was swell before. It doesn't seem like much. I guess it was just——"

They found time during that first week, occupied though the two men were with their business, to make a short trip or two. They lunched well in the sun-drenched patio of the inn at San Angel, once a monastery. They drifted down the Xochimilco canals and came home with armloads of violets and roses. They whirled down the dusty roads across the plains to the pyramids at San Juan Teotihuacán.

Leonard Starrett, long silent as he looked out at the Mexican countryside unfolding before their eyes, said slowly, "It's more mysterious than Egypt."

"Egypt's finished and done. This thing's just begun. You can feel the Indians boiling and seething underneath. Someday—bingo!"

Muriel looked about mildly. She was very careful to protect her fair skin from the straight rays of the Mexican sun. "Mysterious! Why, I was just thinking it looked a lot like the places outside of Los Angeles."

Muriel had a tiny camera, not more than four inches square. With it she took pictures of pyramids, mountains, rivers, cathedrals, and plazas. She had difficulty in pronouncing the Mexican names.

"Just call everything Ixcaxco," Jeff cheerfully advised her, "and let it go at that."

After a week Leonard came to her in some distress. "We're not getting anywhere. At least, we've just made a start. They don't do business here the way we do at home. They talk for hours. They only work about four hours a day. Jeff and I will have to be here a month, at least—maybe longer. I'd like to put you on the boat at Vera Cruz. They say it's a beautiful five-day trip. You'll land in New York, take the Century home, and we'll all be happier."

"I'm sorry my being here has made you and your friend unhappy."

"Oh, Muriel, for God's sake!"

"Please don't think I'm enjoying it. But I know what my duty is. And if you have to be here a month, I'm going to look for an apartment."

"No!"

But for the next three days Jeff, stricken with dysentery, was wan and limp. That decided it. Muriel, with the aid of an agent, found an apartment in a good new building just off the magnificent Paseo de la Reforma. It was the apartment of some Americans named Sykes. They were returning to the United States for three months. Sykes was a mining expert. Mrs. Sykes showed Muriel all over the place. Very nicely furnished, and in good taste. A grand piano. There were even some good American antiques. A mahogany four-poster, a drop-leaf table, a fine old couch.

"These have been in the family for generations," Mrs. Sykes explained. "I'm very much attached to them. That's why I've never rented this apartment before, to strangers."

"I understand," Muriel said, with some hauteur. "I am a member and, in fact, an officer of the Pioneer Daughters of Illinois."

"Oh, well, then," Mrs. Dykes said, reassured. She looked happily, pridefully, about her at her dear belongings. "You'd never know you were in Mexico, would you!"

Muriel repeated this to Leonard and to Jeff as she, in turn, showed them the apartment. "You'd never know you were in Mexico."

"You certainly wouldn't," they both said; and roared with laughter.

"What's so funny about that?"

Mrs. Sykes had left her servants with Muriel. "They're very good," she had assured her. "As good as you can get— in Mexico. Jovita—the bigger one—she's rather handsome, don't you think?—is the cook. She's a—uh—I mean to say, she's a very good cook. She's used to having her own way. I wouldn't interfere with her if I were you." Then, as Muriel's eyebrows went up, "I mean, unless you're used to Indian ways—yes, she's Indian, and very proud of her ancestry— you might not understand. She does all the marketing."

"I always prefer to do my own marketing. It's the only way to get the freshest, the best. In Chicago——"

"But this isn't Chicago. Mexico is different. They wouldn't understand. Another thing. You'll find she sometimes has one or two of her children here for a day or so. They're very quiet. She has four."

"Oh, she's married!"

"No."

"Oh, I understood you to say four——"

"Jovita has four children, of four different fathers. She has never married. She does not believe in marriage. She is the finest cook in Mexico City. She used to pose for artists. She is highly respected. I wouldn't part with her for the world. I'd rather not let the apartment, really, if you——"

Muriel related this to Len and Jeff, expecting from them masculine indignation. They seemed impressed, but not in the way she had expected. At their first dinner in the new apartment—Jeff dined with them—she saw the two men regarding Jovita, who assisted Lola in serving. The Indian girl, Jovita, bore herself magnificently. Her eyes were large and black; her skin was a rich copper; her bosom was deep; her shoulders were superb; her hair was straight, black, abundant.

"I really don't feel quite comfortable about Jovita," Muriel confided to the men, as they sat sipping their very good coffee, after dinner. "Having her here in the house, I mean."

"Well, I shouldn't think you would," Jeff agreed, with a great laugh. Muriel said, afterward, that she never realized how vulgar Jeff was, until the last two weeks. You really have to travel with people to know them.

Besides Jovita and Lola, there was the Indian boy, Jesús. Muriel had objected to the name, but Mrs. Sykes had assured her that it was very common in Mexico among the Indians, and that he would be terribly offended if called by another name. The three servants were capable, quiet, and rather consistently dishonest about small things, according to American standards.

"Custom of the country," said Len. "Don't fuss about it. You're not going to live here. Take it as it comes."

"Jeff is always talking about how magnificent the Indians are, and how the race has survived in spite of everything, and how they'll rule someday. A lot he knows about it. If he can tell his precious Hank about her cousins the Indians I guess I can tell her a few things, myself."

Muriel was horrified to learn that Jovita usually slept on the floor of her little bedroom, rolled in her blanket, instead of on the very decent little cot bed provided for her. The boy, Jesús, had conceived an enormous and instant liking for Leonard. They discovered that he was in the habit of sleeping outside their bedroom door, like a faithful dog.

"I'd like to send them packing," said Muriel, again and again. "The whole dreadful kit of them. Oh, how wonderful it will be to get back to my own lovely clean house, and to Junior, and to Katy and Ellen, and a good thick steak and sweet butter and fresh cream and waffles and a big devil's food cake with fudge icing."

They had asked Jeff to share the apartment with them, but he had declined, a little embarrassment in his high-colored, boyish face.

"It's mighty nice of you to want me. But I think I'll just stay on at the hotel. I kind of like to bum around the restaurants and cafés and streets. I like to see the way the people live, and talk to them. But if you'll ask me to dinner once in a while I'll certainly appreciate it."

Muriel, with her fine, fair skin, her coils of copper-gold hair, her plump, firm figure, attracted attention when she went out alone. She was accustomed, at home, to walking. All her Chicago friends walked for the good of their figures. She found that almost always now she was followed home by some amorous Mexican.

Her admirer always used the same tactics. He would pass and repass her. He would double on his tracks. He would appear at unexpected and impossible corners. She would think she had evaded him. She would jump hurriedly into one of the crazy little Ford taxis marked Libre. But when she reached her own flat there he would be, miraculously, lounging against the building, in his bright-blue suit, his feet, in their American tan shoes, negligently crossed, a cigarette between his slim brown fingers.

She complained to Leonard and Jeff about this. "Horrid creatures!"

"Hank would get a kick out of that," Jeff grinned.

"I suppose she would."

"They don't mean anything," Leonard assured her. "It's the Latin way of showing admiration."

"They frighten me, the nasty leering things."

"Try taking Jovita along as bodyguard."

"Oh, well, if that's all you care. I don't understand you lately, Leonard."

"It's the altitude," fliply.

The servants made her nervous. They were in and out of the room without a sound. She would look up from a letter she was writing to find Jovita standing there, silent, waiting.

"Goodness, how you startled me. What is it?"

Jovita spoke very little English, understood a little, thanks to the Sykeses.

Jeff came to dinner two or three times a week. He and Jovita would speak together in Spanish. Suddenly Jovita's dusky, impassive face would grow vivid with a flashing smile.

Muriel didn't like it. "What are they talking about?" she demanded of Leonard.

"He's going down to Milpa Alta on business Thursday. She heard us talking and caught the name. She's telling him it's her native village, where two of her children are. She says it's very beautiful, and that there is a festival down there next week—an important festival when everyone dresses up and there are fireworks and dances and big doings. Let's all go."

"Don't be foolish, Leonard. Those festivals are childish and stupid; the sun blazes down; you can't eat the filthy food, nor drink the water. You know it as well as I do. It's a mercy Jeff has been able to take the necessary business trips into the other districts. I'm glad, now, that you brought him along. I'd never have let you take them. Never. You would have, though, if I hadn't been here. You're like a child. Really, sometimes I think you need as much looking after as Junior."

"Yes," Len said thoughtfully. "I would have taken all those trips into the country, by motor and by mule, with the hot sun beating down by day and the cold coming on at night; sleeping, perhaps, on straw mats on the floor of some pueblo hut—if it hadn't been for you."

"Well, then! And the way Jeff looked last time. Remember? Though you can't tell me that was only the hardship of the trip."

Jeff was off to Milpa Alta. If this trip proved successful they could leave at the end of the week; the last, then, of their six weeks' stay. Jeff would be gone four days.

Next morning Jovita was not there. She simply was not there. No word, no explanation. Lola and Jesús shook their heads, spread their palms in innocent denial.

"I'll tell you what I think," said Muriel, with the abrupt coarseness of the good woman. "She's gone down there to be with Jeff, that's what I think."

"I hope so," said Leonard.

"What do you mean, Leonard Starrett!"

"I was just thinking."

"Thinking what?"

"I was just thinking how pleasant it would be to live for a year or two with Jovita in an old pink house, with a garden, in Cuernavaca, and paint pictures of the Indians, and of Jovita and her children, and sit in the sun, and in the evening look at Popocatepetl and the Sleeping Woman against the sky."

"Leonard Starrett, have you gone crazy!"

"A little," said Leonard, "a little. But not enough."

Jan Gabrial

VOYAGE TO THE SHORES OF CUAUTLA

TRINIDAD walked through the open door of the wineshop that was called "El Tigre," moving in a slow and deadly way, as though inside she were hung with the weight of each moment that had elapsed since Pablo left.

The wineshop was small and dark, and behind the long counter, which served also as a bar, were stacked row on row of the barrels of sweet wines.

Through the doorway from the back room of the shop came Bernardino, and when he saw Trinidad his solid face fitted together more closely and he moved forward and put his fists down on the bar and looked across at her without speaking.

"They are in Cuautla," she told him harshly.

Bernardino looked over his shoulder and called into the back room. "Arnulfo," he called.

Arnulfo came through the door and stood just inside it, lounging against the frame, a cigarette between his lips. He stared at his father, ignoring Trinidad.

"They are in Cuautla," Bernardino said. He turned back. "Go on," he said.

"They have been there ten days. I know the house. I can tell you where it is."

"You will come with us," Bernardino said.

She wrapped her shawl more tightly about her face. "I have work here," she said. "My Señora. . . ."

"We do not do this thing alone," said Arnulfo, speaking to her for the first time. "He is your husband, Pablo. Luz is Bernardino's wife."

"You will come with us," Bernardino said again. He wet his lips.

It could be that it was right so, Trinidad thought. She had wanted to come in here when she heard where Luz and Pablo were, to come in here and tell Bernardino and then to go away again, and let what she knew must happen be apart from her. But it could be it was the task of both of them, of her and of Bernardino, and she bowed her head, saying nothing. The bitterness and the pain and hatred welled so fiercely in her that the very skin upon her bones felt taut, stretching to cover it.

Bernardino opened a drawer in the counter and took out a gun and placed it in the pocket of his coat. He looked at Arnulfo, who was watching him.

"Now," Bernardino said, and there was a kind of triumph in the way he spoke.

Arnulfo took the cigarette from his lips with his thumb and forefinger and sailed it out past Trinidad in a curving arc, through the doorway to the street. He looked like the North American film star—what was his name?—Bogart. He was older than Luz, he was the son of Bernardino's first wife, and nothing like Bernardino, who was a rock in a man in motion.

"Together we do this thing," said Bernardino to her. "If we do it right no one knows afterwards, and then no one will ever know, because we do it together, you see, and we none of us will forget we are doing it together."

"I do not like the gun," Trinidad told him. "It is not animals you are hunting. A man carries a knife."

"A man carries what he has," said Bernardino. "I am a

man of position. I have no wife, perhaps, but I have a gun. And I take this gun with me."

Some of the hatred welled up towards him. "I do not like it," she said, loud and defiant. "That you should understand at least I do not like it."

She went out into the street to wait for them. They joined her presently.

"We will take the truck," Arnulfo said. "On a bus we would be perhaps remembered. We will take the truck, loaded as it is now. There are deliveries to make. When we return we will make them. Should there be any questions later on."

She stood with him before the shop and Bernardino went around to bring out the truck. It was a very old truck, a 1920 Dodge, with one seat in front, roofed over, and an open body piled with the barrels full of wine. She climbed in and Bernardino moved over towards her and let Arnulfo take the wheel.

"Cuautla, you say?" Arnulfo repeated.

"Cuautla," she said. "I know the house. It is on the outskirts, well on the outskirts. We had better leave the truck in town and walk from there."

The truck fumed noisily and started down the dusty streets towards the highway.

It was like the one that ran as bus between Acapulco and Pie de la Cuesta, where she had been born. When she had married Pablo, eight years before, she had ridden for the first time in such a truck, riding from the Pie, beside its broad beautiful lagoon, back to Acapulco. She had wanted to stay there, near the beat of the sea and the smells it threw up towards the town, with the sounds of singing from along the shores in the bright evenings.

That was before the children came, when she was eighteen, as full and soft as Luz, as mixed with laughter. That was when Pablo was porter at the Miramar Hotel, restless already, with plans so complex that she could not comprehend them. A bar, he told her . . . yes, a *pulquería*, . . . in the City of Mexico they would have a *pulqueria*. . . .

He was telling that to Luz no doubt, now, at this moment, and Trinidad's face, which had relaxed with looking backwards, hardened again, and she folded her hands more relentlessly in her lap. The shawl about her head slipped but she did not bother with it.

"I did not stop at the Señora's," she said to Bernardino. "I should have told her I would be away this day. She is expecting lunch."

"She is *Americana*," said Arnulfo. "Not so strict as the others. You can think of something to tell her later on."

Beside her Bernardino stretched, and she could feel the tremendous muscles of the man beneath the heavy curtain of his flesh. Silent and purposeful he sat beside her, consecrated, as were they all, to this day for which they had lived a fortnight, this moment of fulfillment leading them towards Cuautla.

And towards the house—

As the truck careened over the cobbles she saw the house once more, knowing each board, each corner, and every wave of the corrugated roof, for in this house she had herself lived for three years with Pablo and the children, when they came up from Acapulco. Two of the niños had been born there. Pablo had been attendant at the mineral pool near by, and there was a little land where they had made a garden. Chucho and Pepe and Maria had been the niños' names. And for one three-years' time she had thought only of their days together, like a consistent act of love. In the dark months that followed it had seemed to her they lived out all their lives, not just the niños, but Pablo as well, and she, there in that place, and that they had nourished it with their brief happiness.

Afterwards, after the niños' deaths, when Pablo refused to stay there any more, they had moved on at last to the City of Mexico, but the house remained. A house of death, a house of evil fortune. And now Pablo had gone back to it, with the Luz of Bernardino.

With a harsh gesture she gathered the shawl about her face. They were on the road now. The Tepoztlan Mountains loomed ahead, clear and sharply etched, then they were in the Canyon of the Wolves. To their left, granite mountains rose bitterly, to their right sank the dark, muttering ravine; the truck steamed on, noisy and insecure.

"We must have water," Bernardino said. "We must stop in Yautepec."

He sounded eager now, and Trinidad could feel the purpose that carried him everywhere in his formidable life beating out in this truck, like a web winding about them. Blood did not flow in his veins, but pride and inflexibility.

She looked at him squarely, and the eyes he turned towards her gleamed with kindness; sweat stood on his forehead, and in the ridges around his mouth was a gathering content.

Meeting his eyes she thought that, consecrated though they might be to this act of vengeance, all else between them was wary, tense. I too would have gone away from him, she thought. Or else I would have somehow killed him first.

Arnulfo began to whistle, softly, smoothly, as though he were near a girl who was pretty and whom he wished to win over and possess. There was something appalling about the silky way in which he whistled. It was not love of Luz, but love of punishment—whereas with her, revenge was the continuation of her love.

And thinking this, she remembered the night when she had known—

It had begun three months before, at fiesta time, on an evening when she had walked in the plaza with Pablo and they had encountered Luz, alone, wide-eyed. Bernardino, she told them, was busy in the wineshop, and she was lonely.

They had stood together beneath the Ferris wheel, she and Pablo and Luz, and the wheel had sailed up into the sky, and hesitated, sailed down, and stopped.

"Come," Pablo had said, taking her hand. "Come, we will ride up there, no?"

"Oh, no," she had protested. "You go then. But I am afraid."

"I am not afraid," Luz cried, laughing, lonely. "You do not mind, Trinidad, if I go up there with Pablo? It is so lonely . . . see how near the stars. . . ."

And she had smiled, content and sure, sorry for the little Luz.

Then one night, two weeks ago, she had risen, restless, more than restless. She had put on no dress or shoes, but softly had gone down to the gatekeeper's house where Pablo slept, thinking to creep in and lie beside him and wake him with her body. She had moved so quietly that at a little distance even she could hear the voices.

They were not voices raised in conversation, they were more sounds than voices, and one of them was Pablo's, but one—she had stopped then, naked in the darkness, appalled and confused, listening and aghast, and at last had crept back to her room, crouching down in her bed as though never again would she be warm or safe.

I must not let on to Pablo that I know, she had thought desperately. I must not ever let it come out in words between us. If it will only pass.

That was what she had decided, despite the fury that battled with her judgment, but it had all been useless. For in the morning, Pablo was gone, and Luz.

It was then that the hatred had begun, she thought, feeling it steadying her once more as they rattled across the old bridge into the town of Yautepec.

They stopped for water and for gasoline.

"It has one door, this house?" asked Bernardino. "There is no back way, perhaps?"

"One door," said Trinidad.

"We will move up," said Bernardino to his son, Arnulfo, "quietly, you see. You on one side, I on the other. When they run I will shoot."

At the ominous excitement rising in his voice, Trinidad fought with an impulse to protest, and growing in her too was dread of how they might carry out their vengeance.

Dread was no new companion, but this was unlike the fear

which had walked beside her for the past four years, which had taken hold in that tragic house in Cuautla. That was a fear of insecurity, even of life, which had been worst in the City of Mexico, where Pablo and she had been unable to find work, where their money had slipped away, peso by peso, till they were sleeping on the streets with the other lost, forgotten ones, and where the searing winter had brought dreams of Acapulco and its warm, blue sea.

But she had prayed to the Virgin of Guadalupe and the Virgin had brought them to the Señora Bell who had given them jobs with her in Cuernavaca. And gradually the fear had lessened and the insecurity began to ease away.

Then Pablo spoke of leaving. To take work in a *pulquería.*

For the first time, he became to her incomprehensible.

"Here we are safe," she wailed. "Here we can make a life— niños. Oh, Pablo, here we have all we need!"

He grew argumentative, then he grew sullen, and finally apathetic.

"The *pulquería,*" he insisted doggedly. "The *pulquería.* . . ."

And from the constant battle he had withdrawn at last. With Luz, who was young and who had not yet tasted fear.

They passed the hacienda of San Carlos with its old aqueduct, and drew into an arid stretch from which the vision of the volcano, Popocatepetl, gleamed on the far horizon.

A doubt was gnawing at the edges of Trinidad's mind: she had wanted security for herself, but what meaning did it have if it was not for man and wife, if it was not for both of them?

They passed two villages and now at last they were approaching Cuautla, and an equal tension possessed them all.

As they drew up beside the railroad station, Trinidad saw on their right the plaza, vivid with jacaranda and mamey.

"How far?" said Bernardino, turning to her.

"Maybe two kilometres," she said. "Maybe a little over. Maybe three kilometres."

"We will park here then," Bernardino said.

When they climbed down from the truck, she hesitated. "I

will tell you where it is," she said to Bernardino. "I will tell you how to get there. I will wait here for your return. I have thought, Bernardino; I do not wish to go."

"Tell us then," Bernardino said, not looking at Arnulfo.

"You go west," Trinidad said. "It is outside of San José, near the mineral springs. You cross the old bridge at the Cuautla River and the road ascends. When you can see Popocatepetl you then turn right." She spoke almost dreamily. "The first house, quite apart. There is a plaque of the virgin above the door. . . ." She stopped.

Bernardino turned to Arnulfo. Arnulfo nodded. "I will know it," he said.

"Here, then," said Bernardino. She sat upon a nearby bench and her strength flowed out of her as she looked at them. "Here," she said faintly.

"Good," said Arnulfo, and they started off.

She sat as if carved from stone; there was a ringing in her head and something was wrong too with her breath. She put one hand to her throat and the fingertips felt icy and wet and she swallowed against them. Here in the plaza, on this very bench, she had so often sat with Pablo and the niños.

"*They drank milk, do you see?*" the doctor had said to her. "*It was the milk, do you understand, it was the milk that caused the illness.*" But she had not understood. Milk was good for the niños. Everyone knew that milk was good for the niños.

Hands fell upon her shoulders and she jumped. She looked up. Bernardino and Arnulfo stood beside her.

"You must come with us," Bernardino said. "It is what was decided."

"We do not do this thing alone," Arnulfo said. "You must come with us too."

The confusion settled into a desperate wish for flight. They were smiling at her strangely and she knew that she was trapped by them, but she said, speaking very slowly, "I will wait here. I will sit here."

"You will come with us," said Bernardino, and his fingers tightened upon her shoulder.

"You understand," said Arnulfo, looking at her tensely.

She rose. She moved down the street beside them as if by instinct only, and out to the west they walked together towards the town of San José.

Along this route Pablo and Luz had moved.

If they would give her the knife, not the gun but the knife, she would go forward alone and erase what had taken place. But this was not to be her act—she was an instrument like the gun, a weapon. . . .

Ahead of them the bridge stretched over the Cuautla River. In wary silence they crossed together and reached the road which ascended through lemon and banana trees, and then on the horizon rose the peaks of the volcanoes, startling and white and sharp.

Trinidad's mouth was dry as the dust on which she walked, and there were bands within her head which were destroying thought and will; she made a desperate effort to break them, to regain control, and then her feet slowed and she stopped where she was. For ahead of her rose the house!

Bernardino jarred her shoulder and she came alive, sucking her breath in with a gasping cry, and started forward, and began to scream, running and screaming, shrieking and running, "Pablo, Pablo, take care—Bernardino and Arnulfo—Pablo, take care, take care."

Her voice rang out high and vibrant and into it she put all of their lives, the nights on the Acapulco beaches, the days they had played with the niños here, the nights in the City of Mexico when they had suffered together. "Pablo," she shrieked, "Pablo, watch for yourself!"

She fell. Bernardino, leaping past her, had struck her violently, but it was Arnulfo who paused to draw from his belt the slender knife and thrust it brutally, his face distorted with fury, into her side. She fell forward and lay there, her eyes open and fixed upon the house, with no strength now to move.

The two men, dimmer in her sight, threw the door back and plunged in and she tried to scream again but something was wrong with her voice. She dug her nails into the earth in an agony of watching.

. . . the garden was so overgrown . . . it should have been kept up. . . .

The men came ploughing out, baffled and violent. They circled the house and went for a way into the fields, still searching.

Then they came back and stood near her and she could make out a little of their conversation.

Pablo had gone. She closed her eyes and lay more heavily. Pablo and Luz had gone. Restless as ever, Pablo had moved on.

When she opened her eyes again, Arnulfo and Bernardino were gone from sight. She tried to move but she was far too tired. She gazed instead at the house. But the house wasn't important any longer because in some way that she couldn't bother now to understand, she could feel peace.

Her fingers, clutching the earth that had been their garden, relaxed a little, and she laid her face against it.

Jan Gabrial

NOT WITH A BANG

A SOUND of fumbling and stumbling and shuffling began outside the door (all her life Catherine would associate such sounds with Michael) and her heart pounded wearily, and she turned in the bed, her mouth half open in protest and her brows drawn close together.

A key was fitted into the lock and then the door swung inward and two bellboys appeared, half propping Michael up between them. They stared roundly and sheepishly at her, the pale hair covering her shoulders, the robe on the other pillow.

"Here is the Señor," one of them said proudly. "Here he is once more Señora, the Señor."

Michael drew himself up and flung them off, straightening his shoulders with drunken dignity. "What the hell do you think you're doing?" he shouted, and stalked over and sat heavily on the bed.

Catherine roughed back her hair with one hand and the other bellboy said confidentially, "We could hardly push the Mister into the elevator."

"That's a goddam lie," Michael said. His mouth was heavy and loose in his swollen face.

Catherine looked in between the bellboys and said carefully, "Thanks very much. He'll be all right now. You can go."

"Just a proper tin Jesus, aren't you?" Michael said.

The bellboys bowed and swung out.

"I might have known it," Catherine said without bitterness. "I might have known the one night I'm tired enough to go to sleep at nine o'clock I'd be honored by a visit. I haven't any money, if that's what you want. We're out of money. We don't get a check until tomorrow. Tuesday, remember? You get your father's checks on Tuesdays."

Michael stared at her analytically. His sea-blue eyes were almost buried in the liquored flush of his cheeks. "A wife," he said. "A wife is a legally kept woman who eats you out of house and home. So I have to have a wife."

"It's the luxury of it," Catherine said. "After you hocked both my working cameras, I settled back into a life of ease." She waved her hand around the disordered room. "Mexico City," she said. "The Paris of the Western Hemisphere."

"You're a great woman," Michael said extravagantly. "You're the greatest woman in the world, but why the hell do I have to listen to you?"

"I'm the tiredest woman in the world," Catherine said. "Period."

"Tired!" Michael echoed. "Tired, oh my God!"

"Why don't you come to bed?" she asked him reasonably. "Why don't you get some sleep?"

"Sleep?" Michael said, shuddering. "But that I should answer a cry of yours with a counter cry must show you how fast nailed I am to the eagle-baffling mountain."

She sighed and edged down further in the bed. "Night life," she said. "I don't know how I do it. Last night you came in at one, the night before you came in at five, the night before that you didn't come in and I waited for you. If it means anything," she said, studying him gravely, "you look like Saint Sebastian when they'd been shooting arrows at him."

"I feel like Saint Sebastian," Michael said, "when he was very dead."

He had been holding his coat bunched up on one side, and now he drew it apart and peered within and turned back to her and laid a finger on his lips. "Don't talk so loud," he said warningly. "You must be very quiet. It's asleep."

She was beginning to shiver in the badly heated room. As she reached for her robe she watched him. His face had taken on a look that was profound and sly. "It's asleep," he said again, very tenderly.

A feeble wheeze came from beneath his coat, belying him.

"Michael," said Catherine, "what have you got there? What is it, Michael?"

He smiled gently at the coat and her heart contracted.

"It's a dog. A little, little, little dog who is cold and tireder than you will ever know how to be."

He opened his coat and laid on the bed beside her a small black-and-white puppy, a few weeks old, a puppy with black ears and a black nose and nervous, agonized black eyes. It lay where he had put it, shivering.

"A man on the street," Michael said thickly, "was selling it. I bought it for you."

The puppy had started to sniff about the bed; suddenly it planted its four small legs more firmly. Catherine snatched it up and dropped it on the floor, where it whimpered loudly.

"Look," Catherine said, "you don't have to sleep here. You practically never sleep here. I do."

"It's such a little, little dog," Michael repeated.

"It isn't a question of size," Catherine said. "It's a question of I have to sleep in this bed and they only change them once a week."

"You are a bitch," Michael said violently. He bent over and picked up the puppy and held it in his arms. "It's everything I have in the world to love," he said. "Everything I have in the world and that's all I have. My wife is a legally kept woman who is only after what she can get, with an eye on every man who passes."

Catherine put both hands to her head and shut her eyes. "There are all kinds of women," she said harshly. "Some of them like dogs. Some of them like husbands. I'm funny that way. I don't want a small dog that isn't housebroken in place of a husband whose whereabouts I don't know for days at a time."

She was beginning to cry inside and she knew that it meant that the need was there, as it was always there; that she wanted Michael, wanted his nearness and his tenderness. But he wouldn't give her that. He would give her a dog, a symbol, saying in effect, "This innocent, helpless, gentle creature is your husband Michael; look after it and mop up after it and cherish it and give it your protection."

"Michael," she said, "oh but Michael, don't you see—"

But he was already getting up, bundling the puppy back underneath his coat, swaying a little on his feet.

"I love you," he told her with excessive firmness. "God damn it, how I love you, because you are a wonderful woman. I am not doing anything destructive. If you would only understand that I am not doing anything destructive."

He began to make his way carefully toward the door.

"Michael," Catherine said remorsefully, "stay, Michael. We'll keep the dog. Don't go."

He didn't answer her. He pulled the door open, teetered back on his heels for a second, then strode out into the hall, slamming the door upon her.

When he had gone Catherine sat in the bed, very still, feeling as though the world had gone away and left her in emptiness.

The picture of him striding out the door, with his face set and lonely, rose up a dozen times so that the empty, quiet room was filled with Michaels, turning in misery from her on her seat of judgment.

And crying a little with weariness and pity, she thrust the covers away and slid from bed.

When she went out of the hotel, the bellboys stared at her, and the night clerk half leaned across his desk as if to ask her to call upon his competence. But she pushed through the doors of the hotel into the bitter night of the Avenue of the

Fifth of May, and stood, holding her coat about her face, de-
liberating: just where would Michael be?

A list of bars had formed within her mind and one after
another she visited them: the hotel bar, a near-by saloon,
Mac's, Paolo's, Butch's Manhattan Café. Michael had been
to none.

Then she remembered a cantina they had sometimes gone
to, in the small streets back of the Teatro Nacional, where
children lay at night, huddled upon the pavements, with
posters torn from the walls and newspapers gathered from
the gutters piled over them for a memory of the warmth of
sunlight. She hailed a cab and gave the address of the Maria y
Marta.

Her emotions were suspended within her now, suspended
in anxiety like a foetus in alcohol, stillborn, insistent, waiting. The night took on an unreal quality and the taxi, as if in a
dream, sighed through the streets of the great quiet city.

As it pulled up she saw Michael sitting on the pavement a
little to one side of the cheerlessly lighted entrance, his coat
bundled beside him. His head was in his hands and he looked
forlorn and somehow inevitable, as though all the days of his
life had prepared him for this moment of sitting on a curb on
this street of violence and tragedies, as though there were no
further place for him to go, as though the pages stopped here
and there wasn't any more.

Catherine walked over and touched his shoulder; he didn't
move, didn't raise his head.

"Michael," she said, and squatted down beside him.

When his white gaze had focused on her he stared, but he
still said nothing.

"You'll be cold," she said. "Put on your coat, you'll be
cold. I followed you, Michael," she said, putting her hands
upon his knees, trying to hold his stare. "Why do we do these
things? why do we do them to each other, Michael?"

"You're a good person, Cathy," Michael said. "But you
can't tie the wind to a cliff. The rock has claimed your
Sisyphus."

"Michael," she urged him, "oh Michael, please. I get so desperate. I'm lonely. You shut me away from you."

His brow puckered and his voice came faint and lost, bewildered. "I?" he said. "I shut you away? Oh, little Cathy, oh, God, help me then."

"I can make you happy if you'll let me," she cried out to him. "I can. I have. I don't know why I want to go on doing it, but let me, Michael, try."

But he shook his head, so slowly that every movement seemed to cost tremendous effort. "It isn't any good," he said. "The trimmers, not good enough for heaven, poor devils, not bad enough for hell. It isn't any use."

"Oh, Michael, you're so *wrong*," Catherine said desperately. But he had set his face backward in time.

"Michael," she said, speaking now very softly to him. "Michael darling, remember the good things, the good parts of our life together: our winter in Taos; the old reading rooms in the library where we worked; the party Ben gave for your first book of poems; Martha's Vineyard, where you taught me to play tennis. . . . Oh, Michael, all of it, like a tapestry—you can't renounce it, it's woven all through us. It's a part of us."

Michael's hands covered hers. His finger tips were icy. "The hotel room at Lake Patzcuaro." Now he was looking at her.

Her laughter pleaded with him. "And when we turned, the bed sighed like a wind, and we could see the butterfly boats out on the lake."

"Tzintsuntzan," Michael said. "Place of the Humming Birds."

He caught up her hands and put them across his eyes. She could feel tears behind them. They might have been children abandoned together in hostility.

"Won't you come home now?" she asked almost humbly. "Won't you come home at last? I can't go on asking you, Michael. Please come with me; we won't talk about anything that's happened."

He sighed and she could feel the tortured breath against her wrists. And then he put her hands away from him.

She waited, and she could feel him going past her, the moment going past.

"No," he said. "No," clinging to this resistance because resistance meant that he was still a man. "No," he said then more loudly like a child.

She let her hands fall in between her knees. "Well, put your coat on. Please put your coat on anyhow."

He looked down at his coat. "The little dog," he whispered. "It's asleep."

She had forgotten about the dog. She started to open the folds of the coat, but he checked her, trembling. "No," he protested. "No. Don't you understand, it's asleep. You must let it be asleep."

"It must be smothering, Michael. Let me just look at it."

She pulled the folds back and the little dog, its head on its paws, peered at her, moaning plaintively.

"It isn't asleep," Catherine said. "Michael, it's sick."

"It's asleep, I say. Oh, damn you, it's asleep."

She laid her hand on the dog and was shocked at the cold tremors of its body. "Michael, feel it yourself, it's too chilly for it here. Take it into the bar, then. Please, Michael, take it inside, please."

"I love it," Michael said, beginning to break, his voice beginning to break, to sing with tears. "It's all I have to love. I'm all it has. It's my little dog," he sobbed. "It's my little dog. I love it."

"You have me," Catherine said. "Don't you know you have me, Michael?"

"You?" he said. "But you want it to die. You want everything I've ever loved to die. You've always wanted it. God and I and the pigeon who is the eye of God, we see through everything, we see through you."

She tried to pick up the dog but he struck her hand away. "Let it alone," he shouted. "Let it alone, you hear? You think you can control me, don't you? You think you can manage me, don't you? You think I don't see it? Well, let me tell you, I know everything. Because I am a great person, you see? I am a great person, all my life I am a great person, even though the stupid, mealymouthed, crumbling little bellboy people will want to destroy me for it." He grew a little quieter. "You are a great person too," he said, "but you waste yourself. God, how you waste yourself!"

"Oh, all right, then," Catherine said. "So I waste myself. But take the dog inside, anyhow. Or put your coat on. Or something, Michael, *please.*"

"Oh, to hell with your chatter," Michael said, stumbling to his feet. "Chatter, babble, chatter, babble, that's all you do." He gathered up his coat, holding it and the dog closely beneath his arm, and scowling and muttering, staggered into the bar.

After a moment Catherine followed him.

It was a small cantina that had seen several murders and that stank of urine. Four booths lined one wall and there were scattered tables in the center; unshaded bulbs glared from the ceiling. Michael went directly to the bar and put down his coat upon it and summoned the bartender.

"Tequila," he said loudly. Then he looked at the man next to him and put an arm on his shoulder. "And one for my friend here. Two."

The man had a stubble of beard and wore the blue jeans of a workman. He looked surprised but pleased, and he smiled at Michael ingratiatingly.

Catherine sat at a small table that was near-by. I could use a drink, she thought. I don't have to get drunk but I could certainly use a drink in the worst way.

"Parras," she called, and the barman brought her a small glass and a larger one that held carbonated water. She looked about her as she drank the liquor.

It was early but there were already a few people there. Michael was pointedly ignoring her, but at a near-by table a dark good-looking man, probably half Indian, was staring with interest, and when he caught her glance he smiled.

She looked away, but the man's face stayed in her mind, hanging there in the foreground of her thoughts like the grin of the Cheshire cat.

I could show Michael, she thought. It would help me to put up with Michael and I might get a night's sleep for a change. I could show Michael, she thought again, bitter because he had resisted her when she was open to him. Then she thought, I'm really too tired to drink. So I'd get back at Michael. I'd wake up tomorrow in a strange room with a guy I couldn't talk to. It isn't much good if you can't talk to him afterward. I ought to know.

She knocked on the table and the bartender brought her another drink. The dark man was looking at her half expectantly. She frowned at him, and his glance grew hurt and surprised, and he looked abruptly away. There, that was that. She had frowned at him.

Michael was telling the man at the bar that he had flown in the Battle of Britain. Every time he gets drunk enough he flies in the Battle of Britain, she thought; it's a substitute for action. He always comes down in flames because even his visions must be couched in self-destruction.

Then as she looked at him, she noticed with an awakening shock that while his right hand, holding his glass, was waving, his left hand and arm were leaning on the coat. And she was sure that in that moment she could hear the pitiful gasping whimper from within. She set down her glass and ran up to the bar.

"Let me alone," cried Michael as she tugged at his arm. "Let me alone," he cried, suspecting fresh rebuke, and he pressed his left hand more firmly on the coat.

The puppy was suffocating; she could hear its gasps, its long faint struggling breaths.

"The dog," she said. "The dog, Michael—you're hurting it, Michael, you're choking it!"

He raised his left arm then and struck her; the back of his hand caught her across the neck so that she staggered backward and grabbed at a chair to save herself from falling.

The man in the blue jeans seized Michael's arm, looking shocked and unhappy.

While they were struggling, Catherine flung back the top folds of the coat; the puppy was shaking terribly; suffering stood out in every line of its tiny feeble body; its mouth was open, and its eyes—looking at nothing—were partly shut and dull; the piteous sounds came irregularly from its small wet throat.

"It's dying," Catherine cried, feeling the horror in her. "Michael—it's dying—don't you understand?"

"It's thirsty," Michael said desperately. "That's all, it's thirsty. Water!" He turned to the bartender. "A little water," he called, "for my little dog."

But as the puzzled bartender turned for the water, with the other man standing watchful in case Michael should break out once more, the puppy struggled and its head sank forward against the roughness of the coat; the noises ceased, and it lay still, and alien.

"It's asleep now," Michael said. "Never mind the water."

"Michael," Catherine whispered, "don't you see—it's dead."

"That's a damned lie!" Michael shouted in agony and loathing. "It's asleep, I tell you! Look!"

She gazed in desperation at the bartender. He touched it and looked at Michael firmly. "*Muerto,*" said the bartender. "Dead. Dead, Señor. Yes."

Michael's mouth opened childishly. He looked as though he were about to cry. "But I loved it," he insisted, as though that could make all the difference. "It's my little dog. I was going to look after it."

Catherine turned her white face toward him and stared at him, at all the things in him she had cherished, which had grown stretched and loose in his flight headlong from the meaning of life, his backward flight to a lost world on which the walls of history were closing.

And she thought. Already it is happening to me. I catch

myself thinking that if I sleep with the man in the dark shirt I can get back at you.

He turned on her, his voice harsh with his own fear. "You wanted it to die," he stammered, "you want to destroy everything that loves me, you think I don't know—"

The dark man at the table had risen, as if in readiness; the man in the blue jeans was standing watchful; the bartender looked tense. But Catherine stared dispassionately at Michael, as though he were an enemy whose strength she was now gauging to protect herself.

"—You think I don't know you are destroying *me!*"

One day all of it cracks, just like this, and falls away, and you discover yourself enmeshed in a jelly of pity for the man you married, and making that your life. . . .

"But God and I," Michael said, "and the pigeon who is the eye of God—"

She walked over to the table and put down the payment for her drinks. Then she went out into the street without another look at him.

She wanted to think ahead to life, but the thoughts wouldn't come.

And then, across the surface of her mind—I hope they don't steal Michael's coat. . . .

She stopped, staring before her into the night. But I don't have to worry about that any more, she told herself. I don't have to worry about Michael any more at all.

And harshly, violently, she began to cry, because she knew that the boat that was Michael had slipped its moorings in her life, and was even now putting out to the darker sea to which she could not follow him.

John Graves

THE GREEN FLY

I N the one-room cottage he had rented at the rear, near the stream and the steep-rising green mountainside, Thomas Hilliard awoke each morning early, sometimes at six with the clean tolling of the bells in the village below, often before. An old man named Celestino brought fruit and rolls and coffee from the kitchen at the main house of the hacienda; and afterward, Hilliard would walk a few minutes along the stream, watching for fish, then would go back to work until noon at his typewriter.

In the thin, high foreign air, undistracted, his mind moved spiderlike, weaving and linking with a precision that he had not really expected; the work went well. Though he had half agreed, laughing, when Wright Forsythe had told him that Mexico was a hell of a place to go to finish a dissertation in English literature, it nevertheless went smoothly and fast. Within a few days his existence at the hacienda had shaped itself into a life, a backwater life without conflict or crisis or betrayal, to last only until Wright and Deirdre drove down to join him later and to take him back northeastward, but a life, full enough.

There was the fishing. In the afternoons Hilliard fished, because for a man who prized trout it was beautiful fishing, the best he had known. It flavored that life indispensably, and when old Dr. Elizondo came, it was through the fishing that they met at the start, and the fishing gave their meeting its meaning. In the rich water of the rapids and pools, in the small dammed lake at the stream's end, before it plunged to the valley below and the river, the trout moved thick among broken walls and aqueducts and insignificant stone masses that had had use in the long-gone days. The Mexican families at the hacienda, clumsy with worming gear, took small fish by the basketful, but in the smooth water of the pool-heads the big rainbows lay haughty and selective. It needed a pretty fly on a long, fine leader, deftly cast from downstream, to hook them.

No other Americans came. Hilliard did not miss them. Within the formal limits of his acquaintance with them, he liked the pleasant, prosperous Mexicans vacationing in the other cottages and rooms. In the evenings by the fireplace in the big house they would talk, quietly and with their friendly foreign distantness, to one another and to Hilliard, enduring with grave humor his faulty Spanish and the incomprehensible fact that he spent half of each day flourishing a *caña* over the stream.

They came and went away and one evening in Hilliard's third week a new man appeared at dinner, graying and bald-ish, alone, with a strong Iberian nose and tawny well-shaped eyes that gazed, afterward in the sitting room, with remote gentleness into the fire while the others around him talked. Then the next day Hilliard, casting into white water where the stream debouched from a jumble of huge weathered build-ing stones into a pool, glanced up to see him watching from the bank. In that moment the line twitched and Hilliard raised his rod tip against the tug of a stout fifteen-incher that thrashed up and down the pool before coming finally ex-hausted to the net.

"*Bien hecho,*" called the man on the bank.

Smiling, Hilliard wet his hand and held the fish up for a moment for the other to see before he shook the fly from its lip and dropped it back into the water. For a moment, spent, it hung there and then with a drunken flirt of its body rode the current downward out of sight. Hilliard waded ashore.

"You released him," the man said, in the flat courteous Spanish manner that is neither statement nor question. In the sun he looked older, his face hollow, leathery old-man's wrinkles radiating from the corners of the alert, almost golden eyes. He was dressed to fish, in a tie and a rusty black coat and patched wading boots, and held a long, old-fashioned English fly rod with close-spaced silk windings. Before that battered old-world formality Hilliard, in khakis and glittering American equipment, suddenly felt shabby.

He said, "I let most of them go. What I care about is the fishing."

Nodding, the old man smiled. "They're noble fish. Permit me. I am Juan Elizondo."

Hilliard took the old, slim hand and then, with the ease of strangers who share enthusiasm, they talked for a while. The doctor—he said he was a doctor, and fished little nowadays—asked politely, in measured Castilian, about the personality of the stream and its trout. Of specific spots and lures he said nothing and Hilliard, watching him finally trudge off downstream, the long rod bobbing, comprehended the painstaking pleasure he would find in learning those things for himself.

And from that meeting—because, as the doctor remarked later, no one else at the hacienda was insane enough to possess an *afición* for angling—a mannered, mild comradeship sprang up between them. On the stream they met often to smoke and talk, nearly always of fish, and in the evenings by the fire. They traded flies, the doctor tied his own, European patterns strange to Hilliard, which he whipped together deftly and with care. "*Esta,*" he would say with love, holding up a gaudy tuft of tinsel and peacock herl. "This one. She did much killing on the Gallego. My colleague, Aguirre, used to call her the Green Traitor."

That sufficient basis for friendship widened itself without effort on Hilliard's part. From the voluminous morning gossip of old Celestino he learned that the doctor was Spanish, a Republican *refugiado;* it explained the coolness, the distance apparent between him and the upper-class Mexican guests. Having listened well in good places, Celestino knew also that the doctor had once been a surgeon very noted, Señor, but now, with exile and political discredit, was lucky to have work in the medical office of a tile factory, in Puebla. Devoutly religious, the old servant found pleasure in the fact that the doctor was poor, and that his wife and daughter in Madrid, *franquistas,* did not write him, not a word. . . .

Hilliard said curtly that morning, ashamed to have listened, "All this is none of my business, or the señora's, or yours."

Celestino, making the bed, patted a pillow. "*Pos, quizá,*" he said equably. "Maybe. But the suitcases of this doctor, how barbarous. You should see."

Talking to the doctor himself, Hilliard had other glimpses of a past that had been clearly busy, full of high accomplishment. Vienna-trained, he had traveled through all Europe, and had fished most of it. "The medicine and the sport were companions," he said, smiling. "Sweethearts. With the scalpel, the rod."

That with their association the other guests' coolness toward the doctor came also to envelop him did not disturb Hilliard. He understood it, so well that when the señora, the unworldly patrician widow who owned and operated the hacienda, approached him about it he nearly avoided anger, nearly but not quite. He liked the señora. She stopped him in her office, a tiny room baroque with the sculptured furnishings of Diaz' day—at the hacienda they were all *porfiristas,* forty years out of date—and when he grasped what she was saying he flared at her with a quickness that brought terror to her diffident, velvet-wrinkled face. She was trying, unskillfully, to draw him out about the doctor—no, Señor, he had done nothing, but she felt . . .

Hilliard said, "Then why did you let him come here, Señora?"

Her shy hands writhed against the black silk of her skirt. "Don't mistake me, Señor 'Illiard. He was sent by a friend in the capital. A cousin, but with acquaintances most strange . . ."

Hilliard, opening the office's carved door, said with finality, "*Pos.* He is more *caballero* than anyone I've seen here. They won't suffer."

"I meant only . . . you're American. You can't know."

"Yes, I can," Hilliard said. He had seen fights between Spaniards in Mexico City cafés and, though they were not his people and it was not his fight, had felt the acrid, hating pain still knife-sharp after a dozen years. As much as one could understand others' hatreds he thought he understood, as he understood also the señora's sequestered fearfulness, but when it touched the doctor it made him somehow furious. "*Con permiso, Señora,*" he said, and as he went through the door she answered with the automatic, "*Pase usted.*"

It aligned Hilliard. The doctor had begun—when, he did not notice—to call him by the familiar *tu,* like a son. They ate together now in the dining room, at a corner table, and he knew, without always being able to say how, a great deal more about the old man.

The Forsythes had been good friends to him. Wright Forsythe, seven years older than Hilliard, was one of the young emergents of the university's faculty, and it had been important that someone like that should have taken keen interest in him—almost as important as that a warm and graceful woman like Deirdre Forsythe had made him welcome always in her home. They were intelligent and balanced each other in a life built around the quiet, unexuberant luxury of inherited money, and they had treated Hilliard as a younger brother.

And yet, he had never thought of them apart from the university and its town, so that into that hypnotically pleasant regularity of work and fishing and friendship with the old doctor, the letter that came finally from the Forsythes, already in Mexico City, arrived as a mild shock, as though he had forgotten them—almost, he had. The letter came on a Wednesday, ten days before the doctor was to leave, and when he had read it Hilliard sent off a wire by the hacienda's rickety telephone, telling them to drive up immediately. At lunch he told the doctor. "I'm content to hear it," the old man said in his courtly Castilian.

"You'll like them," Hilliard said.

"I'm certain. And for a change you'll have some compatriots."

It was somehow an odd thought. "Yes. I will, won't I?"

That Wednesday became entirely remarkable when in the afternoon the doctor, as a sort of climax to his vacation, took his seven-and-three-quarter-pound trout, stalked it laboriously in the spot where he had first seen it weeks before, teased it to his gaudy peacock fly, and played it with a half-century's skill on the delicate old rod before dipping it at last from the water. He quit fishing then, and came almost running up the streamside path to where Hilliard was wading, his reserve shattered by tremendous pleasure. "He is handsome, no?" he demanded, holding the big trout across his palms, its living iridescence not yet dulled. "He is noble?"

"Beautiful," Hilliard agreed, as happy about it as the old man was, for he knew what it meant and would mean to him. When they had weighed it on the doctor's old brass scale, he wanted badly to offer to have it taken to the city, for mounting, but he did not. It was not the kind of thing one could offer the doctor, not conceivably, and when they carried the fish to the big charcoal-pungent kitchen of the hacienda, the fat head cook, Felix, bellowed in unaffected astonishment.

And that night, at dinner, when Felix had brought the trout in on a plank, with ceremony, its smoky pink flesh perfectly baked, and had offered it around at the tables, even the wry Mexican bankers and lawyers smiled to the doctor and raised their glasses in congratulation. He was quietly triumphant. In the trout's honor, Hilliard ordered a bottle of wine and afterward, instead of his usual one, the doctor smoked two thin, dark cigars. "An insanity, to excite oneself over the murder of a fish," he said. "But he was big, no? On the plank. I wish your friends had arrived for him."

Hilliard grinned. "They aren't fishermen. The small ones will be good enough."

"People of intelligence," the doctor said. "Common-sense Americans, not like you. *Caray,* what a fish."

Nor were they like Hilliard, the Forsythes. He felt it more strongly than he ever had after lunch the next day, when they emerged from their car into the quiet air of the old courtyard like a robust, alien breeze—handsome, blonde people, congenitally crisp and Northern. It was good to see them. On the long, tiled gallery of the big house, when he had introduced them to the señora and they had seen their rooms, the three of them talked.

"You look healthy," Wright Forsythe said. "Unscholarly as hell."

Hilliard answered, "I've worked. I've gotten a lot done."

"I wouldn't," Deirdre said, gazing from a huge leather chair out across the stone-walled court where a gnarled ahue-huete tree clung to dry life and two brown children scrambled obscurely in the dust. Her small, sandaled feet rested on the veranda's railing; after the decorous Mexican ladies the pose seemed odd to Hilliard, but like everything he had ever seen her do it looked also fitting. She sighed, making a face. "Work? Not here. How did you ever find it?"

"Divination," Hilliard said. "And you'd better reserve judgment for a while. For one thing, the plumbing's haunted."

Wright wore a checked gingham shirt and flannels and looked inevitably like a scholar. He grinned, poking with a twig at his pipe bowl which he held three inches before his face because he was not wearing his glasses. "We had a year of Venetian *pensiones,* after the war. What gets me is how you've stood it."

Hilliard said that it had not been a matter of standing anything; there were people and fishing.

"Fishing," Wright said, grimacing. "You wrote about it. I did bring a pole, for trolling if they've got a lake."

"They have," Hilliard said, with a smile because Wright, who knew the nomenclature of everything, had said "pole" with deliberate amateurism, to bait him. Nor did he say anything about the trolling which, being a fly-fisherman, he disliked; he had found long before that the ritual of angling, like most rituals, was not logically defensible. "I know a Spaniard here," he said. "You'll like him."

"I might, if he speaks English."

"He doesn't," Hilliard said. "Or very little. He's a refugee."

Wright lifted an eyebrow humorously. "A kumrad."

Hilliard said, "No. I don't think so. It wouldn't make much difference. He's a doctor."

"Doctor, schmoctor," Wright said idly. "It always makes a difference." He regarded a buzzard, wheeling above the ahuehuete in the domed mountain sky. "Read anything decent in between fish?"

"Not yet, please," his wife said. "It's too nice here. Let's just talk awhile about things that aren't printed on paper."

"As though anything worth talking about," Wright said, smiling, "hadn't been printed on paper."

The doctor smiled warmly in the dining room that night, bowing to Deirdre. His English was labored. "How do you do. It is good."

"It is good, indeed," said Wright in tweeds, with grave irony as to an Indian chieftain.

Hilliard said, "I spoke to Felix. We're all to sit together."

Comprehending, the doctor touched his arm. "With permission," he said in Spanish. "I'd rather . . . you with the friends alone." Nor would he reconsider, making the gentle semicircular gesture with an outward palm which is polite, firm refusal. "You have enough to say," he said. "For knowing one another there is time later."

Wright grinned after him, and glanced at Hilliard. "Exclusive?"

"It's not that. He didn't want to be in the way."

"He's fine, Tom," Deirdre said. "Like someone from a long, long time ago."

"So long ago," Wright said, "that it might not count. He

looks like the emperor Vespasian, on a coin. Maybe with a hammer and sickle on the obverse. And let's sit down."

Quite simply it did not work. The chemistry was wrong. After dinner, by the fire, for the first time since Hilliard had met him the doctor seemed awkward, not self-possessed. He sat for a time listening, politely uncomprehending, to their conversation in English, and once he and Wright exchanged a few remarks in French, but it had no warmth. Hilliard knew that it was not going to work, and when finally, earlier than usual, the doctor had gone upstairs, Wright chuckled. "With all respect, I'm afraid your old revolutionary's something of a dud, Tom. Or maybe," they had talked of the doctor's big trout, "he's still dazed from wrestling that seven-pound whale."

Deirdre said, "He's only shy."

Hilliard, flipping a chip of eucalyptus at the fire, did not want to discuss the doctor. He said, "He's not shy; just hard to know, I guess. He's all right."

"*De gustibus,*" Wright said.

Hilliard grinned, wryly. He had tried before in his life, and failed, to bring people together when the chemistry was bad. "*De gustibus,*" he repeated.

So he did not try to mix them again. On the two afternoons of the following week when Hilliard was not wrangling over his dissertation with Wright, who liked it, or wandering with the warm, unbookish Deirdre around the neighborhood, gossiping about Mexico and the university town they lived in, he went to the stream to fish and the doctor was the same, gentle and friendly and glad to stop fishing and talk awhile on the soft, drooping grasses of the bank. He asked courteously after the Forsythes but avoided them, either going to his room in the evenings early or reading alone in the corner of the great sitting room.

The señora, approving of the Forsythes, grew friendly again. Wright developed mild dyspepsia from the seasoning so that his food had to be cooked separately; and Deirdre

tumbled harmlessly from a burro on a trip to the Toltec pyramid around the mountain, where the conquistadors had built
a chapel; and Hilliard's work began to take final shape. Then,
abruptly, one day it was Saturday. The next day Dr. Elizondo
was to leave, to go back to his factory and whatever existence
was there.

Hilliard felt relief when Wright, who had wandered along
with them to the stream, grew restless and said that he was
going to try fishing from the battered canoe in the lake.
"Leave a few," Hilliard said as Wright set off.

"I intend," answered Wright over his shoulder, "to wipe
your puristical eye. Trolling."

"What says the friend?" the doctor asked, smiling up from
a knot in his leader. Hilliard translated, and the old man
laughed. He was in a good humor, buoyant, as though the
imminence of his departure made the day not worse but
better. "Some troll," he said. "Some pull nets like San Pedro,
but you and I, we fish with reeds and spider threads. *Pos,*
who is crazy?"

They fished together, watching one another cast into the
alternating stair-step pools. Unmuddied by recent rain, the
stream was clear and full and the fish fed well, with just sufficient caution to compel stealth. They talked much, resting
frequently, and before it was at last time to stop they had between them caught and freed nineteen heavy, healthy trout,
one within a pound of the doctor's record. Never, the old
man said as they walked in the almost-dusk back toward the
hacienda, not anywhere had he known fishing like that of this
stream.

"Not even on the Gallego?" Hilliard said, slyly because the
doctor had always kept special reverence for the Pyrenean
rivers.

The doctor grunted humorously. "*Bueno,* not even there.
No." It had been an afternoon good enough to make trivial
its finality, its quality of farewell.

Nearly among the first cottages, Wright's voice called to
them from ahead, and they saw his white shirt luminous

against the black-green of the stream's deep glen. His wife stood behind him, and when they approached Hilliard saw that his hand was wrapped in a handkerchief. He said to Hilliard, with a slight wryness of pain, "The trout rodeo's over. I need your friend."

Deirdre held a heavy bass-stringer festooned with small dead trout. She said, "The fish weren't big enough. He decided to catch himself."

"What a comic," Wright said, taking the handkerchief away. Pendant from the flesh web between his thumb and forefinger, one point of its coarse treble hook inbedded above the barb, dangled a heavy red-and-white trolling spoon.

Carefully the doctor leaned his fly rod against a bush, and taking the hand, examined it. He looked up into Wright's face and smiled, touching with his finger a small white scar on the back of his own left hand and another on his cheek, near his eye. To Hilliard in Spanish he said, "The mark of the angler."

"It's nice everybody gets such a boot out of this," Wright said.

"All right," said Deirdre. "Who stuck that in you?"

The doctor had brought from his pocket a pair of long-nosed pliers that Hilliard had seen him use as hook disgorgers with the trout. "To pull it now will relieve him sooner," he said. "This serves as well as any instrument I have."

"Yes," Hilliard said from personal suffering with hooks, and then without hesitation, moving surely, the doctor grasped Wright's wrist in his left hand, seized the hook at its bend, and in one strong pull drew it free.

Wright, who had not expected it, wrenched his hand away and glared furiously at the doctor. He said, "Good Jesus Christ!"

The doctor smiled uncertainly at Hilliard. "Tell him . . . there had to be pain. At the hacienda we will clean it."

Watching Wright, Hilliard said, "Take it easy. You have to pull hooks that way. Or push them through and cut them."

His friend, pale, did not answer. No one spoke as they ascended the hill to the main house, and Wright said nothing until the three of them stood waiting in the courtyard while the doctor went to his room for bandages. Then, whimsically, he looked at Hilliard. "You said he was a bone specialist?"

"I think so," Hilliard said shortly.

"T-bones," Wright said. "He's a pure butcher, that boy."

Silently, Hilliard dismantled his fly rod and when the doctor returned he cleansed the wound of its black, crusted blood, bandaged it, then glanced up at Wright, who had not winced, with a slight quirk of his mouth. "Thus," he said in Spanish.

"Good as new," Wright said. "Barring gangrene."

Hilliard said to the old man's interrogative face, "The friend thanks you."

The doctor nodded politely and for a moment, on the ancient weed-tufted paving stones, they stood awkward, without speaking. There was nothing to say until Wright, twisting to reach his hip with his left hand, brought out a wallet. Hilliard saw suddenly that he was very angry.

His wife said, "Wright."

The doctor looked at the billfold and at the sheaf of money which Wright's finger had brought half into view. Hilliard said sharply, "Put that away."

The corners of Wright's mouth turned downward in stubborn amusement. "I pay my way," he said. "Ask him how much."

Even as Hilliard spoke, he felt the hurt shock in Deirdre's eyes swinging to his face. He knew that it was the end of something. "You bastard," he said clearly to Wright. "You complete bastard."

Staring back, Wright was not grinning now, but after a long moment he lowered his eyes, slipped the wallet into his side pocket, and stood looking away, strumming his thumb against the inside of the fingers of his left hand in an odd gesture Hilliard had seen him use in classrooms. To the doctor finally, who watched with stoic perception, Hilliard spoke quietly: "There was a fault of comprehension. The friend . . ."

"I am sure," the doctor said.

But this time, for once, the courtesy was language only. It was not in his tone, nor in the tawny eyes that turned from Wright Forsythe to Hilliard now, and to the pretty young woman at his side, flicking them. In the eyes was the end of something else: a rebuff of sympathy and of friendship, ancient pride that had stood long years alone and would stand again alone for the years that might remain. There was no anger. The doctor picked up his rod from against the old ahuehuete, then bowed slightly, a bow that held not politeness but condescension.

"With your permission." It was the formal pronoun.

"Pass," Hilliard answered mechanically.

Without glancing again toward him the doctor turned, and the three Americans stood silently watching as he walked away toward his room and the meager packing he had to do, the delicate, long, antiquated rod in his hand waving up and down with the slow rhythm of his old-man's stride.

John Graves

THE AZTEC DOG

WHEN, on sandal-shuffling feet, the young Indian maid had taken away the last plates, the two of them sat at the table smoking. The boy was reading a book, as he had been doing throughout the meal. The old man's bored forefinger made squares and triangles of crumbs of tobacco. The dining room was wide, floored and wainscoted with patterned green tiles, its three windows mullion-paned, but it had no ceiling and the roof that showed dimly above rough-milled rafters was of corrugated steel. Of furniture it held only the heavy table and the unmatched chairs in which they sat. In a corner, where the old man had tossed it before dinner, lay a quirt.

He had a gray mustache, cold dark eyes, and the face of a falcon, and wore a gray short riding-jacket and a white shirt buttoned at the throat without a tie. He said distantly, "Would you want a game of checkers?"

The boy raised book-focused blue eyes. It was poetry, the old man knew. He had glanced through the book where it lay on a chair that afternoon and had seen that it was poetry, in English. Not even good poetry, as far as he considered himself qualified to judge . . .

The boy said in formula, "No. No, thanks."

He had been living at the hacienda for six weeks and had learned nearly all of his Spanish, which was good enough, in that time. It was one of the reasons given for his being there, to learn Spanish. When his father came again he would perhaps notice its excellence, not that the old man, whose name was Fernando Iturriaga, cared greatly.

Nor did he care about the checkers; the invitation was a nightly convention. At the beginning of the six weeks while feeling each other's temper they had played every evening. Later less, and later still not at all. But he went through the ritual of the invitation each night because irony and formality made living with the boy possible. He would have enjoyed carrying the formality to the point of coffee and cigarettes in the salón de estar, but that was not feasible because the salón, like the rest of the house except the dining room and two bedrooms and a kitchen, was without even a steel roof above it. Raw edges of mortared masonry left white marks on your clothing if you walked much about the unfinished parts of the house, though they had been unfinished for eighteen years. The porch lacked railings, and outside the back door gaped a staired, never-covered cellar-entrance into which a hog had once fallen to break three of its four legs. Much pork, that had been.

Rats danced sometimes in the moonlight on the tiles of the salón de estar. Fernando Iturriaga had seen them. It had seemed well.

The boy coughed and lit another cigarette. The old man went to the window and swung it open and looked out in the late dusk at his flower garden beneath old aguacates. Pallid small roses speckled the gloom and he smelled them. From a hole in the great wall beyond the garden, water he could not see trickled audibly. He was reassured by the roses and the sound of the water running from a wall his people had built two hundred years before and by the knowledge that among the roots of the aguacates violets bloomed as they had since his mother's time.

For a wife his father had gone to Spain—to Asturias—and she had brought the gardening with her to the moist valley where the hacienda spread, big in those days. His father's family had been hard, harsh, rawhide people, precipitate in pleasure and in work, and it was only now, after nearly seventy years of living, that Fernando Iturriaga could feel a little of his mother in himself.

Having made the bet with himself he forgot to time it, but he thought the guess had been good. When the boy came back with the blue-glass liter bottle of aguardiente it was his turn to be ironic. He sat it on the table and asked Fernando Iturriaga if he wanted a drink.

As always, the old man refused. He drank, sometimes too much, but not with the boy. He valued the formality too highly.

The boy's father planned, or said he planned, to make the hacienda into a guest ranch. Fernando Iturriaga believed by now that the boy, who was there because he had slapped a professor, or had fecundated a girl, or something of that sort, was the only guest that particular guest ranch was ever likely to have.

Watching the boy pour yellowish liquor into a glass, he said, "You rode into the upper valley today?"

"Yes."

The boy took a piece of bread and soaked it in the liquor. Fernando Iturriaga heard a quick tapping of claws on the tiles.

"You shouldn't," he said. "I've told you, with the elections coming on. You went into the cantina?"

"I do every day," the boy said. "Vidal! Look, Vidal!"

"You shouldn't," the old man repeated, risking a loss of formality in the irritation that cooled his belly when he thought of the boy speaking with the peasants of the upper valley in a brushwood bar, about Fernando Iturriaga.

The boy said indifferently, "Oh, it's all right. I get along with them."

The dog barked, dancing on quick white feet. It was tiny, brindle above and white below, with fragile legs and shadings of black about its muzzle and eyes. Before the American boy had come, the dog had never entered the house, though Fernando Iturriaga had played with it on the veranda in the afternoon, quietly, and had dropped bits of tortilla and meat to it out of his dining-room window when it begged from the garden. It was two years old and he had named it, whimsically, Vidal, because in his country's capital there was a street called that where the French mistress of a friend of his had once lived. It was of the ancient breed of alert Mexican mongrels from which the Aztecs had bred their even tinier bald dogs, and was symptomatic of a gentleness that had troubled him now for five or six years.

He had never seen gentleness as desirable, except in women. Insufficiently gentle, his own wife had left him eighteen years before, taking his sons, when the house was half-rebuilt and the money had run out and she had found out about his relations with the cook they had had then.

He conceded now that there had been enough for her to be ungentle about. But he had several grandchildren whom he had never seen.

"Stand up," the boy said.

Fernando Iturriaga watched as the dog skipped on two legs before the boy. It snatched the piece of liquor-wetted bread from the air when he dropped it, gulping without chewing.

"Salud," the boy said sipping from his glass and grinning. "Salud, Vidal."

The old man said stubbornly, "They're troublesome people. Sooner or later you'll meet one of them drunk."

"One?" the boy said and laughed, glancing at him. "The half of them always are. They let me shoot a pistol at a cactus today."

"Sons of whores!" Fernando Iturriaga said forcibly through clamped teeth.

And wished that he had not, since it only meant that the boy had once more broken through the formality. Iturriaga sat for a moment swallowing anger like spittle, then went to his room to change his slippers back to half-boots and to shave. When he passed through the dining room twenty minutes later the dog was drunk. It had no capacity for the liquor. Neither had the boy, who crouched laughing on the floor, teasing it. It ran in short circles about him, yapping and dashing to tear at the flickering hands with its teeth.

Fernando Iturriaga thought that it was much like the rats' dance in the drawing room.

In the moonwashed court before the house a fresh horse stood saddled, as it did every night whether or not he wanted to use it. From the great wall's shadow two Indians' cigarettes pulsed; they murmured inarticulate courtesies and he grunted back in the same spirit. Leading the horse through the gate, he mounted in the road by the river. It shied, bouncing under him, a gray he had not ridden for several days. As he reined it into darkness under the cottonwoods lined along the little river, he was conscious of the valley's wide concavity to either side, more conscious than he had usually been when the valley had belonged to him. He had been there only occasionally during most of that time.

At its mouth, below the town toward which he rode, the earth fell away two thousand feet to malarial jungle, where the river ran turbidly wide to the sea. On clear days, from the flat top of a granary at the hacienda, the old man had often seen the shimmer of sun on salt water a hundred kilometers to the east.

Inland, the valley rose and flattened into a grassy bowl beneath the high peaks. His family's cattle had grazed there for seven generations, but now it was checkered into irrigated holdings of Indian agrarians. In the days of the change he had killed one of them. That had cost him a good part of the money he had had left, and they had nearly killed him later, skipping a bullet off his ribs as he passed a canebrake, six months before his wife had left him.

In the mornings the miserable dog had hangovers. Like a Christian, with thirst and groaning, and when you rolled back the thin black lids, the balls of the eyes were laced with blood.

He thought the gringos had begun to spawn rare ones, finally. Maybe they always had, but before, except for their nervous accessible women in the capital and the resorts, they had sent usually the meaty big ones like the boy's father, who knew cattle or oil or cotton or some other one thing completely and whom Fernando Iturriaga had always disliked a little because they profited from change and he did not.

But without obsession. Without what he thought of as the national obsession. He rode along on the pleasantly tense gray gelding toward the town where he would clatter dominoes and sip habanero with a drugstore owner and a grain-dealer and a fat incompetent doctor who—though, with less reason than he, they shared his political bitterness—were not really friends of his. The kind of people he had chosen for friends lived in France, or the capital, or New York. Or were dead. He had not chosen well; he recognized that. Even the survivors had comfortably forgotten him when he had left that world.

But he had lived for five years in Paris and had known how to eat and drink and had bayed after actresses and gringas and such quarry, as a man of his background had been expected to do, and had spoken good English and French.

The gringo boy and his father did not know about all that, not even about the English, which he had never spoken with them. They thought of him as decayed indigenous gentry left over from feudalism.

That kind of feudalism had not existed since Iturbide, or before, but the old man granted that he was at least, sufficiently decayed.

Riding, he thought without obsession about the gringo boy, and the dog, and gringos, and actresses with generals in long touring cars riding out to bull ranches, and how there ought to be green peace in the valley when, finally, you wanted peace.

Drink made the boy dizzy. He did not especially like it; it

was a thing to rasp the old man's feelings with, like speaking of the cantina in the upper valley.

His name was John Anders and he was at the ranch because he had driven a pink unmuffled sports car into a culvert-rail near Amarillo, on his way to Hollywood with money from a considerable check forged in his father's name.

He had not known why Hollywood. An unpleasant hitch-hiker with a ducktail haircut, sitting beside him, had died in the crash, but the boy had waked up on his back among prickly pears with a state patrolman bending cold-eyed over him and nothing at all broken in his slight body.

"No," he said to the dog sternly. "You've had enough."

He put down the book. It was Dylan Thomas; the boy's mother had had two nervous short stories published when young and all his life, in lieu of comprehension, had besieged him with literature. Some taste for it had stuck. He was nine-teen, with one expulsion from college behind him and an-other school to try in the autumn, four months ahead now, and for two or three years poetry and kindred queerness had been serving him for armor in prep schools and around coun-try-club swimming pools, where he did not fit well. Queer-nesses and a willingness to fight. . .

His mother had wept emptily in her dove-gray bedroom and he had watched her, not for the first time or the fiftieth, and afterward had listened to his father's bellowing querulity in the same mood and had ridden with him on the peremp-tory trip down into Mexico, not-listening all the way. He had learned to do that before he had been twelve.

When he got up from the table he found that the raw aguar-diente had him in the legs, if not in the head. He lurched; the quickly counterpoising sole of his half-boot screeched in un-swept grit on the tile. He stood, resisting the sudden idea of going out to see the Indian maid in her room beyond the laundry-court.

Foggy guilt swirled in him when he thought of the maid, and he cursed aloud.

Turning, he walked through a hall to the old man's room and snapped on its light. It was monastic under the bare bulb's glare—a blue floor, a dresser of scarred oak, a table, a bed made of scroll-bent rods of tarnished brass, and a little wall virgin. The boy stood resisting it. The old man's dignity was there like a smell, but did not explain itself. On the dresser stood a silver-framed photograph, cloud-haired, of an actress he somehow recognized to be Jean Harlow. It was a publicity picture of a special vintage, but was affectionately inscribed and signed. It did not fit with anything else that was there. He stared at it.

It stared back.

Him, the old bastard, he thought—but principally with puzzlement . . .

In the beginning he and the maid had talked at night in the laundry-court outside her door. She was shy, and alone a good bit, and giggled at his ragged confident Spanish, correcting him. Her people had worked there always and she would not talk to the boy about Don Fernando. She was not unhappy. She had a young man in the upper valley who possessed some education and would one day, maybe soon, be a power in the ejido there. But she saw him only on Sundays; Don Fernando did not encourage the upper-valley people at the hacienda.

"You have no life at all," the boy had said to her roughly, three nights before. He felt his own sophistication to be relative wisdom, and was enraged that ignorance and immobility could so brace the heavy contentment she expressed. "None of you," he said. "The ejido. Maybe they'll let him weigh sacks of grain."

"Maybe," the girl said, placid in the pallidity that came through the open door of her room. "Maybe so, señorito," she said. "But he won't end in the cantina, waving a machete with shouts. And there is no hurry . . ."

Feeling wise still, and miserable, the boy said, "There's always hurry."

"Not in the valley," the girl said quietly.

She was young, with the Indian shyness and a round, brown, velvet face. Abruptly he put his hand on her cheek.

She sucked in breath sharply through her teeth and ran inside, closing the door behind her.

That had been all, but it had shamed him; he had not wanted to be alone with her since.

He made a big embarrassed X-mark with his finger on the glass that shielded inexplicable Jean Harlow against the eatings of time, and left the room, the little dog's claws clicking along behind him.

He would apologize . . .

You rode the bay horse (your father having paid for it, sight unseen, when Don Fernando had said someone was offering it for sale) hard up the valley by the river, under the big poplars, and then left the river before you reached the cantina, not wanting to go there first. Rising, the horse's flanks straining against your calves in labored effort of ascent, you passed oxcarts and laden strings of timid people in a roadlet than ran between terraces of irrigated grain and fiber, green. The world there smelled of green, and leather, and dung, and of charcoal and toasted maize in the huts between the fields, and on the higher mountains mists lay. The boy had not in his life known a freshness like that of the green upper valley as your horse mounted its side toward the mists.

Except that long before you were near the real mists you came to an almost vertical belt of cactus and stone and gray-green clawed plants, the trails were there that led to villages in the sierra. Clanking, clicking, short-haired burro-trains came along them. One trail ran simply parallel to the river, far below now. Taking that trail, you stopped somewhere along it and dismounted and sat on a rock, the cold feel of the mists above and behind you on your neck, the horse tearing irritably at clumps of inedibility among the stones, the quilt-patched green of the valley troughed below you, smoke-tufted, split by the roving line of the river's trees.

Sometimes he would sit there for hours smoking Elegantes, coughing-strong. Once he yelled aloud in ferocious exultation of aloneness, "By God!"

The upper valley was, too, the brushwood cantina on the

way home, and the taste of tepid black beer with loud peasants crowding toward his oddness. They liked him. He liked
them, or thought he did, and was a little afraid of them—it
was the main reason he went there. He would not talk to
them about the old man, toward whom they felt the frank
reflex hatred of crows for a crippled owl. They asked him
about the States United and the flogging of wetbacks, and
told him with pride that they were Reds. Once, when a stum-
bling-drunk Red with a drawn machete had cursed the boy
and had gone outside to ride the bay horse away, one of the
others had maced him from the saddle with a shovel and had
courteously tied the horse again to its post.

"It is that at times one drinks," the courteous Red said.

"It is so," John Anders said with the solemnity of that dia-
lect, and they laughed to one another to hear their intonation
in his mouth, and slapped his shoulder.

And sometimes he ran the bay horse all the way back to the
hacienda, the long-pounding lope downhill, and walked him
cool in the courtyard there, and rubbed him slick with a cob.

The fact was, he liked living in the valley. It was a recent
admission, and had had no effect on his prickling-war with
the old man, who perplexed him. He had been at war with
many adults, but had managed to touch most of them more
painfully than he could touch Fernando Iturriaga.

Maybe, he thought, it was because the others had given a
damn . . .

He paused in the open door, winking against night's dark
assault, and saw a yellow line beneath the maid's door. When
he started down the unrailed steps, the aguardiente took him
to the right. His foot pawed vacancy. Blackness jerked him
cartwheeling down into the unroofed cellar-pit; he landed
among shards of bottleglass, right-side-up and sitting, his
right leg twisted back under behind him.

At first he knew only a shallowness of force-emptied lungs
and fought to get his breath. Then a knowledge of the leg
ascended through him like nausea. In sick shock, he knew
that he was about to faint, but the little dog's whine cut into

his ken and it was jumping at his face, licking. He took it in
his hands and held it, speaking to it as it squirmed and licked
and as the sickness went down, and waited while the dull but
sharpening pain rose.

His hand was bleeding. The Indian girl was standing above
him at the edge of the hole, uttering a mooing sound. He
supposed he had made noise.

"Look for help," he told her.

She went away, still mooing. Without shifting, the boy
held the dog and met the leg-pain full face and decided that it
would probably be bearable. . . She came back with the gardener, Elifonso. Elifonso gritted down the steep steps of the
pit and loomed over the boy, smelling of peppers.

"If this is bad, señorito!" he said. "If this is very bad!"

"Don't touch me yet," the boy said.

But Elifonso grabbed him by the armpits and yanked
upward, and the boy yelled and struck at him, and when
Elifonso let go the hurt was twice what it had yet been. The
boy's hand touched a stick; he flailed out with it and Elifonso
went back up the steps. The boy shouted upper-valley words
at them, and they murmured between themselves in the darkness, above him. He quieted, ashamed but still angry. After a
time he asked the girl to bring the bottle of aguardiente from
the dining room; when she gave it to him he drank five gulps
of it, cold and oily, without stopping. It warmed him and
pushed the pain down for a while, and he drank more. Then
he vomited and for a long, long time sat coldly full of pain
while the quiet Indian voices murmured on above him.

Finally a flashlight glared down into his face, reawakening
dull rage. Fernando Iturriaga held it.

After a moment he said quietly to the boy, "You are a
disaster."

John Anders said, "You aren't going to touch me."

"Go for the doctor Rodríguez," the old man told Elifonso.

Walking around the pit and down its steps, he knelt beside
the boy and played the flashlight on the leg.

"How handsome," he said.

"Don't touch me," the boy said, and raised his stick.

Fernando Iturriaga took it from his hand and dropped it among the broken glass.

"Boy, I will touch you," he said. "I will hurt you, too. Shut up. You, Luz, come. . . ."

They were careful, but the pain was a twisting shaft up inside him, though it seemed that when the responsibility was no longer yours maybe the pain was not, either. The maid mooed all the way. When they had him on the bed in his room, waiting for the doctor, the leg as straight as they had dared put it with the big splinter sticking through the flesh above the knee, the old man said matter-of-factly. "It will have hurt like ten demons."

The boy rolled his head negatively.

"Don't lie," the old man said. "I know hurts. It will have hurt."

He considered, hard eyes candid. "Fat Rodríguez will hurt you more when he comes," he said. "He drank a lot this evening."

Weakened by the bed's comfort against his back, the boy began to cry. He cried because he hurt, and because the doctor would hurt him again, and because the old man clearly did not give a damn about him, and because he was a thousand miles from even a home that he despised—having, therefore, no home—and because the green foreign valley had turned on him and bitten him and was foreign now altogether, and hateful. He laid his forearm across his eyes and sobbed.

Astonishingly, the old man was patting his shoulder.

"Child, child," he said. "It will pass."

The boy stopped sobbing, and after a time uncovered his eyes. The formal hawk's face was smiling gently at him.

"I suppose it will," he said.

"Yes."

"All right," the boy said.

He was listening.

"At least a telegram," the boy's meaty father said ernestly,

down-wiping damp hands against the front of gabardine
trousers. "Don Fernando, a letter that sat in the club in Mexico City for three weeks was . . ."

Fernando Iturriaga dropped his shoulders, flashed the
cupped palms of his hands briefly upward, and turned away,
unapologetic. He felt some pity for the big man, but he felt a
little bit nationally obsessed, too. He considered that a telegram would likely have cooled in that club for three weeks
also, awaiting the big man's arrival, and even had he known
how to telephone him he doubted that he would have tried to
do so. The bone had been set.

Crookedly, yes, healing with a bend like a pruned tree
fork. Fat Rodríguez, gold spectacled, standing nervous now
against the whitewashed wall while the slim young doctor
from the capital felt with long fingers the boy's humped fe-
mur—Rodríguez had thought of a thick fee but had not earned
it. But Rodríguez had been all that there was; even the boy
had understood that.

The slim capitaleño did not glance toward Rodríguez as he
spoke to the boy's father.

"It will need rebreaking," he said. "There is also infection.
A question of various months . . ."

"The hell it will," the boy on the bed said in English.

"Close your mouth," his father said. "For Christ's sake,
you make any more trouble now and I'll . . ."

"I'm not going to let them bust it over again," the boy said
unemotionally. "I watched them with Phil Evridge at school
and he still limps."

The big man's voice shrilled. Rodríguez, his nervousness
requiring expression, said to the slim doctor, "It is that sometimes, despite what one can do . . ."

The slim doctor turned on him for an instant two liquid
slits, said, "Sí, señor!" and looked away, closing thin lips in
punctuation.

Fat Rodríguez shuffled.

Fernando Iturriaga grinned and turned to go outside. My
nationals, he thought. But the slim contemptuous capitaleño
was of his nationals, too. Did he mean, then, those of his nationals who would end in a place like this valley?

Maybe.

On the gallery he dropped into a big hard chair of aguacate-wood, and the little dog's nose shocked cold against his dangling hand. He caressed the bulb of its head and not looking felt its warm eyelids with his thumb.

Changing, he . . . Gentling. A week after the boy's fall, three agrarians from the upper valley had come to the hacienda. With some pleasure he had gone out to tell them to go away again. But in their stubbled faces before he spoke, and in their politeness, he saw an actual concern for the boy. He had not expected that. Quietly, he led them himself to the boy's room, and afterward spoke to them about that year's crops . . . .

You are effeminated, he told himself.

Prepared for the big-meaty-gringo anger, he was a little disappointed when the father came out, alone, with cold control on his face.

He said, "Don Fernando, it was not well done."

"No."

"I don't mean that fat fool!"

His voice trilled at the end and Fernando Iturriaga glanced up hopefully, but the control was still there. The blue capable eyes glittered down at him like tile-chips.

"There will not be a guest ranch."

"No," the old man said, and sighed courteously. Even in childhood, the line of the mountains where he was now looking had seemed to have the shape of a woman lying on her side. In childhood he had ridden there, on the high rocky slopes under the clouds, and the gringo boy had told him of doing the same.

Gently he pinched the small dog's ear.

"What a very great shame," he said in exact British English.

"By God!" Anders said, and stood above him for a moment longer, and then went out to the long brown-and-cream car to bring back a blanket.

The old man watched as all of them, the maid and the gardener and the doctor and even hopeful Rodríguez, bore armloads of books and clothes to load them into the luggage compartment. At last the capitaleño and Elifonso brought the blanketed boy between them through the door. They paused with him beside the chair.

"Well," the boy said. "Many thanks."

"Nothing, son," Fernando Iturriaga said. "May they make you a good oilman."

Crooked amusement split the boy's face, and he said a word from the upper valley that made the gardener laugh. They carried him to the car, and the old man watched still while the father strode past him unspeaking and managed to direct them into ramming the boy's head into a doorpost and the back of the front seat. At the end, the maid Luz ran out with the whittled crutches she had bought for the boy in the village, which he had refused to try.

By then, however, the car was moving; the maid stopped behind it holding the crutches and began foolishly to weep. Fernando Iturriaga saw the flash of the boy's face toward him from the rear seat. In the narrow gateway of the wall a stone tilted the big car's rear, and he felt a reprehensible surge of national pleasure as its finned fender gritted against the arch.

Fee-less, fat Rodríguez stood in the courtyard with the maid, his hands clenching and unclenching at his sides. Then he walked with head down and wagging to his old Ford, and drove away in it.

"Well, then," Fernando Iturriaga said aloud and for some reason in French.

He stared across the sunlit, slab-paved court at a section of wall where, mixed among the pocks of revolutionary bullets which in 1911 had killed his brother and a cousin and the peons who had stuck by them, were newer gray marks where he and the boy's father had held pistol practice some months before, speaking of the grandeurs of guest-ranching as they shot. It gave him satisfaction to think about how easily he had beaten the big American; then it disturbed him to recognize the satisfaction.

You are becoming nationally obsessed, he told himself.

He felt quite alone. Diffidently, the Indian girl came and asked if he would want his midday meal. He said that certainly he would. Hearing his calm tone as permissive, she said, "They left money. The big one said it was for room and food."

"Shut up," he said.

"Caray!" she protested.

"Shut up. What was he doing there in the laundry-court, beside your house?"

She went back in. He was half-certain she was his daughter, the child of the cook that had cost him his wife and sons. The cook had died quietly and quickly one winter, after the way of Indians, and the child had grown up there. He would give her something when she married her prim young man from the ejido. Not much. There was unhappily little to give.

The old man walked to his room, looked about it for a moment, and in leaving lightly, affectionately flicked the picture of Jean Harlow with his forefingernail. He had not known her; the picture had been some sort of joke from a friend, its point lost now. Or maybe he had bet and won it.

He went around to the shaded garden between his breakfast window and the wall. At its gate he examined the small perfect roses with pleasure, and he moved into the green gloom of the great aguacates slowly, so that hens in the path edged aside with only ritual cackling. He would tell Elifonso that the violets needed water; the outlet in the wall when he looked at it was closed with a whittled plug. Diverted riverwater, cool and vocal, ran in all the circumference of the peripheral wall. Two hundred years before when his people had raised it—first, his father had said, the wall first of all for protection—the old Moorish water-love had made them build conduits inside it that ran into the houses, the gardens, the washwomen's court, the stables. . . . As a child he had leaned against the wall and listened while the water spoke its words.

Now he went to it again and put his ear against it and heard the water. In the pigpens these days there was only a drip from hairy green slime; he had meant for years to have it cleaned. A man lived in the town who could do that, some-how, with hook-ended wires.

Beside him there was a sound. It was the dog, squatting, one foot held delicately before it in the air as though in sup-plication. Its bright dark eyes were on his face.

"Vidal," the old man said.

The dog yipped at its name.

Fernando Iturriaga said, "You miss him, poor Vidal."

The dog whined and pumped the air with its foot and sat up as it had been taught. Commandingly it barked. The old man leaned down and picked it up, stroking its head as he glanced about himself. Against one of the aguacates leaned a section of rusted pipe. It had a familiar look. Holding the dog gently in the crook of his arm he walked to the tree and picked up the pipe, half a meter long, heavy, plugged with dirt. They had used it one year, he recalled now, as a stake for strung sweet-peas.

He hefted it, and then in one deft motion, with Indian grace, he swung the little dog downward, holding its hind legs together in his left hand, and even as it yelped in surprise hit it a swift uncruel blow on its skull.

At the base of the tree he laid the dog and the pipe down beside each other, beyond the violets his mother had brought from Asturias, and rubbed the palms of his hands horseman-wise against his hips.

Now, he thought. Now maybe we will have peace here.

Jack Kerouac

A BILLOWY TRIP IN THE WORLD

AS I pulled up the car at the gas station near the gates of sunny Gregoria a kid came across the road on tattered feet carrying an enormous windshield-shade and wanted to know if I'd buy. "You like? Sixty peso. Habla Español? Sesenta peso. My name Victor."

"Nah," I said jokingly, "buy señorita."

"Sure sure!" he cried excitedly. "I get you gurls, onnytime. Too hot now," he added with distaste. "No good gurls when hot day. Wait tonight. You like shade?"

I didn't want the shade but I wanted the girls. I woke up Dean. "Hey man I told you in Texas I'd get you a girl—all right, stretch your bones and wake up boy, we've got girls waitin for us."

"What? what?" he cried leaping up haggard. "Where? where?"

"This boy Victor's going to show us where."

"Well lessgo, lessgo!" Dean leaped out of the car and clasped Victor's hand. There was a group of other boys hanging around the station and grinning, half of them barefoot, all wearing floppy strawhats. "Man," said Dean to me, "ain't this a nice way to spend an afternoon. It's so much *cooler* than Denver pool-halls. Victor, you got gurls? Where? A donday!" he cried in Spanish. "Dig that, Sal, I'm speaking Spanish."

"Ask him if we can get any tea. Hey kid, you got ma-ree-wa-na?" The kid nodded gravely.

"Sho, onnytime mon. Come with me."

"Hee! Whee! Hoo!" yelled Dean. He was wide awake and jumping up and down in that drowsy Mexican street. "Let's all go!" I was passing Lucky Strikes to the other boys. They were getting a great pleasure out of us and especially Dean. They turned to one another with cupped hands and rattled off comments about the mad American cat. "Dig them, Sal, talking about us and digging. O my goodness what a world!" We all got in the car and lurched off. Stan Shephard had been sleeping soundly and woke up to this madness.

We drove way out to the desert the other side of town and turned on a rutty dirt road that made the car bounce as it never bounced before. Up ahead was Victor's house. It sat on the edge of cactus flats overtopped by a few trees, just an adobe crackerbox, with a few men lounging around in the yard. "Who that?" cried Dean all excited.

"Those my brothers. My mother there too. My sistair too. That my family. I married. I live downtown."

"What about your mother?" flinched Dean. "What she say about marijuana."

"Oh, she get it for me." And as we waited in the car Victor got out and loped over to the house and said a few words to an old lady, who promptly responded and turned and went to the garden in the back and began gathering dry fronds of marijuana that had been pulled off the plants and left to dry in the desert sun. Meanwhile Victor's brothers grinned from under a tree. They were coming over to meet us but it would take awhile for them to get up and walk over. Victor came back grinning sweetly.

"Man," said Dean, "that Victor is the sweetest gonest franticest little bangtail cat I've ever in all my life met. Just look at him, look at his cool slow walk. There's no need to hurry around here." A steady insistent desert breeze blew into the car. It was very hot.

"You see how hot?" said Victor sitting down with Dean in

the front seat and pointing up at the burning roof of the Ford. "You have ma-ree-gwana and it no hot no more. You wait."

"Yes," said Dean adjusting his dark glasses, "I wait. For sure Victor m'boy." Presently Victor's tall brother came ambling along with some weed piled on a page of newspaper. He dumped it on Victor's lap and leaned casually on the door of the car to nod and smile at us and say "hallo." Dean nodded and smiled pleasantly at *him*. Nobody talked; it was fine. Victor proceeded to roll the biggest bomber anybody ever saw. He rolled (using brown paper bag) what amounted to a tremendous Corona cigar of tea. It was huge. Dean stared at it popeyed. Victor casually lit it and passed it around. To drag on this thing was like leaning over a chimney and inhaling. It blew into your throat in one great blast of heat. We held our breaths and all let out just about simultaneously. Instantly we were all high. The sweat froze on our foreheads and it was suddenly like the beach at Acapulco. I looked out the back window of the car and another and strangest of Victor's brothers—a tall Peruvian of an Indian with a sash over his shoulder—leaned grinning on a post too bashful to come up and shake hands. It also seemed the car was surrounded by brothers for another one appeared on Dean's side. Then the strangest thing happened. Everybody became so high that usual formalities were dispensed with and the things of immediate interest were concentrated on, and what it was now, was the strangeness of Americans and Mexicans blasting together on the desert and more than that, the strangeness of seeing in close proximity the faces and pores of skins and calluses of fingers and general abashed cheekbones of another world. So the Indian brothers began talking about us in low voices and commenting; you saw them look, and size, and compare mutualities of impression, or correct and modify, "Yeh, yeh,"; while Dean and Stan and I commented on them in English. "Will you d-i-g that weird brother in the back that hasn't moved from that post and hasn't by one cut hair diminished the intensity of the glad *funny* bashfulness of his smile. And the one to my left here, older, more sure of himself but sad, like hungup, like a bum even maybe, in town, while Victor is respectably married—he's like a gawd-dam Egyptian King that you see. These guys are real CATS. Ain't never seen anything like it. And they're talking and wondering about us, like see? Just like we are but with a difference of their own, their interest probably revolving around how we're dressed—same as ours, really—but the strangeness of the things we have in the car and the strange ways that WE laugh so different from them, and maybe even the way we smell compared to them. Nevertheless I'd give my eye-teeth to know what they're saying about us." And Dean tried. "Hey Victor, man . . . what you brother say just then?"

Victor turned mournful high brown eyes on Dean. "Yeah, yeah."

"No, you didn't understand my question. What you boys talking about?"

"Oh," said Victor with great perturbation, "you no like this mari-gwana?"

"Oh yeah, yes fine! What you TALK about?"

"Talk? Yes, we talk. How you like Mexico." It was hard to come around without a common language. And everybody grew quiet and cool and high again and just enjoyed the breeze from the desert and mused separate national and racial and personal high eternity thoughts. Everybody was very high.

It was time for the girls. The brothers eased back to their station under the tree, the mother watched from her sunny doorway, and we slowly bounced back to town.

But now the bouncing was no longer unpleasant, it was the most pleasant and graceful billowy trip in the world, as over a blue sea, and Dean's face was suffused with an unnatural glow that was like gold as he told us to understand the springs of the car now for the first time and dig the ride. Up and down we bounced and even Victor understood and laughed. Then he pointed left to show which way to go for the girls, and Dean, looking left with indescribable delight and leaning that way, pulled the wheel around and rolled us smoothly and surely to the goal, meanwhile listening to Victor's attempt to speak and saying grandly and magniloquently "Yes, of course! There's not a doubt in my mind! Decidedly, man! Oh indeed! Why, pish, posh, you say the dearest things to me! Of course! Yes! Please go on!" To this Victor talked gravely and with magnificent Spanish eloquence. For a mad moment I thought Dean was understanding everything he said by sheer wild insight and sudden revelatory genius inconceivably inspired by his supreme and glowing happiness. In that moment, too, he looked so exactly like Franklin Delano Roosevelt—some delusion in my flaming eyes and floating brain—that I drew up in my seat and gasped with amazement. In myriad pricklings of heavenly radiation I had to struggle to look to see Dean's figure and he looked like God. I was so high I had to lean my head back on the seat; the bouncing of the car sent shivers of ecstasy through me. The mere thought of looking out the window at Mexico—which was now something else in my mind—was like recoiling from before some gloriously riddled glittering treasure-box that you're afraid to look at because of your eyes, they bend inward, the riches and the treasures are too much to take all at once. I gulped. I saw streams of gold pouring through the sky and right across the tattered roof of the poor old car, right across my eyeballs and indeed right inside them; it was everywhere. I looked out the window at the hot sunny streets and saw a woman in a doorway and I thought she was listening to every word we said and nodding to herself—routine paranoiac visions of people due to tea. But the stream of gold continued. For a long time I lost consciousness in my lower mind of what we were doing and only came around sometime later when I looked up from fire and silence like waking from sleep to the world, or waking from void to a dream, and they told me we were parked outside Victor's house and he was already at the door of the car with his little baby son in his arms showing him to us.

"You see my baby? Hees name Perez, he six month age."

"Why," said Dean, his face still transfigured into a shower of supreme pleasure and even bliss, "he is the prettiest child I have ever seen. Look at those eyes. Now Sal and Stan," he said turning to us with a serious and tender air, "I want you par-ti-cu-lar-ly to see the eyes of this little Mexican boy who is the son of our wonderful friend Victor, and notice how he will come to manhood with his own particular soul bespeaking itself through the windows which are his eyes, and such lovely eyes surely do prophesy and indicate the loveliest of souls." It was a beautiful speech. And it was a beautiful baby. Victor mournfully looked down at his angel. We all wished we had a little son like that. So great was our intensity over the child's soul that he sensed something and began a grimace which led to bitter tears and some unknown bitter sorrow that we had no means to soothe because it reached too far back into unnumerable mysteries and time. We tried everything, Victor smothered him in his neck and rocked; Dean cooed; I reached over and stroked the baby's little arms. His bawls grew louder. "Ah," said Dean, "I'm awfully sorry Victor that we've made him sad."

"He is not sad, baby cry." In the doorway in back of Victor, too bashful to come out, was his little barefoot wife with anxious tenderness waiting for the babe to be put back in her arms so brown and soft. Victor having shown us his child, he climbed back into the car and proudly pointed to the right.

"Yes," said Dean, and swung the car over and directed it through narrow Algerian streets with faces on all sides watching us with gentle wonder and secret fancy. We came to the whorehouse. It was a magnificent establishment of stucco in the golden sun. On it were written the words "Sale de Baile" which means dance hall, in proud official letters that seemed to me in their dignity and simplicity like the letterings on stone friezes around the Post Offices of the United States. In the street, and leaning on the window sills that opened into the whorehouse, were two cops, saggy-trousered, drowsy, bored, who gave us brief interested looks as we walked in and stayed there the entire three hours that we cavorted under their noses, until we came out at dusk and at Victor's bidding gave them the equivalent of twenty-four cents each just for the sake of form. And in there we found the girls. Some of them were reclined on couches across the dance floor, some of them were boozing at the long bar to the right. In the center an arch led into small cubicle shacks that looked like the places where you put on your bathing suit at public municipal beaches or bath houses. These shacks were in the sun of the court. Behind the bar was the proprietor, a young fellow who instantly ran out when we told him we wanted to hear mambo music and came back with a stack of records, mostly by Perez Prado, and put them on over the public address system. In an instant all of the city of Gregoria could hear the good times going on at the Sale de Baile. In the hall itself the din of the music—for this is the real way to play a jukebox and what it was originally for—was so tremendous that it shattered Dean and Frank and me for a moment in the realization that we had never dared to play music as loud as we wanted and this was how loud we wanted. It blew and shuddered directly at us. In a few minutes half that portion of town was at the windows watching the Americanos dance with the gals. They all stood, side by side with the cops, on the dirt sidewalk leaning in with indifference and casualness. "More Mambo Jambo," "Chattanooga de Mambo," "Mambo Numero Ocho," all these tremendous numbers resounded and flared in the golden mysterious afternoon like the sounds you expect to hear on the last day of the world and the Second Coming. The trumpets seemed so loud I thought they could hear it clear out in the desert, where the trumpets had originated anyway. The drums were mad. The mambo beat is the conga beat from Congo, the river of Africa and the World, it's really the world-beat. Oom-*Ta,* ta-poo-*poom*—oom-*Ta,* ta-poo-*poom*. The piano montunos showered down on us from the speaker. The cries of the leader were like great gasps in the air. The final trumpet choruses that came with drum climaxes on conga and bongo drums, on the great mad Chattanooga record, froze Dean in his tracks for a moment till he shuddered and sweated, then when the trumpets bit the drowsy air with their quivering echoes like a cavern's or a

cave's his eyes grew large and round as though seeing the
Devil and he closed them tight. I myself was shaken like a
puppet by it; I heard the trumpets flail the light I had seen and
trembled in my boots. On the fast Mambo Jambo we danced
frantically with the girls. Through our deliriums we began to
discern their varying personalities. They were great girls.
Strangely the wildest one was half Indian half white, and
came from Venezuela, and only eighteen. She looked like she
came from a good family. What she was doing whoring in
Mexico at that age and with that tender cheek and fair aspect
God knows. Some awful grief had driven her to it. She drank
beyond all bounds. She threw down drinks when it seemed
she was about to chuck up the last. She overturned glasses
continually, the idea also being to make us spend as much
money as possible. Wearing her flimsy housecoat in broad afternoon she frantically danced with Dean and clung about his
neck and begged and begged for everything. Dean was so
stoned he didn't know what to start with, girls or mambo.
They ran off to the lockers. I was set upon by a fat and un-
interesting girl with a puppy dog who got sore at me when I
took a dislike to it because it kept trying to bite me. She com-
promised by putting it away in the back, but by the time she
returned I had been hooked by another gal, better looking
but not the best, who clung to my neck like a leech. I was
trying to break loose to get at a sixteen-year-old colored girl
who sat gloomily inspecting her navel through an opening in
her short shirty dress across the hall. I couldn't do it. Stan had
a fifteen-year-old girl with an almond colored skin and a
dress that was buttoned halfway down and halfway up. It was
mad. A good twenty men leaned in that window watching.
At one point the mother of the little colored girl—not colored but dark—came in to hold a brief and mournful con-
vocation with her daughter. When I saw that I was too
ashamed to try for the one I really wanted. I let the leech take
me off to the back, where as in a dream, to the din and roar of
further loudspeakers inside, we made the bed bounce a half
hour. It was just a square room with wooden slats and no

ceiling, a bulb hanging from the hall roof, an ikon in the corner, a wash basin in another. All up and down the dark hall
the girls were calling "Agua, agua caliente!" which means hot
water. Stan and Dean were also out of sight. My girl charged
thirty pesos, or about three dollars and a half, and begged for
an extra ten pesos and gave a long story about something. I
didn't know the value of Mexican money, for all I knew I had
a million pesos. I threw money at her. We rushed back to
dance. A greater crowd was gathered in the street. The cops
looked as bored as usual. Dean's pretty Venezuelan dragged
me through a door and into another strange bar that apparently belonged to the whorehouse. Here a young bartender
was talking and wiping glasses and an old man with handle-
bar mustache sat discussing something earnestly. And here
too the mambo roared over another loudspeaker. It seemed
the whole world was turned on. Venezuela clung about my
neck and begged for drinks. The bartender wouldn't give her
one. She begged and begged, and when he gave it to her she
spilled it and this time not on purpose for I saw the chagrin in
her poor sunken lost eyes. "Take it easy baby," I told her. I
had to support her on the stool, she kept slipping off. I've
never seen a drunker woman, and only eighteen. I bought her
another drink, she was tugging at my pants for mercy. She
gulped it up. I didn't have the heart to try her either. My own
girl was about thirty and took care of herself better. Still with
Venezuela writhing and suffering in my arms I had a longing
to take her in the back and undress her and only talk to her—
this I told myself. I was delirious with want of her and the
other little dark girl. Poor Victor, all this time he stood on the
brass rail of the bar with his back to the counter and jumped
up and down gladly to see his three American friends cavort.
We bought him drinks. His eyes gleamed for a woman but he
wouldn't accept any, being faithful to his wife. Dean thrust
money at him. In this welter of madness I had an opportunity
to see what Dean was up to. He was so out of his mind he
didn't know who I was when I peered at his face. "Yeah,
yeah!" is all he said. It seemed it would never end. It was like

a long spectral Arabian dream in the afternoon in another life, Ali Baba and the alleys and the courtesans. Again I rushed off with my girl to her room; Dean and Stan switched the girls they'd had before; and we were out of sight a moment and the spectators had to wait for the show to go on. The afternoon grew long and cool.

Soon it would be mysterious night in old gone Gregoria. The mambo never let up for a moment, it frenzied on like an endless journey in the jungle. I couldn't take my eyes off the little dark girl, even after the second time, and the way, like a Queen, she walked around and was even reduced by the sullen bartender to menial tasks such as bringing us drinks and sweeping the back. Of all the girls in there she needed the money most; maybe her mother had come to get money from her for her little infant sisters and brothers. Mexicans are poor. It never, never occurred to me to just approach her and give her some money. I have a feeling she would have taken it with a degree of scorn and scorn from the likes of her made me flinch. In my madness I was actually in love with her for the few hours it all lasted; it was the same unmistakable ache and stab across the mind, the same sighs, the same pain, and above all the same reluctance and fear to approach. Strange that Dean and Stan also failed to approach her; her unimpeachable dignity was the thing that made her poor in a wild old whorehouse, and think of that. At one point I saw Dean leaning like a statue toward her, ready to fly, and befuddlement cross his face as she glanced coolly and imperiously his way and he stopped rubbing his belly and gaped and finally bowed his head. For she was the queen.

Now Victor suddenly clutched at our arms in the furor and made frantic signs. "What's the matter?" He tried everything to make us understand. Then he ran to the bar and grabbed the check from the bartender who scowled at him and took it to us to see. The bill was over 300 pesos, or 36 American dollars, which is a lot of money in any whorehouse. Still we couldn't sober up and didn't want to leave and though we were all run out we still wanted to hang around with our

lovely girls in this strange Arabian paradise we had finally
found at the end of the hard, hard road. But night was coming and we had to get on to the end; and Dean saw that, and
began frowning and thinking and trying to straighten himself
out, and finally I broached the idea of leaving once and for all.
"So much ahead of us man it won't make any difference."

"That's right!" cried Dean glassy eyed and turned to his
Venezuelan. She had finally passed out and lay on a wooden
bench with her white legs protruding from the silk. The gallery in the window took advantage of the show; behind them
red shadows were beginning to creep, and somewhere I heard
a baby wail in a sudden lull, remembering I was in Mexico
after all and not in a pornographic hasheesh daydream in
heaven.

We staggered out; we had forgotten Stan; we ran back in to
get him, like the boys run to get Ollie the seaman in "Long
Voyage Home"; and found him charmingly bowing to the
new evening whores who had just come in for nightshift. He
wanted to start all over again. When he is drunk he lumbers
like a man ten feet tall and when he is drunk he can't be
dragged away from women. Moreover women cling to him
like ivy. He insisted on staying and trying some of the newer,
stranger, more proficient señoritas. Dean and I pounded him
on the back and dragged him out. He waved profuse good-
byes to everybody, the girls, the cops, the crowds, the children in the street ouside, he blew kisses in all directions to
ovations of Gregoria and staggered proudly among the gangs
and tried to speak to them and communicate his joy and love
of everything this fine afternoon of life. Everybody laughed;
some slapped him on the back. Dean rushed over and paid
the policemen the four pesos and shook hands and grinned
and bowed with them. Then he jumped in the car, and the
girls we had known, even Venezuela who was wakened for
the farewell, gathered around the car huddling in their flimsy
duds and chattered goodbyes and kissed us and Venezuela
even began to weep—though not for us, we knew, not altogether for us, yet enough and good enough. My dusky dar-

ling love had disappeared in the shadows inside. It was all over. We pulled out and left joys and celebrations over hundreds of pesos behind us and it didn't seem like a bad day's work. The haunting mambo followed us a few blocks. It was all over. "Goodbye Gregoria!" cried Dean blowing it a kiss. Victor was proud of us and proud of himself. "Now you like bath?" he asked. Yes, we all wanted wonderful bath.

And he directed us to the strangest thing in the world: it was an ordinary American type bath house one mile out of town on the highway, full of kids splashing in a pool and showers inside a stone building for a few centavos a crack, with soap and towel from the attendant. Besides this it was also a sad kiddy park with swings and a broken-down merry-go-round and in the fading red sun it seemed so strange and so beautiful. Stan and I got towels and jumped right into ice-cold showers inside and came out refreshed and new. Dean didn't bother with a shower and we saw him far across the sad park strolling arm in arm with good Victor and chatting volubly and pleasantly and even leaning excitedly towards him to make a point and pounding his fist. Then they resumed arm-in-arm and strolled. The time was coming to say goodbye to Victor so Dean was taking the opportunity to have moments alone with him and to inspect the park and get his views on things in general and in-all dig him as only Dean could do and does.

Victor was very sad now that we had to go. "You come back Gregoria, see me?"

"Sure man!" said Dean. He even promised to take Victor back to the States if he so wished it. Victor said he would have to mull over this.

"I got wife and kid—ain't got a money—I see." His sweet polite smile glowed in the redness as we waved to him from the car. Behind him was the sad park and the children. Suddenly he jumped after us and asked for a ride home. Dean was so bent on the road he was momentarily annoyed by this and brusquely told him to get in. And we went back to Gregoria and dropped Victor a block from his house. He didn't understand this sudden businesslike grimness on the part of Dean, and Dean realizing it began talking pointing out what he could to him, and finally they were straight again and Victor walked down the streets of his life.

Margaret Shedd

THE DWARFS OF XLAPAC

IT does sometimes happen that out of the endless similarity of travelers to distant places some, extravagantly grotesque, will put in an appearance. They do not belong where they have appeared, but then they may not belong anywhere. Or are they looking for a home?

There were two tourists in the Mayaland car that morning; the chauffeur was also the guide. These three and a man with a Victorian beard, surely a professor, who must have come by bus since there was no other car in sight, were the only people at the Maya site.

The guide got out and waited a minute before he went to the closed-up booth where tickets and booklets were sold. He knocked and called, "Don Angel," once or twice and then went back to the car. He stretched, putting his hands up to head height, and flexed his back. He was a stolid-looking man with a fine Maya profile, but his name was Rodolfo Yáñez, so he could not have been all Maya. In any case, no one would have guessed from his looks that he was subject to the flights of imagination he had been indulging in all the way from Mérida. He had invented stories for this couple not because of their enthusiasm (which might have been the case with, say, a load of teachers) but because their extreme oddity intrigued him. But the woman had been silent all the way and the man had badgered him with unknowledgeable insulting questions to get his money's worth out of the tour.

When at last the guide opened the car door (they within having made no move until he did so), the man and woman descended into the great jewel box of sun, the moment and place embellished as well as enclosed by the transparent frames of sunlight. Stepping onto earth alongside the unchallengeable pyramid of Xlapac, they were conspicuous. The grave sophistication of the explicit Maya buildings was surely alien to these two; yet there they were, their hate and love and their deformities voicing themselves loudly.

Yáñez almost found himself saying, "Go back to your hotel. I'll make the trip for nothing." He did not know why he wanted to say this, and of course he wouldn't for anything have given them back a centavo, but he thought, watching first the woman uncramp herself from the car, that it was not right to have brought them here. Then Yáñez noticed the professor leaning against a nearby wall, and he was comforted: here was a countryman who knew his way around and who could be called on, if need be, although Yáñez had no idea for what he might need the professor.

But the professor, so elitely bearded, was perhaps not going to be any too available. He had been looking the tourists over and reading a book, but then he picked himself up and walked away—and they soon found out he could walk faster than anyone any of them had ever seen—to the foot of the pyramid as if he planned to go up the 187 steps without drawing a breath. But he did not; instead he found himself a shady spot and went on reading.

The woman, whose name was Martha Gilpatrick, wore a dark blue rayon print with a bloused back, and her fatuous, forward-sitting hat assumed that no one could see the ugly back of her head covered with rough hair in perfunctory beauty-parlor curls. She carried a cane and her hands were twisted, but she had the beautiful deep-seeing eyes of a cripple, and that itself would have been moving, but on top of trust, dependence, understanding of other people's weakness, there was an overlay of frantic anger.

She had pushed herself out of the car, ejected herself, really, because she had to slide to the edge of the seat, then dangle her short legs and jump with the help of the cane. She had looked at the professor, their eyes meeting. That was when he decided to leave, even while his hand was in his pocket to take out a card and introduce himself, which would have been in line with his old-fashioned looks.

The woman was a hunchback. At first glance you might have thought she had got it from stooping too long at labor too hard, but then you realized it was a hump born with her. She was very short and thin, as against her husband's great girth and height and weight. She looked the scene over while the lumbering man took his turn to get out.

Once he might have been handsome, but he was a monstrosity now. Having passed the line of decent appearance, he had hurried on as far and as fast as possible into grossness. You could see money in the man but he wore it simperingly—his vulgar obesity, his insulting tones of voice, the way he had of resetting his fine silk jacket over his fat haunches. The horrid little boy, the immature young man, were present in all this, and the oafishness was that much more unpleasant. When you got beyond his mere bulk, you saw that of the two the man was the self-adorner. The woman looked as if she had gone into a cheap store, put thirty-five dollars on the counter and been equipped for this trip from top to toe, while her husband's tie probably cost thirty-five dollars and his studs matched the embossed gold edging of his wallet.

She was certainly paying him no mind; that was all given to the place around her. What she saw first against the blue sky were the circles that kingfishers make in flight, their long tails meanwhile in lesser, separate, but not less beautiful, circular motion. Under this, another layer of color moved everywhere—mauve butterflies, their flights beginning and ending like a young girl's short and uninterrupted song. And then Martha Gilpatrick raised her eyes to the buildings of Xlapac, purple in the strong light, the pyramid with the nuns' house behind it and over on the hill to the left the governors' palace. (She knew the names and places.) She was becoming aware of the beauty of detail, but she had no way to express her delight in the enmasked façades enriching the strong horizontals and, on the building corners, the rain-god's elegant snout over and over. And all lifted up, brightened, illuminated by the un-shadowed morning light so that the space between her and the buildings was neither near nor far. Distance was different and so was time.

She did not think in words and was engulfed in silence; she started when her husband spoke. He whined, full of sincere self-pity, "Are you going to stand here all day, Martha? I can get sunstroke even if you can't."

She put her head sideways to see him, a fugitive, small-animal look which the beauty had surprised out of her. She was vulnerable just then. Yáñez saw that and so did the professor over by the pyramid—distance so changed that he was really among them or rather among and apart at the same time. And the four of them were drawn together by the defenselessness of the woman, although not all of the bonds were pity. The professor was chivalrous. Yáñez was not exactly that. He had seen women bullied before; not that he liked it, and this man looked the complete bully. He watched them mostly with curiosity, and he saw the woman step toward the man, no obvious menace in it (how could a frail, sick, ugly thing menace a giant like that?) but the man wilted, or wrinkled like a balloon slowly seeping air. The woman watched him, her face changing with each jot of different emotion from primordial flight to cruelty. Yáñez came alongside her, and they began to walk in the direction of the governors' palace.

The professor was speeding away across a drained lake bed where the high comb of a building came out of the earth and the earth out of the possessive foliage of trees. The old man walked so fast that he created his own breeze and his beard floated around his neck and behind his head. Mr. Gilpatrick pointed to the professor and spoke to Martha, "I can keep up with him." He galloped ahead as if he were going to do it; the old thin one moved as if he did not know he was going fast, the fat one agitated speed into a travesty of itself. Shortly he pulled back to join Martha and Yáñez and then trailed them up the incline.

The guide was saying, "Should I tell you the story of the king of this place?"

She answered, "Yes, the story of the hunchbacked king of Xlapac. Tell it to me."

Yáñez helped her on the bouldery path to the governors' palace, an arm under her thin elbow. In the field in front there was a double-headed stone jaguar, a throne in other times. Yáñez sat her on it and himself on the ground beside her. A long-legged, long-winged, pillage-minded hornet kept attacking the guide's green shirt, but he didn't seem to mind. The swallows, not hundreds but thousands and more, swished in and out of the palace doors and windows as if the restoration had been all for them, their endless swoops a pattern too complex to trace.

"Once upon a time—you begin your stories that way?"

"Yes," and looked at her husband chomping about at fallen masks and rain-god heads. "Go on."

"You see, white stone roads went from here into the jungle to other cities—the chicle cutters meet them today—and a prince from this very palace took the white road to another city to find a bride. She never would remove the veil off her face. At last he made her take it away before he would marry her and she was very ugly. But a baby was already borning, only the veiled princess was also a witch and arranged that the baby hatch from a turtle's egg. He was a dwarf. And they made him many trials. His real father made them—not any turtle because, you understand, that was a deception. He won every trial and I can tell you them and he became king of here. If you would climb the steps of the pyramid you would see his little room on top there, a little room for him with a bed no bigger than a child's. And I will show you him also on the kings' wall in the nuns' house." Perhaps nobody but a Latin could have done it, but Yáñez talked easily about a dwarf to Martha, who was one.

The husband came over to them and was immediately attacked by the ravenous hornet and, battling it, left. Martha and the guide got up and followed him, Yáñez ready with more of the story, his mouth open to begin again when the low voice of Mr. Gilpatrick spoke, and, like the heat around them, carried its intensity in tactile, quivering waves.

"Martha. Why did you ever bring me here? We could have gone to Acapulco. We could have gone anywhere but here."

She answered across the guide, who then stepped out of the path of the words and looked away politely at the professor, who had loped back to the pyramid and was examining the long steep staircase.

Martha said, "You know why we came. We had to. You know that. You know he wanted to—"

The fat man sighed. "Look, Martha, I've heard it all before. Look. Are we here to do penance for Lyman? He wanted to be an archeologist. You've told me that a hundred thousand times. Am I supposed to crawl over all Mexico on my hands and knees because of that? What did Lyman himself ever do about being an archeologist?"

Yáñez's perfectly natural curiosity was rattling around in him. Whoever this Lyman was. Yáñez moved away, not out of his earshot but out of their eyesight. Maybe they needed this very place, its grandeur like a poultice drawing out their anger.

She spoke fiercely and directly, not like the sly deflation by the car. "You put him where he is. You never listened to a word he said. You wouldn't let him be himself. You made him into a thief." Between each accusation time was charged with a past accretion of overheld silences.

The man spoke softly, coldly, "Not only a thief, Martha, a murderer. You think I made him that too? You don't think your spoiling him rotten soft had anything to do with that?"

It seemed to Yáñez he ought to interrupt them because now

they were too indecorous. But the woman was already answering in a great shout. Who would have thought she had that voice in her improper head and body, crying out from the Maya summit in the glittering heat down the white roads to far, dead, purple cities, "You never let him have a room or a thing of his own or time for himself. He couldn't have been anything but what you made him."

The man was beet red, the shame maybe only for her shouting, because he said, "I didn't bring you into this foreign country to have you act like a wild witch. Pull yourself together, Martha. I was fool enough to promise you to come, and I have. We'll look at every cranny of this damned sepulcher and then we'll get us to a civilized place and the rest of this vacation time we'll stay there."

The word *sepulcher* flushed Yáñez from cover. "Sir, pardon me, sir, this city was not for burying. It was a great festival city. Here on this plateau you must imagine the dances and the elegant kingfisher robes—very gay and very splendid." He was reproving a child not only for the one gaff but for general obstreperousness.

"Yeh? Say, what's that old man doing now?" The professor was waving to them from the pyramid top. Even Martha looked up, who had been hanging her head as if exhausted by her outcry.

Yáñez spoke quickly, "It's a very hard climb, sir. I would not advise it."

"If he can, I can."

"Forty centimeters each step. One hundred and eighty-seven of them. Besides, sir, just for the present moment, the chain alongside the stairs for pulling on is gone away. They are repairing it." Yáñez looked candidly at his client's bulk—

"You think I'm too fat?"

"Well, sir, no, I don't think that. But everybody use that chain."

"Except the old man who's up there now."

"But this is a sun and a climate you are not accustom to. It is wise to be a little careful."

"I'll decide for myself. Let's not waste any more time. Are you the guide or aren't you? There must be more to see than this one building."

They went down the hill in single file, the guide, offended, giving perfunctory lore as they walked through the ball court, explaining it had been only for practice because the ceremonial games were held at Chichén-Itzá.

"What do you mean ceremonial? Was it a game or wasn't it? You always hear about their great ball games. Well?"

"Not a game the way you think of it, sir." The guide was as disgruntled as his client.

But in the nuns' house Yáñez could not remain vexed. The four great sides with partly restored façades, the kings' side— a carved, ordered, and disciplined entanglement of serpents feathered with corn tassels and, sure enough, the dwarf sitting on a throne—renewed his optimism. He wanted to finish the dwarf king's story.

"He ruled for many years but with too much power. You understand these Maya people were not a very war people and finally they got tired of the little man's strength," looking up at the short-legged figure carved on the wall above them, "and they turned their back on him."

"What did he do?" asked Martha avidly.

"He went to the top of the pyramid and lay down on his little bed and he died."

Mr. Gilpatrick laughed. "What kind of thing was that? They didn't want their king to have power so he laid down and died? What did they think he should have been doing?"

"Well, sir, those people, their wise men and priests you understand, they loved to study."

"Study?" For once Mr. Gilpatrick gave his contempt volume.

Yáñez answered doggedly, "About the stars, the eclipses— they knew more maybe than we know today. I could show you in Chichén-Itzá—"

"Nobody is going to show me anything more than 'these people'—"

Yáñez took himself away, now really angry, and sat down in the shade; the Gilpatricks were left stranded in the middle of the court. The professor, still up on the pyramid, looking down, or God looking from heaven, might have felt pity for these two beings, except that the emotion of each was so arrogant that it pushed even against the peace of an open space surrounded by unrestraining walls, whose proportion was born in some intimate study and passion for time, where every day was garlanded with its special virtues and a day ten thousand years ahead or behind was known and valued now. Not time's ticking passage but its flavor of eternal continuity was what had been preserved in that court.

The woman may have felt it as a blind man feels the sun and moves to find a warmer ray. Why would she not be blind, living the pain she was living because her son was a convicted murderer and was beginning to serve a life sentence for it? She could not visit him for three months and only because of this she had been persuaded to come on the trip. And then the idea of seeing the places he had said—oh, much earlier—that he longed to see had sped the trip, had consecrated it for her. And the neighbors, speaking plainly and understanding little, urged her to go because time, they said, was the best cure.

To his father, Lyman as hopeful archeologist had climaxed the fancy absurdities that the boy and his mother had devised. He had possibly even beaten Lyman for wanting such a cockeyed thing. But does that make a murderer, he asked himself, because his wife's wild accusations were repeating themselves to him, and he looked all around the court hunting for escape—one of those doorways led out to the plain, but he was not sure now which one. He looked at the pyramid, overpoweringly above them. My back aches, he thought, all this climbing. She knows I can't do it. I need to get back to the hotel room, such as it is. Why doesn't she ever think of me?

292   GRINGOS IN MEXICO

She spoke. "I'm going to climb the pyramid."

"You can't."

"I will, though."

"All right, I'll do it too." He laughed. "I'll race you, Martha."

From his refuge Yáñez heard them, and it was more than he could bear. Bad enough for the man to climb: an attack of vertigo or of the heart. But for this ugly little dwarf woman to even approach those peremptory stairs was an idea he could not face. He kept saying, "Madam, please, madam, I cannot permit—"

"I saw a big shade hat in your car," she answered.

He tried appealing to the husband, but some implacable line of battle had been drawn between these two, which Yáñez with all his experience of crazy tourists could not define nor alter. They walked happily, Yáñez thought, to the bottom of the pyramid. And he got the hat; what else could he do?

One could not have helped seeing that this was something for which they had prepared for years. One who had known why these two married in the first place would also have known the course they were running now. He had been a boy with a small head and a body so tall that he was out of place with the pretty girls who liked normal-sized boys. And it was she, Martha, who was the wooer, the devotion in her eyes balm for other rejections. But marriage even to her whom he did not love, or especially to her because she doted on him so, made him into a big handsome man, and the boyish impulse to marry a hunchback soured into regret in the face of manhood and a hundred eyeing, unexpressed queries—how can a man like this have taken a wife like that? And they had the son. The queries were now compounded by the presence of the boy. The man's solution, perhaps the most honorable one, was to turn into the gargoyle that would have married another of the same. The son was no gargoyle. He was a fine boy but they mangled him in the wheels of the competition which had become the one live thing between them. The murderer, their son, killed them both in effigy.

Martha changed hats, put down her cane, and started climbing a little ahead of her husband.

For him it was the difficulty of lifting that weight. He sweated and groaned, but even so it seemed an ill-matched race. The woman was strong armed and weak legged and her chest crowded by the humping of her shoulders could not give her the air she needed. Every breath was a separate struggle, with boundaries around it, not growth of one into the other but full stop, the heart's plunging beat audible between breaths, and the act of breathing itself cut into segments. So she lived forever on each step (having pulled up the incompetent short legs), but this forever had nothing to do with continuity. It was the forever of blank cessation, eternal stop. This kind of struggle had shaped her life—a battle for each move: to get Lyman to the right school, to get him a bicycle, or to conceal a report card from his father. There had been no sequence in these, she had had to muster her whole strength every time. And the battle of his trial was the same; she had lived each day separately with heart-gripped, scarring determination. So climbing the stairs was not as hard for her as it looked to the two men who watched from below—or at least to Yáñez. The professor had seen her face as he passed her, he coming down. He said to Yáñez, "What is this? What's happening?" He sounded lighthearted.

Yáñez answered abruptly, to the point of bad manners, "You tell me. You're the man of education."

"Are they interested in Xlapac?"

"The woman, yes, a little. The man's a beast. But they came here to fight, not to see anything."

"Yes?"

"Somebody named Lyman, they say he's a murderer, they say they came here because of him. The man's a real brute."

"So what are you going to do? Stand there and let the brute

push her off, or what do you have in mind, my friend?" The professor spoke mildly.

Yáñez was still angry. "If one or the other falls, it's not my concern. Other gringos have fallen. Maybe they shouldn't come here. Maybe it's too rich for their blood."

"Your business is a guide?"

"Up to a point. If they give me madmen?"

"If only one survives it will be the woman." The professor permitted himself a smile.

Those daily, segmented battles had always been against the man she married, as was this contest against him—in the beginning. Used as she was to fighting him, power the only balm for humiliation, she began on the stairs to enjoy this final effort (of its finality she had no doubt), her perpetual effort to snatch a place on earth for her ungainly body. He had never granted her this. Instead he had expanded his own body to fill as much space as possible, thus negating her needed space. But her need would not have to be proved any more; this climb would be conclusive.

Her simian arms with their warped hands were not weakening, but her breath came even harder. Mr. Gilpatrick was groaning and heaving close behind her and she knew that for all his fat he was stronger than she. As he surely must, he passed her, that sweating, bullish bulk. He even took time to stop and remove his tropical silk coat, fold it and lay it on the step above her. And then an event of the greatest oddity occurred: this time she did not feel the hate that always surged up at his crass little brutalities. It was not forgiveness, of course, but a quick perception in her chest, burning up as it was, that this time she was not racing him. She could not have stopped; she had to get to the top, but that need was within her own head and for herself, because at the top there was going to be an end. Was it the dwarf's hard little bed which she knew was waiting for her? No, this was going to be something more terminal than death: this was going to be the end of time. Victory over Mr. Gilpatrick would never be an end, because every contest had a false finish which presupposed the next race; now there would be no more contests, she was sure of that. She was reduced to the muscles which commanded her knees to lift and place themselves on the next step, and now her inhalation, exacerbate as ever, was nevertheless continuous from breath to breath.

For him, the contest was beneath scorn and utterly compulsive. Up to now, at least, he was a human being who had been able only to think of himself, as if a nerve surgeon had cut off all other lines of communication. So the climb was not hard for him because inside himself he had a source of energy untapped during all the fat days; he had never spent himself. Even the living daily battle with Martha had not begun to use it all.

Now he released that force, and with delight felt the sweat roll off every part of his body, and thought exultantly, "Let this teach her for good, let this be an end of her beating her silly wings." The image amused him. But then, absorbed as he was in the simple pleasure of drawing on that secret energy, he did not notice where his mind wandered nor the emotions that had been hidden in with that concealed power and now released with it: unwittingly he remembered Lyman. Related to himself, of course; every memory must be that for him. The two of them walking—and this was when he had still been a handsome huge man—and his face was looking down from on high, that was his recollection, at the eager small one that talked, and his own face listened. He had listened. She said he never had. But then another face impinged, the one in the courtroom, white, frightened, and full of hate, looking straight at his own lardy face, although the boy was answering a question from the district attorney, straddlelegged in front of the witness stand, "Get advice from my father? I couldn't have. He never had time to find out I was alive." Mr. Gilpatrick was almost at the pyramid top, so far ahead of Martha that he could afford to pause again.

Yet the satisfaction that he had won this race so easily, that there she was still crawling up like a spider, these thoughts would not lodge firmly enough to give him comfort. He was panting dreadfully but he would not sit down until she got there; here at least habit dominated, made him stand triumphant for her defeat.

She did not rise from the last step but lay face down. She was neither angry nor cringing; he could tell this from long acquaintance with her humped back. She was resting.

He waited.

Still face down she said, "What's at the top here anyway?" Then she sat up.

A race has a finish line, the broken tape a symbol of achievement, one runner faster than the other, a record which shatters time. Now they both looked around and there was nothing up there except time unshattered. She saw this. He, always suffocated by his own body, saw less. But he said, "I must have lost ten pounds on the way up."

There was the dwarf's room, that truly. There was no bed in it but a stone slab. Martha went there and lay down. It fitted her but she did not die. She breathed easily.

He sat outside the room, panting for a long time, looking down along the unrestored side of the pyramid at the jutting rock points. What if he fell, purposely rolling down? But he said in a loud voice, speaking to her too, "We got up here; we'll get down." And he hummed something that resembled an old ditty, "The king of France and all his men, Went up the hill and down again."

Mr. Gilpatrick was first, joining Yáñez and the professor. He stood by them. He looked up at Martha and shook his head, "She shouldn't try to do those things. She's not able." Both men heard the absence of spleen in the words, and Yáñez marvelled. He handed Mr. Gilpatrick his coat, which he had retrieved, and he was almost respectful, giving a small bow which seemed not very incongruous. Then he started up the stairs to help Mrs. Gilpatrick.

The professor spoke quietly, "I thank you most sincerely, sir, for your interest in one of my country's great monuments."

Mr. Gilpatrick was still catching his breath and he waited quite a while before answering. In fact he sat down on a pile of rock, sighing and settling in his padded bones.

"If I'm rude, excuse me, but are you by any chance an anthropologist or, what is it, an archeologist?"

"At your service." The professor nodded and now proffered that card, which read, *Profesor Porfirio Jiménez y Jiménez K., Universidad Autónoma de Guadalajara, Guadalajara, Jalisco.*

The fat man took plenty of time to read the card, mispronouncing the name half aloud. Then he said, "My boy wanted to be one."

"Yes? Well," and the professor shrugged questioningly, "it's a profession in which time can hardly be counted."

Mr. Gilpatrick looked puzzled, for a minute watched the flight of swallows in and out of the inner temple of the pyramid.

The professor said, "I mean it takes a long, long time, sir, to understand what it is to be an archeologist."

There was another pause, this time Mr. Gilpatrick watching Yáñez, who gently aided Martha's slow descent. Then he said, "Well, my boy has all the time there is, Professor." He looked at the card again, not trying to say the name. "What I wondered was if you would tell me some books to give—to send him. About this place—" and he looked around it, "or others—that one Chich—" He struggled with the pronunciation, and the professor left him alone, but then answered with an extra, grave benignity which exactly matched him and his beard, "Of course." He waited a minute, then added, "We shall speak about it at more length? Perhaps you and your wife will do me the honor to have a refreshment with me? A beer?"

Mr. Gilpatrick looked surprised. "Where?" There had been no sign of beer or a place to drink it when they came in.

But now the site was alive although there was hardly what you would call bustle. The caretaker booth was open and just outside the entrance gate, under a big ceiba tree, there was, sure enough, a cold-drink stand, with goats, people, and dogs around it. "Thank you, Professor, a beer would be just right." He got up and they walked together.

And Mr. Gilpatrick moved his eyes slowly over all the site. He was an ill-bred fat man, but the place looked handsome to him, and besides that it looked familiar, in some ways more like home than any place he had ever been.

"Martha," he called back to her where she was coming along with Yáñez. They were talking so intently that he surely must be telling her another story. They acted like old friends. "Martha, hurry up." But he was in no hurry. None of them were.

Margaret Shedd

I HATE YOU, CRUZ RIVERA

IT was not only his looks we held against that little boy, Cruz; it was the way he dangled the half-dead, struggling iguana. At least that was the way I felt. For the past few miles, country children had been holding them up for sale, but not so cruelly. The directions they gave us in Mexico City were look for your turn-off after you meet the children on the road selling iguana. They had also said the iguana were good eating, but although my precious Robert and I agreed on very little we did agree that that was the last thing on earth we'd eat.

Our reasons were different. Robert made one of his orations about how anyone but a fool could see that this was a pre-historic giant hooded and bedecked as any colossus should be, that this small dragon was a symbol of times past not understood, majesty ineluctable (what a word), ancient earth curves which the shrunken heart cannot quite forget. Of course Robert had been drinking along the way. Iguana don't affect me poetically. I think that they are rather sinister and that the meat would probably be slimy.

It was a fact, though, that the one Cruz had was impressive if you like the fantastic: purple, armoured, the crest along his head and back like a war-bonnet. As our car approached, the boy pushed the iguana onto the hot macadam on its green-fingered feet and then pulled it back with the cord and hung it in the air. The turn-off was right beside him, kilometer 144. We had to stop. At once our car was surrounded by ugly children.

"Go away," I said angrily.

Robert closed the window on his side as if this would protect him from them.

The leader, Cruz, as we later found out, put his dragon's head into my window. I knew something more than words was necessary. I took out ten pesos. That dirty boy (in size like an American six-year-old, but he looked about a hundred right then) didn't reach for the money until I pushed it at him.

"Look, we'll buy all your iguana. But don't keep them dangling around. Kill them right away."

Cruz said, "Why shouldn't we take them back to the river? Why not, Miss?" With the car stopped we could hear the water.

"How silly can you get, Julia?" Robert sounded perfectly drunk. It had caught up with him all of a sudden and I was glad we were standing still because he would not give up a wheel once he started to drive no matter how much he drank. "Julia, you know perfectly well that he'll keep them alive to sell them again. Why give him money? Look at him." Robert laughed. "You want to demoralise him, don't you, dear little Julia?"

Indeed Cruz was eyeing my purse and I thought triumphantly (why was that?) that there was very little he wouldn't do to get hold of it. I took out another ten pesos, maybe to annoy Robert, or maybe it was some funny idea of letting Cruz see the roll of money I had.

Meantime I said to Robert, "You listen to me. I want him to kill them just so he can't sell them again. Anyway, let him get them away so we don't have to look at them. Go on, get them away."

Cruz shrugged, but the absurd deal was made and the iguana were dangled off by two of the smaller boys. Now a wad of girls crowded round, filthier than the boys. They kept saying, "Give me a five centavos."

"Talk about demoralise. Look at them, Robert. Your architect friend must have put in his oar."

Robert didn't answer because he was going to sleep, his curly head on the steering wheel and his hands clutching it like a life-preserver.

One girl spoke rapidly. She was taller than the rest, almost fair, and wore a dress that had once been blue, with inset lace around her breasts and the skirt, but was now the same dirt colour as the others' garments, which looked as if they were made of flour sacking. I was sorry I knew some Spanish because what I could understand was an itemizing of me; she was making fun of me and telling the things she could do for Robert. I looked away from her. I was frightened. Cruz was back at the window doing lassoing tricks, the coil of rope in his iguana hand. He said belligerently, and his animosity was a relief after that pale blue girl, "Are you waiting for the jeep from the ranch?"

"Yes." I admitted it reluctantly. It was going to be dark all too soon. We had no idea where the ranch was, only that its name was The Pomegranates. We had been told you went up a mountain road which only a jeep could manage and that our host would meet us at kilometer 144. Instead, here was a village with a lot of children, and no adults as far as we could tell, and an unpronounceable name you could never hope to get used to—t's and z's so tightly crowded together that they vibrated and made the word into a weapon that left you helpless, however, since you did not know how to use it. The place was old, with a rundown church and a jail and mud houses. Probably we had driven through many villages like it, but this one seemed outlandish.

As far as that went, we didn't know our host either, nor could I imagine why he would want a house in such an out-of-the-way place. I had never met him; Robert barely once or twice, and had heard him lecture. Naturally he was interested in him because he was an architect and famous, Eric Something, and Robert was so excited about being invited up there that it had become the high spot of our trip. He said this house was the most beautiful thing that Eric Whateverhisnamewas had ever designed and that finally he had bought it from the people who had him build it and lived there himself.

All the way out from Mexico City Robert kept saying, with his hands moving rhythmically on the wheel, "What a place for a honeymoon, Julia." I realised now it had been the banking up of drunkenness, not mere repetitious lust. We were on our honeymoon, true enough, well into the third dire week, and we had known each other a weary long time before that. Robert also said repetitiously that Eric hardly ever asked anyone to come there. By now I was wondering if maybe this invitation had somehow been forced out of him by Robert and if maybe he never intended to meet us.

Amid his whirling rope coils Cruz remarked, "The jeep is broken."

"How do you know?"

"I heard yesterday that the oil all came out on one of the steep grades."

I thought he was saying this to torment me. I did know from his voice that the place and children were not only strange, they were our enemies, especially Cruz. I saw I would have to make a friend of this enemy if I could.

"What's your name, boy?"

He told me Cruz Rivera, without tacking on the usual abracadabra about at your service and I am your loyal servitor.

"How old are you?"

"Eleven years." And he went right on, "What's your name, Miss?"

"Mine? My name? Why, it's Julia." I answered without even thinking. That was because he was staring at me so hard.

He said it softly, the 'j' like an 'h', Julia.

His eyes were black and large but they were opaque. What was he looking at? The car, stylish and ugly; two gringos, the blond big man half asleep. I had on a white sweater and white slacks. I had known they were foolish for a trip in a jeep but I wanted to look my best. Why? Who knows? Somehow the unknown host with his perfect house was a challenge I had to try to meet. Robert too was dressed in light colours; he always wore blue to match his eyes, so his sweater was that, and his slacks pale grey. I could see ourselves refracted off the blank eyes of Cruz Rivera, and we looked unripe.

Cruz was dressed in light colours too, that classic floursack white that had never been washed. There were wraparound pants and a shirt. Every visible part of him was dirt—worn, and not temporary, by any means—deep into his skin. He reached out his hand and touched my bare arm resting along the window frame. That small hand was cold, and not exactly scaly but as dry as scales.

"Don't do that. Please don't."

He laughed, and his eyes peeled back their unlighted surface and I saw a little boy, a laughing boy. For that moment I wasn't afraid.

He said it right out. "Don't be afraid of me, Julia. I'll take you up to The Pomegranates. If you have one of those electric torches we'll be fine. I know the road even in the dark. That electric light would be for you so you shouldn't fall. Part of the road is along the top of a precipice."

He was absolutely tender and compelling. I thought I never before had met such a virtuous child. I was ready to take the flashlight out of the glove compartment, leave Robert sleeping there, and climb the mountain road with Cruz.

I said, "You better get yourself awake, Robert. Your fine friend has evidently forgotten us, so we'll have to go on foot." The last thing I wanted was to take that winding drive back with Robert. The walk up the mountain now seemed dangerous to me, but less so than a three-hour ride with a drunken man, husband or no.

Anyway, Robert wasn't going to miss his big treat for anything. He climbed out of the car, locked it laboriously, and stumbled down the short incline Cruz showed us was the beginning of the way. Cruz led.

It wasn't dark yet. In fact there was a fine sunset, unfurling distances one after the other, and brash mountains halved in prehensile struggle, purple on slashed sides and rolling blue where rocks and earth were not afraid to make a slope slanted for the rain. The wash of good evening light was filtered by Indian laurels in the table-land which the path was following. No time like early evening, I thought, while a goat tribe picked its way across the terraced cow paths of a slope on the other side of the valley from us.

We could hear the river, softly, for we were far above it.

I think I agreed with Robert that happiness is for fools, but here was a place plainly mine—the earth's tilt so particular that I needed not to hide from myself, at least. It made me joyful to see this appropriate beauty. Even the words to match came into my mind, although I laughed at Robert when he used that kind of language. Morning glory vines grew thickly along the path and I saw one flower blooming, a mistake of course, but the blue-purple was just as reminiscent of childhood mornings as if it had been morning instead of day's end.

The darkness reached us when we were on a plateau of small up-ended rocks and a prickly shrub that had taken the place of the laurels. A family of dogs barked far away, high-pitched country baying, not the clack of city dogs. And, too, as dark came we heard cow bells. The two sounds offset each other and the whir of grasshopper legs threw the balance toward peace.

Cruz was first, I came next, and Robert last. Although Robert was not staggering now, he slipped occasionally on a loose rock. So did I, that small shattering jerk more disturbing than a fall. Only Cruz walked surely on his tough, bare feet. I think if the twilight had only lasted longer we would have been friends. It was the darkness that set us on edge again, because it got harder and harder to know who we were, and Robert and I certainly had no idea where we were. Perhaps that made me think again that Cruz was my enemy. In the sundown light and especially in the presence of those wild flowers, growing in every space a flower could find, mostly small with open faces and golden hearts, I was able to

watch the boy and take him as part of the place. It was different in the dark.

The first thing was that Robert and I began to stumble
badly, and there was Cruz surer of himself without a light
than we were with it. Robert kept calling me to share the
torch with him, and I tried and did, but if I put the light behind me too much of the time I was left in the dark myself.
Then he demanded that I give it to him. That I would not do,
having learned in these three weeks that his first and last
thought was for himself. He came up to me. I felt his hand on
my wrist, so tight that I was going to have to drop the torch.
Above the water's din—the path was descending and we were
directly over the river—I shouted to him that if the torch fell
it would break.

"Then give it to me, you fool."

We hated each other so much just then that it was a straight
black unpolished unbendable shaft between us. And it was
right at that moment that Cruz called out, his voice not
frightened but peremptory, urgent. "Give me the light this
way, Miss, this way."

I wrenched my arm free, obeying that child voice which
had to shout to be heard and in doing so had shed everything
but childishness. I threw the torchlight wildly, hunting for
Cruz, because in the hullaballoo with Robert I had lost what
sense of space I had managed to hang on to in the dark. The
beam moved wide, found a lightning-struck, crippled tree
crouching over the path on one side, felt its way into the drop
on the other, not far to the river but steep, and finally caught
Cruz.

I had been very anxious to find him. Perhaps I thought he
had fallen. But, no, he was standing as straight as he could
and he had let down those white wrap-around pants and
there he was, male child. Why was he exhibiting himself?
Why the command to throw the light on him?

The sounds Robert made were not of disgust but of fierce
and pungent anger. "The miserable, foul little son of a bitch,"
and the words were mixed with action, scrambling rage,

sound changed into literal motion. In one arc he grabbed the torch and pushed me out of the way and pounced toward Cruz. I followed, of course. The hate blazing in me was for the compound of the two, not Cruz, not Robert, but an amalgam of both. No, I hated Cruz Rivera.

The beam of light skittered this way and that, fragmented by indecent motion. The three of us were also fragmented by the light until we were more than three, a crowd, a mob of hunters and the hunted, jeerers and the jeered. Cruz fell to the mob.

Perhaps he had called because while he stood there with his pants down he had suddenly found he was too near the edge and had shouted, unmindful of his exposure, but his voice had not sounded like that. Now, with us both scrabbling at him (I do remember that my hand touched him once) he was falling and we heard a rock we had loosened go down after him, and then many more. And we heard one scream, as far-off and penetrating as the memory of a nightmare.

We went down the bank, almost a precipice. Most of the time I was sliding. It was the only way for me to get there. I was not grieving for Cruz. I had to see him before any feeling could begin.

A big rock had caught him and he lay bunched in among the loose ones which had followed him. He was stripped of his dirty clothes—rolling down had done that, I suppose—a dying little child. He was gasping and you could hear it above the river's wash, overpoweringly near. Once the flashlight touched up the ropes of water tossed down from the mountain above. Cruz had fallen at the foot of a waterfall.

I could still hear him gasp, and I heard him call my name, "Julia, Julia, this is where we find the iguana." It seems he wanted badly to say that, because it cost him a great effort. I think his neck was broken. He straightened out then, arched up once, and his head fell back. There was no doubt that he was dead.

There was enough light spilling over from the shaft Robert had on Cruz so we could see each other. Our clothes were neither blue nor grey nor any colour but that dirty white that had never been washed.

Robert said, "It was you who pushed him, wasn't it, Julia? You know that, don't you, Julia?"

To get back up the precipice was a black time, the waterfall to one side of us dulling all sound of effort. We didn't help each other except that Robert shone the torch my way from erratic time to time. In the dark I clung to whatever there was, a trunk or root or rock.

When we got to the top we were confronted by lights, suddenly, as if they came on for us, although I think simply we couldn't see them until we climbed the overhanging lip of the bank. It was a house illuminated for a festival, light pouring in layers onto great trees that surrounded the house. There was a wall and a gate in front, both lustrous bright. It occurred to me that Cruz might have been calling out to say we had reached The Pomegranates because it looked as if we were back on the path at the place we had left it. Here was the little promontory on which Cruz had stood. But lights there certainly had not been before.

Now the electric torch seemed ridiculous. I don't know whether Robert put it out, or if it was invisible in the majestic brilliance of the lighted foliage and of the beautiful granite wall and of the wooden gate that belonged in that setting. We stood for a while, certainly not looking at each other but at the gate. Finally Robert walked over to it and knocked. The knock sounded strong and it comforted me. We did exist. Our knock was audible.

There was a long wait before the gate was opened. That man was Eric, but he was nothing like what I had expected. Small, ancient. And in the first moment I saw that he was invincible, not a man you could urge to anything.

"Who are you?" he said loudly.

"Eric, Eric." Robert's voice was weak, unlike those fine knocks he had made on the gate. I don't think Eric heard him at all and I could tell Robert was afraid of him. "Eric, you asked me to come."

"No, I don't know you. Who are you? You seem to be in trouble and I'd gladly send you down in the jeep, but I have just this moment dispatched that to the village for a friend of mine and his bride, who've been waiting there a long while. We are having trouble with the jeep." He spoke just like that, slowly, pedantically. And he closed the gate.

He closed the gate, but first I saw past him to the house. Between us and it, even between the gate and the house, flowed a quiet river, the same one that made the waterfall. Beyond the gleaming, sparkling river, the house of glass, lighted to greet the bridal pair, stirred because those trees around it moved in the wind.

Edmund J. Robins

A SNAPPED STRING

SHE stood one step above Luis on the set-rock stairway that led from the terrace, steeply, to the slope of orchard. Her fingers dug into his shoulders and she dropped her head so that the point of her chin rested in the thick black crest of his hair. He spread his legs quickly for support, swaying slightly under her weight, then steadied and leaned back against her, his head between her breasts.

"We could take a nasty fall," he said, his voice acid.

"But you love the place, darling? I couldn't be happy unless you loved the place just as I love it!"

"It's beautiful," he said, and the two of them stood quietly, looking across the glossy green of the citrus trees to the red-tiled roofs of the village, set at every angle and always the right angle, and beyond to the lake, gray today with the mist dropping from the purple peaks like skeins of spun glass upon the water.

"Then you have decided on this place?" Luis declared.

They had looked everywhere—in the north of Mexico, in the south, along the two coasts, but even curling down the road from Toluca into this mountain-circled valley with the long lake, even through the metronomic beat of the wind-shield wiper, which couldn't quite keep clear the streaming glass, she had seen only beauty, which her eager cries had told him: "Oh, Luis, those pine trees marching up that ridge! Do you see those two arm in arm? It's enchanting! Oh, darling! We've found it! Oh, really, we have found it!"

He shrugged her hands from his shoulders, turning and mounting to the terrace. She climbed with him, clutching his elbow, running her hand down his arm to find his hand.

"We will be beautifully happy here," she said. Her voice choked so that she put up her other hand to her throat, fingering the scar of her operation.

Through the wrought-iron gateway onto the snaky street, the urchins who had crowded about the station wagon called shrilly. "*Quinto, señorita!*" "*Quinto, señor!*" "*Allo, señorita.*" "Me name ees Chucho, *señorita.*"

"The darlings," Mary said. "Oh, Luis, the first thing I'll do is teach them English!"

But she spoke to them in Spanish, the excellent Spanish with which she always amazed him. The couple of Russian songs which she had had in the concert repertoire she apparently had patiently memorized, much as she appeared to have done with the German *leider;* but she had studied intensively French and Italian and, of her own volition, had moved into Spanish: "The words sing themselves!" She was no fool, certainly. And could one even call a person so consistently affected, affected?

Standing with magenta bougainvillaea behind her, she seemed unusually attractive, almost young. Her abundant and beautiful still-dark hair was drawn into a long pony's tail, tied with a bow of lilac ribbon. Her forehead was wide and white above her carefully arched brows. All the bones of her face showed finely through the smoothly drawn skin. Perhaps her slightness, the suggestion of hollowness to her cheeks were kindly to her: before the operation, she had been a noteworthy Mimi, but for him she lacked the voluptuousness for what had been her favorite, Carmen. Luckily, she no longer attempted to sing, though she kept in her handbag a pair of handsome castanets (they reminded him always of bulls' ears he had seen cut in the Plaza), dragging them out in the most incongruous places, in a lunchroom, in a railway station, to warm them between her palms, to clack, clack, clack them just enough to make both herself and him conspicuous, not quite long enough for him ever to have made a derisive comment. "They're like tiny kittens! They need warmth and love!" She would raise to her lips the smooth black ovals tied together with red and yellow yarn. "Poor dears! I don't fondle them enough. Their little bellies sound perfectly hollow!" And to his jaded, yet experienced ears, they did sound "clock, clock, clock." It was so with the guitar too, which she would never relinquish to any porter. How many miles, Luis wondered, had he carried the black case from which she lifted the instrument as though she were lifting an infant from its cradle, gently, gently, running her fingertips sensitively along the polished wood?

He had known her only shortly in her profession. At nineteen, he had finished a secretarial course at a Los Angeles night school and, perhaps because of his appearance, had found the only immediate position, that of waiter in a Laguna restaurant. Mary Donovan? The name meant nothing to him when the manager, along with the head waiter, ushered her party in. "A tip, m'boy. Tips!" the manager had whispered too close to his ear, a hand too softly laid seconds too long across his own. However, the job paid well. As usual, he did not withdraw his hand though he felt the hairs at the nape of his neck tightening in their follicles. "I understand," he said, straightening the napkin across his arm, flipping expertly the leaves of his order pad.

He had seen far too many well groomed women to be impressed, but her eyes had caught his on the diamond pendant lying between her breasts. She smiled at him. "Mexican?" she asked. "Yes, madam," he answered, his English certainly as American as her own.

It was only when she coughed so savagely, flashing her

hands to her throat, that he really noticed her. Smoothly, he poured another glass of water. Suavely, and honestly kindly, he asked how he might help her.

"Nothing. Nothing." She had green capsules in her gold mesh bag. He held the carafe, waiting, while she swallowed two.

"You're a dear," she said, her eyes still weeping. And her still wet eyes looked him up and down, coolly, appreciatively.

"You're a handsome boy," she said. "You make a beautiful Don José." She stretched out a thin hand and stroked his arm as she might have stroked a cat.

"But"—But—" He felt himself flushing; he saw the half-smiles on the faces of her companions. "My name is Luis, madam."

"A lovely name! All of the Spanish names are lovely names. Like uncomposed music!"

Then he had escaped, remembering the peculiar huskiness in her voice, the sharp rasp as again she held her throat, the almost electric clinging of her palm to his forearm.

Now he was called her secretary; he had been with her, on and off, for seven years.

But the children beyond the gate were pressing eager, laughing faces through the black tendrils, between the wrought-iron leaves. "Allo, mees." "Allo, meestair." "*Quinto, señorita?*"

"The darlings! Luis, haven't we got some coins?"

She shoved her hand into his trousers pocket, scrabbling for the money.

He squirmed back from her touch, excited and annoyed. "Let me," he said, drawing out a handful of copper pieces, warm from his thigh. He watched her dividing them among the cupped brown palms, and suddenly was conscious of his own hand lying loosely upon the balustrade, palm up and cupped. Luis clenched it tightly, watching the tendons tauten under the smooth pinkish-tan, the oval pink nails whitening with the pressure.

"*Adiós Adiós!* Tomorrow! Until tomorrow!"

Her voice was high; her voice was happy. She turned to him her lighted face, alive, gay, her blue eyes sparkling.

"Oh, Luis!" she said. "Were you a charming little boy like these? Like the little one without any panties?"

"I never begged," Luis said coldly.

Seizing his arm, she laughed. "But with those marvelous dark eyes, those extraordinary eyelashes!"

Throwing her arms about him, she pushed her face against his chest. Her words were muffled and hot through his yellow sports shirt: "Oh, darling! Darling! It's like finding home!"

"Home?" he asked slowly, thinking of New York, thinking of San Francisco and Chicago. "Home?" And he thought of his father, nattily dressed behind the shined counter of his liquor store in San Diego; his mother, tying his sisters' sashes, examining their ears before she sent them down the palm-lined block to school.

Thoughtfully, Mary lifted her face. "Here I can be one of you!"

"One of *us?*" he asked, and he seized her shoulders, pressing her away from him, looking deeply and perplexedly into her blue eyes. Holding her so, he swung his glance across the circle of landscape: the brilliant splotches of clothing on the balconies down in the village; the steep cobbled street where the burros in strings of three and four moved slowly up or down like fat gray lice; the lush mallow and dock and morning glory growing unheeded among the orange trees; the veils of blue smoke oozing from under the eaves of chimneyless houses; a *barrio* fountain, like a dark eye below him, where he could just distinguish the flash of a couple of oil cans a barefoot child was filling; the tiled dome of the crumbling church. . . .

"María," he said, "are you sure this place is for us, us two?"

"Forever!" she said, pressing her forehead against his cheek.

He shrugged—into another round of time. They had spent two months in the Adirondacks, three months on the Oregon coast, a month in Vancouver, a few days here, a few weeks there; only one long period, a full year, back in Laguna after her operation, when each day served more brutally to prove to her that she no longer had her voice. Then he had been truly sympathetic; there had been many friends, many visitors, an active, pleasant, and, for him, a growing life, even though daily he watched her spirits wane until she knew the truth, and accepted the truth. Still, he had found it a relief to be drafted, to be forced away from her without any break between them. He appreciated her gifts, her letters. In mess hall, the clerk who distributed the mail asked him, "That isn't *the* Mary Donovan?" Luis blushed, pleased. "Yes, I've been her secretary close to two years." "Say, guys, did you know Pérez was Mary Donovan's secretary?" "Mary Donovan?" "Sure, the famous opera star." "Fat, like real opera?" He showed them her photographs—Mary svelte, charming— photographs from years back, but with "Affectionately, your María," "To Luis, to keep you from forgetting!" There was a delightful warmth to this reflected glory. The kidding was flattering: "I thought the old girl was old enough to be your mother! Jeez, what a set-up!"

Mary Donovan was old enough to be his mother. Part of that facial smoothness was explained by two thin crescents, pale lavender scars hidden by her ears. Still there had been some talk of starring Mary in a movie, the voice, of course, dubbed in from her own recordings, from which she drew excellent royalties. "I'm much too young to act out my own life! It's hardly begun!" She flashed her own firm white teeth, rejecting immediately the barely suggested offer.

It had been different with the publisher. When Luis had re- turned from Korea, Mary had been demanding: "Of course you'll continue with me! Now I need a secretary more than ever." Already Luis had taken from her dictation copious notes: "My Fear of Farrar," "My Amiga Anderson," "Friend- ship with Flagstad," chapter headings, anecdotes, favorite dishes, stage business, costumes—all for Mary's memoirs. "Quite Contrary" she now spoke of as an amusing title.

Settled once more—for how many weeks, Luis won- dered—the scrapbooks, the photographs, the letters, the diaries, the record-player and the records came out of the jammed trunks. "Work, work, work, in the mornings!" Mary exclaimed, clasping her hands tightly under her pointed chin. "And Life in the afternoons!"

Though it was the rainy season, the sun flooded the terrace until one or two o'clock. It was the pleasant time of day for the barefooted children to be about. "Are the oranges ripe, *señorita?*" Their straight broad noses pushed through the wrought-iron gate; their slim hands clung to the bars.

"The little monkeys! Let them in, Luis! You mustn't *pick* the oranges, children, but you may have any you find on the ground." She stood watching them scurry through the trees.

"Shall we continue, *señorita?*" Luis asked, biting the tip of his pencil. She came to him, laughing. "Where were we, darling? Oh, about my insisting on changing the score!"

"Right, *señorita.*" And the dictation continued through the shouts of the children along the slope, while the clouds billowed up over the mountains, first white and pearly and fat, then spilling over the blue and verdant ridges, opalescent, trailing across the evergreens, down to the gray lake.

At first her children left before the rain. "*Muchas gracias, señorita, señorita.*" "*Adiós, señorita.*" Then they stayed longer and longer, peering over the balustrade of the terrace, giggling, whispering, running back down into the orchard like frightened mice when Luis, glaring at them, tapped his pencil nervously against the table, so that when the clouds opened, spurting their burden in great sheets, "But the children!" Mary would cry. "*Niños! Niños! Niños!*" Steely rain would blot out the village. "They'll be sopping!"

"Listen, María. These kids were living here years before you saw the place."

"Poor darlings! Come along! Come along!"

Tittering, they would push each other up the stairway, stop shyly at the open doors, their eyes entering the room first, inquisitive little mice, finding this bright pillow, that basket of rusty apples.

"How pretty, *señorita,*" "Are those apples yours, *señorita?*"

Their ragged white shirts bulged with limes and oranges. The pockets of their stained cotton trousers were tight-packed with treasure.

"Come in, boy. Don't be frightened."

They came in hesitantly, very politely, removing their straw hats, scratching their heads, sitting gingerly in the seats of wood and woven reed, smiling when Mary smiled, sobering when she became sober.

"Please, María. We've got enough fleas without adding lice to them."

"But when you were a child, darling."

"When I was a child," Luis said, "I lived in the United States. There were plenty of Mexicans who went barefoot and dirty, but I didn't. My father—Oh, hell!"

She eyed him lovingly. "Lucky, lucky Luis!"

"Why is your son angry, *señorita?*"

"He isn't her son; he's her boy-friend."

The children looked at one another, looked at Mary and Luis, laughed heartily, holding their chests and bellies to ease the laughter.

"You're letting them make fools of us," Luis said.

He rose quickly, grabbing his folded raincoat.

"I'll leave you with your friends." He clanged the gate behind him.

"But darling! Darling!"

Rain washed down the cobbled street. Before he had reached the plaza, his American Oxfords were squishing with wet. He turned in to the first refreshment stand, threw off his raincoat, and hunched down at one of the blue-painted tables.

"Good afternoon, *señor.*"

He looked up into pale-gray almond eyes, the lashes so long and straight, they seemed a fringe of black pins.

"*Buenas tardes,*" he said, sitting up straight, startled and charmed.

He sat there the rest of the afternoon and evening, drinking the sickeningly sweet *refrescos,* palely colored sugar-water, watching her slick black hair, parted in the middle, drawn back in two thick plaits braided with cerise ribbon, watching her waxen cheeks, her lips, almost purple when the light was turned on.

"What is your name, *señorita?*" he asked with the third drink.

"Ramona, señor." She tipped her face shyly to one side, though her pale eyes were fixed on his eyes.

"Ramoncita? Where I come from, we have a very pretty story about a Ramona, but a very sad story."

"You're from the United States? But I don't like sad stories."

Outside, the rain beat down, lessened, beat down again. She waited on other customers, swinging her hips under her tight green skirt, glancing at him from the corner of an eye. Her breasts pushed out the blue-checked bib of her apron. Her belly rounded pertly from the tightly tied apron string. She was pregnant, he suddenly realized. Standing close to him, feet slightly spread, she emitted a vaguely acrid odor like the smell of charcoal smoke and the scent of some crushed herb.

"How old are you, Ramoncita?"

"Seventeen, *señor,*" she answered; palms on her hips.

He felt that she was very willing, but when the proprietor began to put down the shutters, a boy stopped inside, sandaled, hung with soiled white shirt and shapeless trousers, straw hat pushed back from his forehead. A machete was tucked through his wide embroidered belt.

The girl was wrapping her shoulders in a green-and-yellow-striped *rebozo*. "My brother always takes me home, *señor.*" She smiled at Luis.

"Your brother?"

The boy's face was bronze, though his eyes too were almond-shaped and seemed even paler in his somber face. Down hung silkily over the sharp corners of his wide, dark mouth.

"But he really is my brother," the girl said, laughing, and Luis was conscious that her dangling earrings were of plastic, her hands grimy, her ankles bare, her shoes shapeless. He walked out with them, into the thin drizzle.

"Wouldn't your brother like to go to the movies?"

"There are no movies tonight, *señor.*"

"Tomorrow?"

"Who knows, *señor?*"

He shook hands in farewell, dropping her limp hand quickly. The brother's fingers barely touched his palm.

His soles slipped on the slick cobbles; the way was all up-hill. The high walls of the gardens, the dark fronts of the windowless or shuttered houses made the street bleak. At a couple of corners, dim street-lamps scarcely managed thin globes of yellowish light. It seemed like midnight; yet, when he checked his wristwatch, it proved to be shortly after nine. As he made the final turn, the voice of Mary Donovan came to meet him—a recording of *La Paloma;* and he walked more slowly. On the closing note, he unlocked the metal gate.

She was alone, her back to the door as he entered. Quietly, she lowered the top of the record-player.

"María."

His damp soles made unpleasant sucking sounds as he crossed the red tile toward her. He caught the faint odor of the perfume she had used ever since he had known her. Her eyes were incredibly blue. Against her hollowed cheeks, pendant diamond earrings shot sparks of clear color.

"Don't touch me!" she said abruptly. "You've been with some woman."

Luis flushed uncomfortably.

"This is news," he said.

"But true," she said.

"You say it."

"Do you deny it?" Mary asked.

"I'm not discussing it."

His raincoat crackled as he put his hand out toward her. She moved a step backward.

"Was she pretty? Was she—young?"

Luis smiled wrily. "You're talking city-talk. I know as little about this village as you do yourself."

"These are your people."

"My people." His forehead wrinkled in puzzlement. He looked at her white throat, and at his hand, which he had not withdrawn. Through his mind's eye, vividly as though the boy were present, he saw Ramona's brother, the lean hands coffeedark, the broad bronze face, the unshaved down, the chafed ankles, roughened with exposure, the horn-like toe-nails sticking through the sandals, the unbuttoned fly. He brought his hand to his chin, running his sensitive fingertips along the slight prickle of his sparse whiskers, dropping his hand abruptly against the rustle of his coat.

"My people?" he asked himself, then asked her, "For you, what am I?" He shuddered, seeing again those horny nails.

"I must change my shoes," Luis said. "My feet are sopping."

Slipping the records into their cases, she said quietly, "We must hurry with the book tomorrow."

Sun gleamed on the terrace in the morning. Luis sharpened his pencils, reread the last few paragraphs. Mary had walked down to the village for fresh hard-crusted rolls. "Bread, *señorita?*" "Do you have candy, *señorita?*" "Don't forget me, *señorita.*" He heard the voices before the gate had clicked open. The children followed her onto the terrace, appeared to fill the terrace, ragged, hungry, laughing, begging. They seemed to surround him; they surrounded Mary, their sticky fingers clinging to her skirt, their hands lifted to where she held the parcel aloft.

"Wait! Be careful! Chucho, stop pushing!"

She was laughing with them, radiant. She unwrapped the butcher paper, passed out the rolls. "Will two each be enough for lunch, darling?"

"One," Luis said, dropping his eyes to the scratchings he was making on the pad. He was horrified at the line of animal paws, the claws, sharply curved, emerging from the fur. The point cracked under the pressure.

He had not heard Mary dismiss them. But their voices were less demanding down among the trees. He picked up his second pencil as Mary sat down beside him.

"Where were we, darling?"

Her chin was against his shoulder as she leaned toward his work. He tore out savagely the scribbled sheet, crumpled it in his fist. "You had just started lessons for your dance in *Carmen*." He jabbed the pencil at the last word. The brittle snap brought him to himself.

"Damn," he said.

Tenderly, she laughed, closing her fingers about his fist. "Let's not be angry, darling."

"No. No, of course not. Let's get on with the work."

He searched about him, on the table top, the chair beside him, the floor; felt in his trousers pocket. "Have you seen my knife?"

"Your pocket-knife?" she asked.

He jumped up, looking toward the orchard.

"One of those damned kids! Chucho! Chucho!"

Already the golden glow of the sun was graying. The wispy clouds that had been driving rapidly across the sky had clabbered into dark rubbery masses.

"Don't be silly, darling," Mary said.

"Next," Luis said, "it will be your diamonds."

"That's ridiculous!" she said, but her hands moved swiftly to the lobes of her ears. She dropped her hands quickly. "You have always been interested in my diamonds!"

His mouth opened. He looked down at her in complete consternation.

"I? I?" With wide eyes, as though he had never seen her, he watched her rise. Her laugh shook him.

"Isn't that your knife?"

He followed her eyes to the balustrade of the terrace where he had placed the knife against the base of the wooden pillar. He was confused by the blood pounding into his temples. The quick lash of rain relieved him. He raised his hot face into it, feeling the sting of the vicious drops.

"The children! Oh, the children!"

But after the numerous days, they no longer needed summoning. Their bare feet splattered on the stone steps, on the tiles of the terrace. They were into the house before Luis could carry in the chairs.

"Does your boy-friend play the guitar, *señorita?*" "We like the guitar very much, *señorita.*" "Will he play for us, *señorita?*"

They sat on the edges of the woven chairs, rubbing their chapped ankles with the soles of their bare feet, eyeing the black guitar case, propped in a corner like a miniature coffin.

"We must have music!" she cried, twirling so that her skirt sailed about her. The children grinned. She ran quickly into the other room, returned immediately, adjusting the castanets to her hands.

"What are they, *señorita?*" "Do you eat them, *señorita?*" "They're castañuelas, stupids!"

One arm she held above her, the other across her breast, posturing, stamping, clicking the castanets.

"How pretty!" "How nice!" "But *la guitarra, señorita?*" "*La guitarra, señorita!*"

Lovingly, she cradled the black ovals in her palms, then held them out to Luis, who sat silently, his face down, his fore-arms on his knees. Lifting his head, he received them into his cupped hands. The wood was warm from her flesh, slightly oily from her handling. It held brief fragrance of her own perfume.

Leaning behind him, she lifted the guitar case. Like a clumsy nursing child, it lay against her. The breeze, cold, damp, swept in from the terrace, pressing her skirt about her legs.

"Close the doors, Luis."

She placed the case on the coffee-table, gently removed the guitar. Lightly her fingers held the neck, fitting themselves to the strings. The fingers of her right hand plucked tentatively. At the sour notes, the children snickered.

"Oh, Luis! The damp! The damp!"

Holding the guitar against her, she slowly tightened the strings.

"It feels damp!" she lamented, twisting the creaking keys.

There was the sudden clop of the bridge breaking, the sharp twang of a snapped string.

"Oh!" she cried. Her free hand grasped at her throat. Where the string had struck, a tiny bead of red formed against the pink of the scar.

The children were shouting, bouncing on the chairs with laughter.

"They love it," Luis said. "You're really entertaining them."

She stared at him as though he were a stranger, then lowered her eyes to the broken guitar in her hand. Passionately, she hugged the guitar to her breast, her eyes glaring at the children.

"Get out!" she screamed. "Get out! Get out, all of you!"

The children slid from their chairs, their faces somber, their eyes distended with astonishment and terror.

"All of you! All of you!"

She stepped rapidly to the terrace doors, threw them open so violently the glass rattled.

They were gone like mice, the children, as though there had been no sound, no movement; she followed after, Luis behind her. But with the clang of the gate upon them, metal between them and their enemy, the children turned back, their faces sullen. Chucho reached down to grab up a loosened stone.

Luis glanced at her quickly. She was still staring at the children.

The smallest child, the one with only a shirt and the chapped naked bottom, pressed his face through a tendril of iron. Like an angry little cat, he spat viciously at Mary.

"Your public," Luis said. The castanets clacked hollowly as he dropped them from his cupped hands.

Mary turned her face from the children. As though the guitar had become a dead weight, she dropped it at her side, her arms dangling. She looked at him, her whole face tired, lines that he had not been sure existed etched deeply into the skin. On her throat, beside the pink scar, the bead of blood hung ready to fall.

"Not a Mexican in this village would have been cruel enough to say that," Mary said softly.

"I'd rather you had spit."

Edmund J. Robins

A PRIMITIVE

BECAUSE Mrs. Fransome was listening to a bird sing and because she saw only the loose white trousers of the boy, she made no haste about answering the knocking. From the door of the cottage, she called, quite sharply she later realized, "Well, what do you want now?"

"Mrs. Fransome? Edith Fransome?"

Whether she first heard the English words or first saw the tweed suit, she couldn't have said, but she was suddenly conscious of her denim shorts, her bare legs, and her *huaraches.* Hurrying down the path, she pushed back the fluff of blond hair from her forehead.

Her tones were apologetic. "Oh, Mr. Dahn!" Her blue eyes were bright with exasperation. "These Indians—."

The metal clicked as she pulled the key-ring from the pocket of her shorts.

"Then you did receive my letter? But I'm afraid I'm a good week later than I said. Two exhibitions in the City—friends of mine."

She had opened the padlock and withdrawn the heavy chain. With an effort, she dragged the gate toward her, grating it on the flags.

"Like a fortress," he said, lifting the gate slightly with one suntanned hand.

He was distinguished looking. She supposed that he was distinguished. A painter. Parlor portraits, she understood: women in satin and lace with pale, slender children standing beside them or roly-poly rosy-cheeked babies cuddled in their satin laps. He had been a friend of her husband—much older, of course. . . .

"So my sister Helen saw you in New York?" she said.

"Your sister, yes. Of course, I was coming to Mexico— here as a matter of fact. But I shouldn't have known you were here—Oh, the boy. He showed me up from the plaza." Dahn fumbled in his pocket. "What is usual?" he asked.

"He'll probably expect more," she answered harshly. "He knows you're a tourist. But—give him twenty centavos. That's adequate."

She stepped back so that Dahn might enter.

"*Muchas gracias,*" the boy said. He had removed his straw sombrero. Now, as he raised it, he added, "*Muchas gracias, señorita.*" He stood quietly as Dahn entered.

Snapping the padlock, Mrs. Fransome laughed shortly. "They all call me 'Miss.' I suppose it's my blond hair."

"Possibly," her guest said, his eyes following her trim tanned legs. "And possibly because you're young—and look even younger than you are."

"That's gallant."

"That's true."

It was a small cottage, but the living room faced the lake. The eye moved farther than the picture window, across the garden wall with its wicked glass teeth to the ochre hills, fountained with maguey. Beyond was the steely sheen of water and the low mountains, rising amethyst beyond purple beyond blue.

"This is a lovely spot," Dahn said, stepping to the window. "And primitive!" he added.

"That's what I adore," she said. She had not followed him; she had not seen the rebozo-ed woman, baby on back, squat awkwardly among the maguey plants, her magenta skirt well raised above her fat dark buttocks.

Mrs. Fransome dipped her head. "That fellow's still planting *maíz*."

Across the ravine on a slope too precipitous for him to find footing on one level, a white-clothed figure jabbed savagely into the soil with what appeared to be a heavy javelin. He rotated the point, withdrew it, stooped to drop something in the hole, and smoothed the earth carefully with his foot.

"The digging stick," Mrs. Fransome said. "Just as his forefathers did. If he were close enough, you'd see how he's tied his front shirttails together: a pouch for the kernels of corn."

Her eyes sparkled. Her cheeks were pink and young.

Turning back to the view, Dahn saw two youths threading through the maguey. Laughing heartily together, unconscious of either the woman adjusting her skirt or of himself in the window, they fumbled at their flies. The sun caught the arcs.

"It's all—" Dahn turned again to Mrs. Fransome—"very natural."

"I love it," she said. "Quiet—"

There was a sharp click on the glass, and both of them started. A clack and a second clack told them that something had struck the outside wall.

"These damned savages," Mrs. Fransome said bitterly.

"Boys after birds?"

"Boys!" Her nostrils constricted. Her knuckles were white from the grasp of her hands on the edge of the table. "Does a Mexican ever grow up? Boy and man, there isn't a male in the village who doesn't carry a flipper." Her upper lip looked hard, as though stretched too tautly across her teeth. "I spoke to Carmelo about it this morning. That's the boy—."

"My guide. Yes, he told me about it. At least I think he told me. Speaks much too rapidly for me. Says you're crazy about birds. *Loca* does mean *crazy*, doesn't it?"

Mrs. Fransome eyed him narrowly. "*Loca* does mean *crazy*," she answered slowly. "But I'm quite certain—no, I'm

sure there isn't any such expression. If Carmelo said *loca*—"
she released the table and stood erect, her feet slightly apart—
"he definitely means I'm insane!"

"Great guns, my dear!" Dahn's smile was exasperated.
"I'm not trying an exact translation. Actually, Carmelo ad-
mires you. He says you're blonde. He says you're beautiful.
He say you're a real mango—which I understand is even
more delicious than a peach."

Color crept up her throat, into her cheeks.

"That's city slang," she said.

"But spoken very nicely by a country boy. Besides," Dahn
added, "I think he has a gift for you."

"A gift?" Mrs. Fransome frowned. "When I scolded him
this morning?" She sighed. "I never can tell what they understand—they're so polite." She thought a moment. "He kept
nodding. A feather had floated down between us, just soft
and white, but it was like silver in the sunlight. I pointed at
it with my toe—" Both she and Dahn glanced at the ver-
million nail.

"I don't always wear these," Mrs. Fransome said abruptly.
"I'm told my feet will spread and I won't be able to get them
into my regular shoes."

"And Carmelo?" Dahn suggested.

"Carmelo?" She had to adjust her thoughts. "Oh, well, I
appealed to his pride—reminded him of the exquisite feather-
work his forefathers had done, asked him if he, too, didn't
find the feathers lovely. I pointed to the trees. A bird was
singing—it's a charming bird, tiny and squat like a wren, but
lemon-yellow—and I said that birds sing beautifully, almost
as beautifully as Carmelo does. He does sing nicely," she said
apologetically, "and then I think they like flattery. And I said
would he like to die—"

"What did he say?" Dahn asked.

Mrs. Fransome looked at him perplexedly. "One of their
regular *dichos*," she answered shortly. "'*Es la vida.*' 'That's
life.' They're always saying things like that. *Ni modo; es la*

vida; la vida es dura: it can't be helped; that's life; and life is hard."

"Sounds as though they accept the truth," Dahn said.

Mrs. Fransome's face stiffened. She clasped her fingers tightly together and watched Dahn from under her penciled brows.

"Mr. Dahn," she asked, "exactly why did Helen want you to call on me?"

Then, as though she felt she had been rude, she added ruefully, "You understand you're very welcome; Howard often spoke of you, wanted me to meet you; I was delighted to receive your letter. And I haven't been very hospitable, have I? You'll have tea, of course." And before he could answer, she disappeared through the door into what apparently was the kitchen.

Dahn glanced about the room: lacquer from Uruapan, animal masks from Quiroga, an obsidian knife. He looked thoughtfully out the window. On a less precipitous slope, lying like a mustard rug among the blue-green of the maguey, a farmer followed his yoke of heavy oxen. They reached the green on the right, the parallel furrows growing into a deep-brown woven pattern against the clay-yellow field.

A shrill whistle made Dahn jump. It expired in a soft snuffling.

Mrs. Fransome, smiling, her eye on the tray she carried, stood in the doorway.

"A whistling tea-kettle! Everything about this house amazes. Architect from the States, I suppose?"

"No. It's strictly Mexican. Built by a newspaper man in the City. His own design, he says."

"But it's perfectly modern. All the comforts of home."

"I'm lucky to get it. You noticed the hovels as you came up the hill."

"At least, they're picturesque. I thought one house was on fire. Apparently no chimney. Smoke poured from between the top of the walls and the eaves."

Small talk. Keeping the ball rolling. Holding back the decisive moment.

"Lemon?" Mrs. Fransome asked.

Her long white fingers, nails brilliant, closed delicately about the yellow-green lime—bright and beautiful as an Easter egg.

"Thanks." Her guest shook his head slightly. But he accepted the proffered cup and saucer, sniffing politely at the aroma. He tried a sip. "Delicious," he said. "Better than any I've had in the City."

"Chinese," Mrs. Fransome said. "Though a friend brought it down from the City. No tea here—that is, what I should call tea." Her spoon clicked against the china as she stirred. "The natives, of course, use different herbs. *Té del monte* has a quite pleasant minty flavor. Sundays, the Indians bring it down from the hills. And everyone uses *manzanilla*." She sipped at her tea, blue eyes far off across the lake on the skeins of cloud dragging themselves between the ridges of the mountains.

"In the rainy season," she went on, "it's like a Japanese print: the little trees on the horizon seem sharp, but the slopes are covered with mist."

"Helen tells me that you've travelled a good deal." He turned his eyes from the window to the tiny white clay "spirits" jauntily perched about the rim of the incense-burner from Oaxaca; the carved fibre monkey with the inset shell eyes from Guatemala; the framed photographs of Chichén Itzá. . . . "But you prefer the primitive, I see."

Mrs. Fransome looked at him gravely. "That's principally what I like about it here, the closeness to nature. The people are simple. They're born, live, have children, and die close to the fields, among these lovely mountains. They don't fret about canned goods and electric refrigerators. Tortillas, beans, the good green corn—."

"And pulque," said Dahn. "Your friend Carmelo and I had to sidestep an old woman lying face down on the walk near the plaza. I thought she'd had a heart attack or been knifed, but Carmelo said no, she was drunk. No expression on his face. And the villagers stepping around her as they do around the curled-up curs."

"Poor old soul!" Mrs. Fransome flushed with pity—or with annoyance. "I don't judge them."

"I suppose that I was judging her," Dahn admitted. "It's a characteristic of our culture."

"A culture built on money and on time!" she declared hotly. "And a pretended belief in a Golden Rule!"

"But a culture out of which we've grown," said Dahn, "one that has our actions, if not our beliefs, pretty well regulated. Maybe unfortunately. I'm doubtful because we're so close to it."

Her eyes were uneasy; they evaded Dahn's.

"Sometimes I think that we're too civilized," she said, devoting eyes and tremulous fingers to the pouring of more tea.

Dahn reached for a tea-cake. Save for the exceptional view and the cold tiled floor with the rush mats, they might have been sitting in any living room in any city in the United States. His eyes examined her curiously, a bit quizzically, sympathetic and a little sad.

"But we," he said, "you and I, are used to that civilization. I'm still fairly well satisfied with it. My shoes and socks are really quite comfortable—habit, I suppose. And I honestly relish tea." His mouth quirked at the corners, and he eyed her carefully before he added, "The theory of the Noble Savage is nice—Jean Jacques Rousseau, Mrs. Aphra Behn, James Fenimore Cooper, and, for short, Tolstoi, perhaps, all rolled into one. But I can no more see the Last of the Aztecs sitting unhygienically erect in a beautifully sanitary lavender-tile-and-white-porcelain bathroom than I can see myself squatting in the nearest bed of poison-ivy when the spirit—to put it politely—moved me. I do, you see"—his voice was apologetic—"rather approve of modern conveniences."

"But that's a matter of education!" she burst out heatedly. She set down her cup with a clatter.

"Mr. Dahn, you're laughing at me!"

"Not laughing," he said. "And certainly not at you. I'm smiling a little at our inconsistencies. And I'm grinning like a death's head at Escape."

"Escape?" she asked, but her rising color disclaimed any misunderstanding.

"Escape," he repeated slowly. "Running away. Doping one's sensibilities. Kidding oneself. Whatever you choose to call it. Your Helen—"

"Helen's a fool!" Mrs. Fransome exclaimed. "She never could leave me alone! Because she's a few years older, she has always wanted to lead my life for me!"

Dahn sipped at his tea. "Contrariwise," he said gently. "She doesn't care for the life you lead. Perhaps, she'd like to *guide* you—to help you." Watching her lowered lids, he continued softly, but emphatically, "Helen is terribly fond of you, Eddie."

Mrs. Fransome's spoon clashed in the saucer. When she looked at him, her eyes were panicked.

"Pardon me," Dahn said. "Howard always spoke of you that way. I've always thought of Howard's wife as Eddie."

"But only Howard ever called me that!"

"And now with Howard dead, there is no Eddie?" He went on quickly, but as though he were thinking to himself. "I like the name. More than a nickname. More than a wife's name. It's a young name. It's a comradely name. An Edith, I think—yes—can be aloof, can separate herself from the world, can push aside all of the little loves—relatives, quick acquaintances, old friends. And—yes—the great loves: there are other Howards." He held up a hand to stop her. "Yes, an Edith can forsake all of her own people; and Edith *can* live solitary. But an Eddie can't stand loneliness and cold."

"Mr. Dahn—."

Again, he held up his hand.

"Other wives lost husbands in the war."

"I hate it! Oh, I hate it!"

"Wives have always lost husbands in all wars."

"He had so much to live for!"

"Because he was an artist? Plumbers and masons have much to live for too."

"The shame of killing!"

"Any time, any place—boys after birds," said Dahn softly.

"I have been happy here!"

She spoke so desperately that Dahn reached abruptly to touch her hand. She lowered her eyes. His words were slow. "I certainly have no right to interfere with happiness." He drew back his hand.

"Helen, of course, did ask me to come. But I came as a friend, as Howard's friend, your friend. I know that I sound sententious. But I have been places too. One doesn't just give up suddenly the Louvre, El Prado, or the Metropolitan Museum. People, I suppose, once talked in grunts and snorts, but most of us prefer the language of Bernard Shaw and Flaubert. Eddie—Mrs. Fransome, there is no escape. You're made for civilized life. You need pretty things. You don't have to have an electric toaster, but in daily existence it's really more convenient than sharpening a willow twig and hanging over the speared blackening bread while the smoke reddens your eyes."

Mrs. Fransome had not raised her head. She sat looking at her hands.

"I've been rude," Dahn said. "I hope that you are happy. If you say that you are happy—" he hesitated—"then I accept your happiness."

As she failed to speak, he placed his cup and saucer on the tray, glanced through the window, and rose to his feet.

"That's what I'll tell your sister," he said cheerfully.

"But don't those dropping clouds indicate storm?" He tipped his head toward the mountains.

Mrs. Fransome lifted her face.

"It was thoughtful of Helen," she said quietly, "and it's been awkward for you."

She, too, rose. Against the window, a spray of gloria, like an arc of tiny white stars, swished in the rising wind. They listened a moment to its clicking on the glass.

"You'll call again?" she asked.

"I leave in the morning," he said, lifting his hat from the table. "But one of these days—" he held out his hand for hers—"I shall certainly see you."

"Goodbye," she said at the gate.

"Until we see one another," he answered, smiling. Holding his hat against the wind, he strode up the hill. At the crest he stopped. Her face twisted as he looked back quickly and waved his long tweeded arm in a comradely farewell.

In a moment he was over the cobbled rise of the street. She watched him disappear—knees, thighs, shoulders, the crown of his gray felt hat—as though he had sunk in quicksand.

"Oh!" she said, and took three running steps before she halted. She had meant to send some little thing—the filigree butterfly, the beetle brooch in the tortoise-shell and silver— to her sister Helen. Well, someone else would call, in a week, a few weeks, a few months. . . .

The wind pushed at the gates as she forced them closed. The chain chilled her fingers as she wrapped it about the center palings, clicking it together with the squat padlock. Overhead, the clouds scudded: it would rain shortly.

"Senõrita! Señorita!"

Half up the walk she paused, her bare legs prickling in the chill of the wind.

"Señorita!"

She turned from whatever was her dream.

"Señorita!"

"Carmelo!" Her voice was almost glad.

"*Un chiquitito regalito, señorita.*"

"A little gift? For me?"

Again, she unlocked the gate.

"How nice," she said, taking the cardboard box from his extended hands. Carefully she lifted the lid. It dropped with a dull clop upon the flagstones. The chain clanked. The padlock made a heavy metallic thump.

She lifted her eyes from the yellow, the black, the grey, the tufted red to his delighted grin.

"Oh, thank you! Thank you!"

Without warning, she burst into sobs.

She wanted her handkerchief; she wanted the chain and the padlock: her hands were filled with dead birds. Uninterrupted the tears rolled down her face; she tasted them on her lips; she felt them dripping, slowly, regularly, from her chin to her breast.

"But señorita, what is it? Are you ill? Have you hurt yourself."

"*Nada!*" she sobbed. "Nothing, nothing, nothing!"

Her eyes were slimy with the tears. Her nose was running. Abruptly, she turned about, stooped, and set the box carefully on the flagstones. Rising, she wiped her face on the puffed short sleeve of her smock.

Through rainbows she saw Carmelo's black eyes wide with wonder, his hand scratching the black forelock under his pushed-back straw sombrero.

"Nothing. Nothing at all," she said, shoving the gate to, lacing in the chain, snapping the padlock.

"I'm so happy," she said between the palings. "*Muy contenta. Muy contenta.*"

"Thank you very much, Carmelo. *Muchas gracias! Muchísimas gracias!*"

Eugene Garber

AN OLD DANCE

THE sun requires blood. Our dancers know how to signify that—stooping, hanging their arms down together like huge lolling tongues. We are, all four of us, enthralled by the lurid set bathed in red, the deep pounding of drums, and the dancers' high-stepping pantomime of angry hunger. Behind the scrim is the shape of the great pyramid with the god-house atop. A priest stands there, his obsidian knife raised on high. On the backdrop is painted a huge stylized heart, stubbier than a chicken heart, with twin volutes sprouting up, the aorta. It looks a bit like a space capsule plunging earthward. Our younger son, Lane, tells us that it ought to be pointed skyward. He has read the gruesome accounts of human hearts swiftly cut out and held, still beating, up to the sun. So there ought to be an upward motion, he says.

It is fortunate that these pantomimes of blood sacrifice are extravagant and melodramatic. For if they were vivid, they might disturb Lane deeply, despite his mother's initiatory rites, just as his reading in Meso-American mythology disturbed him earlier. He is still too tender for this world. It is a question of certain endowments, emotional and physiological, involving empathy and the introjection of the feelings of all kinds of creatures. Lane's mother has said that it is like living with an emotional hemophiliac, an apt image, for it has often seemed that a deep bruise to his feelings would be fatal. This is the story of Lane's initiation in Mexico. His initiator was his mother. All the ancient rites call for the father to initiate the son, but I could not have done it.

Lane's older brother, Michael, Mike, could have done it if it had been absolutely necessary, though they are only two years apart, fifteen and thirteen. Here is the difference in a nutshell. Just a few minutes ago we saw *The Ball Game,* danced with a big plastic globe half the size of a weather balloon and only just heavier than air so that it bounced about among the dancers in an elegant lento paradoxically mixing images of inexorable momentum and weightlessness. On the one side of us Mike went through a passionate thermomuscular dream of participation, unconsciously moving hips and elbows in imitation of the dancers. On the other side of us Lane whispered the possible significances: the ball was a human head buffeted by the contrary winds of fate but destined ultimately to pass through the hoop of immortality; or, the ball was the sun that went up and down, designating those to be sacrificed; or, the ball was the cosmos, the hoop the cosmos' own eternal round. And so on.

And here is an image of Lane's mother. Some days ago at the *charreada,* the rodeo, when the young man bit the tail of the brahman that had fallen into a wise placidity to avoid further lassoing, she laughed lustily and called, "Nip the loafer!" So she was the one who said of Lane, "He can't go through life like this. We can't go on protecting him."

"What are you going to do?"

"I'm going to show him things, show him everything."

"You'll kill him."

"Better his blood on my hands, who bore him, than for the world to kill him as soon as he steps out of our house."

AT THE BOXEO

We sat in the twenty-third row. On the white, brightly lit

square down in front of us there were to be five events: three prelims and two features. The finale would pit "El Tigre de Jalisco" against "Ishmael Toboac," the mad Jew of Buenos Aires. This was the first of the initiatory trials which Lane's mother designed for him. We did not at that moment know precisely how many there would be (a Herculean even dozen?) or toward what pinnacle of suffering we were ascending.

While Mike strained forward in his seat, slugging it out with the boxers, Lane provided a gloss based on his extensive reading of Mexican mythology. For instance, the fights were under the auspices of the ancient god Tezcatlipoca, Lord of the Smoking Mirror. Of the smoke there could be no doubt, thick sickening stuff rising from cigarettes and Cuban cigars, hanging in the air like the viscid white gas that magicians pour from milk bottles. (Nothing so delicate as the scrim that partially conceals the priest with his obsidian knife.) The mirror image was less obvious. How, precisely, were we to see ourselves reflected in the two then fighting—a peppery Mexican with a thin mustache and a glistening black who had not kept his guard up and was bleeding from the left eye? Lane and I were the unfortunate Negro and Mike and his mother were the excoriating Mexican? No, because suddenly the black, who had seemed pinned against the ropes, came flashing forth, all glistening like the knife, and cut the Mexican down. The crowd roared. When he could be heard again, Lane tried to explain that the ring (curious misnomer, or is it?) was a four-cornered mandala encircled by the spectators. The fighters, paradoxically an emblem of unity, revolved at the hub, the center of centers, which made the ring, like all mandalas, a quincunx. Precocity—nothing can be clearer— is a curse. Lane's mother hissed at him, "Stop talking and watch. You might learn something about the manly art of self-defense."

So we sat silently through the rest of the bouts breathing the foul air, listening to the crowd howl, watching the boxers, whose leaden gloves prevented what might otherwise have been clean kills. El Tigre and Ishmael, neither in great

shape incidentally, fought to a standstill and fell into each
other's arms, having only occasionally aroused themselves to
a slow pantomime of trading blows. "One of your Aztec
priests ought to finish them off," I said to Lane, but he was, in
obedience to his mother, deep in suffering, his hands clenched,
his face set, and his eyes narrowed but, bravely, not shut. I
feared those images he was storing. (My wife and I had a
friend who, after seeing that eye-slicing scene in *An Andalu-
sian Dog,* had to go to a shrink and later a hypnotist to get the
image removed from his inner eye, and still he lives in constant fear of its return.) "Remember Marvin," I said to her.

"Atta boy!" she shouted to El Tigre, whose fist was making its way slowly toward the thorax of the Jew.

That night Lane had a nightmare. We heard him shouting
out in his sleep. "Stop! No, stop!" We hurried toward his bed
in the adjoining hotel room. When we got there Mike was
still sleeping, albeit restlessly, and Lane was just struggling
up from the abyss of fear, whimpering piteously. My wife
shook Lane's shoulders. "Wake up, Lane." She had snapped
on the ceiling light and flooded the midnight room with
blank glare. Lane blinked his eyes. "What's the matter, son?"
she said.

Lane looked at his mother's face. Some moments passed
before her presence displaced the images of his dream. Then
he said, "He was after me."

"Who was after you?" my wife said, at which moment
Mike suddenly sat up in his bed. The question had struck
through his sleep and alerted him that information of interest
was about to be revealed. He looked at us brightly, angrily.

"El Tigre," said Lane, "with his claws." So the dream figure was of much greater ferocity than the slogging boxer of
some hours before.

"No, he wasn't," said my wife. "You have been here in the
room with Mike all the time, and nobody else has been here.
Isn't that right, Mike?"

Mike fairly glowered as he nodded his head—Mike the
empiricist. All things material glow in his eye with luminous

solidity. Not for him the second images, afterimages, fleeting auras of dreamers.

"See?" said Lane's mother, who possessed the same bird-bright eyes as her Mike. I should have shouted, "Be quiet, ignorant inquisitors! Blind in your inner eye, you know nothing of dreams and dreamers." But I was silent while Lane, aware of the futility of arguing, merely nodded assent. "Then go back to sleep," his mother said. "And put your mind on *not* dreaming. Mike is here with you. And we're next door."

Mike nodded peremptorily, as though to say that his role as guardian of Lane's sleep was too piddling to warrant full acknowledgment. If, on the other hand, there had been a real tiger at the gate, let it be said for Mike that he would have gladly thrown against it all the strength of his young body.

"OK," said Lane.

My wife snapped off the light and we were back to our room, where I said, "This is a dangerous game you're playing."

She looked at me sharply for a moment. "Game?"

"Tactic then—of suddenly filling Lane full of fearless macho."

She shook her head slowly. "I'm not that stupid. I know it will not be suddenly—if ever."

"Why not just let him be whatever it is he's going to be?"

"What? Cringing, hypersensitive, maybe gay? You would be satisfied with that?"

"I would learn to love him whatever he was."

"Yes, of course. So would I. But why give up without trying? Why not work for something better?"

I had no ready answer for that. My wife lay back down in her bed, turned her back to me, and soon fell asleep.

The dancers have assumed a different posture. No longer do they hang their arms down in front like bloodlapping tongues. On the contrary, they are standing erect. They have thrown their heads back and are addressing themselves to the gods of the red sky. Into their mouths they have inserted long feathered things like Halloween serpents that uncurl and whistle when you blow in them. These scrolling songs, sayings, chants, or whatever, Lane tells us, are very similar to those seen in the codices. So, everything in this extravagant performance retains an element of authenticity. That's good to know, but the truth of the matter is that we are too caught up with the dancers to pay much attention to Lane's gloss. What's fun is to figure out the nature of each of these plumed orisons. For instance, one tall male is suavely waving a spray of peacock blue—obviously the language of court flattery, the Aztec equivalent of *The Book of Common Prayer*. One of the women is making an undulant motion with a golden spray of softly sweeping mariboo feathers, an aspirant to celestial courtesanship. I plan to try to identify each of the eight dancers and later test my characterizations against my wife's, which will be just a hair too cynical. But now Lane whispers, "I like the green one best." He's a nice choice all right, a maize man, tall and straight, with a topknot of yellow tasseling. Not only does he aim his spume at the sun, but in his fervor leaps up into the air. Perhaps even my wife will be pleased with Lane's choice. In the meantime, Mike is saying, "Mine is the red one." Of course. He's a brilliant crimson. Byronic, out of patience with the gods, he shakes his red plume at them ferociously, like a fist.

And what do the gods do, these ungentle Aztec superbeings who live in sun, volcano, and thunder? Why, at least for the moment, they are much like our modern gods—entirely otiose.

AT THE CORRIDA

This was the most predictable and the most lachrymose of poor Lane's trials of manhood. Even so, there were some omissions from the scenario which would have made the event even darker. For instance, none of the picador's horses were gored. None of the banderillos were thrown, though that would have been luckless and untoward indeed. No young boys were impaled on the bulls' horns. One did jump over the wall with a cape—but half-heartedly, I fear—and was quickly thrust by the matador's assistants back up into the stands. "What was he trying to do?" said Lane.

"He was like those boys we saw in the park yesterday with capes, only he wanted to try it out on the real thing," said my wife. "Pretty brave, huh?"

Lane nodded. He tried to please his mother by taking, like Mike, a great interest in the particulars of the corrida. But when the second bull had fallen to his knees vomiting blood, and there were four more to come, Lane could not fasten his mind to the events in the ring. Instead, he began his mythical meanderings. *Mumble them softly to me,* I wanted to say to him, *so that your mother doesn't overhear.* And for a while it happened that way. He whispered to me about the acrobatics of the great bull-leapers of ancient Knossos, about the laby-rinth in the center of which bull and man were one. But Labys was the name of the Ax God and he didn't see how that fit. Needless to say, I could not illuminate the matter for him, though, God knows, if a large displacement of time be al-lowed, there was before us ample butchery and blood to image a great deal of axing. In fact, the third bull was at that very moment being dragged away, and the fastidious rakers of the sand had not yet appeared to cover the blood.

From the labyrinth of Knossos it was an easy step to the omphalos, which we had already seen, you remember, at the *charreada* and at the boxeo. And because the matador wore a cap with black bull's ears and his hair in a pigtail, it was easy to see that, appearances of conflict notwithstanding, bull and man were actually one, just as boxers were one with each other and ropers were one with calves and ponies. Well, I thought to myself, Lane's is a complex case. Either all this comes out over and over again because of the intolerable pressure his mother puts on him, or he is a hopeless ob-sessive, or he is a true mystic, which in the contemporary world is defined as insanity. Which should I hope for? Mean-while, his mother inevitably overheard some wayward remark about how the initial allegorical procession, led by the sombre premonitory figure of the black horseman, was tied in with the ring's cosmic divisions—inner and outer circles, *sol y sombra*. And she came down on him like the Mexican eagle on the hapless serpent. "Lane, for God's sake look at what's really out there instead of at that childish myth stuff in your own head!"

Later that night I made my wife a witty discourse on the metaphorical nature of all perception. "I admire the single-minded way you are handling Lane," I said. "I really do. But you can push your empirical line too far, you know, and undermine your own position—I mean insisting that everything simply *is* what it is. For instance, as you know, there are no colors in the universe, only light waves of certain lengths, which the optic nerves choose to represent as colors. And there are no caresses, no kisses, dear—only the repulsion of electromagnetic fields. So a person may make out of a bloody sandpit a number of things."

To give credit where credit is due, my wife tried to take that seriously. She even went so far as to say that she bet some ancient philosopher had said that the best thing to do was to assume that what we saw was what was really out there. I told her that I didn't know of such a person, though Mike might grow up and say something like that. But she wasn't listening to me because she had gotten the giggles. "Kisses . . . caresses . . . electromagnetic fields," she repeated in a high whinnying voice, and then collapsed on our bed under the insupportable burden of mirth. So I was merely playing the pedant to her wholesome fleshy grasp of life. But the fact remained that Lane was genuinely suffering. Maybe it was true that the bullring was exactly a bullring and the matador exactly a brave killer and the dead bull a dead bull, but if Lane wasn't allowed to mythologize it, he got sick. So when the fifth bull fell dead, Lane got up and went down to the low concrete wall at the edge of the stands. He leaned over and vomited a yellow stinking mess onto the sand below. Good, I thought. He's made of it a toilet bowl, a piss pot, Mambrino's helmet revealed for what it is if myth is to be denied. And like all spiritual vomiters, he experienced a relief much more profound that can be explained by the ejection of indigestive elements. He looked back up at us with a smile that perhaps he intended to be sheepish, but that was really, at least momentarily, beatific. I said, "Lane and I will skip the sixth bull. We'll explore the nether regions of the ring. Maybe we can discover the place where they saw the animals up and dispense them to the poor." Neither my wife nor Mike acknowledged our departure.

So that night when my wife had recovered from the near hysterics that my philosophizing had plunged her into, I said, "All right, laugh. But let me ask you one serious question. Are you keeping a careful eye on exactly how far he is from the edge?"

"No," she said flatly.

"Well, that's interesting," I said. "You just plan to keep pushing him until he drops over?"

"No, but if necessary until just *before* he drops over, in which case I'll catch him."

"My God. What monumental presumption. What if you don't see him start to fall? What if you're not nearby when he starts to topple?"

"Where would he be?" My wife seemed genuinely surprised by my question.

"Off, dear, in some pre-Columbian Aztec temple where the priests of Huitzilopochtli hunger for more blood sacrifices." I kept my tone serious, but she didn't answer me in kind. "Phooey! I'll still reach out and catch him."

I shook my head skeptically. "I hope for your sake, as well as for his, that your mother intuition works out. Because if it doesn't, there will . . ."

"Be quiet," she said. "I know it."

After the acrobatics of *The Ball Game,* the lurid ceremonies of *The Sacrifice,* and the extraordinary synesthesia of *Feathered Song,* we examine our programs to see what's coming up. First, a ten-minute intermission, which here in Mexico will be more like twenty, and then three more big numbers: *The Clash of Flowers, The Plumed Serpent,* and *Coatlicue.* Meanwhile we stretch and blink in the light that has gone up in the theatre. We seem to each other suddenly pale, watery-eyed, and vulnerable, as though the light has caught us out in a moment of private self-communing that ought to have remained hidden in the dark. Even the tough ones, my wife and Mike, appear momentarily weak, but they quickly stir themselves and hurry off to the lobby to see what's doing there. Left alone, Lane and I do not talk. Our silence is comfortable. We are both thinking that this, our last big event in Mexico, is really his. It is almost as though the choreographer had designed these dances precisely as a tribute to Lane's successful passage through the severe trials of his mother's making. That may make it sound as though the issue were never in doubt, as though there were not moments when our presence here now would have seemed unlikely indeed. Even so, we both feel strongly that the dance is Lane's. And I for one am glad that the sacrifice at the pyramid came early in the performance and is done. So now, though I haven't read the descriptive blurbs about the dances coming up, I somehow feel both relaxed and titillated, a mood which is not disturbed when Mike comes back saying, "American guy in the lobby says the finale is almost too much to take." I am not disturbed, either, by my wife's sharp glance. She suspects that Lane and I have had soft and emasculating communications, a suspicion I will relieve her of later. But in the meanwhile, I am not disturbed by the perverse reversal of roles my wife's distrustful glance implies. The lights dim and presently the curtain rises on *The Clash of Flowers. Blossoming War,* Lane whispers to me, "is how they ought to have translated it."

I see his point. The dancers who thrust and dart at each other are not just flowers, though they wear pale leotards embroidered gorgeously with luxuriant sprays of color. And there is not exactly a clash between them. In fact, it becomes clear that the dancers are also the bees and the hummingbirds and the butterflies that transfer the pollen. And as they stretch and leap, not quite vertically, they are also slant rain and shafts of sunlight. Toward the end they gather in and fan out to show the blossoming that results from the war. *War, blossom*—curious but the dancers show that the paradox is true, leaning out from a sunburst center in petaled splendor.

AT THE MERCADO LIBERTAD

We entered from the plaza through a narrow corridor of flower stalls, fresh and fragrant after the swarming heat of the wide Calzada Independencia. But these pleasures were short-lived, for presently we passed into the dried flower section, which made Lane sneeze. A moment later we encountered a branching of ways—leather goods down one aisle, straw down another, and vegetables in a distant offing. "Which fatal fork here, oh trusty leader?" I said to my wife, who immediately whisked aside a hanging blanket of Indian zigzags to reveal a stairway. "Up!"

Up was the eating section, a long series of once white-tiled stalls, behind which women and men prepared the famous chicken and corn soups of Mexico, the famous tacos with varied filling, the pigs' feet, the ribs, and huge crisp chunks of pigs' skin, the messes of brains and kidneys, the shrimps and fishes, the pickled vegetables, and so on. And at the stalls, sitting hunched over plates, were the midafternoon eaters, spooning up soups, gnawing flesh from bones, crunching skins and crustaceans, rolling up tacos like fat cigars and engorging them in two bites. A grindery, a human mill for reducing objects of nature to the homogeneous pulp of alimentation. And all around the place rose the heat, noise, and odor of mass ingestion. Did our leader whisk us through these unpleasant precincts? No, slowly, looking carefully left and right in order to take in the varied offerings of each stall, she proceeded deliberately, nay lovingly, like a connoisseur. And we behind, perforce, at equal pace. But I noticed that not even Mike savored these refections. And Lane began to discolor. Fortunately we reached the end of the stalls before his stomach turned as it had at the corrida.

We passed among trinket stands and then entered not an alley or a cul-de-sac exactly but a sort of close or mews, a congeries of tiny stalls selling herbs and other curatives. "Are you going to get us a joint as a consolation for that trip through the gastric inferno?" I asked our leader. That got a giggle from Mike, but it was perfunctory because we were all immediately fascinated by the wares—tangles of rank-looking weeds (purgatives, no doubt, strong enough to un-bind a mule), delicate sprays of dry lacy flowers (aphro-disiacs?), ugly black worts that looked as though they had been blasted by a hundred early winters, and much else. Our group broke apart as each of us found different centers of in-terest. Turning a corner I bumped into my wife buying a little packet of black powder: "Sal Negra, Contra Malos Vecinos." I chuckled and passed on, browsing aimlessly until I happened on Lane standing agape in front of a stand which featured the hanging pelts and bones of small animals, also snakeskins, strings of snail shells, and other zoological rem-nants. But it wasn't these that had so dramatically seized Lane's attention. It was the vendor, an old crone whose head seemed to hang there among the animal parts as within the wicket of an entry into the underworld. And what's more, so wrinkled was she, so withered her mouth and forehead, so warted and moled all over, so scraggly with hair on chin and head that for an instant I thought she was hanging upside down, the famous sibyl in the bottle. But when she spoke I saw that her mouth was after all below her nose. "¿Que quieres, niño?" She spoke in a high insistent quaver, but Lane said nothing. I nudged him. "She asked you what you want."

"I know that," he shot back petulantly, so I waited for him to say something to her. But he said nothing, just stood there looking at her, not looking at the interesting wares, but obsessively staring into the old woman's face. I grew em-barrassed and blurted out, "Medicina contra una mala ma-drastra." *Medicine against an evil stepmother.* Well, I didn't have to dig very deep in my unconscious to discover where that came from. Fortunately Lane didn't know the word. (I hadn't known until that moment that I knew it.) "What's a *madrastra?*"

"Hell, I don't know. Something I read in one of the other stands. You weren't saying anything."

He didn't say anything to that either. The old woman's mouth began to work, obscenely, like an agitated anus. At length she said, "Muy raro, muy caro." *Very rare, very expensive.*

"Vamos a ver," I said. *We'll see.*

She took down a little jar from a high shelf and set it on her tiny counter. I looked with amazement at the hand that set it there. So did Lane, I'm sure. The hand was not gnarled, knobbed, or warted. The nails were not cracked or necrotic. In fact, the hand was hardly wrinkled. I peered sharply at the woman in the wicket to see if the ancient countenance was really a mask. If it was it had been put on by a make-up man too clever for me. Meanwhile the anomalous hand was turning the jar so that we could read the label: "Malas Madrastras." So maybe I had actually seen the word displayed on something in a previous stand. I picked the jar up and inspected it closely, like a connoisseur. I perceived that a certain gamesmanship was necessary with this hag. I handed the jar to Lane. "Eye-ball it carefully, son." Then I addressed myself to the hag. "Me parece heces del buho." I may have said that purely out of orneriness, but the fact is that the stuff did look like owl pellets, and I decided to make the pellets feces. But I could never have predicted the response I got. The crone threw back that withered rotten-apple head of hers and screeched like a moon-haunted owl—a screech so raucous and inhuman that it absolutely unnerved me. Lane widened his eyes, set down the jar, and would have backed off, but I was right behind him, standing my ground. I had to. "¿Cuánto cuesta?" I said, noting uncomfortably the thinness of my voice compared to the old woman's rich ululation.

"Una dosis cuesta veinte pesos."

"¡Ay, caramba!" I exclaimed, striking my forehead as in a
seizure of penurious grief. "Muy caro." Well, everybody had
told us that you ought to get anything in the market for half
the initial asking price. But did I really expect the hag to
come down? No, I did not. She puckered her anus mouth and
said, "Vale mas, señor. Vale mas." *It's worth more.*

"Bueno," I said. "¿Es suficiente, una dosis?"

"Si, si. Mire, señor." She opened the jar with great care
and sifted a tiny pellet out into the palm of her hand. Then
with her free index finger she ground the gray substance into
a fine powder, like graphite. "Miren, señores." She lifted the
stuff ceremoniously, like a priest raising a chalice—up over
Lane's head until it was very close to my nose. Then suddenly
she leaned forward and blew sharply. Out of her hand rose a
puff of gray smoke that flew over my shoulder. Did I say the
mouth looked like an anus? The breath seconded the image—
or was it the odor of the puff of gray dust? I didn't have time
to unravel this, because I heard a coughing and a disgusted
poohing in my ear. I turned to find my wife beside me, her
face bearing evidence of the hag's ashy ministrations. I couldn't
keep from laughing. And once having started, I though I had
as well be hung for a goat as a sheep, so I let rip a series of
raucous guffaws that bent me over against Lane and rattled
my ribs. The crone joined in and treated us to another of her
unearthly ululations.

When I was sufficiently recovered to receive communication, my wife said, "Why don't you pay up and let's be on our
way." First I had to settle accounts with the crone, who was
holding out her gray-smudged hand. I fished up a twenty
peso bill and laid it in her hand, tapping the paper significantly. "Mire," I said. "El famoso templo de Quetzalcoatl y
Tlaloc."

As we passed through the last of the herb stands on our
way to the stairs, Mike having formed up with us at this
point, my wife said, "How long do I have?"

"According to the hag," I said, "not long. Any minute
now you will start shriveling up and melting into the floor

like the Wicked Witch of the West." But Lane wasn't smiling. I feared he was feeling guilty, thinking that we had perpetrated on his mother some aggressive act. "How about it, Lane?" I said lightly.

"She wasn't really a hag," he said. "She was an aspect of Tezcatlipoca, smoking mirror."

Down we went. Even before I saw anything, I smelled the odor of flesh and blood rising up the stairwell. "Wife," I whispered, "I think we have seen enough of the great Libertad." But she continued to lead us down without comment. Perhaps if we had come early in the morning we would have seen attractive displays of chops, roasts, rolled skirts, and the like. At least we would not have seen the absolute dregs— hearts, livers, brains, sheets of tripe, and organs I couldn't even identify. From long strings of hooks hung hogs' heads and feet and a few scrawny yellow-gray chickens. Elsewhere, on beds of bloody ice, large fish were beginning to make odorous announcement of their not so recent death. As we passed one stall, the butcher ladled briny water up from a rough tun and doused his festooning of hogs' heads, which then dripped prettily from their pale lashes, pert ears, and gently smiling mouths. Noting—or to be more charitable, misinterpreting—Lane's gaping dismay, the butcher said, "¿Quieres un puercito, niño?" With his fingers he widened the smile of a dead pig. Lane sidled away. But my wife approached. "¿Qué se puede hacer con una cabeza de puerco?" *What can be made with a hog's head?* The butcher rattled off something and then kissed the tips of his fingers, those very fingers which had formed the inviting smile on the hog's face. My wife went on playing the game, inspecting the heads closely, and Mike egged her on. "Get the one with the spotted ears, Mom."

"¿Cuál, señora? ¿Cuál?" The butcher was anxious to take one down and wrap it for her, become the first butcher of the Mercado Libertad to sell a hog's head to a gringa. "Para usted, señora, un precio especial." That was the last of the exchange I heard, because out of the corner of my eye I saw that Lane was at the end of his tether. A wave of pity rolled over me. Nightmares, vomitings, what would he have to suffer next? Fainting? How did I guess? I had something of the same feelings myself—that burred quality of all sound, the tendency of the whole spectacle of carnage to wheel as though one's spine were affixed to an axle of perpetual suffering. So I grabbed his arm and hustled him toward a splash of daylight I spied in the distance. The prospect of escape braced him. He walked most of the way under his own power. But before we reached the open air, he went limp, so I had to pick him up and carry him through the final hive of blood and flies. The patch of daylight I had spotted was a small interior patio surrounded by stalls of straw goods. I laid Lane on the stone floor. Several women approached clucking. But presently his breath came more regularly, his eyes fluttered hopefully, and he said, "I'm all right."

By the time his mother and brother had found us, he was standing, albeit weakly, drinking a 7-UP I had found nearby. "Lane and I are ready to be liberated from the Libertad," I said.

The dance of *The Plumed Serpent* is a disappointment. The costumes are gorgeous—scintillant green leotards, headdresses of purple feathers, diaphanously winged arms. The dancers lock themselves together to form the long slithering image of the great god Quetzalcoatl. But the dance is inert— something to do with the god's profound benignity, which does not lend itself to drama. My attention begins to wander. I have an image of my father holding a forked stick like a witching wand, but he is not witching. He is stalking something that is running on the ground before him, a snake. I follow close behind him until finally he plunges his stick down like a little pitchfork and pins the snake's tail. "Watch!" he says. The snake struggles for a moment and then suddenly is on his way again. "Look," says my father. In the fork of his stick is two inches of the snake's tail. "It was a glass snake." He hands me the section of tail, broken off precisely along a seam of scales. And it does feel like glass—smooth, dry and brittle. "How does he do it?" I ask. "I don't know," my father says. I try to hand him back the tail. "Don't you want it?" he says. "No," I say and drop it into the grass. My father says, "A coyote will chew off a paw to get out of a trap."

Even when the temptresses of Quetzalcoatl come out in their whorish black pelerine-like garb, the dance will not come alive. (They are agents of Tezcatlipoca, I know this time without Lane having to tell me.) So my mind wanders again, this time to an episode in the childhood of one of my sons. I can not remember which. He is sitting beside a tiny fence of white wickets that surrounds my wife's flower garden. Inside the wickets a little grass snake has been sunning. It is summer. The babbling of my baby boy has awakened the snake and set his little red tongue to flickering in and out. The two stare at each other a long time. Perhaps a primordial trust is rebuilding which will erase the effects of the fall. But then my son reaches out a fat meddlesome hand. The irrepressible urge to possess is upon him. And away darts the little snake toward his hole, but he does not make it. The blade of a spade comes plunging down and cuts the snake's head off as clean as a guillotine. The executioner? My wife, of course. The baby— I still do not remember which—sets up a piteous howling. "Bad snake," says my wife. "Bad snake!" But the baby, horrified by death or, more likely, peeved by deprivation, will not see the snake as evil. He continues to whimper and sob, and even crawls forward to retrieve the severed body, but my wife snatches him up, hugs him, and tries to console him. I cannot sympathize with her. I say, "What do you expect, killing a perfectly harmless garden snake?"

"Goddam you! I know it was perfectly harmless, but do you want him to get in the habit of ogling and petting every snake he sees? What if the next one is a rattler?" And curiously, perversely I think, the child stops crying and looks at me reproachfully as though it has suddenly understood that its mother is its protector and I am a dangerous sentimentalist. I turn away from them both. I will not accept the idea that to protect ourselves from a few evil things we must kill much that is innocent. Which son was it? I still cannot remember. Lane, maimed by the image of phallic destruction, or Mike, strengthened by his mother's unswerving tough-mindedness? How approximate are our histories. Unsortable even in cases as dramatically different as those of Mike and Lane.

Now the snake dancers are climbing one upon the other, making a pyramid. The music is rising triumphantly. A resurrection is taking place, or a translation to the skies, but I haven't been paying attention and therefore don't know what's going on.

AT TEOTIHUACAN, CITY OF THE GODS

The question was whether to start with the Pyramid of the Moon and end with the Temple of Quetzalcoatl and Tlaloc or vice versa. We decided on the latter. Actually I was suffering a mild case of Moctezuma's revenge, and so the first sight of the vast expanse of the ruined city tended to depress me. But the Temple of Quetzalcoatl and Tlaloc was very moving because, finally, the disparity between Quetzalcoatl's benevolence and his representation as a curve-toothed serpent resolved itself for me. While Mike scooted around saying *wow* and looking from every conceivable angle, Lane and I studied the faces of the plumed serpent and the rain god. My wife walked the course set out for the visitor, slowly, giving the temple its due, but pretending no reverence. Anyway, as I said, the benevolence of the serpent came clear to me, although I cannot say exactly how—something in the deepness of the hollow eyes, something in the intricate scrolling of the ears—though all around loured gray stone, bare hills, and dry dusty plains inhospitable to man. No wonder Tlaloc seemed strained, popeyed. What will, even divine, could wrench from those desiccated skies water necessary for maize? So I found myself in a state of mildly mournful peace. But how precisely was Lane taking it, I wondered. He had come through the boxeo, the corrida, as well as the witch and carnage of the Libertad, but in what condition, having suffered nightmares, nausea, and dizziness? Was he weaker or stronger? At the moment he shared with me the sense of repose afforded by the shadow of the grinning serpent. I felt that strongly. But like the serpent heads themselves, braced with iron rods, his balance was precarious. Some final test of equilibrium was to come, the last rigor of his mother's tutelage.

From the Temple of Quetzalcoatl and Tlaloc we went to a recent excavation revealing bathing stalls and some badly faded frescoes among which Lane thought he spied the Teotihuacano emblem of cosmic paradox, the flaming freshet, *Burning Water*. When we emerged from this underground place, we were met by a flautist. He was making a slow high glissando on a little clay pipe that was molded in the shape of a man. So the stops, as it were, represented perhaps a multiplicity of navels, or maybe the cruel perforations of the priest's obsidian knife, although the little face just under the mouthpiece was complacent, almost smiling.

The flautist was a willowy young man not much older than Mike. He wore the inevitable huaraches on his feet. His pants were rolled up to the knee and were tied at the waist by a piece of rope. He wore a shirt the sleeves of which seemed to have been brutally hacked off with a dull knife. He had a little knapsack slung over his shoulder. He was a mestizo, his hair black, his nose sharp, his eyes narrow, his forehead broad, and his cheekbones flat. As I came up the steps from the excavation, I saw him silhouetted against the gray-bright sky, his fingers arched delicately over his pipe like a spider's legs. It was an image I knew I was destined to remember. We tipped the attendant who had guided us through the excavation, and he pointed us toward the ball court. The flautist followed us. "How do you like the music?" my wife said.

Mike said, "I don't like it. It's fruity."

"Well, get used to it," my wife said. "The guidebook says these tooters hang on like leeches. There's no shaking them."

"I like the music!" Lane said.

Mike didn't pay any attention to that. "What does he want?"

"He wants to sell us a pipe," my wife said. "About forty pesos, as I recall."

"Then let's buy Lane a pipe and get rid of this guy." I looked sharply at Mike, but I knew I wouldn't find any malice—thinking cruelty maybe, but never malice. Give credit where credit is due. Meanwhile, the flautist was tooting a gay little scherzo that would've had us all marching in step if it hadn't been for the stony ground which broke the rhythm of our walking.

"It won't work," said my wife. "If one member of a group breaks down and buys, then he hangs on until everybody does. We'd have to buy four."

"To heck with it, then," said Mike. "Let him follow us around. I'll bet he won't climb to the top of the pyramids."

Lane lifted his eyes to the Pyramid of the Sun. "You mean you're supposed to climb that?" Actually, his question was already answered by the presence up there of a half-dozen early-bird tourists. We could see them milling around against the gray sky.

At the ball court Mike decided to run, "just to get the feel of it," he said. So while we sat at the top of the stone stands he dashed around down inside the court. The flautist made proper music—a nervous, sometimes almost shrieking screed of presumably athletic sounds—but I myself found that the fluting had a decidedly hysterical edge to it, which reminded me that Lane had mentioned something about the ball being a human head. My wife, however, was at this moment reading aloud from the guidebook. "In this cosmic game, the ball, presumably the sun, which the players had to keep aloft lest it descend into eternal night, was made of hard rubber and probably embellished with carvings and golden paintings." She read on about the noble captains of the players, the probability of a hoop, the extant representations of players in elaborate collars and greaves. Meanwhile I watched our son Mike make swift runs along the sides, dash across the ends, feint, and pivot as though he'd been playing basketball down there in the rocks and dust of Teotihuacan ever since it was founded some seventeen centuries ago. Something about his absolute grace in that confined space gave me goose bumps. (The music also added to the effect, the flautist inspired by Mike to great flights of trilling and shrilling.) I admired Mike, but my admiration contained an element of horror. There would always be, I was thinking, a class of noble warriors (Eagles, Jaguars were they here?) for whom war was as natural and necessary as breathing. And what could the peaceable weaklings of the world, like Lane and me, do to keep them from destroying us? Make up games, like the ball game—keep 'em running. That was the only hope. "Hey, let's give him a hand," I said. "Come on, Lane!" So we clapped and whistled and yee-hooed. "Who's winning?" my wife hollered. Mike drove under for a lay-up, then came running up the stone seats shaking a fist in the air triumphantly. The flautist produced a reasonable imitation of a tantara of victory, but I noticed that everything came out of that pipe in a minor key. Mike stood in front of us, arms akimbo, breathing only a little faster than usual. "That freak still following us around? Let's see if we can lose him on the pyramids."

So we trudged off down the Avenue of the Dead, the Pyramid of the Moon directly ahead, the Pyramid of the Sun off to the right. It was toward the latter that Mike turned us when we drew abreast of its grand frontal steps. "Hey, wait a minute," I said, "don't you want to do the tallest one last?"

"No," said my wife. "The book says the visual effect is wrong. Also the Moon is steeper and ought to come after you've gotten the hang of it on the Sun."

At the foot of the steps I looked up and shook my head. "How many steps does the book say it has?"

"It doesn't say," my wife said. "Just start climbing and counting and you'll know when you get to the top."

"Nope," I said.

"Aww!" said Mike, disgusted. "You're not going to climb it?"

"Nope. Moctezuma is raging in my stomach, I'll try again when we get to the Moon." I turned to Lane. "You going to keep your old sick Daddy company?" Actually I was not feeling that bad, but I thought I would give Lane an out. He suffered mild acrophobia. However, to my surprise he said, "No, I'm going up. You can sit over there in the shade." He pointed to a stand of three low scraggly trees—I don't know what, stunted peppers perhaps. So, he had seen through my ploy and was rejecting it. He wanted to brave it out, both pyramids, the whole thing. In my heart love and respect surged up—tempered, though, by worry. What if something happened and I wasn't up there to do anything about it? "Well, then . . ." I began. Lane shook his head, almost pleadingly, I thought. "Rest under the trees." He wanted to do this alone with the two fierce ones.

"OK." My anxiety subsided. There would be no crisis on the Pyramid of the Sun. Something in its slope, gentler than that of the Moon, reassured me—something also in the timing, the arch of the day, which had not yet reached its crest. So, as they mounted the steps, I headed toward the meagre grove. The flautist followed me. When I reached the trees I looked back and saw that the three of them had already reached the break that ran around the middle of the pyramid like a tightly cinched band. Mike led, his mother and brother keeping equal pace behind.

I sat down in the shade and leaned against the trunk of the largest tree. I gave the flautist a ten-peso coin and told him to play me something soft. "Tócame algo muy suave," I said. I don't know if that was right, but he took my meaning and began to play a marvelously plaintive melody. I shut my eyes. The first thing I noticed was that the air was completely odorless—and in that heat too. Heat will usually stir up some kind of smell—a faint exudation from the vegetation, a hint of pollenous dust in the air, the odor of stone and earth itself if nothing else—but there was nothing. And there was a breeze, too. Why didn't it pick up something? Because it wasn't really a breeze. It was a huge mass of air moving slowly from one quarter of the world to another, odorless. It was unnatural. The flautist went on playing his plaintive tune. And I, sitting in that invariable mass of moving air, felt like an old fatalist. The Sun rises and drinks blood. The Sun falls, and the Four Hundred Warriors of the starry sky arise and guard their Mother Moon. The wind circles the earth. The summer rain pits the dust. The small corn tassles and makes a flaxen noise at night. And the Sun also rises.

I smiled wryly at myself. It was time to open my eyes, look up. We Americans are not fatalists but climbers and conquerors, sons of Cortés and not of Moctezuma. So if I had stayed behind this time to listen to the flautist's mournful tune of old mortality, it was only an interlude. I must up and prepare myself to mount the Pyramid of the Moon. But when I opened my eyes to see where my three conquistadors were, what caught my attention was a butterfly flitting before me in the near distance with an eerie irregularity—that is to say, sometimes I saw it and sometimes I didn't. I realize that these weird instants of invisibility were the result of the butterfly's getting its wings and body in a thin plane exactly horizontal to my eyes. Also the undulance of the hot air, as well as my Polaroid sunglasses, probably contributed. But I chose to see it as a metaphysical phenomenon—the butterfly flying back and forth across the border of two layers of reality: the now and the, what? the eternal present (the perpetual cycle of Sun, Moon, and Stars). Why not? Hadn't Lane told me that *Mariposa,* the butterfly, was closely associated with Quetzalcoatl—its transformation from worm to creature of gorgeous pennons an apotheosis, resurrection, translation to the skies in fluted, voluted, venus flight? And as if this wacky skein of images wasn't enough, the flautist suddenly said his first and, it turned out, his only word of our association: "Mariposa." Whereupon he immediately began playing *allegretto,* and I swear the butterfly picked up the beat and flew even more swiftly in and out of whatever it was flying in and out of. I couldn't take it. I got up waving my hands wildly and shouting, "¡Basta! ¡Basta!" I figured that if I didn't get free of the butterfly I would stumble into an ontological fault like one of Kafka's poor devils and forever wander around in some old city or island thronged with absurdities.

My three companions were halfway back down the pyramid, so I trudged over to meet them, somewhat peevishly, because my stomach was growling and because I had the sense of having been excluded from an adventure. "I'm glad you didn't lose our friend the fluter," my wife said. She looked at me closely. "You look a little peaked. Want some more Pepto-Bismol?" She fished the bottle of pink liquid out of her purse and handed it to me. I unscrewed the top and took a couple of swallows of the slimy, minty stuff with the faint redolence of paregoric. That was all I could get down without gagging. I handed it back to her, rubbed my mouth with the back of my hand, belched, and Bogart-like said, "Thanks, doc."

"I forgot to tell you. Don't worry when your stool turns black."

"Why would I worry?"

"Because in other circumstances it might signify internal bleeding."

"Oh."

"You OK, Dad?" said Lane, the exuberance of the successful climb flushing his face, but I knew that his trials were not over.

"Sure, I'm OK."

So we walked the last couple of hundred yards down the Avenue of the Dead from the Pyramid of the Sun to the Pyramid of the Moon, Mike in the vanguard, not because he wanted plenty of distance between him and the flautist, but because he always had to be in front. He was not proud or self-promoting. He simply had to be first, a human antenna, but a hell of a lousy one for Lane and me, because he would always call back, just as now from the foot of the Pyramid of the Moon, "Hey! It's a cinch. Come on." So he started up and we came behind lifting our knees high to climb those big stone steps. "It's steeper," said Lane, and I should have taken account right then of the hint of a quaver in his voice, but the truth is that I had dropped a little behind and was watching my wife's legs with fascination. Nothing erotic. On the contrary, I was noting that, though half a foot shorter than I, she was taking the steps more easily. Obviously she had more spring in her feet, more power in her knees, and twice as much flex in her pelvis, the whole apparatus apparently very rubbery—whereas I felt like I was doing the splits, suffering some kind of male episiotomy. So I said, "According to the original canons of the use of these structures, women were not permitted up here. That's why you're finding the climb a little strenuous."

"No doubt," she said. But Lane corrected me. "In the old days," he said, "there was probably a wooden god house up on the top, and women adjutants to the priests may have had minor offices."

"That's a consolation," my wife said, pulling a little farther ahead of us.

"I thought the highest the women got was to be sorceresses or occasional sacrificial victims by strangulation," I said panting.

"You're thinking of the Aztecs," Lane said.

I was weak, dizzy, and a little nauseous, so it didn't occur to me to try to distract Lane from the vertigo he was bound to suffer on those steep steps. In fact, when we reached the middle platform of the Pyramid, I looked back down where we had climbed, breathed deep, and said, "Jesus Christ! You guys already scaled one of these monsters and are stupid enough to do another one."

"It's steeper," said Lane, this time his voice weaker, his face grayer. But I didn't take note of these important changes. In my minor sickness I was busy rebelling against my wife and Mike, especially in view of what they were doing at that moment. Mike was restlessly pacing the perimeter of the platform as though this paltry plane of the middle air was too low, too confining for his vaunting spirit—a regular Manfred. And my wife was ecstatically taking in great gulps of air as though she had mounted to some clime of vast spiritual refreshment. My irritation with all this superabundant health prevented me from seeing how fearfully Lane sought the middle of the platform, staying as far as possible from all vertiginous edges. "Tired, old timer?" I said, still missing the mark by a mile. In fact, at this moment I found Lane's weakness as irritating as Mike's and my wife's vigor, mirroring, as it did, my own.

Consequently, when Mike lifted his arm, pointed up the final flight of stones, and shouted "¡Arriba!" I gave Lane a rough slap on the back. "*Arriba,* the man says."

I don't remember much about the top of the Pyramid of the Moon. No doubt it was more or less flat and at the same time rubbly and wind-gnawed. No doubt it had the inevitable grass or saxifrage growing in crannies between stones—the kind of stuff that is supposed to make the traveler marvel at the mysterious ubiquity of green life. In fact, I think my wife remarked on precisely this matter of unaccountable verdure, and I said, "Bird shit," although I could not myself have been thoroughly convinced of that explanation because I hadn't seen a bird all day, hadn't heard one. I remember then hearing the flautist again. He was below, on the middle level, playing a mournful tune. I remember that Mike scrabbled around and found a chip of obsidian, a piece, he instantly concluded, of an ancient sacrificial knife. Lane had sat down in the middle and was looking at nothing in particular. I gazed down along the Avenue of the Dead to the far end of the ruinous city where I could see the museum, the restaurant, and the parking lot, which spoiled the profound antiquity of my Pisgah view. I was about to call back to my wife peevish observation of that fact, when suddenly I heard behind me a squeal, a grunt, and the sound of scuffling. I turned to find my wife lying on top of Lane not far from the edge, his limbs thrashing beneath her weakly. I rushed over. Mike rushed over. My wife said, "Vertigo. He got up to look over the edge and started teetering."

Almost instantly Lane stopped thrashing. I pushed my wife roughly aside, and Mike and I pulled the now unconscious Lane back away from the edge. I kneeled over him. His breathing was uneven and his face ashen. "Prop up his knees," I instructed Mike while I chafed his temples. The truth is that I had no real knowledge of the efficacy of these procedures, but I needed desperately to be doing something because I was filled with anger and shame—my wife alone had stood between Lane and death while I had not been vigilant, had not even been thinking of him. And my wife, I'm sure, was wise enough to see my need. How else explain her patiently standing aside at this point? At any rate, I was greatly consoled when last Lane came to and looked up at me, but the fear in his eyes undercut the consolation. Weakly he began to speak: "I can't . . ." His voice trailed off. But I divined his meaning immediately. "Don't even think about it," I said. "You don't have to walk back down. You don't even have to look." Lane first registered pained disbelief. Probably he thought I was merely telling comforting lies. But his desire to be relieved of the prospect of the dizzying descent was so intense that he necessarily seized on my words and gave them his faith. As a result, he relaxed and began to regain a little color.

Meanwhile, Mike and my wife eyed me with disapproval, believing that I was using false hopes to quiet Lane down. So, when I next spoke I made sure that my voice carried authority. "We'll need your skirt, dear." My wife hesitated, not out of misplaced modesty of course, but because she did not for a moment understand my intention. And during that brief interval we heard the flautist's mournful music rising brokenly up to us against the stones and the wind. "For a litter," I said. "It's good stout denim, right?" She nodded. The skirt was one of those wraparound things made of the same material they make kids' jeans out of, tough stuff. Still, my wife hesitated, probably this time questioning the feasibility of my plan. "Go ahead, dear. Take it off," I said gently. "Mike and I have a good grip. And you'll lie very quietly, won't you, Lane?" He nodded. There was perhaps even a wisp of a smile playing in the corner of his mouth.

My wife stood up, untied the belt, unfurled the skirt, and

took it off. It made something of the same motion as a matador's cape. It wimpled in the wind. In the ring the matador's
assistants would hasten to wet it down, for nothing is more
dangerous than a windblown cape. These irrelevant analo-
gies passed quickly, leaving me peering stupidly at the black
shadow of my wife's mons veneris under the sheer cover of
her panties. Mike peered too long also before he turned his
glance aside. Lane looked up steadily—and though I did not
think that his age and innocence really did permit him that
indulgence, I didn't rebuke him on this occasion. Fortunately
my wife paid no attention to our staring. "All right," she said
and spread the skirt out on the stone beside Lane. "Hem at
the head and waist at the feet, right?"

"Right. Here's how we'll work it. We'll wrap him up tight.
Mike takes the feet, I take the head. You go down right in
front of us, backwards, just in case." Actually I should have
put Mike at the head, the heavier end, but I wasn't ready to
admit that my fifteen-year-old son was stronger and better
balanced than I. So we rolled Lane up snug, from shoulder to
knee. My wife smiled and said, "What will hatch from our
little cocoon?" Her tone was tender, but touched with irony
at that—as how could it fail to be, given the comical dis-
abilities of us men?

Mike and I heaved up our burden, awkward but not heavy.
"Give it a good shake," I said. "If it's going to rip, we want to
find out now, not later." So we tugged on the skirt and gave
Lane a good jostling. The cloth proved stout. We carried our
burden to the edge and started down. My wife descended
two steps ahead of us, backwards, keeping her weight against
the steps. That was a great comfort to me, because I began to
feel a little queasy. I even considered suggesting that she take
the litter and let me be the emergency man, because I knew
that this was no place for foolish pride. So if I had continued
to feel wavery on those first steps down I would have called
on her strength. But quickly I began to get the feel of the litter, picking up the rhythm from Mike who coordinated our
steps with the short swing of Lane's body. So my crisis of

confidence passed. In fact, about halfway down to the middle platform I turned my attention to Lane's face. He lay perfectly still in the litter, his eyes shut, his expression a paradoxical cross between deep placidity and repressed terror. I essayed a joke. "I hope, dear, that the God of the Moon will receive the homage of your white buttocks flashing in the mid-morning sun and not tumble us down."

"*God* of the Moon. Can that be, Lane?" my wife said.

"Goddess," he whispered sibilantly, like one in a trance. "Tlazolteotl, eater of filth, purifier of sinful man."

I started laughing. I couldn't help it. I had to stop and let the litter rest on the stone, which irritated Mike because he couldn't see any humor in what Lane had said. I didn't hold it against him. All the great warriors of the Jaguar and the Eagle were grim, humorless types. I said to my wife, "Not a scrap of consolation for you bloody women's libbers in the mythology of these ancient Mexicans."

"Keep moving," she said. So I stopped my laughter and heaved up my load again. Below, along the Avenue of the Dead groups of bus-borne tourists were just beginning to make their way toward us. I considered how sagacious we had been to come early. Otherwise, in our present predicament we would have had the curious and the prurient to contend with.

Down we went. On the middle platform waited the flautist, his face as blank as the stones of the pyramid, his music unchangingly mournful, as though there were absolutely nothing unusual in the manner of our passing. I said, "What a sense of show biz this guy has. If we had all stripped to the skin and come down in the form of a human pyramid, like the kids at Muscle Beach, he would have just kept playing that three-note dirge of his." Mike, as I said, did not appreciate these sallies of humor. I suppose they detracted from the seriousness of the manly business of carrying one's younger brother to safety. But for me, funny or not, they kept vertigo at bay.

"Keep moving," said my wife. So we commenced the descent of the last long flight to the ground, the flautist behind, sending down his constant plaint.

On level ground at last, we laid Lane down in the dust. And then my wife suffered an enormous shiver, of terror just past. I think I've never seen anything quite like it. It seized her shoulders and gave them a violent shake. It curled her lips back from her teeth and momentarily palsied her head. I thought her legs would buckle. And then it passed, almost instantaneously. She stepped toward Lane. "Get out of my way," she said. So Mike and I moved back. She stooped and unwound the skirt, lifted Lane up, and held him to her. He put his arms around her. Surprisingly neither wept. In fact, there was not so much as a snuffle, a telltale hitch in their breathing. So I didn't feel I would be a callous interloper if I spoke. "You were right, dear. You did snatch him back from the edge. I apologize for doubting you." She didn't reply. I said, "Maybe you ought to put on your skirt, dear. Here come some British tourists." About two dozen of them, and I didn't need to be a master of fine observation to identify their nationality—pink-faced men with pipes, women in pumps with carious smiles.

My wife stood up with Lane, paused a moment to make sure he was steady on his feet, then gathered up her skirt and wrapped it around her. Meanwhile I motioned to the flautist, swaying as he approached, "Bien hecho, bueno y confiable sirviente." *Well done, good and faithful servant* was what I meant. I pulled out my wallet. "¿Cuánto cuesta una flauta?" I said.

"Cuarenta pesos." So I gave him two hundred. "Cuatro, y el otro cuarenta es para un marcho por la Avenida de los Muertos." I motioned with my hand and arm to show him that we would march straight back to the museum. "Hasta el museo." He nodded and pulled out of his little sack four pipes. I gave one each to wife and children with the flourish of an Italian circus impresario. "El señor Lane en frente," I said, stationing him at the head of our column. "Después, el señor Miguel." Mike took the pipe but gave me a deeply suspicious glance. "Be ready to play and march on signal," I said in a momentarily changed voice that left no room for argument. "Después, la señora." My wife fell into line smiling. "Después, el flautista profesional." The Mexican took his place. I brought up the rear. "¡Toquemos! ¡Vámonos!" The Mexican sounded the first note for us. Lane quickly stepped off tooting vigorously. We were on our way. Such a gay cacophony you never heard. The British tourists broke apart like the Red Sea. And we all marched toward the promised land of Lane's manhood.

"Who is this Coatlicue?" I whisper to Lane just as the lights begin to dim for the Finale.

"Coatl—serpent, cue—skirt, Earth Goddess."

"Interesting," I say, but I am thinking, *snakes again. All these phalluses. Mexican macho.*

"Guess what," says Lane. "I just figured out who the guy with the flute was yesterday."

"Pan."

"Nope. A *pochteca,* combination of traveling salesman and missionary of Quetzalcoatl."

"Ah," I say. "That explains how he conjured up a butterfly in midair and then made it disappear." Lane looks at me and starts to say something, but the curtains are parting and my wife is shushing us.

The stage lies in utter silence and darkness, the primordial void, I suppose. Presently a tiny cheep of premonitory fluting creeps out from the pit. "Hey," I say, "they got our boy in the orchestra."

"Sshh!"

Slowly a grayish light seeps down from the flies to reveal in the middle of the stage a huge bicephalous mass. The thing is composed of dancers all twined together, standing on each other's thighs and shoulders, roughly in the shape of a pyramid. The two at the top wear serpent masks with long curving teeth. They seem to be trying to kiss. The rest is a congeries of coiled limbs which the eye cannot untangle except that at the breastbone there is the image of a huge heart and around the heart a fan of human hands. It is these that move first, stroking the heart, coaxing into life the great pump that will send vital blood out into Creation. The action of the hands increases in tempo, in erotic importunity until at last the heart (the artfully masked head of a dancer) begins to beat. Drums in the pit rise rapidly to a thunderous crescendo, at which moment the strange goddess bursts apart. The dancers that once were her fling themselves out into a sudden green light that obviously signifies the greening of the earth. There are, it turns out, a dozen of these living fragments of old earth undulating in the verdant light like creatures of the ur slime—tadpoles, spermatozoa. Now other dancers come out from the wings and meet the original fragments. The stage is animated, peopled. And what an incredible facility the dancers have for representing various forms of life. The eye can hardly keep up with all the transformations. We distinguish turtles and dolphins, eagles and butterflies, elephants, tigers, and coyotes, monkeys and men, and much more.

The audience can not contain itself. Loosed from the ordinary bonds of decorum by these images of irrepressible vitality and by the wild improvisational pizzicato of the orchestra, we begin to shout and clap. But our joy is short-lived. The pizzicato rapidly gives way to a sibylline scraping of the strings. The multi-colored lights sink into a crepuscular gray. The variformed dancers vanish. And then slowly the light contracts into the center of the stage, where a skull appears, larger than a Greek tragic mask. No doubt it is atop a tall dancer, but to us it seems to float in midair. Presently, like a lodestone, it begins to draw the dancers out of the dark. They come to the center and gather behind the grim memento mori. They climb each other and twine as before. Within moments all is still again—the stony pyramid with its twin serpent head, its serpent skirt, its breastbone of hands and heart—all as before except that this time there is the death's-head. The plaintive flute gives a final call. All is silent, gray, monolithic. Slowly the light fails. The stage is dark. We hear the rustle of the closing curtain. Hesitantly at first, still in deep darkness, we begin to applaud. But quickly we clap louder and louder. The house lights go up. Some of us begin to stand and shout "¡Ole!" The curtain parts to reveal the entire company, all somehow miraculously changed into simple black. The applause and shouting is thunderous. There are three curtain calls. In addition, the orchestra gets the spot, stands, and takes a bow. Finally the applause dies and the performers are permitted to depart toward a well deserved rest.

As so often after a moving performance, we do not know how to make the transition back to ordinary life. We have trouble putting away these unusual feelings. Our hearts, dilated by the dance, and our eyes, dilated by the dark, are equally vulnerable.

So I take it upon myself to be the clown. "Well, so much for happy endings." No one pays any attention to what I say, but the breaking of silence allows Lane to speak. "Heart and hands are the mandala, the quincunx. And at the omphalos the skull and the navel are the same."

"That says it all," I say, still clowning, but I think I do in fact see what he means.

"Tomorrow back to the good ol' USA," says my wife tugging Mike affectionately on the shoulder. She sees, as I insufficiently have, that this has been perhaps a little too much Lane's day. Furthermore, the program was arranged all wrong for Mike, beginning with the wonders of *Ball Game* and *Sacrifice* and then dwindling down to feathers, flowers, serpents, and earth mothers. And even Jaguars and Eagles have feelings. But Mike smiles. He's OK. And Lane of course is marvelously set up by the dance—high as a mountain.

And I? I am dreaming back to Teotihuacan. In one timeless moment I see my wife's beautiful bare legs there on top the Pyramid of the Moon. I see those same strong legs and tight buttocks going down before me. I see her unwrapping and hugging our son Lane. I see her marching in my comic victory parade down the Avenue of the Dead. That is my moment, snatched out of the gray wind that blows forever over the ruined City of the Gods.

Dorothy Tefft

SERENADE

ACROSS the dark apartment, barefoot over the eggshell-colored shag, walks Joanne Holmes de Rivera. Her mother is the only one who calls her Joanne. The Rivera she is "de," or "of," calls her Jo. Her Mexican friends usually say Yo, but some have difficulty with the pronunciation of the "j" and call her Ho. What is she doing out of bed at that hour, chilled and angry, very angry? It is two o'clock in the morning. Why isn't she asleep?

Her husband, José Antonio Rivera, J.A. for short, has not come home, that's why. She is worried, some, and mad, very. This is the third night in a row out on the town, *de parranda,* for Sr. J.A.R. There are always plenty of parties around for the son of Rodolfo Rivera, Mexico's greatest bullfighter. Plenty of drinking partners, too, you bet. Plenty of drinks sent over to his table from plenty of *aficionados* who had admired his father in the bullring. Plenty of time alone, now, in the new apartment, watching the baby, for Joanne Holmes de R., who used to be right there beside him, enjoying the drinks and the attention as much as he.

The question is, why doesn't she want to play as hard, now that the baby is here? That's the big, fat, million-dollar question. Not the baby's fault, certainly—a most satisfactory baby, Teresa, much prettier and smarter than most at sixteen months. Nicer, too, Joanne, or Jo, or Yo, is sure. But too small to be left alone or with maids who can barely read. Isn't it time to settle down? Not so, thinks José Antonio. Life should be fun, lots of fun.

Joanne considers things hard there in the dark by the window. Is he driving while drunk? Has he found a new playmate? Is he going to do anything he wants to, in this much-fought-for marriage that has to last forever? As his father does. Is she going to let him? As his mother does.

She goes to the kitchen and without turning on the light takes milk and a custard from the refrigerator and carries them to the sofa so she can go on thinking.

Thinking mostly about what kind of reception she should give José Antonio when he comes home. Some sort of a drama will soon be along. Silence, all the next day? Used too much, lately. Screaming—a shrew? Unpleasant and unrewarding. Outraged dignity? Also overplayed. A "final" showdown? "I'm leaving for the States!" Impossible. The last time she said that he answered, "Well, go along, then. Bye-bye!" Tears? She's madder than sad. What about acting as if nothing at all has happened? That's what she did the night before—probably why he's out again tonight for more "fun." José Antonio is drinking far too much and too often; that is certain. Is he going to be like her father?

She hugs her knees and thinks of her father. That time she heard the children next door laughing at the funny way he was trying to get the car into the garage. She feels sick.

That's the sound of their car driving up! There he is! She runs to the window, her heart flickering around her throat like a moth. He has brought a serenade! Ducky. The top of the car down, that awful Juan Lopez in the front seat beside him, three *mariachis* lolling all over the back, and guitar cases sticking out everywhere. Well, at least he's here, safe.

She watches as the musicians get out their instruments there in the street and take their places under the street light, in moonlight, too. The curtain at this, her observation post

(eggshell bleached muslin, finished that afternoon for a surprise), is already limp at the ruffle—at cheek level. At this rate
the curtains will be worn out in a month. She smiles in spite
of herself at the way they always make the trumpet player
stand twenty yards off so he won't drown everyone else out.
Funny. Sweet. Latins can be sweet, all right. And it's not true
that they're lousy . . . . No, that part is still just as it should
be. Sweet. Secret.

A blast of *mariachi* music rolls down the empty street. The
ugliest one would sing: they always do. Sure enough, the
squat, toady one begins. She strains to understand the words,
her Spanish failing her, at times, from the effort. There, now,
she has it.

How about that! "Ah, love, don't love me so much / Don't
suffer any more for me." That *sin vergüenza* rat husband!
Singing louder than anyone else, of course. Happy J.A. No
remorse to speak of, serenading at two o'clock in the morning, telling her not to care for him so much—not to suffer.
The nerve of it made her laugh, and she felt better. It was
probably Juan's fault they started drinking. Some friend. See
if I make any more U.S.-style dinners for you, Juan Lopez!

Should she turn on the light to acknowledge the serenade?
You were supposed to. There were now lights on in other
apartments. No wonder: that *mariachi* trumpet would blow
anyone out of bed. She was not the only one hearing her husband enjoin her to "forget it all; it's only going to cause you
pain . . ." Dear God, he doesn't really mean that, does he?
No! No! He couldn't! Listen, listen closely in the dark.

There now, this song is really romantic; that's more like
it. How does it go? ". . . so many lights you have lit in my
soul / Only God knows how I'm going to put them all out
now." Lovely words. Difficult to imagine a husband in the
States singing them aloud, at three o'clock in the morning.

Now this one he had explained to her before. It was called
"The Abandoned One," or something like that. Abandoned,
who? He or she? He, in the song. Good! She listens closely.
". . . you despise me, woman, just because I'm poor, and

have the misfortune to be married . . ." Misfortune! Some
accident, marriage. ". . . three vices I have, deep-rooted / I'm
a gambler, a drunk, and a Don Juan . . ."

Isn't that just like a damn *macho* Mexican? Poor, married, a
gambler, a drunk, and a chaser, but still right in there pitch-
ing. The ungrateful wretch abandoned him, of course, only
because he was *poor*. Well, her serenade seemed to be over.
Now she could get some sleep. It had been beautiful, after all,
and her wayward Mexican was home. Should she invite them
all in, for a drink? No. They'd wake the baby if they started
singing again, and they were sure to, with drinks. Mexicans had a lot of songs in them. How should she look when
J.A. came up the stairs, properly repentant, loving? To the
window.

Good Jesus, *everyone's* getting back into the car, J.A. too.
Where are they going now? To take another serenade, to
some other woman? To take the *mariachis* back? Frantically
she tries to get the window down, to call. Too late. They
have all driven off, the *mariachis* sitting every which way in
the car, re-playing the last mournful bars of *El Abandonado*.

Well, we'll see who's going to be an *abandonado. You* are,
J.A. Rivera. It is now three o'clock, and Joanne H. de R. (no:
flick that "of Rivera" please) is, as they say in Spanish, *hecha
una furia,* turned into a fury. Which will it be? Let's see. Furies:

Erinyes, or Furies—three goddesses who punished un-
avenged crimes. Their hair consisted of serpents, and
they tracked their victims relentlessly, terrifying them
with appalling visions. Their names were Alecto, Tisiphone, and Megaera.

So be it. I'll be Tisiphone. But first I'll fix it so he can't get
in here tonight. Let him sleep in the hall. Then, tomorrow,
I'll take the baby and go to Cuernavaca for a few days, without telling him. There'll be no taming of this shrew!

She pushes the sofa (with great difficulty: it's heavy) along
the wall until one end rests against the fireplace wall. Getting
the desk into line takes longer, because she has to empty

all the drawers before she can move it even one inch. There: wedged tightly against the sofa. Only two yards to fill and he won't be able to open the door when he gets back, because it opens inward. Ha! A solid line of furniture now, from door to wall, that's what we need. She smiles grimly as she begins to take things out of the bedroom bureau. That will just fit. Continue the line. Hold the line. The solid grey line. She should have married Paul Petry, the jerk, that time when he asked her, after the dance at West Point. Then she wouldn't be moving furniture like an idiot, at three o'clock in the morning.

There. At last. The sofa, the desk, the chair, the bureau. From door to chimney wall. Solid, fast, invincible. Let him try to move that door inward. She lies down on the sofa and falls asleep.

He is trying to get in! She laughs with nervous satisfaction as he tries key after key. His own fault! Now the fool is leaning on the bell. Hard. Again. That's right, wake the neighbors up once more. She smiles. He'll have to sleep the rest of the night there in the hall.

Silence. The sound of footsteps moving toward the stairs. He's going off again! Desperately she pushes and pulls the furniture aside and opens the door. Please, God. Don't let him go away again! She bursts out into the hall.

Two arms grab her tightly from behind and swing her around into the air. "Goddamn you, José Antonio Rivera. You just pretended to go downstairs!"

Brandy breath. Repelling. Exciting. Childhood. Love. Fear. Insecurity. Father!

"Didn't you like your serenade? Why didn't you come to the window? Come on. Let's go to bed."

Dorothy Tefft

THE DIG

"**R**EMEMBER, you can't tell anyone about this, or they'll lose their little piece of land. They're supposed to report everything they dig up in an archeological zone." Lupe said this as we zipped cleanly through the last red light in Cholula. The traffic policeman leaning against a store at the corner pulled himself up and saluted the big station wagon with the MD on the license plates.

"I won't tell anyone. Tell me, do you always go the wrong way down streets like this?" I asked. I had known Lupe for some three months but I had never driven with her before.

She just smiled at the question, but Carla, twelve years old, answered for her mother. "In Cholula we do. The chief of police is a good friend of my father's."

We wriggled through the web of small streets and turned finally to leave the town by a country road at one side of the big pyramid.

I turned around and looked at the packages in the back. All the fashionable young matrons in Puebla drive long station wagons, and Lupe's is always the longest. "What have you got back there?" I asked.

"Beer and Cokes, mostly. Three chickens I had in the freezer. Some boxes of rice. The tortillas we just picked up in the market."

"Who's going to do all the cooking?"

"María doesn't mind a few extra people. She has a lot of kids. Wait till you taste her *mole*. She cooked for us for years—until Carla was born. After that, I made her Carla's nurse because she was the most intelligent of all the servants. When she left to get married she asked me to be the godmother of one of her children. Which one was it, Carla?"

"Pepe."

"So now María and I are *comadres*. I don't believe there's a translation for that in English."

"Maybe 'co-godmothers,'" I said. The road went through fields of daisies, snapdragons interlaced with alfalfa, and larkspur bluer than the sky. I sat back and thought about how wonderful it was to be back in Mexico. The immense pyramid of Cholula, the ancient yellow church clinging to its top like half a flower, looked even more impressive out there in the country. It towered over the little houses that huddled at its base.

"I think this is the right road. I was only there once before, when they dug up the other grave. I hope they find something that isn't broken, for my collection. Anyone digging around Cholula is bound to dig up something as soon as the shovel hits dirt. *Cabecitas,* they call them—the little heads—no matter what it is they find. María can't imagine why I make such a fuss about them, but she lets me know whenever they dig. When they built the outhouse they found one grave. Now they're making a garage for the truck and they've found another."

"There's Pepe, waiting for us," said Carla. A boy about her own age stood by a wall near an unpainted metal door barely large enough for the station wagon to squeeze through. He was holding an exquisite grey poodle in his arms. There were no trees and no pavements there outside the town—just dust and dirt and adobe.

The boy opened the door and we drove in. He closed the door quickly. The lot was surrounded on all sides by an adobe wall that was about six feet high. A small house stood against the wall on the road side. It had only two windows, and they shone in the sun.

To the left of the lot, towards the back, there was a shed for animals. Several pigs and some chickens scratched around comfortably.

To the right there was an outdoor toilet, with the door open. In the middle of the space between these two buildings there was a large, deep hole, with a boy inside, digging intently, some four feet down. Only the top of his head showed. Three children sat with bare feet dangling into the hole, watching the boy at work.

"That's Mariano, digging," said Carla.

"Heavens, I don't know how you remember them all," Lupe answered. "I can't tell them apart."

The children welcomed us shyly as we got out of the car. More children came out of the house, followed by María, plump, clean and kindly. After she had exclaimed over the food, the older girls carried it into the house to be cooked. Pepe was reminded that he should kiss his godmother's hand. Wooden chairs were brought from the house and we sat around the hole to watch the boy at his digging. Scattered all over the yard, in the dirt, were shards—orange and black fragments of ancient cultures. The children, including Carla, squatted in the dust, trying to fit the largest pieces together.

"We're sure it's going to be another grave," Mariano said as he swung his pick, "because this morning we found that, about one meter down." He pointed to a *molcajete,* the three-legged stone mortar that Mexican Indian women have always used to pound and grind their delicious sauces. The well-worn black stone *mano*—the pestle, or "hand"—lay at its side. I touched it with reverence, wondering how many hundreds of years it had lain there beside its owner.

The ancient volcanoes looked on serenely, glitteringly aloof from the dusty yard where the boy was taking pieces of Mexican past from the earth. We sipped beers and chatted while María made rice and *mole* sauce for us in the kitchen. The little grey poodle frisked around joyfully, jumping into the hole again and again, using Mariano's stooped back to climb out, to the delight of the children.

After a while we went inside to get out of the sun. The house was cool and dark. There were only two rooms—a spacious one that was living room, kitchen and bedroom, and another, without a door, that seemed to be packed solidly with more beds. María was cooking on an old gas stove, using the high-handled earthen dishes peculiar to Puebla, and stirring with big wooden spoons. A blender with an elaborately embroidered cover stood on a table next to a *molcajete* that was exactly like the one we had seen outside.

She served us cold beer from the refrigerator in beautiful pink glasses with hand-painted roses that she took from a locked cabinet with a glass door. Lupe and I sat around the table talking while she worked. The children and the dog entered frequently, but chickens were quickly stopped at the door.

María told us about the little dog *Gris,* which had been the smallest in a litter of poodles belonging to the family of an American professor at the University. When they returned to the States they gave *Gris* to Pepe as a prize for high marks at school, and it was his treasure. He had taught it tricks and had learned to clip it himself.

Lupe asked about María's health. "Not very good, yet," she answered. "The hemorrhages are still frequent."

"Why don't you go to see my husband, *Comadre?* He said you stopped going to his clinic," Lupe asked.

"We have gotten a little behind, *Comadre,*" María answered quietly. "And the *consultas* and the *medicinas* are very expensive. Each time we go to the doctor, it costs several hundred pesos. When we get caught up once more, I'll return to my *compadre*'s office." I resolved to have a talk with Lupe, later.

Lupe took some photos out of her purse—snapshots that she had taken during the last excavation. Some were pictures of small heads and figures that had come out of the other grave, and some were pictures of the children—washed, combed and posed for the occasion. The children clustered around to see themselves in the photos, passing them to Carla first, touching them reverently. In one of the pictures Lupe posed, smiling, beside a line of the *cabecitas* placed on a windowsill. "I wonder how much they would go for at Parke-Bernet," I wondered idly.

"Speak in English. They don't know these things are valuable," Lupe said, sharply.

At a shout from Mariano we went outside to see the simple grave he had uncovered. The clean bones of a woman lay there in the pit at our feet. She had been buried lying on her side, her hands crossed on her breast, her legs drawn up slightly. At each corner of the grave there was an unglazed pot, beautifully decorated. Two were broken. Five clay figurines, about three inches high, lay scattered around among the bones. That was all. It was the tomb of a poor woman.

Each of the clay figures had a different face—some attempt had been made to make them human, perhaps recognizable—but the little bodies were stiff and awkward. It was impossible to tell if they were masculine or feminine. "Unisex," said Carla, and the children all shrieked with laughter and ran in to tell their mother.

She came out, wiping her hands on her apron, and stood by the grave, looking at it silently for a minute. The children fell quiet. "And they put her *molcajete* in with her," she said finally. Turning to Pepe she said, "Help your brother dig a hole for her over there where we put the other one. They'll be all right there. If we take them to the churchyard everyone will know we dug them up and someone might tell. Father Miguel says these old ones didn't believe in our Lord, or His Blessed Mother, so I guess it's all right if they don't lie in holy ground."

She led us—Lupe and Carla and me—into the house and we sat down at the table where three elegant places had been set with plates and glasses from the cabinet. Each child was given a Coke, a wooden spoon and a tin plate filled with chicken, *mole* and rice. Three steaming tortillas were laid on top of each plate, like lids, so they could be carried outside.

María and the oldest girl waited on us, refusing to sit down in spite of our pleading. It was a superb meal. María was delighted each time we refilled our plates.

After dinner I helped Lupe wrap each of the pots and figures carefully in squares of newspaper and put them in the station wagon. "I'm going to have someone at the University determine the age of the *molcajete,* so I can get a good price for it," Lupe said. "I already have three."

We thanked María and got into the car. Just as Pepe opened the door, holding the poodle so she wouldn't run out into the street, Carla whispered something to her mother. Lupe nodded.

"*Comadre,*" she said. "Would you like to sell the little dog? Carla is so crazy about it, I'll give you one hundred pesos."*

María hesitated. She looked at Pepe, who watched her with the most emotionless face I have ever seen. The dog struggled to get down from his arms. Then María nodded her head the tiniest fraction, and Pepe walked over to the car and gave the dog to Carla. Lupe rummaged in her purse for some bills and Carla gave them to the boy. He took the money to his mother; without looking at it she tucked it into the pocket of her faded apron.

As we went out through the metal door, Carla hugged the dog tightly; it was struggling to escape. She said tenderly, "The other dogs are just going to love my little *Gris.* Do you know why I wanted her?"

I didn't trust myself to ask.

"Because Pepe has taught her so many tricks." She was silent for a minute. "I wonder how he did it."

*at this time worth about five dollars

Carolyn Osborn

LETTER TO A FRIEND FAR AWAY

Austin

DIANE, things are not going at all well here. I came down to the office with the camera. After two months in Mexico I've gotten so used to carrying one I can't leave it at home. My third eye, my reality screen. Yes, I will take pictures of the office, I said. What did I see? A pile of boards—old shingles, hand-wrought. Shining in the pecan trees high above browning grass and withered bushes, a new tin roof, unfinished. Nothing here to photograph but wreck and reconstruction. I've seen so much of that in Mexico the novelty's worn off, so I left the camera in the car.

I walked in through the back kitchen door, open in June, one of our most air-conditioned months. My artistic landlady shouted, "Welcome!" over her air-conditioner's roar.

"Don't you want me to shut the door?" Remember, if you can way up there in New Hampshire, our Baked Alaska summers—cool inside, flaming out.

"Oh, no," she said. "I'm painting my studio."

While I was gone she'd painted a dozen or so enormous pictures. Why must the walls be painted now? Other people's sequences confuse me.

"A show," she explained. "I'm having a show."

I handed her a tablecloth, green, white, maroon, color-fast—the clerk said—bought in Puebla, Mexico, a place I've been lately. "This is for picnics."

"Thank you. I think I'll use it for a shawl."

How is it one's original intentions get so warped? Think of that time I bought an abstract painting and when I hung it at home the meaningless lines immediately became Portrait of Fu Manchu with Bad Teeth. And the time you installed the big window in your back sitting room because you wanted to watch the birds. Then had to put a curtain up to prevent kamikaze flights.

I thought about that on my way to the porch. The office building is a Victorian frame house. Somebody walled and windowed the porch, gave it a door, stuck an art deco light fixture in the ceiling. Five naked light bulbs—clear glass—sway above my chaise lounge. What do I do here? Mind my own business. Thank God my father left me some to mind. I don't have a phone. There is a typewriter. I write compelling letters to stockbrokers, real-estate agents, etc. Behind me there's another office where book designers work. Behind them in the former back bedroom a graphic artist letters anything and draws a lot. The book designers have a Cuban flag on their wall, not for sympathy, for love of design. I gave them a hand-embroidered pillowcase. The graphic artist got an onyx heart, already cracked, from X—I have forgotten the town's name. In X the sidewalks were paved with onyx. Small boys stood behind high walls cutting stone with power saws, without safety goggles, without gloves. Natives told me to be careful of dogs in the streets. Everybody looked hungry. Amidst the walls was an empty crumbling cathedral surrounded by a tall spiked fence. A disturbing town on a gray day, full of incipient violence and three-hundred-year-old ghosts—cardinals, grandees, overseers, stonemasons, slaves.

I was with Monroe who ordered onyx candlesticks for his

shop. The shop is not yet built. I've known Monroe for almost thirty years. He drinks. He's a little crazy. I'm wandering. Too much to tell.

Coming back here is the reverse of turning up in Madrid right after Franco's death when so many of the street names were changed. Here the names are the same, but the streets have changed. A block from the office all the buildings, all the trees have been blitzed so a new bank can be built. I can hardly remember what was there before.

One of the book designers is drawing maps showing the movements of African tribes. They will scarcely stand still long enough for the book to be published.

To return to X. I met a woman there who had twenty grandchildren. The youngest ten lived with her. One hip was permanently out-of-joint from child carrying. That's the way they manage the youngest—wrapped in a shawl, balanced on a hip. She did not seem to mourn her fate. Her life has moved in an undeviating line from childhood, puberty, courtship, marriage, children, to grandchildren. Death and fiestas interrupt, naturally. No, it isn't simple, but it is organized. Yes, we're organized here. However, the organization is continually disrupted. Possibilities for derangement are endless.

My wall calendar still says May when it's late June. I like the May picture, *A Bacchante,* a costume design by Leon Bakst of a plump woman dancing with a billowing piece of material. She's wearing a gauzy print fastened at the thighs with jewels. Her long black hair flows through another strip of material. How could it have been tied? In 1911 Leon Bakst was not very practical. Someday I will check to see if he got more practical.

My friend Monroe, the demi-alcoholic who ordered the onyx, is not very practical either. He used to be more so, then he got tired of pragmatism. He's now in a muddle. Being rich keeps him in servants. Being drunk he forgets which ones he fires, so they all stay on. Though we never correct each other, I hit him—but not hard—when he goes too far, when he tells me things I don't want to know. Then he says, "Do it again." So I have to stop in order not to indulge his perversity.

There are a good many things I don't want to know these days. Here are some of them: (1) who anybody is sleeping with other than his/her legally wedded spouse; (2) why anyone got divorced; (3) how many people the gunman shot in the grocery, house, church; (4) what has happened to Horace's last client; (5) how hot it was in Wichita Falls yesterday.

Horace hides the morning paper from me because I salt the eggs with useless tears if I read of atrocities before breakfast.

As I said, things are not going well here. What would you do if you came home from a two month's vacation and your scales were missing? I looked under all the children's beds. They are now 16, 19, and 21 and still hide things from me, a habit they must have picked up from Horace. April just returned from a college in California and poked a grass skirt under her bed. She's not going back out there. Then Allen called to say he has my scales under his bed at camp. He's the nature counselor and should be collecting items like butterflies, fossils, and arrowheads.

"Mother, I had to weigh a big raccoon. He was twenty-eight pounds minus the tow sack. Then the kids wanted to weigh Cleophus, the rooster, and the possum. His name is Adolph."

I will never put foot on those scales again.

News of the youngest. Alicia's in Europe. Sold her clothes, sold old newspapers in order to go. Now she's wandering around Rome carrying a light suitcase. I gave her a camera and told her if she looked through the viewer the little square that framed the picture would, for an instant, collect the world. I find cameras soothing. Horace generally prefers that I leave mine at home. He sometimes fears I'll get over-enthused and slip inside his office to snap pictures of his clients. This is a fantasy he insists on. Most of the clients are criminals. In the years you knew him, Horace was a civil lawyer. Now he's taken up with criminals. Says it's more exciting. I hope a similar desire for excitement will not take Rodney out of his classroom and onto the stage, a logical step for a drama professor though not always a preferred one. Should he be tempted, try to turn him toward mountain climbing, or soaring, or some other essentially private danger.

That was the reason I was in Mexico—the danger. Somebody got sent to the pen in spite of Horace's excellent defense. The minute the cell door locked behind him he started sending evil messages. "Your wife's going to come up missing." So Horace sent me to Oaxaca, to a sixteenth century convent which served as a jail in the Juarez years. It is now a hotel. Historical information is relaxing to one who must spend nights in a strange bed. I had two bodyguards—Horace's idea. My room overlooked a patio with a fountain—burble-burble—and orange trees grouped around. The oranges were as green as the water in the fountain. Underneath the arches musicians played and sang for people eating lunch and supper. A good place to honeymoon or to hide out.

The bodyguards, Fernando and Miguel, slept outside my door. Fernando was short with a bandito mustache. Miguel was also short and rather skinny—too skinny to block a bullet we used to say. They went with me everywhere, to the market, to the plaza to watch the people go by—I sat like sandwich filling between the two of them, our backs to the bandstand—to Monte Alban, to Mitla, and to every museum. All my pictures from Oaxaca show either Fernando's or Miguel's profile in the foreground. It was odd. Because of those two several of the Oaxaqueños thought I was in some way kin to the presidential family. The questions on certain faces told me they were dangling from the furthermost limbs of a genealogical tree. The rest didn't bother their heads. They accepted the situation. I did not. As much as I liked Fernando and Miguel, I found their continual presence tedious and my continual absence questionable.

If I bargained in the market, they outdid me. Once I got a

seller down from twenty-five to twenty pesos for a straw hat. Miguel put his hand on his shoulder holster and the price moved to ten.

"If you do that again, we will part company," I told him.

"But, Señora, it's too high."

"You're taking unfair advantage."

"Si, Señora."

The whole conversation went on in Spanish. Mine improved considerably as I had little to do in the evenings but read my dictionary.

As you have guessed by now, I had to leave. Made friends with some people from Connecticut. Told them I was being held against my will. Goth-thick. Lady imprisoned in a second-story tower. Hoisted my suitcase out the window, climbed down the ladder I'd bribed the gardener to leave in the patio. (We did learn something in that expensive boarding school.) My Connecticut friends took me to Puebla to stay with Monroe.

"For God's sake, Annabel! Come in!" That's what he said over the loudspeaker. It was comforting to be welcomed even by an amplified voice. He had a system. You buzzed, he answered. The steel garage door rolled up for the right people. His front door is used only for ceremonial occasions such as large cocktail parties. I'm giving you the following conversation entire so you can judge the quality of Monroe's muddle.

"Monroe, has it occurred to you that you live in an environment that resembles a pen on the outside?" We were drinking gin and tonic by his swimming pool where yellow hibiscus blossoms floated.

"But don't you feel safe here, Annabel?"

"Oh yes."

"Most everyone in Mexico who can afford it lives this way. Broken glass on top of the walls is also decorative. See how it catches the sun. Poorer people make do with watch dogs on their roofs. Functional use of flat roofs. Everyone needs privacy and protection. Enemies are easy to acquire here."

"Do you have some?"

"Of course."

"Who?"

"Oh, they are out there." He waved one hand toward the wall. "Yesterday someone threw a mango at my houseboy."

"Maybe he has enemies."

"My enemies are his."

"Monroe, perhaps I'd better go home."

"Nonsense. Have another drink. You're safe as houses here."

Most accidents happen in the home. Every night I crossed my fingers and pushed the rug against the door to keep paranoia from slithering under. The pope had come to Puebla. Why shouldn't I be happy there? Because I was not El Papa.

To take my mind off my troubles Monroe took me to X. At one point he decided someone was following. I had to scrooch down on the floor until he decided otherwise.

When we returned to Puebla we went to see a woodcarver who carved animals for merry-go-rounds—elephants, swans, giraffes, horses. I bought an elegant horse, wood-colored, not painted, horse-colored, sorrel after Monroe rubbed him with twenty coats of wax. (He consoles himself by doing small tasks with his hands.) The horse was rearing on his hind legs, his mane flowing in a brisk wind. I looked again and saw a frightened animal shying at something, his own shadow maybe. I left him with Monroe.

"You can use him in your shop," I said. "I've talked to Horace again. He says it's all right for me to come home."

"What about his killer client?" Monroe doesn't believe in explanations yet he goes on demanding them.

"That's really rather sad. He killed himself."

"In jail?"

"They think he took an overdose of something. No one knows what yet. The autopsy isn't finished."

"Why doesn't Horace do something less dangerous?"

"He likes to face it head on."

Monroe drank bourbon and purified water when his chauffeur drove us to the airport in Mexico City. Waving one hand at the gray polluted sky he said, "Just breathing here is dangerous." Then he put his head on my lap and went to sleep while the chauffeur played war games in the traffic.

I flew home with twenty children carrying tennis rackets to a tournament, their coaches, and several young women going home to visit their mothers in San Antonio—they took their children with them and bade their husbands fervent good-byes. Passion drenched the waiting room at 7:30 a.m. Each young woman was accompanied by a chaperone disguised as a smartly dressed aunt. There were also at least two men returning from a trip to Acapulco with their secretaries. One secretary's eyes were slightly crossed. However, she was, as you might expect, all bosom, a cliche of voluptuousness. The children ran up and down the aisles, the beautiful Mexican mothers put on more lipstick, the tournament players sat still and hugged their rackets, the secretaries exposed their cleav-ages. Horace's secretary has one she covers up in the office. I do not know what else she covers up.

I looked out the window at the snow-covered volcanoes and wondered when they would erupt again. If they do the U.S. will get blamed for it. Why not? They think we're up to no good all the time.

While I was there Monroe opened the front door and gave me a party. Embassy people drove down from the city. The scientific attache told me we were currently being cursed for causing drought. We sprinkled the clouds around hurricanes' eyes with magic dust, they said. This dispersed them, kept the rain from falling on Mexico.

"Did we really do that?"

"Of course not. We made experiments once—far out over the Atlantic away from anyone's coast. But as soon as the eye began to expand, when it began to lose force, it gathered it-self together again and moved to Texas, Corpus Christi, I think."

I choose to believe the scientific attache. I prefer to think the rain keeps on falling on the just and unjust alike, and there's nothing anyone can do about it.

This all sounds a bit addled. It's the heat. Roads are buck-
ling, chickens are roasting on their roosts, people are keeling
over. It's 114 degrees in Wichita Falls. I was forced to hear
this on a car radio waiting next to me at a red light. There's
no way to keep bad news out. Several days ago an old lady
died at home in bed. She had the gas fire on. 111 degrees in
her room, 105 degrees outside. (I found the paper that morning after Horace left.) How cold was she to keep a fire on?
The final chill? Perhaps.

Today in the graphic artist's office I saw a sign printed in
Bodoni bold: For FUN or for MONEY

but *not*

for FREE!!!

Now who is it meant for? There are also some new pictures
of mournful cows, fat ones with black splotches on them. I
understand very little of what goes on in there. I understand
even less of what goes on in my own house. Last night when
I pulled the bedspread back I caught a glimmer of a gun shining under our bed.

"Horace," I said, "it's one thing to send me and the camera
off to Mexico, but this is something else."

"It's loaded. Don't touch it."

"Who is after you now?"

"The guy who overdosed has a brother. He was the one
who was going to get you originally I guess."

"But we don't have to sleep with a loaded gun."

"Revolver, Annabel. It's a revolver, a twenty-two." You
know how exacting he is.

"What's it doing on my side of the bed?"

"There's another one on my side, a thirty-eight."

I told him we couldn't live like that. I told him anything
could happen any day. He could get food poisoning and
nearly die like I did in Oaxaca. He could have a heart attack, a
plane might crash on the roof, he might get run over while
crossing a street, or he could suffer a number of other mun-
dane ends. I suggested he go stay in Puebla with Monroe.
They could indulge each other. I suggested he have a good

long talk with his mother. I even suggested that the graphic
artist could make him a sign: Criminals Will be Dealt With
Severely, or some other more potent warning of his choice.
He said he thought he'd keep his mother out of it for her
safety's sake, that he couldn't possibly run off to Mexico because he had to practice law in Texas, that signs were inef-
fectual, furthermore, he wanted me to call the burglar bars
people tomorrow.

I must rush. Instead of calling the burglar bars people, I
have called a moving company. A small truck will arrive in a
few minutes carrying several pieces of furniture. Little is required to turn this office into a bed-sitter for me and whatever child happens to be at home. There's a kitchen here, as I
mentioned, and a bath as well. I am aware that a camera and a
calendar that says May in June are the flimsiest of protective
devices, but I will not shoot at everything that squeaks in the
night and I will not commence the day staring at the world
through bars. Horace wants an excuse to have those guns on
hand. Well, he can have them. He can't have me too. I can't
tell you what has truly happened to him, particularly when
you remember him as an affable man. All I know is that his
search for something more interesting and his desire to monkey with the dangerous have overwhelmed him. I'm depart-
ing before I get caught in the crossfire.

Being a lawyer's wife has taught me a bit about the neces-
sity of evidence. I'd appreciate it if you'd keep this letter. I
trust it will arrive, though the mail, like everything else, has
been undependable lately.

Love,
Annabel

EDWARD SIMMEN teaches in the Graduate Studies program at the Universidad de las Americas in Puebla, Mexico. A native of Texas, he received a Ph.D. in English from Texas Christian University and previously taught in Texas. He has taught in Mexico since 1973.

TYPESETTING by G & S, Austin, Texas
PRINTING AND BINDING by Edwards Bros., Ann Arbor, Michigan
DESIGN AND PRODUCTION by Whitehead & Whitehead, Smithville, Texas